The Irish Church and the Tudor Reformations

The Irish Church and the Tudor Reformations

Henry A. Jefferies

FOUR COURTS PRESS

Set in 10.5 on 12.5 point Ehrhardt for
FOUR COURTS PRESS LTD
7 Malpas Street, Dublin 8, Ireland
e-mail: info@fourcourtspress.ie
http://www.fourcourtspress.ie
and in North America for
FOUR COURTS PRESS
c/o ISBS, 920 N.E. 58th Street, Suite 300, Portland, OR 97213.

A catalogue record for this title
is available from the British Library.

ISBN 978–1–84682–050–2

Printed in England
by Antony Rowe, Chippenham, Wilts.

For my wife, Úna

Contents

Acknowledgments

I have accumulated many debts while working on this book over the years, and the footnotes are but a pale reflection of my indebtedness. However, I wish to acknowledge especially Steven Ellis and Colm Lennon, two outstanding scholars whose support over many years has been hugely appreciated. I am also beholden to Réamonn Ó Muirí, Adrian Empey and Michael O'Neill, and to Brendan Scott whose comments and advice I very much value. I am very conscious too of my debt to an army of librarians and archivists, but especially to the librarians in Magee College in the University of Ulster, without whom this book could not have been written. I wish to place on record my gratitude to Máireád Nic Craith, the former Director of the Academy of Irish Cultural Heritages in the University of Ulster, for sponsoring my appointment as a Visiting Fellow of the Academy. It is a great honour to be associated with such a distinguished academy, and to have my scholarship recognised by it. Finally, I would like to record my very great regard for, and manifold obligations to, the late Michael Adams of Four Courts Press whose contribution to Irish scholarship was absolutely boundless.

Abbreviations

AFM	Annals of the Four Masters.
An. Hib.	*Analecta Hibernica.*
Arch. Hib.	*Archivium Hibernicum.*
AU	W.M. Hennessy and B. MacCarthy (eds), *Annála Uladh: annals of Ulster from the earliest times to the year 1541* (4 vols, Dublin, 1887–1901).
BD	Bachelor of Divinity.
BL	British Library.
Cal. Carew MSS	*Calendar of the Carew manuscripts, 1515–74*, et seq. (6 vols, London, 1867–73).
CLAHJ	*County Louth Archaeological and Historical Journal.*
CPCRI	*Calendar of patent and close rolls, Ireland, Henry VIII–Elizabeth*, i, ed. James Morrin (Dublin, 1861).
CPL	*Calendar of papal letters.*
CR	*Clogher Record.*
CRP	*Correspondence of Reginald Pole.*
CSPI	*Calendar of state papers relating to Ireland* (24 vols, London, 1860–1912).
ed./eds	editor; edited by/editors.
Fiants	*The Irish fiants of the Tudor sovereigns, 1521–1603* (4 vols, Dublin, 1994).
HJ	*Historical Journal.*
IHS	*Irish Historical Studies.*
IMC	Irish Manuscripts Commission.
JCKAHS	*Journal of the County Kildare Archaeological and Historical Society.*
JEH	*Journal of Ecclesiastical History.*
JRSAI	*Journal of the Royal Society of Antiquaries of Ireland.*
L&P	*Letters and papers, foreign and domestic, Henry VIII* (21 vols, London, 1862–1932)
LPL	Lambeth Palace Library.
NAI	National Archives of Ireland.
NUI	National University of Ireland.
NUIM	National University of Ireland, Maynooth.
OCist	Order of Cistercians.
ODNB	*Oxford dictionary of national biography.*
OESA	Order of Hermits of St Augustine.
OFM	Order of Friars Minor.

OP	Order of Preachers (Dominicans).
OSA	Order of St Augustine.
PRIA	*Proceedings of the Royal Irish Academy.*
PRONI	Public Records Office of Northern Ireland.
RCB	Representative Church Body.
SAM	*Seanchas Ard Mhacha: Journal of the Armagh Diocesan Historical Society.*
SJ	Society of Jesus (Jesuits).
SP	State papers.
Stat. Ire.	*Statutes at large passed in the parliaments held in Ireland*, i (Dublin, 1786).
Stg	Sterling.
StP	State Papers.
TCD	Trinity College Dublin.
UCC	University College Cork.
UCD	University College Dublin.
UCG	University College Galway.
Valor in Hibernia	*Valor beneficiorum ecclesiasticorum in Hibernia* (Dublin, 1741).
Works of Ware	*The whole works of Sir James Ware*, ed. Walter Harris (Dublin, 1747–50).

Introduction

This book has had a long gestation, its conception dating from as far back as my reading of Nicholas Canny's seminal article on 'Why the Reformation failed in Ireland'.[1] Canny argued that the Reformation was not doomed to inevitable failure in Ireland, as had long been assumed, and I was fascinated by the possibility that Ireland could have become Protestant. My study of the Irish Reformation parliament of 1560 reflects my engagement with that possibility.[2] However, my original thesis proposal, focused on the possibility of a successful Elizabethan reformation in Ireland, turned out to be a chimera. The more I researched the subject, the clearer it became that while the failure of the Reformation in Ireland may not have been inevitable, the evidence suggested that failure was extremely probable from an early date.

The failure of the Reformation in Ireland was certainly clear before the 1590s, when one Irish-born Protestant reckoned that there were hardly more than 120 Irish-born Protestants in the entire country.[3] A contemporary report stated that in Dublin itself there were only twenty Irish-born householders who attended Church of Ireland services, and only four of them received communion.[4] Beyond Dublin, Irish Protestants tended to be isolated individuals, usually men whose wives were Catholics. Nowhere in Ireland, not even in Galway, where Protestantism made more headway than elsewhere, were there self-sustaining communities of Irish Protestants.

Canny's intervention in the Irish Reformation debate, published in 1979, the year of Pope John Paul II's visit to Ireland, reflected the *zeitgeist* at a point in time when Irish society was on the verge of turning away from the old verities, and entering into an era of rapid change and profound secularisation. That cultural transformation is clearly reflected in contemporary Irish historical writing. Whereas Irish Catholic/nationalist historians had traditionally interpreted the religious history of sixteenth-century Ireland in the light of their own denominational and political predilections, their revisionist successors tended to project their own secularist mentalities onto the past and deny religion its significance as an important influence in Tudor times – even on the course of the Reformation itself.

1 Nicholas Canny, 'Why the reformation failed in Ireland: une question mal posée', *JEH*, 30 (1979), pp 423–50. 2 H.A. Jefferies, 'The Irish parliament of 1560: the Anglican reforms authorised', *IHS*, 26 (1988). 3 SP 63/207, pt 4/3. 4 SP 63/207, pt 6/126.

Part of the confusion about the prospects for the success of the Reformation in Ireland arises from a misapprehension as to what it was actually all about. To its adherents, it was a positive message of redemption through faith in Christ. There is a striking tendency in Irish academic circles to divorce the Reformation from religious convictions. A corollary of that secularist view is to equate conformity to the Church of Ireland, regardless of the nature of that conformity or the reasons that underlay it, with progress towards Protestantism. In fact, sullen conformity was no more than a parody of Protestantism. The general collapse in conformity in the Pale *c.*1585 exposed the extent of the failure of the Reformation to secure many convinced adherents in more than half a century since Henry VIII's breach with Rome. I cannot see that any more years of coerced conformity were likely to inspire Protestant convictions.

I feel obliged to declare at this point that my efforts to put religion back at the heart of the on-going debate on the Reformation in Ireland do not reflect any religious convictions of my own. I have been both an Anglican and a Catholic, but am now agnostic about the theological controversies of the sixteenth century. I am reminded of Diarmaid MacCulloch's observation that, 'in view of the contraction of Christian practice in modern Europe … [the Reformation might seem like] a story of two bald men fighting over a comb: an ultimately futile struggle over issues which now seem trivial or irrelevant'.[5] My interest in the Reformation in Ireland reflects my belief that religion has been one of the most important factors in Irish history, and understanding the Reformation in Ireland is critical to understanding much of what followed.

---

5 Diarmaid MacCulloch, *Reformation: Europe's houses divided, 1490–1700* (London, 2004), p. 669.

PART I

Before the reformations

Pastoral care

Conventionally, historians believed that there was a degree of disorder in the late medieval Irish Church 'not far short of total breakdown'.[1] In fact, however, there was an extensive network of thousands of parishes and chapelries served by priests in Ireland in the early Tudor period, and there were thousands of churches and chapels, many of them newly built, rebuilt or refurbished, within those parishes. The evidence suggests renewal, not decline.

CHURCH BUILDINGS

The conventional image of Irish church buildings in the later Middle Ages is one of 'tumbledown, disused and makeshift houses of worship'.[2] Yet, as long ago as 1960, Harold Leask highlighted the fact that the later Middle Ages were a time of 'remarkable building activity' in the Irish Church.[3] Not only were scores of new friaries constructed, but the 'larger monasteries of earlier date were busy with alterations and additions: the provision of belfries and the rebuilding of cloister arcades in particular'. 'Rural parish churches were very numerous ... Many were rebuilt in the fifteenth century or had the fashionable features added to them'.[4] This remarkable evidence did not conform to the conventional paradigm of a Church in decline – and was ignored. More recent work has confirmed that the later Middle Ages witnessed an extraordinary programme of church building, remodelling and ornamentation across much of Ireland.

Máirín Ní Mharcaigh revealed that the physical fabric of the Church in south-west County Dublin enjoyed massive investment in the later Middle Ages; reflected in the building of many new churches, and the re-modelling of at least one older church, together with the building of a number of substantial towers to house the parish clergy.[5] Michael O'Neill argued that St Patrick's Cathedral

1 John Watt, *The Church in late medieval Ireland* (Dublin, 1972), pp 182–3.   2 Elizabeth FitzPatrick and Caimin O'Brien, *The medieval churches of County Offaly* (Dublin, 1998), p. 117.   3 H.G. Leask, *Irish churches and monastic buildings*, iii (Dundalk, 1960), p. 1.   4 Ibid., pp 86–7, 1, 79.   5 Máirín Ní Mharcaigh, 'The medieval parish churches of south-west County Dublin', *PRIA*, 97C (1997), pp 245–96. See also Mary McMahon, *Medieval church sites of North Dublin* (Dublin, 1991), and idem, *St Audoen's Church, Cornmarket, Dublin: archaeology and architecture* (Dublin, 2006).

was 'at the fountainhead of the great rebuilding campaigns undertaken in the Pale, which coincided with and were predicated on the economic upturn in the fifteenth century'.[6] He traced some architectural influences of the cathedral on a number of its prebendal churches, and on some churches in County Meath. O'Neill highlighted an impressive body of late medieval details in many churches from across Meath.[7] He concluded that 'the discussion of the architecture of the churches in Meath, in particular the quantity and good quality of the late medieval buildings and the documentary evidence for their furnishings, must surely reinforce the arguments that the late medieval Church in Meath was healthy and, indeed, vibrant'.[8] Brendan Scott, in his study of Meath diocese, concurs with this positive assessment.[9] In his study of the medieval parish churches of County Kildare, O'Neill identified no fewer than eighteen that were built in the fifteenth century, together with another five that show signs of having been re-fashioned about the same time, and he concluded that a 'massive building and re-building programme' took place, not only within the inner Pale but also in the north-west and south of County Kildare.[10]

In the outlying boroughs in Ireland, there is further evidence of a revival in the fortunes of the Church. St Nicholas' Church in Galway was greatly extended after achieving collegiate status in 1485, with the addition of a south aisle financed by Dominic Dubh Lynch, one of the city's merchant oligarchs.[11] The work was completed by his son, Stephen, who also founded a hospital or poor house in the city.[12] Dominic also donated money for the building of the College House, the residence of the collegiate priests, and for the Dominican friary in Galway, which had been founded in 1488.[13] In 1508, an Augustinian friary was founded in Galway, while c.1538 a south transept was added to the local Franciscan friary.[14] A chapel of ease was established on the west bank of the Corrib at Galway c.1509–10.[15] In 1511, Walter Lynch gave his daughter a house near St Nicholas', which was subsequently known as a convent of the Poor Clares.[16] In 1493, James Lynch bestowed a stained-glass window and financed the building of the choir of St Nicholas' Church.[17] From 1538, the French family financed the construction of the north aisle, making St Nicholas' the

6 Michael O'Neill, 'St Patrick's Cathedral, Dublin, and its prebendal churches: gothic architectural relationships' in Seán Duffy (ed.), *Medieval Dublin V* (Dublin, 2004), p. 256.   7 O'Neill, 'The medieval parish churches of County Meath', *JRSAI*, 132 (2002), pp 1–56.   8 O'Neill, 'Parish churches of County Meath', p. 46.   9 Brendan Scott, *Religion and Reformation in the Tudor diocese of Meath* (Dublin, 2006), pp 29–38.   10 O'Neill, 'The medieval parish churches of Kildare', *JCKAHS*, 19 (2004–5), pp 427–30.   11 Leask, *Irish churches*, iii, p. 81.   12 Paul Walsh, 'An account of the town of Galway', *Journal of the Galway Archaeological and Historical Society*, 44 (1992), pp 60–3.   13 Ibid., p. 88.   14 Paul Walsh, 'The topography of the town of Galway in the medieval and early modern periods' in Moran and Gillespie (eds), *Galway: history and society* (1996), p. 46.   15 Ibid., p. 38.   16 Dianne Hall, *Women and the church in medieval Ireland, c.1140–1540* (Dublin, 2002), p. 91.   17 'Pedigree of Dr Dominic Lynch, regent of the college of St Thomas of Aquin, in the city of Seville, AD1674', *The Miscellany of the Irish Archaeological Society*, i (Dublin, 1846), p. 50.

second largest parish church in Ireland.[18] While few records survive of the smaller bequests of more humble folk, such benefactions were certainly made. In 1494, Peter Lynch endowed a chantry chapel that he had erected in St Nicholas' to support a priest to celebrate Mass daily for his soul and that of Ellen Blake, his wife.[19] The collegiate church at Galway built up a significant property portfolio from such grants before the Reformation to finance its services.[20] By the time of the Henrician reformation, there were fourteen altars in St Nicholas', most of them served by chantry priests in addition to the collegiate clergymen.[21] Less affluent people in Galway paid annual sums for anniversary Masses to be celebrated for deceased family members.[22]

Leask observed of St Mary's Cathedral, Limerick, that no other church in Ireland received so many additions in the fifteenth century.[23] The body of the cathedral was almost obscured by the ranges of chapels that were erected outside the nave aisles and on the east side of the south transept – 'evidences of the piety and munificence of Limerick's burger families'. Major additions to the cathedral's furnishings can also be dated to the same time, most notably the choir-stalls of black oak with their carved misericords, the only Irish example of the *genre* to survive.[24] During the episcopate of John Folan, bishop of Limerick (1489–1521), the people of Limerick renovated the nave of St Mary's Cathedral.[25] The massive shell of the Dominican friary built in the 1460s is further tangible testimony to the state of the Church in Limerick in the later Middle Ages.[26]

I have the impression that religious conditions in Cork were analogous with those of the Pale.[27] Its intra-mural parish churches were large and commodious, and seemingly in good order, and were lined with arrays of chantry chapels. They had impressive collections of funerary monuments dating from 1500.[28] A chantry college was founded in 1483 to accommodate the chantry priests of Christ Church in the city. The local Augustinian friary had a tower erected in the fifteenth century, while the local Dominican friary had a south aisle added in the fifteenth century, as well as a tower.[29]

Brendan Bradshaw observed that the state of the pre-Reformation Church in the south-western towns is 'not at all in conformity with the conventional image. The impression created is of a vigorous and flourishing institution which enjoyed the esteem of the lay community – not at all the moribund structure

---

18 Leask, *Irish churches*, iii, p. 81; Walsh, 'Account of the town', pp 60–3. **19** H.F. Berry, 'Documents relating to the wardenship of Galway', *Analecta Hibernica*, 14 (1944), pp 8, 11. **20** Ibid. **21** James Hardiman, *The history of the town and county of Galway: from the earliest period to the present time* (Dublin, 1820), p. 246. **22** Berry, 'Documents relating to the wardenship', pp 10, 16–18. **23** Leask, *Irish churches*, iii, p. 78. **24** Brendan Bradshaw, 'The Reformation in the cities: Cork, Limerick and Galway' in John Bradley (ed.), *Settlement and society in medieval Ireland* (Kilkenny, 1988), p. 449. **25** *Works of Ware*, i, p. 510. **26** Ibid., p. 448. **27** H.A. Jefferies, *Cork: historical perspectives* (Dublin, 2004), pp 101–6. **28** Ibid., p. 75. **29** Ibid., pp 67–8.

which the text-books depict as conditioning the onset of the Reformation'.[30]
William Neely reached very similar conclusions for Kilkenny.[31]

If a revival in the fortunes of the Irish Church in the English lordship in
Ireland conforms to what might reasonably be expected, the situation in Gaelic
Ireland might be expected to have been very different. Yet, as long ago as 1900,
T.J. Westropp revealed that at least thirty-four churches in County Clare had
been nearly completely rebuilt in the fifteenth and early sixteenth centuries, and
many earlier churches were renovated in the same period.[32] Indeed, Sinéad Ní
Ghabhláin, in her studies of the churches in Kilfenora diocese, in north-west
Clare, has shown that virtually *every* extant medieval parish church and chapel
has late medieval features built into it.[33]

Archaeological surveys from across the Republic of Ireland, from Wexford to
Galway, from Cork to Sligo are revealing that in the decades prior to the reformations, very many churches and chapels were being newly constructed, and older
ones were renovated, ornamented or extended, with many altars, baptismal fonts,
bell-cotes, not to mention altar-tombs and tomb-slabs or other funerary
monuments being added to churches at that same time. Indeed, the 'great rebuilding' of the later Middle Ages seems to have been so extensive that the compilers
of a number of the archaeological inventories can claim that 'the majority of
church remains appear to be 15th/16th century (late medieval) in date'.[34]

Elizabeth FitzPatrick and Caimin O'Brien highlighted architectural evidence
from at least thirty-five churches and chapels in County Offaly that 'indicates
some rebuilding or refurbishment' in the late medieval period, while most of the
remaining fifteen or so churches and chapels lack diagnostic features on which
to base an assessment.[35] Priests' quarters, or at least vestiges of them, survive at
ten churches in Offaly.[36] Those churches and priests' residences give tangible
testimony to the vitality of the Church in the Irish midlands in the later Middle
Ages.

Siobhán Scully's study of the medieval churches of south County Leitrim
showed that seven of the eight churches with diagnostic features in her study
area were either built in the fifteenth or sixteenth centuries, or were modified in
the later Middle Ages.[37] Scully concluded that the evidence from south Leitrim

30 Bradshaw, 'Reformation in the cities', p. 452.   31 W.G. Neely, *Kilkenny: an urban history,
1391–1843* (Belfast, 1989), pp 35–7.   32 J.T. Westropp, 'The churches of County Clare, and the
origins of the ecclesiastical divisions in that county', *PRIA*, 3 (1900–2), pp 101, 116 and passim.
33 Sinéad Ní Ghabhláin, 'Late twelfth-century church construction: evidence of parish formation?' in Elizabeth FitzPatrick and Raymond Gillespie (eds), *The parish in medieval and early
modern Ireland: community, territory and building* (Dublin, 2006), p. 161. See also Patrick Nugent,
'The dynamics of parish formation in high medieval and late medieval Clare' in FitzPatrick and
Gillespie, *The parish*, p. 208.   34 Denis Power et al. (eds), *Archaeological inventory of County
Cork*, ii (Dublin, 1994), p. 242, but its sentiment is repeated in several other inventories.
35 FitzPatrick and O'Brien, *Medieval churches of Offaly*, pp 124–6.   36 Ibid., pp 134–6.
37 Siobhán Scully, 'Medieval parish churches and parochial organisation in Muintir Eolais'

indicates that 'the parish may not have been as ineffective as the tales of neglect in the papal letters would lead us to believe'.[38]

The absence of a modern published archaeological inventory for Northern Ireland[39] might create a misleading impression that conditions in Ulster were different to those in the rest of Ireland. However, studies of the dioceses of Armagh *inter Hibernicos*, Clogher, Derry and Dromore have challenged the conventional impression that the Church in those dioceses was in decline.[40] There is evidence that late medieval church building campaigns occurred in Ulster too: the eulogy of Thomas Óg Maguire, lord of Fermanagh (d. 1480), in the Annals of Ulster notes that he built many churches and monasteries.[41] Indeed, there is archaeological evidence to confirm that many churches in Fermanagh were built or renovated in the fifteenth century.[42]

Irish church buildings were extremely similar across the countryside. Typically, they were rectangular buildings, orientated along an east-west axis, with the altar below a window on the east side, a bell-cote on the west gable, and one or two doorways. Most were simple unicellular structures, with a minority being nave-and-chancel structures.[43] The average lengths of Irish medieval churches ranged from 14.24m to 18.13m (with most ranging between 15m and 16m), and 5.63m to 8m in width (with most ranging between 6m and 7m).[44] Undoubtedly, some of the churches were built with money from the local landowners,[45] but others are likely to have been built through the joint efforts of all of the parishioners.[46]

Medieval churches in Ireland were generally built of roughly coursed rubble masonry bonded with lime mortar.[47] Dressed stone, being expensive, was reserved for mouldings, quoins, tracery and arches. Scully suggests that medieval Irish churches were 'probably plastered both internally and externally'.[48] Significantly, perhaps, one of the very few Irish churches to have remained in continuous use since before the Tudor reformations, St Audoen's in Dublin, had a fifteenth-century religious wall-painting, 'in vivid colours'.[49]

(MA, UCG, 1999), pp 13, 40, 45–6, 50–2, 54, 64, 74–5. **38** Ibid., pp 174, 184. **39** The Northern Irish Department of the Environment maintains an up-to-date web-site by which one may access its archaeological inventory. **40** Jefferies, *Priests and prelates of Armagh in the age of reformations* (Dublin, 1997), pp 57–82; idem, 'Papal letters and Irish clergy: Clogher before the Reformation' in Jefferies (ed.), *History of the diocese of Clogher* (Dublin, 2005); idem, 'Derry diocese on the eve of the plantation' in Gerard O'Brien (ed.), *Derry and Londonderry: history and society* (Dublin, 1999); idem, 'The diocese of Dromore on the eve of the Tudor reformations' in Lindsay Proudfoot (ed.), *Down: history and society* (Dublin, 1997). **41** *AU*, s.a. 1480. **42** Jefferies, 'Papal letters and Irish clergy', p. 103. **43** Scully, 'Medieval parish churches', p. 86; V.M. Buckley and D. Sweetman (eds), *Archaeological survey of County Louth* (Dublin, 1991), nos 902, 904, 915, 923, 924, 929, 952, 968, 983, 984. **44** Ibid., p. 93. **45** Leask, *Irish churches*, iii, pp 12–16, 164–5. **46** Colin Platt, *Medieval England: a social history and archaeology from the conquest to AD1600* (London and New York, 1978), pp 138–44. **47** Ibid. **48** Scully, 'Medieval parish churches', pp 103–4, 111; Jefferies, *Priests and prelates*, p. 23. **49** H.M. Roe, 'Illustrations of the Holy Trinity in Ireland, thirteenth to the seventeenth centuries', *JRSAI*, 109 (1979), pp

It is probable that most late medieval Irish churches were roofed with thatched straw or timber shingles.[50] Rural churches normally had clay floors.[51] Occasionally, the floor of the chancel was tiled, though Heather King referred to such tiles as a 'luxury'.[52] The chancel of the late medieval parish church at Kilquane in County Cork was paved with flat stones of irregular shape, a far cheaper alternative but not a common one apparently.[53] Consequently, given the Irish climate, one may well imagine the muddy state to which the rural churches could descend. Lord Deputy Sussex, in 1556, complained that the churches of Ireland, 'not only in the north but also through the most of Ireland, (were more) like stables for horses and herd houses for cattle, than holy places to minister with due reverence the most blessed sacraments in'.[54] In 1571, Edmund Tremayne, clerk of the Irish privy council, also described Irish churches as being 'only like stables'.[55] That there was a pervasive problem in this regard is indicated by the synodal legislation of the province of Cashel in 1453, which decreed that all churches were to be kept neat and clean and that animals, corn and such things belonging to the laity should not be kept inside the buildings.[56]

Scully found evidence of glazing in 'many windows' in her study area in south Leitrim, which suggests that glass was more common in late medieval Irish churches than might have been assumed.[57] Little survives of the internal furnishings of the late medieval Irish churches. There are only 'random survivals of wooden fittings and statuary, metalwork and wall painting so few that it is difficult to ascertain how representative they might be of what once existed'.[58] The altars were generally removed since the Tudor reformations, and that at Ballingly parish church in County Wexford is one of the very few still *in situ*.[59] On the eve of the Tudor reformations, each altar had to be covered with a special cloth before Mass could be celebrated. In a case brought before Armagh's metropolitan court in 1520, a defendant was severely punished for removing the altar cloth in order to prevent the incoming vicar from celebrating Mass in the parish church of Molary.[60]

Archaeologists have been able to identify evidence of the former existence of timber rood screens in a surprising number of late medieval Irish churches, not only in the Pale and outlying boroughs, but also in Gaelic and gaelicised

127, 144–5.   50 Scully, 'Medieval parish churches', pp 109, 110–11; FitzPatrick and O'Brien, *Medieval churches of Offaly*, p. 132.   51 FitzPatrick and O'Brien, *Medieval churches of Offaly*, p. 131; Scully, 'Medieval parish churches', p. 111.   52 Buckley and Sweetman (eds), *Archaeological survey of County Louth*, no. 981. H.A. King, 'A tiled floor at Greenoge, County Meath', *Ríocht na Midhe* (1992–3), p. 92.   53 Denis Power, *Archaeological inventory of County Cork*, iii (Dublin, 1997), pp 380–1.   54 SP 62/1/22.   55 SP 63/32/40.   56 TCD MS 808 (5), nos 3, 69. 57 Scully, 'Medieval parish churches', pp 129–33.   58 Rachel Moss, 'Permanent expressions of piety: the secular and the sacred in later medieval stone sculpture' in Rachel Moss, Colmán Ó Clabaigh and Salvador Ryan (eds), *Art and devotion in late medieval Ireland* (Dublin, 2006), pp 72–3, 96.   59 M.J. Moore, *Archaeological inventory of County Wexford* (Dublin, 1996), p. 120. 60 Jefferies, *Priests and prelates*, p. 23.

parishes.[61] However, with the solitary exception of the rood screen from St Olave's Church in Waterford, which was carefully dismantled and hidden away,[62] none survived the Reformation. A unique rood-gallery in stone survives at Newtown Jerpoint in County Kilkenny.[63]

The provincial synod of Cashel in 1453, with jurisdiction over a province that was overwhelmingly Gaelic or gaelicised in population and culture, decreed that every church should have at least a statue of the Virgin Mary and a statue of the church's patron saint, together with a cross and a tabernacle.[64]. A number of late medieval Irish churches have a recess in a prominent position beside the altar, which would have accommodated a statue.[65] These statues were typically polychrome.[66] In the Armagh court book for the years 1518 to 1522, there are references to penitents being ordered to stand before the statue of the patron saint in their parish church, holding a wax candle, during Sunday Mass.[67]

A number of late medieval baptismal fonts has survived, though the vast majority were destroyed following the later Tudor reformations.[68] Some holy water stoups or basins are still in place in many ruined churches across Ireland.[69] One anthropomorphic carving that was intriguingly common on Irish churches of late medieval date was the Sheela-na-gig.[70] These exhibitionist figures were generally placed on quoin-stones or above windows or doorways. Their purpose is not understood, and I am not convinced by the speculation that the graphic sexual images may have been intended as a warning against sins of the flesh.

While the late medieval churches in the Irish countryside are remarkably similar across the country, there was a small minority of churches in the inner Pale, particularly in north Dublin and Meath, that were somewhat larger and more ornate. Michael O'Neill has observed that twin-aisled churches were 'surprisingly common' in County Dublin in the medieval period (at least compared with the rest of Ireland): they are known to have existed at Lusk, Balrothery, Clondalkin, Finglas, Howth, St Audoen's and Swords.[71] The wealthier parish churches of the larger towns of late medieval Ireland were certainly much more elaborate than those in the countryside.[72] It was not at all

61 Leask, *Irish churches*, iii, pp 33, 183; Buckley and Sweetman (eds), *Archaeological survey of County Louth*, nos 897, 964, 984; Bradley, 'The medieval borough of Louth', *CLAHJ*, 21 (1985), p. 19; Davies, 'Old churches in County Louth', *CLAHJ*, 10 (1943), pp 200–3. Scully, 'Medieval parish churches', pp 143–4. **62** Niall Byrne, 'Reformation in Tudor Waterford, 1547–1603' (MA, UCC, 1998), pp 4–5. **63** Leask, *Irish churches*, iii, pp 183–4. **64** TCD 808 (5), no. 4. **65** Buckley and Sweetman (eds), *Archaeological survey of County Louth*, no. 927. **66** Canice Mooney, *The Church in Gaelic Ireland: thirteenth to fifteenth centuries* (Dublin, 1969), p. 10. **67** Jefferies, *Priests and prelates*, 23. **68** FitzPatrick and O'Brien, *Medieval churches of Offaly*, pp 123–4; Scully, 'Medieval parish churches', p. 139; Helen Roe, *Medieval fonts of Meath* (Longford, 1968). **69** Leask, *Irish churches*, iii, p. 167; Buckley and Sweetman (eds), *Archaeological survey of County Louth*, nos 983, 995. **70** FitzPatrick and O'Brien, *Medieval churches of Offaly*, pp 130–1. **71** O'Neill, 'St Patrick's Cathedral and its prebendal churches', p. 263. **72** Jefferies, *Priests and prelates*, pp 24–5.

unusual for the larger churches to have choirs; the provincial synod of Cashel in 1453 decreed that in cities and other places where there were choirs established, no clergyman was to be advanced to any ecclesiastical living unless he was capable of singing.[73] It can be taken for granted that many of the choirs were accompanied by organ music. Primate Octavian purchased an organ in 1482 from Kilkenny for Armagh cathedral.[74] Obviously that entrepreneur from Ormond found customers enough in Ireland to keep him in business, and there were parish communities in Ireland with the money and aspirations to emulate the liturgical achievements of their fellows elsewhere.

The prevailing impression that the late medieval Irish churches were 'tumbledown, disused and makeshift' is belied by a formidable and growing body of evidence to show that a great many churches were either newly built, re-built or rehabilitated in the decades immediately prior to the Tudor reformations. The shattered and emptied shells of the medieval church buildings that dot the Irish countryside today can create a very misleading impression of the late medieval churches in their heyday.

PARISH NETWORK

It is not known how many parishes there were in Ireland in the early sixteenth century. The conventional estimate of 2,500 is based upon the number of civil parishes, but one cannot simply assume that every civil parish represented a medieval parish. Work on Armagh diocese in the sixteenth century, supported by a late sixteenth-century survey of Leighlin diocese, showed that there were many chapelries within parishes that came to form the basis of civil parishes – indicating that an indeterminate number of the civil parishes were not *de jure* parishes in the Irish Church on the eve of the Henrician reformation.[75] On the other hand, the very fact that many chapelries became civil parishes reflects an ambiguity in their status.[76] Significantly too, one finds churchwardens acting on behalf of the parishioners of Tullyallen, a chapelry within the parish of Mellifont that was served by an unbeneficed curate.[77]

The parish network reflected local fluctuations in economic conditions:

---

73 TCD MS 808 (5), no. 86. St Peter's in Drogheda also had a choir: Jefferies, *Priests and prelates*, p. 24.   74 T.G.F. Paterson, *Harvest home* (Dundalk, 1973), p. 32. I cannot, however, trace the source for Paterson's statement.   75 Jefferies, 'The role of the laity in the parishes of Armagh *inter Anglicos*, 1518–1553', *Archivium Hibernicum*, 52 (1998), pp 73–4. Dónal Moore (ed.), 'A relation concerning the estate of the churches within the diocese of Leighlin, 1585–7', *Archivium Hibernicum*, 41 (1987), pp 3–11. The survey of Leighlin diocese identified sixty-two parish churches and forty-nine chapels within parishes – but both the areas served by the churches and their chapels subsequently formed the basis of distinct civil parishes.   76 N.B. White (ed.), *Extents of Irish monastic possessions, 1540–1* (Dublin, 1943), pp 219, 226.   77 Jefferies, *Priests and prelates*, p. 112.

economic decline made some parishes unviable (sometimes temporarily, sometimes permanently), and necessitated the union of parishes to provide some kind of reasonable financial support for a priest. The provincial synod of Cashel in 1453 observed that 'in many areas where churches or chapels have been united or appropriated, it has been learnt by experience that these churches have been deserted and let fall into decay'.[78] In effect, the parish network was rationalised, *de facto* if not *de jure*, in parts of Ireland before the Tudor reformations.

On the other hand, new parishes and chapelries were sometimes formed when conditions permitted. The parish of Dromore was established in Clogher diocese in 1503/4 at the instigation of the local lord, Art O'Neill, who financed the building of the church and graveyard, and provided the necessary liturgical equipment for the parish.[79] A church was built at Kilcreevy in Armagh diocese in 1458 through the benefaction of Art McKearney, a carpenter from Armagh city.[80] Indeed, several parishes with beneficed clergymen are recorded for Armagh *inter Hibernicos* in Primate Dowdall's register in the mid-sixteenth century whose existence proved to be transient.[81] Peter Nugent found a number of such parishes in County Clare in the later sixteenth century,[82] suggesting a broader pattern whereby the parish network in Gaelic lordships expanded or contracted to modest degrees in response to changing conditions on the ground.

One cannot simply assume that each civil parish was actually served by a priest at any one particular point in time in the later Middle Ages.[83] However, procurations lists in the Armagh registers show that more than sixty churches were being served in Armagh *inter Anglicos* (County Louth, in effect) *c.*1544, with another ten being identifiable from diocesan records dating from a few years earlier. This indicates a remarkable density of churches – of one for every 2,000–2,500 acres within the Pale ditch.[84] That demonstrates that not only were churches very numerous in County Louth, but they were readily accessible. Archbishop Alen compiled a list of churches in Dublin diocese in the early 1530s,[85] and there are procuration lists available for Meath diocese from the late fifteenth and early sixteenth centuries.[86] For dioceses with few if any surviving ecclesiastical records, one may turn to the *Valor in Hibernia*, a record of the value of clerical benefices in 1538–9, and to the monastic extents, which offer indications about many non-beneficed parish cures in 1540–1.[87]

---

78 TCD MS 808 (5), no. 16. 79 Jefferies, 'Papal letters and Irish clergy', p. 95. 80 Jefferies, *Priest and prelates*, p. 67. 81 Ibid., pp 62–8. 82 Peter Nugent, 'The dynamics of parish formation in high medieval and late medieval Clare' in FitzPatrick and Gillespie, *The parish*, pp 195–208. 83 Jefferies, 'Parishes and pastoral care', p. 212. 84 Jefferies, *Priests and prelates*, p. 20. 85 N.B. White (ed.), 'The *reportorium viride* of John Alen archbishop of Dublin, 1533', *Analecta Hibernica*, 10 (1944), and also Charles MacNeill (ed.), *Calendar of Archbishop Alen's register, c.1172–1534* (Dublin, 1950). 86 TCD MS 1060 (5); Dowdall's register, pp 253–68 (129); Brendan Scott, 'Administrative documents relating to the pre-Reformation Church in the diocese of Meath, *c.*1518', *Archivium Hibernicum*, 41 (2008). 87 Steven Ellis, 'Economic problems of the Church: why the Reformation failed in Ireland', *JEH*, 41 (1990). The *Valor in*

Only for Ulster and County Clare, as yet, are there yet any useful indications as to how many churches beyond the Pale were served by priests in the sixteenth century. Archbishop Dowdall's register indicates that *c*.1544 there were forty-four churches served by beneficed clergymen in Armagh *inter Hibernicos*.[88] That would suggest a density of one parish church for every 13,300 to 14,000 acres – a striking contrast with the figures for Armagh *inter Anglicos*, though when one takes account of the chapels that are known to have existed on the eve of the plantation, the density improves somewhat to approximately one church per 10,600 to 12,500 acres, which still means that churches were less accessible to parishioners across a diocese that extended into the heart of Ulster.[89] Bishop Montgomery's survey of the Church in Derry diocese *c*.1607 suggests a density of one parish church per 14,644 acres, though the inclusion of the fifteen chapels identified by Montgomery improves the density to one church per 10,983 acres. The thirty-eight parishes Montgomery reported for Clogher diocese would indicate a density of one parish church per 22,473 acres, though that figure makes no allowance for the now-indeterminable number of chapels in the diocese. Nonetheless, no matter how one looks at the figures, it is clear that across much of Ulster the parishes were extensive in size, and churches and chapels were far less accessible than was true in the Pale. A survey of 1576 identified seventy-six vicarages in County Clare – indicating a density there of one parish church per 10,400 acres, which is not dissimilar to the densities across much of Ulster.[90]

Studies of the Church in Ulster have demonstrated that the uneven distribution of churches and chapels reflected, to no small degree, the physical geography of the province.[91] This seems to have been a general phenomenon, as Ní Mharcaigh found that in south-west County Dublin all but one of the eighteen medieval parish churches were situated below the 400-foot contour, though there were some 'subsidiary churches', chapels of ease I presume, above the 500-foot contour.[92] This suggests that churches were more numerous and accessible in fertile lowland areas where agricultural output was likely to be highest and the population densities were greatest, but least numerous in upland areas that were almost certainly poorly populated.

We have no idea about the numbers of people, nor the proportions of the population, who attended Church services on a regular basis. We might assume

Hibernia* was published as *Valor beneficiorum ecclesiasticorum in Hiberniae: or the first fruits of all of the ecclesiastical benefices in the kingdom of Ireland, as taxed in the king's book* (Dublin, 1741); White (ed.), *Extents of Irish monastic possessions*. See also Charles McNeill (ed.), 'Accounts of sums realised by sales of chattels of some suppressed Irish monasteries', *JRSAI*, 52 (1922), pp 11–37.   **88** 'Dowdall's register', pp 234–6 (119, E); Jefferies, *Priests and prelates*, pp 19–20, 62–5. **89** Jefferies, *Priests and prelates*, pp 64–5.   **90** Nugent, 'Dynamics of parish formation', p. 195. **91** Jefferies, 'The diocese of Dromore', p. 126; idem, 'Derry diocese', p. 200; idem, *Priests and prelates*, p. 63.   **92** Ní Mharcaigh, 'Medieval parish churches', pp 247, 257.

that regular Mass attendance was less likely among parishioners from the remoter corners of large parishes than among members of small parishes, but we have no hard evidence to confirm such plausible suggestions. Nonetheless, one may conclude with this observation: there were more parishes, and more parish churches and chapels *per capita*, across late medieval Ireland than there would be again before the nineteenth century.

PARISH CLERGY'S INCOMES

An Act of 1537 authorised commissioners to be sent to each diocese to determine the values of all tithes, offerings and emoluments (spiritual and temporal) of each benefice and chantry. Deductions were allowed for rents, fees payable, synodals, alms that the benefice holders were obliged to pay, and any pensions payable from the revenues of benefices.[93] Valuations were compiled in 1538–9 for parishes within the English lordship of Ireland and were duly preserved in the *Valor in Hibernia*.[94] It seems clear that the crown commissioners drew their information from pre-existing diocesan records.[95] The *Valor* gives no indication of the incomes of unbeneficed parish clergy.

One striking fact that emerges from the *Valor* is the poverty of the beneficed parish clergy, the rectors and the vicars. Only in the dioceses of Meath (stg£7 11s. 10d.), Ossory (stg£6 4s. 4d.) and Ferns (stg£5 11s.) were the rectories worth more than stg£5 on average. Dublin's rectories were valued at stg£4 19s. 8d. on average. Yet, even in those dioceses, the proportion of rectors whose incomes were assessed at less than stg£5 was no less than 44%, 59%, 64% and 57% respectively. In the diocese of Leighlin, the average value of the rectories recorded was stg£1 6s. 5½d.[96]

In Ferns alone did the incomes of vicars exceed stg£5 on average. In Armagh, Dublin, Meath, and Ossory vicars received an average of between stg£4 and stg£5. In Kildare, the average value was stg£3 14s. 2d., in Waterford & Lismore £3 6s. ½d. (excluding the exceptional vicarage of Dungarvan that was valued at stg£20), in Leighlin stg£2 1s. 9½d and in Cashel stg£1 4s. 4½d. The proportion of vicars whose incomes were assessed at less than stg£5 was no less than 36%, 54%, 60%, 69% and 72% in Armagh, Ferns, Dublin, Meath and Ossory respectively, and 76% and 77% in Kildare and Waterford & Lismore, while all of the vicars in Leighlin and Cashel dioceses had incomes assessed at less than stg£5. Indeed, 93% of Cashel's vicars were reported as receiving incomes of less than stg£2 10s. *per annum*.

---

93 Dowdall's register, pp 193–208 (110).   94 Ellis, 'Economic problems of the Church', op. cit.; Jefferies, *Priests and prelates*, p. 32.   95 Jefferies, *Priests and prelates*, pp 35–6.   96 *Valor in Hibernia*, p. 13.

Calculations based on Primate Dowdall's register suggest an annual average income of stg£1 8s. 6d. for the rectors, and stg18s. 1d. for the vicars in Tullyhogue rural deanery c.1544.[97] One cannot know how the figures were calculated, but they were gathered on the instruction of the archbishop and he, at least, expected that they would accord with reality to some considerable degree. Furthermore, work done on clerical incomes in the dioceses of Dromore,[98] Derry,[99] and Clogher provides broad confirmation of the same pattern across Ulster.[1]

By contrast with England, there were a great many parishes in late medieval Ireland that were appropriated *cum pleno jure*. This meant that the religious house or cathedral chapter that held the rectory kept possession of all of the parish's endowments, and generally employed an unbeneficed priest to discharge the cure of souls, often in return for the altarages of the parish.[2] The value of altarages recorded in the monastic extents for rural parishes in Louth, Meath, Dublin, Kildare and Kilkenny range in value from Ir5s. to Ir£2.[3] The unbeneficed parish priests of such parishes were significantly poorer than their colleagues with benefices.

With their generally paltry incomes, the priests who served the cures of souls sought small monetary offerings from their parishioners three or four times a year.[4] A statute of the provincial synod of Cashel in 1453 decreed that mendicant friars were not to 'quest' on the feast days on which the parochial clergy were accustomed to receive offerings.[5] Another source of additional income was the fees charged for the administration of certain sacraments, including those for baptisms, weddings and funerals, and for the churching of women after childbirth. Masses for the dead could also generate a little additional cash.[6] However onerous such fees may have been, especially for the poor, they did ensure that the laity secured the services they required of their parish clergy – at a price. For a great number of the parish clergy, including both the beneficed clergymen beyond the main tillage regions in the east and the unbeneficed priests everywhere, such fees made all the difference between being able to subsist as a priest, and not.

Despite their low incomes, rectors were normally responsible for maintaining the chancel of the parish church; the laity were responsible for the nave.[7]

97 Jefferies, *Priests and prelates*, p. 71.   98 Jefferies, 'Dromore on the eve of the Tudor reformation', pp 124–5.   99 Jefferies, 'Derry diocese', p. 185.   1 Jefferies, 'Papal letters and Irish clergy', pp 95–6.   2 *Monastic extents*, passim.   3 *Monastic extents*, pp 28, 34–5, 44, 86, 88, 89, 92, 160–1.   4 These payments were not strictly voluntary: Jefferies, *Priests and prelates*, p. 30. 5 TCD MS 808 (5), no. 13. Offerings may have been in the order of 1/2d. to 1d. per adult in the parish: James Murray, 'The sources of clerical income in the Tudor diocese of Dublin, c.1530–1600', *Archivium Hibernicum*, 45 (1990), pp 153–4.   6 SP 60/5/74, presentment xv; SP 60/5/85, presentment liv; TCD MS 10,383, 'Clogher, Derry and Raphoe', fo. 8.   7 For the chancels see *Monastic extents*, pp 225, 253; Jefferies, *Priests and prelates*, p. 37. In Ulster west of the Bann, the rector and vicar shared responsibility for maintaining one third of the parish

Furthermore, all priests with cures had to pay a synodal when attending diocesan synods.[8] There were also the not inconsiderable expenses involved in travel and in finding lodgings wherever the synods were convened, though the dean of Raphoe was obliged to provide hospitality for the clergy attending synods in that diocese.[9] Procurations were more burdensome charges that were payable by beneficed clergy to the bishop, and sometimes to the archdeacon too after visitations.[10] It was claimed in 1537 that during their visitations the archbishop of Cashel and the bishop of Waterford & Lismore demanded either an 'unreasonable sum' of money, or else meat, drink and lodgings for their episcopal retinues.[11]

The beneficed clergy of the Pale were obliged to pay an annual subsidy to the Dublin administration.[12] Landholders commonly imposed cess on the clergy as well as lay freeholders, and one may doubt the effectiveness of Church attempts to legislate the practice away.[13] The provincial synod of Cashel in 1453 demanded that the clergy should not be cessed more than once a year, and never on a Saturday or Sunday so that the clergy could attend to their religious duties in peace and quietness.[14]

Peter Heath, in his study of the English parish clergy on the eve of the Tudor reformations, reckoned that stg£15 was a 'desirable and reasonable income' for an incumbent with a chaplain, or stg£10 where there was no chaplain.[15] Yet, only a tiny minority of clergymen enjoyed stg£10 or more in Ireland. Any meaningful attempt at ecclesiastical reform in Ireland would have had to address the problem of clerical poverty. However, there were no easy solutions to that problem. It was due to three key factors: the under-developed state of much of the Irish economy, the manifold customs that limited the tithe revenues that the Irish Church could effectively secure, and the extraordinarily high proportion of parishes that were appropriated and, in a great many cases, left without an

church and the erenagh for the rest; ibid., p. 78. **8** Jefferies, *Priests and prelates*, p. 37; Charles McNeill (ed.), *Calendar of Archbishop Alen's register, c.1172–1534* (Dublin, 1950), p. 275. Bishops of Clogher collected their synodals at Easter; A.F. O'D Alexander (ed.), 'The O'Kane papers', *Analecta Hibernica*, 12 (1943), p. 100. **9** Ulster inquisitions, appendix, County Donegal, third page. **10** Jefferies, *Priests and prelates*, p. 37. In Dublin diocese too, procurations were related to the value of the benefices: *Alen's register*, pp 277–8. In Derry diocese, beneficed clergymen paid procurations of 2*s.* to 3*s.*: TCD MS 10,383, fo. 9; Jefferies, 'Derry diocese', p. 180. In Raphoe diocese, procurations ranged from 3*s.* to 4*s.* from each rector and vicar: 'Ulster inquisitions', County Donegal. **11** SP 60/5/80, presentment xxxiv. The procurations demanded by the bishop of Kilmacduagh, as recorded on a copy of a document of 1500, also appear extortionate, but they must have included the bishop's share of the tithes; Nicholls, 'The episcopal rentals of Clonfert and Kilmacduagh', *Analecta Hibernica*, 26 (1970), pp 141–3. **12** In Armagh *inter Anglicos* in the mid-fifteenth century, the levied ranged from 8.75% to 13.74% of incumbents' incomes; Jefferies, *Priests and prelates*, p. 37. **13** Jefferies, *Priests and prelates*, p. 37; Mary Ann Lyons, *Church and society in County Kildare, c.1470–1547* (Dublin, 2000), p. 73; H.J. Lawlor, 'A calendar of the Liber Ruber of the diocese of Ossory', *PRIA*, 27C (1908–9), p. 165. **14** TCD MS 808 (5), no. 7. **15** Peter Heath, *The English parish clergy on the eve of the Reformation* (London, 1969), p. 173.

endowed vicarage. The options of either rationalising the parish system significantly to improve the remuneration of a less numerous priesthood, or
rationalising the monastic establishment to divert appropriated parish revenues
to support poorer parishes, were not considered at the time.[16]

Nonetheless, one should not unthinkingly interpret clerical poverty of itself,
or its symptoms (decayed chancels or ragged clothing), as proof of moral
failings. The low incomes of the parish clergy in Ireland did mean, though, that
very few parishes would have offered a graduate priest a financial return for the
heavy investment required to secure a degree. Nonetheless, the priests' financial
dependence on their parishioners would have served to ensure that the priests
could not afford to neglect the needs and wishes of the laity.

PARISH CLERGY

Across Ulster west of the Bann, but in few districts elsewhere, a great many of
the parish clergy were drawn from erenagh clans, families of hereditary tenants
on episcopal lands.[17] The erenaghs were the successors of the heads of early
Irish churches and, according to Bishop Montgomery, they were still popularly
regarded as clergymen in the early seventeenth century.[18] A large number of the
erenaghs in Derry diocese in 1607 were either the rector or the vicar of the local
parish (though the enormous mortality inflicted on the civilian population in
Ulster during the final stages of the Nine Years War could, conceivably, have
made that necessary at the time).[19] Similarly, in studies of the dioceses of
Armagh *inter Hibernicos*, Clogher and Dromore men whose surnames indicate
that they came from erenagh clans are often found among the parish clergy. Men
with erenagh surnames have also been identified among the clergy of the Pale,
often with their surnames under an anglicised guise.[20]

Across Ireland generally, but particularly in Gaelic and gaelicised districts, a
significant proportion of the parish clergy were the sons of clergymen. It is very
difficult to form a judgment as to the size of that proportion. Michael Haren
studied 1,903 papal penitentiary dispensations for illegitimacy among Irish
clergy granted from 1449 to 1533.[21] Fewer than two thirds of the dispensations

16 Indeed, the number of appropriations increased in order to enhance the already well-endowed
collegiate church in Galway. However, Archbishop Alen of Dublin's suppression of the dilapi-
dated convent at Timolin, County Kildare, in 1530 brought six appropriated parishes back under
archiepiscopal control: Brendan Bradshaw, *The dissolution of the religious orders in Ireland under
Henry VIII* (Cambridge, 1974), p. 43. Alen had worked as Cardinal Wolsey's agent in the
suppression of a number of English houses whose assets were redeployed to better use.
17 Katharine Simms, 'Frontiers in the Irish Church: regional and cultural' in T.B. Barry, Robin
Frame and Katharine Simms (eds), *Colony and frontier in medieval Ireland: essays presented to J.F.
Lydon* (London, 1995), p. 179. 18 Jefferies, 'Derry diocese', pp 181–6. 19 Ibid., pp 181,
186–7. 20 Jefferies, *Priests and prelates*, p. 47. 21 M.J. Haren, 'Social structures of the Irish

were granted to clergymen whose fathers were themselves clergymen; fewer than half were granted to the sons of diocesan priests.[22] Every diocese in Ireland is represented, with no fewer than 170 dispensations granted to clergy in the diocese of Killaloe, 120 to clergy in Ardfert diocese, ninety to clergy in both Derry and Meath dioceses (almost half of the latter to men with English surnames), but only fifteen dispensations were granted to clergy in both Clonmacnoise and Kilmacduagh dioceses. There were thirty-seven dispensations to clergy in Dublin diocese (almost half of whom had English surnames).

Unfortunately, the surviving records do not allow one to calculate how many diocesan clergymen were the sons of clergymen: the sixty-four dispensations known to have been granted to clergymen in the diocese of Armagh over the seventy-seven years in Haren's study would indicate that an average of one clergyman every two years from that diocese received a papal dispensation for being the son of a clergyman (allowance having been made for the proportion of fathers across Ireland who were not identified as clergymen).[23] The figures from the other dioceses too are low when considered as an annual average. However, it is conceivable that some clergymen secured dispensations for illegitimacy from their local bishop rather than taking the trouble and expense of securing a papal dispensation.

Interestingly, my survey of the papal registers showed that the mothers of priests' sons were almost invariably unmarried – indicating that the Irish diocesan clergy were far more likely to be intimate with unmarried women than with other men's wives, or former wives.[24] The fact that the priests' sons featured in the papal registers had decided to follow their fathers into the Church may be interpreted as evidence that their fathers maintained an abiding interest in their children's well-being. It seems that clerical marriage was widely accepted in Gaelic society, despite the strictures of canon law.[25] In the more gaelicised parts of the English lordship too, being the children of clergymen carried no social stigma. Indeed in 1552, the rector of Knocktopher, in Ossory diocese, explained to Bishop John Bale that it was considered an honour to have a clergyman for a father, preferably a bishop or abbot or prior.[26] The high proportion of priests with English surnames within Meath and Dublin dioceses who secured papal dispensations for being the sons of priests belies the misconception that clerical concubinage was strictly a Gaelic sin.

Of the backgrounds of parish clergymen who were neither the sons of

Church: a new source in papal penitentiary dispensations for illegitimacy' in Herausgegeben von Ludwig Schmugge (ed.), *Illegitimitat im spatmittelalter: Schriften des Historischen Kollegs Kolloquien*, 29 (Oldenbourg, 1994), pp 207–26. **22** Haren, 'Social structures', p. 224. **23** Jefferies, *Priests and prelates*, p. 79. Note that I mistakenly referred to the fathers as being priests rather than clergymen. **24** Ibid., p. 87. **25** Haren, 'Social structures', pp 221–2. **26** John Bale, 'The vocacion of John Bale to the bishopric of Ossory in Ireland (1553)', *Harleian miscellany*, 6 (1734), p. 447.

clergymen nor members of erenagh clans, little can be written for certain. A very small proportion of priests came from reasonably wealthy families of landowners or merchants, though one can form an exaggerated impression of their numbers because they were more likely to occupy senior positions in the Church and thus feature disproportionately in surviving records. Such men enjoyed the confidence and assurance that wealth brings, but often too they had the advantage of a good education, perhaps even a university degree, to ensure them of promotion within the Church. Even the poorer priests would have come from families that had sufficient resources to afford to have their sons educated, and to support them until such time as they secured employment in the Church.[27]

Information on the training of Irish diocesan clergy is hard to come by. There was, of course, no university in Ireland despite the repeated efforts made to establish one in Dublin. In 1465, an attempt was made to found a university in Drogheda, but the project failed to reach fruition.[28] Only a privileged minority of the clergy from Ireland could afford to acquire a university education overseas.[29] It seems to be generally true that the universities produced more canon lawyers than theologians; training in canon law opened the way to promotion in diocesan administration.

Across Ireland, there were many *studia particularia* conducted by masters who were generally drawn from families who followed as hereditary occupations the various learned professions. The masters were usually 'closely connected' with the Church; in Ulster they were often drawn from erenagh families.[30] The *studia* were sometimes run by graduates and aspired to a more advanced level of education than that available in the grammar schools elsewhere. Matthew Ó Gríofa stated in 1458 that he had lectured publicly for four years in the faculty of canon law at Oxford University, before lecturing for four more years in various schools in Ireland.[31] Thomas Ruth or Magruhert, a cleric of Meath diocese, acquired a doctorate in law and, he declared in 1468, he had also studied and taught canon and civil laws for seven years in various schools in Ireland.[32] Such examples signify that the *studia particularia* in Ireland were not wholly isolated from wider intellectual currents abroad in Europe.

Nonetheless, while acquiring an education was an important step towards priesthood, neither the schools nor the universities actually trained men to become priests. Most priests in Ireland were likely to have been trained through a form of apprenticeship. This training would have produced variable results

27 Jefferies, *Priests and prelates*, p. 47; idem, 'Papal letters and Irish clergy', pp 87, 93.
28 *Statute rolls: Edward IV*, i, p. 369.   29 In 1607, only one beneficed clergyman in Derry diocese, Seán O'Heaney, rector of Banagher, was a graduate (of Glasgow University), though two others were learned in English, and another could speak Scots, which may indicate that they received some of their education overseas; Jefferies, 'Derry diocese', p. 189.   30 Nicholls, *Gaelic and Gaelicised Ireland*, pp 79–83; Jefferies, 'Papal letters and Irish clergy', pp 99–100.
31 Mooney, *Church in Gaelic Ireland*, p. 23.   32 Ibid., p. 23.

depending on the qualities of the teacher and the student yet, in practice, it probably equipped the average priest in Ireland as well as his counterparts in other countries for his vocation. For a satisfactory knowledge of theology and canon law requisite in one who was to have the *regimen animarum*, it would have been necessary to study books such as *Ignorantia Sacerdotum*, which Primate Cromer instructed all of his clergy to acquire in 1526, or else a little priest's manual such as that which Seán O'Connor of Roscommon (d. 1405) is thought to have translated from Latin into Irish.[33] Yet, if one may judge from the legislation of the provincial synod of Cashel in 1453, there were some *studia particularia* that offered an education intended only for candidates for the priesthood.[34] It is not clear whether such schools actually trained young men for the priesthood, or whether they simply offered lectures in theology or canon law. It would be quite remarkable if special schools had existed in Ireland to train priests, as there were few such institutions anywhere in Europe at that time.

Patrons, whether bishops, gentry or religious communities, were generally keen to promote educated clergymen.[35] However, given the low values of benefices in Ireland, it was often necessary to grant graduates a number of benefices in order to retain their services. The problem of losing well-qualified graduates to more remunerative offices elsewhere is well illustrated by the case of Thomas Darcy, a canon lawyer who graduated from Oxford.[36] Darcy already held two benefices in Armagh diocese prior to his promotion in Dublin diocese.[37] He held onto his benefices in Armagh for several years despite gaining a plurality of offices in Dublin.[38] In his absence, his parishes would have been served by unbeneficed curates.[39] It is clear then that if a priest had significant academic achievements to his credit, they did not automatically bring immediate benefits to the parishioners in his charge, though they may have been useful in the administration of the diocese as a whole.

For priests who were not graduates nor blessed with the favour of a patron, preferment could take a protracted period of time, or might never happen at all. Many priests' prospects for promotion were hampered by the fact of being Irish. The Statutes of Kilkenny (1366) decreed that no Irishman should hold a benefice within the English lordship.[40] However, in the later Middle Ages, there

33 Jefferies, *Priests and prelates*, p. 39.   34 TCD MS 808 (5), no. 53.   35 Jefferies, *Priests and prelates*, p. 45. Hugh O'Shiel, for example, seems to have acquired his legal training in a *stadium particularia* before working in Armagh's consistory court and being promoted to a number of benefices: Jefferies, 'The diocese of Dromore on the eve of the Tudor reformations' in Lindsay Proudfoot (eds), *County Down: history and society* (Dublin, 1997), p. 128.   36 A.B. Emden, *A biographical register of the university of Oxford, AD1501–1540* (Oxford, 1974), p. 160.   37 Jefferies, *Priests and prelates*, p. 45.   38 *Fiants of Henry VIII* (Dublin, March 1875), no. 3; Leslie, *Armagh clergy*, p. 98; Jefferies, *Priests and prelates*, p. 45.   39 NAI, Exchequer inquisitions, II, Inquisition no. 12 (1524), fos 27–8.   40 The chapter of St Patrick's Cathedral, Dublin, were zealous in excluding Irishmen from that body; Charles McNeill (ed.), *Archbishop Alen's register, c.1172–1534* (Dublin, 1950), pp 262–3.

simply were not enough men of English birth or descent coming forward for preferment in the Church, and Irishmen were presented to many parish benefices.[41] In fact, it was possible for Irish benefice holders to purchase a charter of denizenship to escape the legal disabilities of being Irish. Irish clergymen were indispensable to staff the parishes of the Pale. Yet, in Armagh *inter Anglicos* in 1518, priests with Irish surnames held only a minority of the benefices, and they generally held the poorest benefices. I would expect to find the same pattern of discrimination among the parish clergy across the inner Pale generally.

Two thirds of the parish churches and chapels in Armagh *inter Anglicos* were served by unbeneficed stipendiary clergymen. About 70 per cent of the parishes in Dublin diocese, and half of the parishes of Meath diocese were also served by unbeneficed priests.[42] Gaelic Irish priests predominated in their ranks, and they were not necessarily local men who had been acculturated to some degree to English mores. Many of the priests in County Louth in 1518 had surnames that suggest that they may have come from erenagh clans in Ulster.[43] A decree endorsed by the provincial synod of Dublin in 1518 shows that many priests from Ulster and Connacht migrated to Leinster in search of employment.[44] The line between the Church *inter Anglicos* and *inter Hibernicos* was very porous indeed.

Beyond the Pale and the towns, the practice of 'Rome-running' reflected intense competition for benefices. Most commonly, this involved delators charging the incumbents of ecclesiastical offices with failings that, if proven, would lead to the deprivation of the incumbent(s) and the transfer of their office(s) to the delator. Two-hundred-and-twenty-two (64 per cent) of the 348 entries in the *Calendar of papal letters*, volume xv, with some reference to Ireland in the period 1484–92, involved delations for benefices or offices in the Irish diocesan Church, with another twenty-two letters (6.5 per cent) requesting confirmation of the supplicants' possession of the offices they held (without delating anyone else).[45] The single most common type of man who delated an office holder in the diocesan church was a cleric in minor orders who did not have a benefice of his own: eighty-three such men can be identified in the *CPL*, xv. Only in three cases did delators explicitly delate their fathers for a benefice, and not always successfully.[46] It is clear from the papal letters that the much-vaunted practice of 'hereditary succession' to benefices in the Irish Church was not at all as common as has been assumed.

---

41 John Brady, 'The medieval diocese of Meath', *Ríocht na Midhe*, 1 (1957), p. 38; Lyons, *Church and society*, p. 56. 42 James Murray, 'The Tudor diocese of Dublin: episcopal government, ecclesiastical politics and the enforcement of the Reformation, *c*.1534–1590' (PhD, TCD, 1997), p. 304. 43 Jefferies, *Priests and prelates*, pp 47–8. 44 Lawlor, 'Liber Ruber', p. 165. 45 *CPL*, xv, 12, 292, 299, 308, 310, 312, 345, 412, 459, 488, 548, 551, 556, 560, 579, 593, 874, 900, 910, 917, 918, 955. 46 *CPL*, xv, 475, 746, 842.

One unavoidable conclusion is that the papal system of delations tended to undermine the authority of bishops beyond the Pale. In an indenture signed in 1534 by Sir Piers Butler, 1st earl of Ossory, it was stated that the papacy had provided to benefices not only men who were unlearned or of an evil disposition, but also men of war who unjustly expelled the lawful incumbents from their cures.[47] In the Pale, by contrast, the English statutes against provisors, ensured that papal interference was kept to a minimum. Even in dioceses where delations *were* made, one should not exaggerate their impact. In Armagh *inter Hibernicos*, only eleven diocesan clergymen were delated over the thirty-one years between 1482 and 1513, and many (if not most) of those suits failed.[48] There were six delations in Dromore diocese in that same period.[49] In Clogher there were seventeen delators who made allegations against office-holders in the diocese, and many of their suits failed.[50] Hence, delations were not at all as common as the secondary literature implies.

PASTORAL CARE

It is not easy to form a qualitative assessment of the Irish parish clergy before the Tudor reformations. In terms of hard evidence, the Armagh registers offer the best basis for forming a convincing assessment anywhere in Ireland. The parish clergy in Armagh *inter Anglicos* have been shown to have been resident in their parishes (the small number of absentees had legally appointed substitutes). The records of the diocesan synods show that the clergy were regularly exhorted to strive for higher standards, but they give no indications that the parish clergy in Armagh *inter Anglicos* were either generally incapable or negligent. The records of Armagh's consistory court point to occasional infringements of the canon law, but the scale of the problem seems to have been modest and manageable. There is much evidence of a very positive appreciation of the Church's ministry by its congregations.

Systematic studies of the pre-Reformation Church are needed for other dioceses, but in the meantime it seems reasonable to assume that the pastoral ministry provided in parishes elsewhere in the Pale was comparable with that in Armagh *inter Anglicos*. Certainly, the records pertaining to Meath diocese in the Armagh registers convey that impression. Beyond the Pale and the towns, the evidence for the quality of the pastoral ministry provided by the parish clergy across southern Ireland is scant, though the late medieval synodal legislation from the province of Cashel shows that the expectations of the clergy were high right across Munster.[51] The widespread evidence of lay investment in their

47 *Cal. Carew MSS*, i, no. 42. 48 Jefferies, *Priests and prelates*, pp 80–1. 49 Jefferies, 'Diocese of Dromore', pp 128–9. 50 Jefferies, 'Papal letters and Irish clergy', pp 90–4. 51 TCD MS 808 (5).

parish churches suggests a more positive appreciation of the pastoral ministry of the parish clergy across Ireland than convention had claimed.

No Irish visitation book has survived from the early Tudor period to reveal how well the Irish diocesan clergy served their parish cures. All we have is the loose document that records the visitation in 1546 of the two northern rural deaneries of Armagh *inter Hibernicos*. It shows that several of the churches visited (25 per cent) were ruinous or suffering from major defects. This was likely to have been a consequence not of clerical negligence but of poverty. The visitors found that in almost every parish church visited, the sacred vessels and other equipment were in either good or satisfactory order. Whatever the state of the churches visited, the Mass was celebrated in them, and the Office was prayed. It is surely significant that the lay people interviewed by Primate Dowdall's commissaries in 1546 told the visitors of several priests who broke the rule of celibacy, but in only one case was a priest reported for failure to perform his pastoral duties. Even with regard to clerical celibacy, the scale of sexual incontinence was rather less than conventional studies would have us believe. A series of studies of the Church across Ulster has challenged the conventional image of a disordered and disorganised Church by pointing to its resilience and to the comprehensive network of parishes, churches and chapels in place, staffed by clergy who were often praised for their piety and learning and hospitality, who resided in their parishes, and who were well esteemed.[52]

The records of delations among the papal letters convey a misleadingly negative impression of the late medieval Irish clergy. Of the 423 holders of Irish diocesan church offices who were delated between 1484 and 1492, 372 (81 per cent) were accused of no fault other than that they 'detained' the office. That is very significant. If these men had been negligent in their pastoral responsibilities, or living sinfully or acting improperly (at least by the standards of the day), their delator would have cited such failings for use against them in order to acquire their benefice. One hesitates to argue *ex silencio* but, given the nature and volume of the evidence available to us about the diocesan clergy of late medieval Ireland, I believe that it is valid in this instance to draw inferences from the lack of criticisms made against the vast majority of the churchmen delated.

Almost half of the remaining delations included allegations that did not reflect upon the quality of the delatees' pastoral ministries, and even if the twenty seven remaining delations were well-founded, and that is by no means certain, they still comprise fewer than four cases a year from the thousands of parish clergymen working in the whole of Ireland. In sum, the papal letters tell us nothing of the quality of the pastoral care afforded by the late medieval clergy in Ireland beyond the fact that a negligible number of the thousands of rectors,

---

52 Jefferies, *Priests and prelates*, passim; idem, 'Diocese of Dromore', passim; idem, 'Derry diocese', passim; idem, 'Papal letters and Irish clergy', passim.

vicars and curates across the island had allegations made against their pastoral ministry. I do not claim that the late medieval Irish Church enjoyed the ministrations of an exemplary priesthood, but the evidence adduced from the papal letters suggests that the parishes of Ireland were not at all as poorly served as has conventionally been assumed. On the contrary, contemporary estimations of the diocesan clergy were often very positive. For instance, my study of Clogher diocese highlighted the many obituary notices in the *Annals of the Four Masters* that praised clergymen there for their piety and learning.[53] Incidentally, I might observe that the provision of hospitality was far more noteworthy to the contemporary annalists than whether the clergyman had a wife or not.

Judged by the novel standards set by Catholic and Protestant reformers in the sixteenth century, the pre-Reformation clergy in the parishes of Ireland may well have fallen short. However, when judged in the context of their time, against the standards set for them by synodal legislation, and the expectations of their parishioners, one must conclude that the Irish parish clergy generally performed their duties in at least a satisfactory manner. Indeed, given the dismally low levels of remuneration enjoyed by the generality of the Irish parish clergy, and the widespread lawlessness and disorders they often had to live and minister through, it is remarkable that so many of them succeeded in providing such a service to their congregations.

RELIGIOUS ORDERS

Brendan Bradshaw's magisterial account of the dissolution of the religious orders in Ireland under Henry VIII has stood the test of time remarkably well.[54] He concluded 'that medieval monasticism in Ireland was sick to death, riddled by the cancer of secularism'.[55] He reckoned that even if a suppression policy had not emerged in England, some drastic action was required to stem the rot in Ireland. Bradshaw's qualitative assessment of the monastic orders has been strikingly confirmed by Roger Stalley's work on the Cistercians in late medieval Ireland.[56]

It is worth emphasising that conditions in Ireland's monasteries and convents were not uniform. Archbishop Walton's account of his visitation of the religious houses in Dublin diocese in 1468 indicated that all was satisfactory there.[57] Mary Ann Lyons found that the monastic buildings in that part of County Kildare encompassed by the Pale were in a 'comparatively sound state' at the time of

53 Jefferies, 'Papal letters and Irish clergy', pp 104–5.   **54** Bradshaw, *The dissolution*.   **55** Ibid., pp 35–6.   **56** Roger Stalley, *The Cistercian monasteries of Ireland: an account of the history, art and architecture of the White Monks in Ireland from 1142 to 1540* (London and New Haven, 1987), p. 27.   **57** H.F. Berry (ed.), *Register of wills and inventories of the diocese of Dublin, 1457–83* (Dublin, 1898), pp 174–8.

their dissolution, and several of those beyond the Pale seem to have been in good condition until the Kildare rebellion and its aftermath.[58] Lest one imagines that only the religious houses in the Pale were in good order on the eve of their dissolution, I have highlighted evidence from Clogher diocese that suggests otherwise.[59] Let me emphasise, though, that I am not attempting to 'rehabilitate' the late medieval monks or canons on the basis of cursory work done on the religious communities in one diocese in Ulster. I concur with Bradshaw's and Stalley's overall assessments of the monastic communities, but I would simply point out that conditions in Ireland's religious houses were not all the same, and were not determined by race or culture.

In terms of the Irish Church as a pastoral institution, I see the secular spirit that pervaded the monastic establishment as having a central significance that is often overlooked: through the system of appropriations, monks and canons exercised great power over the appointment of clergymen to parishes across the east, south and west of Ireland, and they siphoned off most of the parish revenues for their own uses. To my mind, the lax lifestyles of many of the monks and canons in their religious houses was far less significant than the fact that they enjoyed the right to present so many of the beneficed clergymen to parishes, and the stipendiary curates where no benefice had been established, when, seemingly, they were not very often concerned about the quality of the pastoral care provided in the parishes appropriated to them. Sarah Preston arrived at that same conclusion independently of me in her study of the Augustinian canons.[60] It is in their deleterious effects upon the Church in the parishes that the true significance of the monks and canons lay.

In contrast with the monastic orders, the mendicant communities enjoyed an incredible phase of renewal and expansion through the fifteenth and into the sixteenth century. Between 1400 and 1508, no fewer than ninety new communities were founded in Ireland, sixty-eight of them in Ulster and especially in Connacht.[61] As well as new foundations, many conventual communities were won over to the strict Observant cause. In all, two thirds of the Franciscan houses became Observant: the last to do so being in Kildare (1520), Dublin, Waterford and Drogheda (1521), Trim (1525), Limerick (1534), Clonmel (1536) and Cashel (1539). Though the progress of Observatism was less spectacular among the three other mendicant orders in Ireland, it was very significant among the Dominicans and Augustinian friars, perhaps less so among the Carmelites, and its influence was pervasive.[62]

---

58 More tellingly, she found that the monastic life 'still continued to attract young men and women in Kildare right down to the 1530s'; Lyons, *Church and society*, pp 59–62.   59 Jefferies, 'Papal letters and Irish clergy', pp 104–5.   60 Sarah Marya Preston, 'The canons regular of St Augustine in medieval Ireland: an overview' (PhD, TCD, 1996), pp 174–5.   61 Watt, *Church in late medieval Ireland*, pp 193–4.   62 Bradshaw, *The dissolution*, pp 8–11. Colmán Ó Clabaigh, *The Franciscans in Ireland, 1400–1534: from reform to reformation* (Dublin, 2002), pp 58–79. See

Colmán Ó Clabaigh has focused attention on the growth of the Franciscan 3rd Order in Ireland, calling it 'one of the most important developments in the Church in late medieval Ireland'.[63] The regular tertiaries 'were principally engaged in assisting the local parish clergy in their pastoral duties, and in conducting schools for the education of the boys of the district'.[64] Their pastoral and educational activities in large areas of Gaelic Ireland must have been hugely influential, but little or no trace of it now remains.

The Franciscan 3rd Order Seculars were lay men and women, usually married, who lived and worked in the local community but followed the rule of the 3rd Order, which required significant commitment to prayer and fasting, including an expectation of attendance at Mass, daily where possible, and the wearing of a distinctive habit at all times.[65] Membership soared during the fifteenth century and was a 'widespread phenomenon' in Ireland by the eve of Henry VIII's reformation, generally associated with Observant inspiration.[66]

The friars were vigorous in their pastoral involvement throughout Ireland. According to the anonymous author of the 1515 treatise on the state of Ireland, they were the only clergy among the Irish or those of English descent in Ireland who preached the word of God.[67] The Irish annals regularly praised friars, though never diocesan clergymen, for their preaching. The Annals of Ulster praised Aengus Mac an Ulltaigh, OFM (d. 1492), as a 'good and famous preacher'; Dónal O'Fallon, OFM, bishop of Derry (1488–1500), as 'the preacher who did most service to Irishmen since Patrick was in Ireland', while Patrick Ó Feidhil, OFM, (d. 1505) was praised as a 'distinguished and honoured preacher in Ireland and in Scotland'.[68] Ó Clabaigh observed that 'the preaching concerns of the Irish friars were those which were central to late medieval Christianity: the life of Christ, the Eucharist, repentance, right living, life after death, intercession for the dead and the cult of saints, especially of the Virgin Mary'.[69]

Compared with the generality of diocesan clergy, the friars were better educated and trained, and apparently more zealous. Yet, given the relatively limited number of friaries and their very uneven geographical distribution, the mendicants could never play more than a supportive role to the thousands of parish clergy who served their parishioners day by day. The friars might help to deliver the quarterly sermons required of every parish priest, but beyond the environs of their houses, friars were only occasional visitors to most parishes, akin in many respects to the Redemptorist preachers and their counterparts who conducted Lenten missions in Irish Catholic parishes in more recent times.[70]

also T.S. Flynn, *The Dominicans in Ireland, 1534–1641* (Dublin, 1993), pp 1–11; F.X. Martin, 'The Augustinian reform movement in the fifteenth century' in John Watt, J.B. Morall and F.X. Martin (eds), *Medieval studies presented to Aubrey Gwynn SJ* (Dublin, 1961); P. O'Dwyer, *The Irish Carmelites* (Dublin, 1988), pp 67–9. **63** Ó Clabaigh, *Franciscans in Ireland*, p. 105. **64** Ibid., p. 101; Mooney, 'The Franciscan 3rd Order friary at Dungannon', *Seanchas Ard Mhacha*, 1 (1954), pp 12–23. **65** Ibid., pp 84–7. **66** Ibid., p. 85. **67** SP 60/1/9. **68** Ó Clabaigh, *Franciscans in Ireland*, p. 84. **69** Ibid., p. 91. **70** In the early seventeenth century,

I suspect that the burgeoning of the mendicant communities did not simply reflect an increase in lay piety in late medieval Ireland, but contributed to that increase.[71] There is very considerable architectural, archaeological, documentary and representational evidence that reflects the enormous influence wielded by the mendicant friars upon the religious dispositions of the people of Ireland before the Tudor reformations. Yet, the remarkable expansion of the mendicant orders was only part of a wider and quite profound pattern of renewal across the Irish Church before the Tudor reformations.

CONCLUSIONS

With the evidence available, and the relative dearth of research to date, one must be cautious in drawing conclusions about pastoral care on the eve of the Tudor reformations. Nonetheless, one can confidently state that the Church in late medieval Ireland was in far better shape than has conventionally been assumed. It provided a surprisingly dense network of churches and priests to serve the population. The buildings themselves reflect a programme of physical renewal that was widespread across the country, though it was far from complete before Henry VIII's breach with Rome. In terms of the quality of pastoral care, there is reasonably plentiful evidence of its good quality in the Pale and towns, and scatters of evidence from elsewhere pointing towards the same positive assessment. Problems with the provision of pastoral care were far more limited than has been assumed, and tend to be localised in areas wracked by political and economic instability.

only a quarter of Irish friars were preachers; Brian MacCuarta, *Catholic revivial in the north of Ireland, 1603–1641* (Dublin, 2007), p. 71. **71** Jefferies, 'A Church in decline?: the pre-Reformation Irish Church', *History Ireland*, 14 (Nov./Dec. 2006), p. 18.

2

Diocesan administration

A pre-Reformation bishop was entrusted by the pope with responsibility for the quality of pastoral care afforded in his diocese, and for supervising the clergy and laity within it. The papacy reserved to itself the right to provide every bishop to his see with papal bulls. An older system, whereby the dean and chapter of the cathedral church of a vacant see elected the candidate, was not entirely superseded, but such an election was confirmed or ignored by Rome as circumstances dictated.[1] However, because a bishop's authority was underpinned by the revenues derived from often extensive see lands and other sources, he was a figure whose appointment was of great interest to the governing authorities. Not surprisingly, the English crown exercised much influence in episcopal appointments. It had become the established custom in the English lordship, as in England and Wales, for the king of England to issue a *congé d'elire* to the cathedral chapter of a vacant diocese, accompanied by letters missive, naming the single candidate for the see who was acceptable to him. After the election had produced the desired result, the king commended the bishop-elect to the pope. Usually, the pope accepted the king's recommendation and issued the necessary bull of provision. If Rome proved obstreperous, the crown held a trump card: to gain possession of the temporalities, a new bishop had to do homage to the king and renounce those clauses in his provision considered prejudicial to the crown's prerogatives – but the king was free to accept or reject the homage proffered to him, which effectively gave him the power of veto. Oliver Cantwell, OP, bishop of Ossory (1488–1526), was provided by the papacy but he did not gain possession of the temporalities of his diocese for seven years because Henry VII had intended another cleric for the see.[2] Such open conflict was very unusual, however, and the semblance of unanimity between the pope, the king and the diocesan clergy was normally maintained.

From 1492, the English crown maintained a cardinal protector at Rome to refer and expedite its nominations to dioceses, including those of Ireland, though in practice the first cardinal protector nominated to no more than half of the Irish bishoprics.[3] In the early Tudor period, the new appointees to the

1 W.E. Wilkie, *The cardinal protectors of England: Rome and the Tudors before the Reformation* (Cambridge, 1974), p. 54; Duald MacFirbis (ed.), 'Annals of Ireland, 1443–1468', *The miscellany of the Irish Archaeological Society*, 1 (Dublin, 1846), *s.a.* 1444. 2 *Works of Ware*, i, p. 414. 3 Katherine Walsh, 'The beginnings of a national protectorate: curial cardinals and the Irish

wealthiest Irish dioceses – namely Dublin, Meath and Armagh – were almost invariably Englishmen.[4] An English appointee to the bishopric of Kildare in 1449, Geoffrey Hereford, OP, left the diocese after only three years on account of the Irish who drove him back to England.[5] Men of English descent were usually nominated to the poorer dioceses of the lordship, often on the commendation of the local nobility, but not invariably.[6] The English crown made sporadic attempts to impose its choice of bishops on Gaelic dioceses, but Irish lords were not inclined to suffer the presence of royal appointees in their territories.[7]

Irish lords were well aware of the political ramifications of episcopal authority, and sometimes showed themselves to be anxious to harness the power and influence of the bishops for their own ends. In a number of dioceses, the ruling dynasties succeeded in having one or more of their members, or a member of a subordinate clan, provided by the papacy.[8] Doubtless, they supplicated the pope through a cardinal in Rome on behalf of their preferred nominees, but they must also have exercised the power to restrict other aspirant candidates from seeking promotion. In 1525 the 9th earl of Kildare claimed that no cleric in the Ormond lordship dared to seek a papal provision to any benefice there without the prior approval of the earl of Ormond.[9]

It is impossible to estimate how many Irish bishops were the preferred candidates of the cathedral chapters prior to their provision, though a number were so.[10] Furthermore, royal or aristocratic commendations to the papacy do not in themselves signify the absence of local clerical support for a candidate.[11] Indeed, the best candidate was likely to enjoy the confidence of the diocesan clergy as well as that of the local secular authorities. Edmund Courcey, OFM, who was provided to Clogher diocese on 14 June 1484, provides a sorry example of a bishop with no local support.[12] He continued to face insurmountable hostility from the leading clergy in Clogher diocese, presumably with the connivance of the local lords, until he finally resigned in 1501/2.

It would be wrong, however, to assume that political calculations left Ireland without able and conscientious bishops. The English-born bishops promoted by

Church in the fifteenth century', *Archivium Hibernicum*, 32 (1974), p. 78.   4 Steven Ellis, *Reform and revival: English government in Ireland, 1470–1534* (London, 1984), appendix 1.   5 Lyons, *Church and society* (Dublin, 2000), pp 66–7.   6 The 9th earl of Kildare's efforts to have his chaplain promoted as bishop of Kildare in 1523 came to nought; ibid., p. 66.   7 Gwynn, *Medieval province*, pp 152–3, 156–7.   8 Anthony Lynch, 'Religion in late medieval Ireland', *Archivium Hibernicum*, 36 (1981), p. 4.   9 J.S. Brewer and W. Bullen (eds), *Calendar of the Carew MSS, 1515–74*, i (London, 1867), no. 42.   10 K.W. Nicholls (ed.), 'The register of Clogher', *CR*, 7 (1971–2), p. 394; *Works of Ware*, i, p. 254.   11 The 'Letter book' of James V of Scotland contains a copy of a letter sent by the king to the pope in 1536 recommending Art O'Gallagher, dean of Derry, for the vacant bishopric of Raphoe. The dean's promotion was strongly supported by the chapter of Derry: 'The letter book of James V', *Analecta Hibernica*, 12 (1943), pp 179–81.   12 Gwynn, *Medieval province*, pp 166–72.

the early Tudors were invariably men who had demonstrated ability, either as royal chaplains[13] or ambassadors,[14] or had strong connections with Cardinal Wolsey.[15] Most of the English appointees were highly educated men.[16] John Payne, OP, bishop of Meath (1483–1506), had been the prior provincial of the Dominican order in England before his consecration.[17] Indeed, it is striking how many Englishmen of high calibre were provided to Irish dioceses in the early Tudor period. Admittedly, they were often expected to play a role in the English administration in Ireland, yet they were expected nonetheless to be resident and active bishops. Primate Kite and Bishop Wilson of Meath, who found their Irish dioceses uncongenial, were withdrawn from Ireland.[18] There were, of course, some English clerics who held the title of an Irish diocese while acting as suffragan bishops in England, but they do not concern us here.

There were three men from mainland Europe who served as bishops in Ireland in the early Tudor period, including Octavian del Palatio, who was a very able archbishop of Armagh (1478–1513),[19] and Tiberius Ugolino, a Roman parish priest before his elevation to the bishopric of Down & Connor (1489–*c.*1519), who was particularly remembered for the fact that he had 'very much beautified' his cathedral at Downpatrick and augmented the cathedral's building fund.[20] By contrast, an annalist observed that the death of the Greek George Braua, OSA, bishop of Dromore (1483–99) and bishop of Elphin (1499–1530), was of no great loss for mankind.[21]

Of the seventy-nine Irish-born bishops who enjoyed possession of a diocese between 1485 and 1535, thirty bore surnames that indicate English ancestry, while forty-nine had Irish surnames. While recognising that the processes of anglicisation and gaelicisation undoubtedly affected many people in late medieval Ireland, there are some significant differences in the professional backgrounds of the bishops according to their surnames. One trait they had in common was the high proportion (38–42 per cent) of Irish-born bishops who were regular clergymen.[22] The coupled percentages used here reflect the now uncertain status of some bishops.

13 'Kite': D.G. Newcombe, *ODNB*; 'Cromer': H.A. Jefferies, *ODNB*; 'Staples': C. Maginn, *ODNB*. 14 'Kite': Newcombe, *ODNB*; 'Inge': Newcombe, *ODNB*. 15 'Rokeby': Newcombe, *ODNB*; 'Inge': Newcombe, *ODNB*; 'Wilson': in Ware, 'Bishops', p. 154; 'Alen': James Murray, *ODNB*; 'Staples': Maginn, *ODNB*. 16 'Rokeby': Newcombe, *ODNB*; 'Alen': Murray, *ODNB*; 'Inge': Newcombe, *ODNB*; 'Donowe': *CPL*, xv, no. 180; 'Halsey': *Works of Ware*, i, 'Annals of Henry VIII', *s.a.* 1512, p. 60; 'Kite': Newcombe, *ODNB*; 'Staples': Maginn, *ODNB*. 17 'Payne': S.G. Ellis, *ODNB*. 18 *Works of Ware*, i, p. 154; SP 60/1/51. 19 *Works of Ware*, i, p. 89. Ware's positive, if restrained, praise of del Palatio was endorsed in Mario Sughi (ed.), *The register of Octavian de Palatio, archbishop of Armagh, 1478–1513* (Dublin, 1999), p. lx. 20 *Works of Ware*, i, p. 204; Gwynn, *Medieval province*, p. 137. 21 A.M. Freeman (ed.), *Annals of Connacht* (Dublin, 1944), *s.a.* 1530. 22 Those who may have been regulars included: O'Farrell, OCist, in Ardagh; de Courcey, OFM, Cloinin, OESA, O'Connolly, OSA, and O'Cullen, OESA, in Clogher; O'Higgins, OFM, in Clonmacnoise; O'Fallon, OFM, and MacMahon, OSA? in Derry; O'Reilly, OSA? in Dromore; McGovern, OSA, O'Reilly, OSA?, Nugent, OSA, in

No fewer than a quarter of the bishops with Irish surnames – thirteen of a total of forty-nine – were friars.[23] That reflects the high regard in which the mendicant orders were held in late medieval Ireland. A number of the friar-bishops were identified as professors, sometimes specifically as professors of theology, in their bulls of provision.[24] It should be noted, though, that the friars had a quality other than the spiritual, which fitted them well for being bishops in Ireland: their mendicant backgrounds would have prepared them somewhat for the lifestyle they could expect as the bishop of an impoverished Irish diocese.[25] Three of the thirty Irish-born bishops of English descent who ruled dioceses in Ireland between 1485 and 1535 were friars.[26] Again, the pattern of mendicant friars being promoted to poorer dioceses was replicated in colonial areas.

Significantly, only two Irish bishops in the early Tudor period were monks.[27] That suggests a shared concern by the papacy and the English crown not to promote monks to Irish dioceses because their vocational experiences were inappropriate for the active ministry required of an effective bishop. The Augustinian canons were secular clerics, not monks, and had a flexible rule that allowed them to engage in pastoral work, so the canons who became bishops may have had some pastoral experience to bring to their new office. Interestingly, the priors who became bishops were sometimes allowed to retain their priorship *in commendam*, and use its income to supplement the slender revenues of poorer dioceses.[28] Until 1519, no Irish-born Augustinian canon of English descent was promoted to a bishopric under the Tudors. However, that year saw the start of a new strategy to address the problem of under-resourced dioceses within the

Kilmore; Butler, OSA? in Cashel; O'Brien, OSA? in Killaloe; Quin, OP, in Limerick; O'Hurley, OCist, and MacCarthy, OESA, in Ross; Purcell, OSA, in Ferns; Wall, OFM, Dillon, OSA, and Wellesley, OSA, in Kildare; Roche, OCist, and Doran, OP, in Leighlin; Cantwell, OP, and Fitzgerald, OSA, in Ossory; O'Murray, OSA, and O'Fihilly, OFM, in Tuam; O'Congalain, OESA, and O'Flanagan, OP, in Achonry; Magrath, OSA, and Moore, OP, in Clonfert; O'Flanagan, OP, in Elphin.   **23** Clonin and O'Cullen (Clogher), O'Higgins (Clonmacnoise), O'Fallon (Derry), O'Reilly (Dromore), Quin (Limerick), MacCarthy (Ross), O'Fihilly (Tuam), O'Congalain and O'Flanagan (Achonry), Moore (Clonfert), O'Flanagan (Elphin), Doran (Leighlin).   **24** For example, O'Fallon (Derry), MacCarthy (Ross), and Doran (Leighlin). **25** The practice of appointing mendicants to poor sees was not peculiar to Ireland: cf. Glanmor Williams, *The Welsh Church from the conquest to the Reformation* (Cardiff, 1962), pp 304, 307; Denys Hay, *The Church in Italy in the fifteenth century* (Cambridge, 1977), p. 20.   **26** Gwynn, *Medieval province*, p. 146; *CPL*, xv, 333; Augustine Theiner, *Vetera monumenta Hibernorum et Scotorum* (Rome, 1864), p. 529.   **27** *CPL*, xv, p. 64; *CPL*, xii, 180, 208. Theiner, *Vetera monumenta*, p. 529. William O'Farrell, bishop of Ardagh (1480–1516), was only made the abbot of the Cistercian monastery at Granard four years after becoming a bishop. He retained the abbacy *in commendam*, but may not have been a monk prior to his appointment as abbot: *CPL*, xiii, p. 99; W.M. Brady, *Episcopal succession in England, Scotland and Ireland (1400–1875)*, i (Rome, 1876), pp 108–9.   **28** MacMahon (Derry), O'Reilly? (Kilmore), O'Brien (Killaloe), Magrath (Clonfert).

English lordship and beyond by repeatedly promoting Augustinian priors and allowing them to retain their priorships *in commendam*.[29]

Nonetheless, most Irish-born bishops with Irish surnames (perhaps 53–57%) and with surnames indicating English descent (perhaps 67–70%) were drawn from the ranks of the diocesan clergy. Between 77% and 84% of these Irish-born secular bishops came from the ranks of the 'higher clergy'.[30] The most senior of the diocesan clergy, the cathedral dignitaries, would seem to have been the most likely to secure promotion to a bishopric.[31] As officers of the cathedral chapter, they would have had much administrative and liturgical experience. Such senior clergymen were among the best-educated in the diocese and probably demonstrated some abilities or enjoyed powerful patronage to secure the high offices they already enjoyed. The most important of the senior clergy was the archdeacon. Their primary function was to supervise the Church in the parishes under the bishop's jurisdiction.[32] It was no coincidence that so many were later appointed as bishops.

Even with the limited evidence available, it is possible to show that several Irish bishops took great interest in their cathedrals and in the quality of the services conducted in them. One may cite Bishop Ugolini who 'very much beautified' his cathedral at Downpatrick,[33] Nicholas Comin, bishop of Waterford & Lismore (1519–51), who had an arched or vaulted ceiling erected over the choir and chancel of Holy Trinity Cathedral, Waterford,[34] Matthew Saunders, bishop of Leighlin (1527–49), who re-built the choir of St Lazerian's cathedral, and erected a glazed south window in 1542[35] and Milo Baron Fitzgerald, OSA, bishop of Ossory (1527–50), who had a marble altar erected

---

29 *CPL*, xv, no. 360; Brady, *Episcopal succession*, i, pp 23, 350; Augustine Valkenburg, 'Walter Wellesley, bishop of Kildare, 147?–1539', *JCKAHS*, 14 (1968), p. 535; Brady, *Episcopal succession*, p. 362; Gwynn, *Medieval province*, p. 162.   **30** O'Malone (Ardagh), MacCawell (Clogher), Blake (Clonmacnoise), O'Donnell (Derry), MacBrady (Kilmore), MacCarmacain and O'Gallagher (Raphoe), Creagh and Butler (Cashel), Stack, Fitzgerald (Ardfert), Fitzgerald (Cork), O'Cahill and McBrien (Emly), O'Brien (Killaloe), Arthur, Folan (Limerick), O'Driscoll (Ross), Purcell (Waterford & Lismore), FitzSimmons (Dublin), Comerford (Ferns), Maguire (Leighlin), O'Hedian (Ossory), O'Congalain (Achonry), Barret (Killala), O'Mulory and O'Brien (Kilmacduagh)   **31** MacCawell (Clogher), O'Donnell (Derry), MacBrady (Kilmore), MacCarmacain and O'Gallagher (Raphoe), Butler (Cashel), Stack (Ardfert), Arthur (Limerick), FitzSimmons (Dublin), Comerford (Ferns), O'Hedian (Ossory), O'Congalain (Achonry), O'Brien (Kilmacduagh). The senior cathedral clergy were most likely to be promoted as bishops in England and Wales also: S.E. Lehmberg, *The reformation of the cathedrals: cathedrals in English society, 1485–1603* (Princeton, NJ, 1989), p. 260. For a study of Ireland's cathedral staff, see K.W. Nicholls, 'Medieval Irish cathedral chapters', *Archivium Hibernicum*, 31 (1973).   **32** Anthony Lynch, 'The archdeacons of Armagh, 1417–71', *CLAHJ*, 19 (1979); Jefferies, *Priests and prelates of Armagh in the age of reformations* (Dublin, 1997), pp 90–2; idem, 'The diocese of Dromore on the eve of the Tudor reformations' in Lindsay Proudfoot (ed.), *Down: history and society* (Dublin, 1997), pp 132–5.   **33** *Works of Ware*, i, p. 204.   **34** Ibid., p. 256.   **35** Thady Dowling, '*Annales breves Hiberniae*' in Richard Butler (ed.), *The annals of Ireland* (Dublin, 1849), *s.a.* 1542.

within St Canice's Cathedral, Kilkenny.[36] One might also refer to Octavian del Palatio, archbishop of Armagh (1479–1513), who made a grant for the repair of the fabric and for the adornment of Armagh's cathedral,[37] as well as referring to the restoration of the nave of St Mary's Cathedral, Limerick, during the episcopate of John Folan, bishop of Limerick (1489–1521).[38] Of course, there were other cathedrals in a poor state, most notably those at Ardagh and Clonmacnoise in 1517 and 1515 respectively.[39] Yet an architectural study of the cathedral at Clonmacnoise has shown that it had been considerably rebuilt and refurbished in the second half of the fifteenth century.[40] Furthermore, whatever state the cathedral was in in 1515, it had experienced considerable restoration before marauding English troops descended on it in 1552 and smashed the altars, statues and glass windows, destroyed the Catholic liturgical books and stole the bells.[41] The report of 1515 is, therefore, very misleading in terms of the impression it might convey of the state of the cathedral at Clonmacnoise in the fifteenth and sixteenth centuries, and by extension of the state of the late medieval Church across Gaelic and gaelicised Ireland.

The records of bishops restoring and embellishing their cathedrals that have chanced to survive are drawn from wide areas across Ireland and point to a general pattern. In addition, one may cite the initiative of John O'Daly, OFM, bishop of Clonmacnoise (1444–a.1487), who secured papal confirmation for his foundation of a college of four resident canons to sing the Mass and other services in Clonmacnoise's cathedral.[42] Edmund Lane, bishop of Kildare (c.1513–1526), founded a similar college for his cathedral.[43] Dr Patrick O'Cullen, OSA, bishop of Clogher (1517–34), significantly improved the provision for cathedral services at Clogher by composing a new office, and additional vestments were acquired for the cathedral staff during his episcopate.[44] In addition, one can cite some fulsome contemporary eulogies: Dónal O'Fallon, OFM, bishop of Derry (1488–1500), was eulogised in the Annals of Ulster as 'the preacher who did the most service to Irishmen since Patrick'.[45] Thomas McBrady, bishop of Kilmore (1480–1511), was eulogised as a 'paragon of wisdom and piety, a luminous lamp that enlightened the laity and the clergy by instruction and preaching'. He died having consecrated many churches and cemeteries in his diocese.[46] One could cite other eulogies in a similar vein.

---

36 *Works of Ware*, i, p. 414.   37 Ibid., p. 88.   38 *Works of Ware*, i, p. 510.   39 Theiner, *Vetera monumenta*, pp 521, 518.   40 Conleth Manning, *Clonmacnoise* (Dublin, 1994).   41 *Whole works of Ware*, i, p. 174. The rehabilitation of St Mary's Cathedral at Tuam by Christopher Bodkin, archbishop of Tuam (1537–72), is a much better known example of restoration; *Calendar of State Papers relating to English affairs, Rome, 1558–1578*, i (London, 1917), no. 108.   42 Gwynn, *Medieval province*, pp 150–1.   43 Lyons, *Church and society*, p. 69.   44 Nicholls, 'The register of Clogher', p. 377. See also Jefferies, 'Papal letters and Irish clergy: Clogher before the reformation' in Jefferies (ed.), *History of the diocese of Clogher* (2005), p. 106.   45 *AU*, s.a. 1500. 46 *AFM*, s.a. 1511; Gwynn, *Medieval province*, p. 160.

It is not my intention here to portray the bishops of the Irish Church in the early Tudor period as being perfect pastors and faultless. They were not. Yet the conventional image of them is highly misleading. They numbered in their ranks many men of learning, many men of wisdom, many men of piety, and many men who strove as best they could to carry out their responsibilities as bishops in what were often very difficult conditions, as well as a few individuals like William O'Farrell of Ardagh, who did more harm than good.[47] Not every bishop could cope with the pressures, many of them arising from the political instability that wracked much of the country: Diarmuid O'Reilly, bishop of Kilmore (1512–c.1529), 'a man of learning, being a lover of peace and tranquillity, as the times were tumultuous in Ulster he withdrew to Swords in the county of Dublin where for a long time he officiated as vicar'.[48] Nonetheless, my overall impression is of a body of men who were promoted to the bench of bishops because they had demonstrated qualities and possessed experience which made it likely that they would oversee the Church in their diocese to good effect.

EPISCOPAL ADMINISTRATION

It was bishops who ordained men to holy orders, and they should only have done so once they were satisfied that the candidates were suitable. In those areas that had experienced colonisation in the late twelfth and thirteenth centuries, the bishops' right to collate men to benefices was limited by the wide-scale appropriation of parishes to religious houses and cathedral chapters, and by the claims of lay patrons. John Alen, archbishop of Dublin (1528–34), discovered that he could collate clergymen to only four of the twenty parishes in the rural deanery of Dublin (encompassing Dublin city and suburbs),[49] and to only forty benefices throughout his entire diocese of about 192 parishes, and most of the benefices he was able to collate men to were cathedral prebends and not parish cures.[50] George Cromer, archbishop of Armagh (1521–43), found that within Armagh

---

47 Jefferies, *Priests and prelates*, pp 83–4, 94–5; idem, 'Dr George Cromer, archbishop of Armagh (1521–1543)' in A.J. Hughes and William Nolan (eds), *Armagh: history and society* (Dublin, 2001), pp 217–44; James Murray, 'Archbishop Alen, Tudor reform and the Kildare rebellion', *PRIA*, 89C (1989), pp 4–6, 12–13, 15; Mary Ann Lyons, 'Sidelights on the Kildare ascendancy: a survey of Geraldine involvement in the Church, c.1470–c.1520', *Archivium Hibernicum*, 48 (1994), pp 73–87; idem, *Church and society*, pp 68–9, 100–1. Dr Lyons still referred to 'serious organisational and morale problems' (p. 54), though she observes that the negative evidence for the Church in Kildare was 'necessarily anecdotal' (p. 78). Her book was published prior to Michael O'Neill's study which revealed something of the physical renewal of the Church in Kildare in the decades immediately prior to Henry VIII's reformation: O'Neill, 'The medieval parish churches of County Kildare', pp 427–37. Scott, *Tudor diocese of Meath*, pp 39–51. 48 *Works of Ware*, i, p. 229. Swords was a prebend of St Patrick's Cathedral, Dublin, and it is interesting how the cathedral clergy appreciated the pastoral qualities of the bishop from Ulster. 49 *Alen's register*, p. 294. 50 Ibid., p. 279.

inter Anglicos, he was able to collate clergymen to only two prebends and two rectories, and also to a vicarage on two occasions out of three.[51] In Cloyne diocese, there were 130 parishes with a cure of souls in the later fifteenth century, of which seventy were impropriated to religious houses or to the collegiate church at Youghal, twenty-one were in lay patronage, and a number of parishes in the west of the diocese were controlled by coarb and erenagh clans, with the bishop enjoying the right of presentation to the residue.[52]

However, that is not to say that a bishop had no authority at all when it came to appointing priests to parishes where he did not enjoy the right of presentation. In Armagh *inter Anglicos*, whenever a benefice fell vacant, the archbishop commissioned a panel of jurors to conduct an inquisition to establish how the benefice came to be vacant, who had the right of presentation to the benefice, and whether the man being presented to the benefice was suitable.[53] Similar inquisitions were conducted in Dublin diocese,[54] and presumably elsewhere. These inquisitions were useful in providing the bishop with an assessment of the prospective incumbent.

However, the inquisitorial system only applied to parish benefices. For the majority of parishes in the east and south, which were served by a stipendiary curate, there were no inquisitions. Unbeneficed parish priests were obliged to secure a licence of admission from the local bishop, which gave him an opportunity to regulate their appointment to cures of souls, but it is clear from Archbishop Cromer's register that unbeneficed priests often began to exercise their parish ministries before they had been granted admission. That this was a general problem is suggested by a decree of the provincial synod of Dublin in 1518 that insisted that no priests from Connacht or Ulster were to be admitted to parish cures unless the bishops found them to be fit.[55]

Synods
The Irish Church was divided into four provinces headed by the archbishops of Armagh, Dublin, Cashel and Tuam. The archbishops of Armagh were demonstrably assiduous in convening synods for the clergy of their province every three years. There are records of provincial synods convened in the province of Cashel in 1511 and 1514, which could indicate that triennial synods were convened in the southern province too.[56] Random references to provincial synods in the

51 Jefferies, *Priests and prelates*, pp 42–3.   52 D. Buckley, 'Diocesan organisation: Cloyne', *Irish Catholic Historical Committee Proceedings* (1956), pp 8–11; P.J. Corish, *The Catholic community in the seventeenth and eighteenth centuries* (Dublin, 1981), p. 22.   53 Jefferies, *Priests and prelates*, 48–9; idem, 'The role of the laity in the parishes of Armagh *inter Anglicos*', *Archivium Hibernicum*, 52 (1998), pp 75–6.   54 *Alen's register*, p. 263. The inquisition recorded in the archbishop's register was for a cathedral prebend, but the format is so similar to those recorded in the Armagh registers that one may safely assume that it was part of a general pattern for all benefices.   55 Lawlor, 'Liber Ruber', no. 13.   56 TCD MS 808 (5) (20); N.B. White (ed.), *Monastic and episcopal deeds* (Dublin, 1936), no. 83.

provinces of Dublin and Tuam show that they were convened on the eve of the reformations, though one can only speculate as to their frequency (though it seems safe to assume that those for Dublin were triennial).[57]

Provincial synods allowed the archbishops to set forth agendas for good governance and pastoral care in their respective provinces. Unfortunately, few provincial statutes have survived.[58] The most comprehensive collections to have survived are those for the ecclesiastical province of Cashel, which were issued in 1453 and, in revised form, in 1511.[59] In the province of Cashel, the provincial statutes were regularly consolidated into book-form and the clergy were directed to acquire a copy and to read the statutes to their congregations in the vernacular four times a year.[60] This was quite a sensible way of regularly reminding the parish clergy and their parishioners of what was required of them.

The unique series of records of diocesan synods in Armagh diocese have been used to offer insights into the operation of the Church in a particularly interesting Irish diocese.[61] They show that synods were held annually and the clergy were regularly exhorted to strive for the highest standards in their lives, their priestly ministries and the administration of the sacraments. In the 1526 synod, Primate Cromer ordered all of his parish clergy to acquire a copy of the *Constitutions of the province of Canterbury* – better known as *Ignorantia sacerdotum*.[62] This was a schema of Catholic instruction for the laity that was to be expounded by priests to their congregations in the vernacular four times a year. The regular readings of *Ignorantia sacerdotum* and the synodal statutes during diocesan synods may be seen as a form of 'in-service training'.

Unfortunately, the lack of documentation makes it very difficult to discuss the work of synods in other Irish dioceses on the eve of the reformations. However, there were certainly diocesan synods convened in Meath.[63] Diocesan statutes have survived for the northern diocese of Clogher from 1430 and 1557.[64] The bishops of Clogher collected synodals every Easter, which could signify that annual diocesan synods were convened at that time.[65] The same appears to have been the case in the neighbouring dioceses of Derry and Raphoe.[66] The synodals in Dublin were called *cathedraticum*, suggesting that the diocesan synods were

57 *Alen's register*, p. 260; Lawlor, 'Liber Ruber', no. 13. There was a provincial synod in Tuam (*Irish Archaeological Society Miscellany*, i, p. 77). 58 M.A.J. Burrows, 'Fifteenth-century Irish provincial legislation and pastoral care' in W.J. Sheils and Diana Wood (eds), *The churches, Ireland and the Irish* (Oxford, 1989), pp 55–67. 59 TCD MS 808 (5) (20). 60 TCD MS 808 (5), no. 21. 61 Jefferies, 'Diocesan synods and convocations in Armagh on the eve of the Tudor reformations', *Seanchas Ard Mhacha*, 16 (1995); idem, *Priests and prelates*, pp 96–102. 62 Cromer's register, II, fo. 20v (48). 63 TCD MS 1060 (5). For earlier diocesan synods in Meath, see *Octavian's Register*, nos 184, 455, 448; *Prene's register*, no. 432. 64 William O'Sullivan, 'Two Clogher constitutions', *CR*, 15:3 (1996), pp 145–55. 65 A.F. O'D Alexander (ed.), 'The O'Kane papers', *Analecta Hibernica*, 12 (1943), p. 100. 66 TCD MS 10,383, 'Clogher, Derry and Raphoe', fo. 5; Jefferies, 'Derry diocese', p. 180; *Inquisitionum in officio rotulorum cancellariae Hiberniae asservatarum repertorium*, ii, ed. James Hardiman (Dublin, 1829), 'Ulster inquisitions', appendix, Donegal.

normally convened in St Patrick's Cathedral. The Dublin provincial synod of 1518 makes reference to the enforcement of diocesan as well as provincial statutes, showing that they were assumed to be a regular feature of Church life. There is a chance reference in the papal letters to a diocesan synod in Leighlin diocese.[67] For the southern diocese of Waterford & Lismore four statutes of a diocesan synod relating to clerical dress and the conduct of the liturgy have chanced to survive.[68] In 1430, Bishop Art McCawell of Clogher directed that the articles of his diocesan synod of that year be read and expounded to congregations during Mass once a month.[69] It would have been a very effective way of promulgating synodal legislation in the parishes.

Visitations

In Armagh archdiocese, visitations seem to have been conducted annually.[70] Bishops levied procurations on the beneficed clergymen visited,[71] and in most northern dioceses they also collected the rents due from the erenaghs, the head tenants on episcopal land, and also the episcopal share of the tithes. In Derry diocese, the erenaghs paid rents of between 5s. to £1 on the eve of the plantation, but they also had to give refection to the bishop and his entourage whenever he visited their parish – but not otherwise.[72] Bishop Montgomery observed that the refection taken was worth thirty or forty times the cash rents.[73] That gave the bishop a real incentive to regularly visit the parishes of his diocese in person. The 1537 presentments show that bishops in south-eastern Ireland also levied (allegedly extortionate) refections on the beneficed clergy during visitations. The bishops of Clogher used to conduct visitations in May and again at All Hallows.[74]

The visitors would have used a set of articles of inquiry to give focus to their investigations. They would also have attended to any presentments made to them by priests or lay folk. The visitors would have been particularly concerned to investigate the parish clergy's performance of their pastoral responsibilities, to see that synodal legislation was being observed and that, at least minimum standards of morality and religious observance were being maintained. Following a visitation, injunctions were normally issued ordering the remedying of any failings uncovered. The *comperta*, or charges against (allegedly) delinquent priests or lay people, could be dealt with by the visitors during the course of the visitation[75] or, in extreme cases, a delinquent could be arraigned before the consistory court to be prosecuted *ex officio*.[76]

67 *CPL*, xiv, p. 125.   68 TCD MS 842, fo. 57v.   69 O'Sullivan, 'Two Clogher constitutions', pp 152–3.   70 Jefferies, *Priests and prelates*, p. 129. The value of procurations to the archbishops is indicated in Dowdall's register, pp 239–42 (123 A–F).   71 Those in Derry diocese before the plantation ranged from 2s. to 3s.; TCD MS 10,383, fo. 5; Jefferies, 'Derry diocese', p. 177.   72 Jefferies, 'Derry diocese', p. 180.   73 Ibid.   74 'Ulster inquisitions', County Fermanagh; Jefferies, 'Papal letters and Irish clergy', p. 101.   75 Jefferies, *Priests and prelates*, p. 104.   76 *Mey's register*, no. 248.

The only Irish visitation record to survive from the Tudor period is a report on the visitation in 1546 of the two northern rural deaneries of Armagh *inter Hibernicos*.[77] It shows that the visitors drew their information from personal inspection of the church buildings and liturgical equipment. They also questioned the clergy on oath after Mass. The visitation articles investigated the priests' celebration of the Mass, recitation of the divine office and celibacy. Further enquiries were made among lay parishioners.

It is difficult to assess the effectiveness of episcopal visitations in Ireland on the eve of the Reformation. Nonetheless, by taking evidence through personal observations, from the clergy on oath, and by drawing information from lay parishioners, the visitors could form a reasonably true estimate of the state of the Church and clergy in the parishes. John Alen, archbishop of Dublin (1528–34), showed considerable concern for the proper conduct of diocesan and metropolitan visitations in his register.[78] Certainly, the visitation was a long-established and potentially effective instrument of episcopal oversight.

Church courts

His consistory court gave the bishop an instrument through which he could enforce the legislative programmes endorsed in his synods, and discipline persons for religious or moral failings. The church courts claimed competence in all matters concerning faith and morals, a very wide remit indeed, as Archbishop Alen of Dublin made clear in his register.[79] They were founded on the premise that they functioned in a Christian society that was committed to Christian values.

The act book of the court of Armagh in Primate Cromer's register is comprised of records of the *acta* of the court during the period 1518–22.[80] It is very incomplete and any conclusions must be tentative. Nonetheless, it shows that the Armagh court was peripatetic within the archdiocese *inter Anglicos*, and that sessions were held twice a month.[81] Its business may be divided into two broad categories. First, there were the office cases in which the court proceeded against persons who had, or who were suspected of having, infringed the canon law of the Church, or local synodal decrees.[82] The second category of business

---

77 Jefferies, 'The visitation of the parishes of Armagh *inter Hibernicos* in 1546' in C. Dillon and H.A. Jefferies (eds), *Tyrone: history and society* (Dublin, 2000). **78** *Alen's register*, pp 262–3, 266–7, 268–71, 277, 281, 293–4. **79** *Alen's register*, pp 288–9. More generally, see Ralph Houlbrooke, *Church courts and the people during the English Reformation, 1520–1570* (Oxford, 1979), pp 7–8; Christopher Harper-Bill, *The pre-Reformation church in England, 1400–1530* (London and New York, 1989), p. 54. **80** PRONI, MS DIO 4/2/11. The text has been edited in John McCafferty, 'The act book of the Armagh diocese, 1518–1522: a text and introduction' (MA, UCD, 1991). See also Jefferies, 'The church courts of Armagh on the eve of the Reformation', *Seanchas Ard Mhacha*, 15 (1993), pp 1–38. **81** This can be confirmed by a review of court cases, bearing in mind the incomplete nature of our records, but see especially Cromer's register, i, fos 49–51v (67). **82** Houlbrooke, *Church courts*, pp 8, 38–40; Ollivant, *Court of the*

comprised instance cases, which were brought to the courts at the instance of one party against another.[83] Instance cases predominated.

Office cases often followed from information gathered during a visitation. They were generally dealt with by summary proceedings. The defendant was charged upon oath to make true answer to the articles exhibited against him. If he/she denied the charge, he/she was ordered to purge himself/herself by means of his/her own oath and those of a number of compurgators who would swear on his/her behalf, or face punishment by the court.[84] Clerical misconduct was severely dealt with by Armagh's consistory court. Two priests were suspended for simony.[85] Two priests who had eaten meat on a fast day were ordered to repent publicly, and fast on bread and water on a subsequent date.[86] A vicar of Carlingford was temporarily deprived of his benefice after a layman accused him of committing a sin.[87] Office prosecutions for sexual immorality, which were extremely common in English church courts prior to the Reformation, were rare in Armagh. One might suggest that society in Ireland had a more tolerant attitude towards sexual incontinence than was true of the English, and that local people were generally reluctant to bring illicit liaisons to the attention of the church authorities. The single so-called heresy trial recorded concerned a butcher of Drogheda who received the sacraments while labouring under a sentence of excommunication.[88] However, the butcher claimed that he knew nothing of the excommunication and threw himself upon the court's mercy. His demeanour in court, together with the fact that he desired the sacraments in the first place, make it clear that he was no heretic in the true sense of the word.

In the mid-fifteenth century, perjury and debt suits constituted the 'bread and butter' business of the church court of Armagh,[89] followed in order of volume by suits for defamation, and then matrimonial suits.[90] However, the rivalry of the common law courts subsequently reduced the number of perjury and debt suits. About 85 per cent of the instance suits brought before the court of Armagh in 1518–22 concerned matrimonial, defamatory or testamentary matters, or disputes about ecclesiastical revenues. Of the eighty-seven first instance cases recorded in Cromer's register, no fewer than twenty-one concerned matrimonial disputes.[91] A striking feature of the matrimonial suits is

official, pp 21–2; Harper-Bill, *Pre-Reformation church*, p. 55.   **83** The distinction between office and instance suits was less clear in practice than it seems in theory. Some matters, such as suits alleging slander of clerics or suits by clerics to secure what they regarded as customary dues, could be promoted *ex officio promoto*, or as an instance suit: Houlbrooke, *Church courts*, p. 38; Ollivant, *Court of the official*, p. 36.   **84** Jefferies, *Priests and prelates*, p. 108.   **85** Ibid., p. 113.   **86** Ibid.   **87** Ibid., pp 112–13.   **88** Ibid., p. 113.   **89** Perjury and debt cases often came before the church courts because any transaction undertaken with the support of an oath rendered all of the parties concerned liable to the Church's jurisdiction in the event of non-fulfilment.   **90** Swanson, *Church and society*, pp 167–8, 188–9; Harper-Bill, *Pre-Reformation England*, pp 57–9; Jefferies, 'Church courts of Armagh', pp 29–36.   **91** Jefferies, *Priests and prelates*, pp 109–10.

that no less than eighteen of the twenty-one plaintiffs were women. The court regularly recognised the validity of marriages at the behest of the female partner. It defended wives with violent husbands. Women defended their interests in testamentary and debt disputes before the consistory court. Women were frequently plaintiffs in defamation suits, usually to defend their characters against sexual slurs. Quite often, however, women featured as defendants for abusing other women as 'whores' or men as thieves. The courts offered women a degree of security, and an important avenue for redress, in their relationships with men, and other women.

Partial records of eighteen testamentary suits are preserved in Primate Cromer's register.[92] To avoid such suits, the Church authorities took great pains to ensure that wills were properly drawn up and registered. There were five suits brought before Armagh's consistory to secure the full payment of revenues owed to parish churches. My overall impression from the evidence is that Armagh's church court seems to have operated justly and relatively inexpensively.[93]

John Alen, archbishop of Dublin (1528–34), 'Doctor of Civil and Canon law at Rome and previously Master in Arts at Cambridge', as he noted in his register, found on conducting a visitation of the consistory and metropolitan court of Dublin that some aspects of its personnel and procedures required 'reform rather than censure', while others were 'found deserving praise'. Alen issued a new series of statutes for the court in 1530 to address the deficiencies he found.[94] Dublin's consistory court was held within St Patrick's Cathedral on Wednesdays and Saturdays, an indication of a considerable demand for its services.[95] Without a court book, it is impossible to assess its effectiveness – though the volume of business processed suggests that plaintiffs reckoned it was effective enough to warrant their resort to it. I suspect that with the English administration to act as the 'secular arm' in the Pale, the church courts in that region worked well.

According to jurors representing the commoners of Kilkenny in 1537, the official principal of Ossory diocese would not pass judgment in any cause without an initial fee of 6s. 8d. from a poor plaintiff or 40s. from a person of substance.[96] It was alleged that for every judgment, even those concerned with the punishment of sin, the church courts in the region levied financial penalties.[97] Throughout the south-east, fees for sentences in matrimonial causes were graduated according to a plaintiff's wealth.[98] For probate of testaments, the officials of the archbishops of Cashel and the bishop of Waterford & Lismore charged 20d. for each £1 of the value of the deceased's property, while in Ossory the charge was 18d.[99] These damning indictments show that the church courts

92 Ibid., p. 111. 93 Jefferies, 'Church courts of Armagh', pp 25–38. For fees, see McCafferty, 'Act book', pp 57–8; Jefferies, 'Church courts', pp 35–6. 94 *Alen's register*, p. 274–5. 95 Ibid. 96 SP 60/5/64, no. liii. Further fees were payable for the examination of church records to help determine causes. 97 SP 60/5/80, no. xxxvii. 98 SP 60/5/64, no. liii; SP 60/5/76, nos xxv, xxvi; SP 60/5/85, no. liii; SP 60/5/105, no. xxv. 99 SP 60/5/64, no. lii; SP 60/5/80, no.

are likely to have been active in prosecuting offenders against the Church's decrees – if for no other reason than for the fines that might be imposed on them. The financial levies were understandably unpopular among the laity but, given the low values of benefices in the region, fees of some level were unavoidable.

Among the Ormond deeds are many records from the consistory courts of the south-east and they show that the courts conducted their business with great attention to proper procedures. For instance, in a sentence given by John Purcell, bishop of Ferns (1447–79), in a suit for the annulment of a marriage in 1479, reference is made to the original petition being read out in his consistory court, and a copy being sent by the court to the defendant who was cited to appear, together with any relevant witnesses, before the court on a fixed day. When she failed to appear she was declared contumacious and was obliged to come to the court on the next day set. The depositions of all of the witnesses were recorded by the court and copies of them were made available to the defendant. The 'advice of experts in law' was offered before the bishop issued his verdict, which was delayed until both parties were present in the church at Fethard, County Wexford.[1] That is but one of many such records, but one other example is worth citing: the sentence of Bishop John Purcell (1519–39) in a testamentary dispute in 1521.[2] Catherine and Alison, daughters of the late Robert Newell, a merchant of Clonmines, County Wexford, sued the executor of their father's will for possession of their inheritance. The earl of Ormond appointed Christopher O'Connor as the proctor for the plaintiffs. The case was debated over several sittings of the court before the bishop declared his judgment. In his sentence, the bishop explicitly stated that he had taken account of the common law of the realm, and municipal laws, as well as provincial statutes and synodal decrees in coming to his judgment, which vindicated the rights of the heiresses.

The church courts in the south-east were peripatetic, which made the operation of the courts accessible. Care was taken by the courts to record sworn depositions (in one case eighteen witness statements were recorded), though a premium was placed on documentary evidence in court proceedings.[3] Certainly, the church court records from the south-east provide a salutary corrective to the 9th earl of Kildare's hyperbolic claim that the 'spiritual sword' was 'clearly despised' in Ormond's territories.[4]

An intriguing incident recorded by a couple of the juries who made presentments in 1537 was the archbishop of Cashel's use of armed men to imprison a citizen of Clonmel and hold him to ransom.[5] It seems to have arisen from a dispute between the archbishop and the citizens of Clonmel that an order

xxxvii.   1 Edmund Curtis (ed.), *Calendar of Ormond Deeds, iii, 1413–1509* (Dublin, 1935), no. 250.   2 Curtis (ed.), *Cal. Ormond Deeds, iv, 1509–1547* (Dublin, 1937), no. 79.   3 *Cal. Ormond Deeds*, iii, nos 250, 268, 278, 279, 302; *Cal. Ormond Deeds*, iv, nos 27, 39, 91, 177, 183, 275; *Monastic and episcopal deeds*, nos 67, 74, 76, 87.   4 SP 60/1/46.   5 SP 60/5/80, no. xxxiii; SP 60/5/85, no. xxxvii; SP 60/5/105, no. xxxii.

secured from the lord deputy and council of Ireland in May 1536 failed to resolve.[6] Turlough O'Brien, bishop of Killaloe (1483–1525), was another prelate who travelled about with armed retainers.[7] Art O'Gallagher, bishop of Raphoe (1547–61), was noted in the records of his diocese as 'a spirited gentleman [who] went always with a troop of horsemen under his colours'.[8] In the absence of an effective system of law and order enforcement over most of Ireland, it was understandable that at least some prelates employed a number of retainers.[9] Incidentally, the pope employs an armed guard to this day.

An interesting fact that emerges from the 1537 presentments is that almost all of the officials principal in the south-east were Irishmen.[10] Men from Irish legal families, most notably the Leches and Roths, were regularly officials principal in the consistory courts of Armagh and Meath also, though they had to anglicise their surnames to win advancement.[11] That is a useful reminder of the quality of Irish law schools, and of the quality of Irish schools generally. Quite a number of the students of those schools completed their studies in a university overseas.

The church courts in dioceses beyond the English lordship encountered in the brehon law a far less elaborate and bureaucratic judicial system than that operating in the Pale. However, it would be wrong to imagine that the church courts across Gaelic and gaelicised Ireland were ineffective. Some church officials were appointed as brehons by Irish lords.[12] Such 'dual mandates' must have been advantageous to the Church and the lords. In the south-east of Ireland a number of clergymen acted as seneschals with jurisdiction in criminal causes.[13] Nonetheless, it must be recognised that all church courts were dependent on the willingness of local priests and people to co-operate. Where there was a lack of consensus between the Church and secular authorities, the church courts did not have the ability to coerce the clergy or laity to conform to the strictures of canon law, particularly when the sexual mores of the wider society differed from the ideals set down by the canonists.

6 *Monastic and episcopal deeds*, nos 84, 85. 7 *AC*, s.a. 1525; *Works of Ware*, i, p. 594. 8 Jefferies, 'Catalogue of the bishops of Raphoe', p. 109. 9 Michael Tregury, archbishop of Dublin (1449–71), ventured only a short distance beyond the Pale boundary in 1462 when he was seized by Geoffrey Harold, the captain of a marcher clan in south County Dublin, imprisoned and had 'other great affronts and injuries' inflicted on him; *Alen's register*, p. 242; Murray, 'Tudor diocese of Dublin', p. 78. 10 SP 60/5/76, no. xxv; SP 60/5/78, no. x; SP 60/5/80, no. xxxiv; SP 60/5/105, no. xxv. 11 Jefferies, *Priests and prelates*, p. 47. 12 Ibid., pp 85–7; Simms, 'The brehons of later medieval Ireland' in D. Hogan and W.N. Osborough (eds), *Brehons, serjeants and attorneys: studies in the history of the Irish legal profession* (Blackrock, Co. Dublin, 1990), p. 71. 13 SP 60/5/78, nos xiv, xv. See also SP 60/5/76, no. xxviii.

REFORM

In 1496, a petition was despatched to Pope Alexander VI on behalf of Henry VII, stressing that it was 'urgently desirable for the guidance and good government of the metropolitan and cathedral churches' of Ireland that some reform be achieved, particularly in the more remote areas of the island.[14] In response, the pope issued a bull in October 1496, which legislated for the appointment of a panel of senior English bishops to oversee the implementation of a reform programme in Ireland. However, the king's initiative proved abortive and one can only speculate as to why that was so.

There was more sustained interest in the Irish Church under Cardinal Wolsey's auspices.[15] Reference was made above to the number of highly educated, experienced and able men appointed as bishops in the Irish Church in the early sixteenth century, several of them with close connections to the cardinal. In 1528, Wolsey had Dr John Alen, one of his most able and ruthless lieutenants, appointed as his vice-legate in Ireland and archbishop of Dublin, and as lord chancellor of Ireland.[16] This investment of human resources in the Irish Church was expected to reap benefits in Church and state. It was impressive in scale and was curtailed primarily by the lack of bishoprics in Ireland that could support such highly qualified and ambitious Englishmen.[17]

Again, as noted above, from the early 1520s the crown appointed a series of Augustinian priors as bishops, and allowed them to hold their priorships *in commendam* to supplement the revenues of some impoverished sees. It was an easy piece of improvisation that side-stepped the complex causes of those sees being so impoverished in the first place. There seems to have been a naïve assumption that all that was needed for the reform of the Irish Church was the appointment of good bishops.

CONCLUSIONS

It has been shown that many of the men who were bishops in the Irish Church before the Henrician reformation were well-educated and brought administrative experience to their office. Several of them were lauded by their contemporaries as good pastors, and several of them can be shown to have had concern for the well-being of the Church in their charge. In general, their episcopates were more efficacious and effective than has been assumed. The

14 Watt, *Church in late medieval Ireland*, pp 37–9; Lyons, *Church and society*, p. 55.   15 This ties in with Fiona Fitzsimons' fascinating, if confrontationally written, study of Wolsey's involvement in Ireland: 'Wolsey, the native affinities and the failure of reform in Henrician Ireland' in David Edwards (ed.), *Regions and rulers in Ireland, 1100–1650* (Dublin, 2004).   16 Murray, 'Archbishop Alen', pp 8–9, 13–14.   17 *Valor in Hibernia*, pp 2–17.

positive evidence adduced is more voluminous for the more anglicised areas in Ireland, but is certainly not confined to those areas. Nonetheless, the evidence of good order and effective leadership in the Church in the English lordship is especially significant, because it would constitute the key battleground of the Tudor reformations in Ireland. On the other hand, the challenges confronting the pre-Reformation bishops, most notably the problems of finance and its myriad implications, and the widespread political and social disorders that impacted upon the Church and its ministry beyond the Pale and the town walls, were not addressed by the Tudor reformations.

3

The laity

The laity exercised a considerable degree of authority and influence over the Church in the parishes of late medieval Ireland, a fact that has important implications for our understanding of the Church and the progress of the Tudor reformations that followed. Evidence shows that the Church, and its ministry, enjoyed considerable lay support before the reformations, but it was a symbiotic relationship with the Church very much dependent upon the laity, as indeed one would expect.

OBLIGATIONS

Parishioners were obliged to attend Mass on Sundays and holy days, confess their sins to their parish priest once a year and receive communion at Easter, and accept the Church's teachings on faith and morals. They also had a series of financial obligations to meet, most onerously the payment of tithes but also the fees charged for the provision of certain sacraments, particularly at baptisms, weddings and funerals, and the 'canonical portion' levied on the moveable assets of the recently deceased. Parishioners were also charged with the provision of a satisfactory parish church building and the continued maintenance of its nave, the furnishing of their church with a suitable altar, tabernacle, a cross, a statue of the patron saint and oftentimes a statue of the Blessed Virgin, as was required by synodal legislation in the province of Cashel, but possibly in the province of Dublin too if one may judge by a number of references to statues of the Blessed Virgin in parish churches mentioned in the surviving wills that were processed by Dublin's consistory court in the fifteenth century.[1] The provincial synod of Cashel in 1453 also directed that

> the parishioners should have in their parish churches, at their own expense [for the proper celebration of the divine office and the administration of the sacraments], a Missal, a silver or gilt chalice, an amix, alb, cincture, maniple, stole, chasuble, surplice, a baptismal stone neatly constructed and well-covered, and a suitable vessel for keeping the chrism for the sick.[2]

1 TCD MS 808 (5), no. 4. 2 Ibid., no. 3.

What is probably most striking is the scale of the obligations laid upon the parishioners. Nonetheless, they were no mere sycophants, they had their own expectations of the Church and its clergy, and they had means of ensuring that their expectations were met.

THE APPOINTMENT OF CLERGY

The appointment of the priest responsible for the cure of souls in their parish was of direct interest to his parishioners. Whoever was appointed to a benefice might serve the same parish for some considerable number of years.[3] Members of the local gentry enjoyed the right to present men to eight benefices in Armagh *inter Anglicos* on the eve of the Tudor reformations – just over 11 per cent of the churches and chapels in the area.[4] It was unusual for the patrons in County Louth to appoint men of their own surnames to benefices, presumably because the remuneration available was so paltry.[5]

Evidence from parishes in Gaelic and gaelicised Ireland is scarce, though the local lords seem not to have exercised much influence over the appointment of clergy to parishes in Ulster, nor were their children often to be found as clergymen in Ulster's parishes.[6] There were quite a number of Burkes among the parish clergy in Connacht, though one cannot assume a lordly background for every member of that prolific clan. In any event, the right of patronage is only part of the story. The gentry in County Louth, and by implication across the Pale and possibly in other anglicised districts of Ireland, were able to exert significant influence over the appointment of priests to benefices in which they did not have the right of presentation. Leading laymen were consulted before a priest could be instituted into any of the parish benefices in Armagh *inter Anglicos*, and it seems safe to assume that this was the general pattern, not only across the Pale but wherever the common law was enforced.[7] These consultations were formally organised with juries made up of local priests and laymen.[8] The inclusion of laymen on the juries was important, as it gave some of the laity the opportunity of expressing their judgment of the proposed candidates.

3 H.A. Jefferies, 'The role of the laity in the parishes of Armagh *inter Anglicos*, 1518–1553', *Archivium Hibernicum*, 52 (1998), pp 74–5. 4 Jefferies, *Priests and prelates of Armagh in the age of reformations* (Dublin, 1997), pp 43–4. 5 I could identify only one such example in Armagh *inter Anglicos* in the early sixteenth century: p. 44. Significant in this regard too may be the fact that Patrick McLoughlin and Robert McLoughlin were successive vicars of Clonkeen up to 1518, about the time when one John McLoughlin was the tithe farmer there. 6 Jefferies, 'Derry diocese', p. 188. 7 Jefferies, *Priests and prelates*, pp 48–9; Charles McNeill (ed.), *Calendar of Archbishop Alen's register, c.1172–1534* (Dublin, 1950), p. 263. The latter reference relates specifically to St Patrick's Cathedral, but I have no doubt that inquisitions would have been held generally in Dublin diocese, at least *inter Anglicos*, as they were in Armagh *inter Anglicos*. 8 Jefferies, 'Role of the laity', pp 75–6.

MEETING PARISHIONERS' EXPECTATIONS

If a priest was negligent, his parishioners could charge him before the bishop's consistory court.[9] Yet it was not necessary to go before the consistory court in order to have a complaint dealt with. There were regular visitations conducted by the bishop, either in person or through his commissaries.[10] That gave the laity a regular opportunity to report on the performance of their priests. Any failings complained of could be dealt with directly by the visitors, or be referred to the consistory court. It is probable that churchwardens represented the parishioners in the parishes of the Pale, while in the Ulster parishes the local erenaghs were probably questioned along with some other lay people.

Parishioners could act informally against priests who displeased them. The parish clergy were generally so poor that they could ill-afford the loss of even a portion of their revenues. The imposition of various forms of cess levied by lords across Ireland gave them another instrument of control and discipline which could be employed against the parish clergy.[11] The fact that the gentry were in a position to influence the choice of priest appointed to parish cures, and to have erring priests disciplined, does not, of itself, demonstrate that they were necessarily satisfied with the ministrations of the clergy, though it does indicate that they had some power to secure the kind of priest they desired. Contemporary evidence, in the form of lay investment in their parish churches and lay benefactions in their wills, suggests that the late medieval parish clergy generally met the standards expected of them by their parishioners.[12]

CHURCHWARDENS

Adrian Empey observed that the surviving churchwarden accounts for St Werburgh's parish, Dublin, from 1484 to 1597 'were not untypical of similar records in Dublin and elsewhere that have not survived'.[13] Churchwardens were the representatives through whom parishioners fulfilled certain 'collective'

9 Jefferies, *Priests and prelates*, p. 54.   10 Ibid., pp 102–5.   11 Ibid., p. 37; Harold O'Sullivan, 'The march of south east Ulster in the fifteenth and sixteenth centuries: a period of change' in Raymond Gillespie and Harold O'Sullivan (eds), *The borderlands: essays on the history of the Ulster-Leinster border* (Belfast, 1989), p. 58.   12 Jefferies, *Priests and prelates*, pp 50–6. 13 Adrian Empey (ed.), *The proctor's accounts of the parish church of St Werburgh, Dublin, 1481–1627* (Dublin, 2009) [this volume was published after the present book was type-set]; Adrian Empey, 'The layperson in the parish: the medieval inheritance, 1169–1536' in Raymond Gillespie and W.G. Neely (eds), *The laity and the Church of Ireland, 1000–2000: all sorts and conditions* (Dublin, 2002), pp 25–31; J.L. Robinson, 'Churchwardens' accounts, 1484–1600, St Werburgh's Church, Dublin', *JRSAI*, 44 (1914); Adrian Empey, 'The formation and development of intramural churches and communities in medieval Dublin in a European context' (forthcoming).

responsibilities; it was their duty to administer any form of property with which the parish might be endowed for the functioning of the Church in the parish; should such endowments not suffice, it was their business to raise any additional funds required to meet a particular need; they were responsible for the safe custody of the ornaments and utensils to be provided by the parishioners for the services of the church; and they were the acknowledged representatives of the parishioners in any collective action that they might wish or be compelled to undertake.[14] It seems likely that the great church building and/or refurbishing campaigns of the fifteenth century provided an incentive to develop the office of churchwarden over much of Ireland.[15]

The St Werburgh's accounts are unique in having survived, but are invaluable as a palimpsest of a parish of the Irish Church before and during the Tudor reformations.[16] At St Werburgh's, the custom was to elect the churchwardens on the first Sunday in May of each year.[17] Normally, they were local tradesmen with occupations such as armourer, baker, barber, carpenter or weaver.[18] The church-wardens of St Werburgh's managed a portfolio of properties (most of which had been bequeathed by parishioners), which brought in an annual rental of about £5.[19] They also handled smaller sums given by parishioners, to maintain lights, for instance, or as 'pardon money', as well as the fees levied for burials in the churchyard or, at greater cost, under the floor of the church. The churchwar-dens also handled occasional legacies to the parish, such as Anne Archdeacon's bequest of five yards of linen cloth for the altar in St Martin's Chapel in 1484.[20]

The churchwardens organised the maintenance of the church. They ensured that the nave was suitably paved, and they had the chapels tiled. They paid for rushes to cover the floor of the main church at Easter and Christmas, and for St Martin's Chapel at Martinmas.[21] In about 1520, the churchwardens paid 10s. for someone to carve a statue of St Martin, and paid 14s. for a throne to place it in.[22] Around 1520, they paid 9s. for the painting of the Blessed Virgin and St John on the rood screen, and they maintained the rood-light above it.[23] They purchased a printed Missal for 14s. in 1503–4, and a hand-written grail containing the music of the Mass at the same time for 6s. 8d.[24] The accounts for c.1520 refer to the costs of binding the Missal, grail and a psalter.[25] A reference to a payment for the repair of the organs in 1567–70 suggests that an organist had accompa-nied the singing in the Mass for some time prior to that date.[26] Singing, of

14 Charles Drew, *Early parochial organisation in England: the origins of the office of church warden* (London, 1954), pp 5–6. 15 The earliest known references to the office of churchwardens in Dublin date from the fifteenth century (Raymond Gillespie, 'Urban parishes in early seven-teenth-century Ireland: the case of Dublin' in Elizabeth FitzPatrick and Raymond Gillespie (eds), *The parish in medieval and early modern Ireland: community, territory and building* (Dublin, 2006), p. 233), though it is possible that the office existed under the guise of a different title before that time. 16 Robinson, 'Churchwardens' accounts', pp 132–42. 17 Ibid. 18 Ibid., p. 142. 19 Ibid., p. 133. 20 Ibid. 21 Ibid., pp 135–6. 22 Ibid., p. 136. 23 Ibid. 24 Ibid., p. 139. 25 Ibid. 26 Ibid., p. 138.

course, is thirsty work and the churchwardens spent 4*d.* on drinks for the priests and clerks of the church for singing the quarterly dirge for deceased benefactors.[27] They ensured that new vestments were acquired when needed, and that existing vestments were washed or repaired as required.[28] They ensured that bread and wine were provided for the Mass, and that the appropriate candles were available for the liturgy, including the 'Sepulchre light' and the 'Paschal light', and that the chalices used were 'hallowed'.[29]

All in all, the St Werburgh churchwardens' accounts give the impression of a parish in which representatives of the parishioners played a central role in ensuring that their religious expectations were satisfied. Empey observed that they reveal 'the very marked growth of the power and participation of the laity in the life of the parish church over the period extending from the second half of the thirteenth century down to the eve of the Reformation'.[30]

It seems probable that the experiences of St Werburgh's were replicated in parishes across the most anglicised districts of Ireland because not only can one find references to churchwardens carrying out their responsibilities in urban parishes elsewhere, throughout Dublin city and even including the very small parish of St Olave's, Dublin, and as far west as that of St Nicholas' Collegiate Church in Galway, but references to them can also be traced in modest rural parishes and chapelries in the north of the Pale.[31] In 1521, a churchwarden, acting on behalf of the parishioners, sued the vicar of Termonfeckin and the prioress of Termonfeckin in Armagh's consistory court for failing to maintain a chaplain to augment the church services in their parish church.[32] The churchwardens of Tullyallen sued the monks of Mellifont to increase the stipend of their curate.[33] Interestingly, one of the churchwardens of Tullyallen was an Irishman and the other had an English name, a reflection of the mixed population in the Pale. In both cases, from Termonfeckin and Tullyallen, we see churchwardens acting assertively and successfully to realise the expectations of the parishioners who elected them.

Beyond the Pale and the towns, the lack of records precludes any detailed discussion of the role of the laity in the routine operation of parishes. It seems clear, however, that in those parishes which had a coarb or an erenagh the responsibility for maintaining the nave of churches was generally limited to the

---

27 Ibid., p. 134. 28 Ibid., p. 140. 29 Ibid., pp 134, 140. 30 Empey, 'Layperson in the parish', p. 31. 31 Jefferies, 'Role of the laity', pp 77–8; Empey, 'Layperson in the parish', pp 27–31; idem, 'Intramural churches and communities' (forthcoming); Roderick O'Flaherty, *A chorographical description of west or h-Iar Connaught, written AD1684* (ed. James Hardiman, Dublin, 1846), p. 230. For elsewhere in Dublin, see Edmund Curtis (ed.), *Calendar of Ormond deeds, iv, 1509–47* (Dublin, 1937), no. 232; White (ed.), *Extents of Irish monastic possessions*, p. 87. Even the tiny St Olave's parish in Dublin had churchwardens, a sign of their well-nigh universality in urban settings: Richard Haworth, 'The site of St Olave's Church, Dublin' in Bradley (ed.), *Settlement and society* (1988), pp 182–3. 32 Jefferies, *Priests and prelates*, p. 112. 33 Ibid.

erenagh's clan.[34] That would help to explain why parish church and chapel buildings in much of Ulster were generally so modest in scale and design compared with those in the Pale, and why they sometimes seem to have been in a less satisfactory condition.[35] The erenagh's clan simply did not command the kind of financial resources at the disposal of the entirety of the parishioners in parishes to the east and south. However, over most of Ireland there were neither churchwardens nor erenaghs, and it is not yet clear who occupied their places. One can only speculate that in the absence of churchwardens it is likely that local lords and ladies exercised much influence over the life of the Church in their parish.

The extensive establishment of the office of churchwarden in parishes across the Pale and beyond is a significant manifestation of the increase in lay participation in regulating the life of the Church in the later Middle Ages. It formalised lay influence and even a degree of control over a considerable number of parishes. While the office of churchwarden was not universal in Irish parishes, critically, it was well-established in the most anglicised areas in Ireland – the key battle-grounds of the Tudor reformations – and conceivably it could have played an important part in mediating parishioners' experiences of the reformations as occurred in England.

CONFRATERNITIES

Confraternities were associations of lay men and women who came together in a kind of spiritual guild. Thanks to the work of Colm Lennon and Adrian Empey, there have been considerable advances in our knowledge and understanding of these institutions in Ireland.[36] They were generally headed by a master and two proctors or wardens elected annually on the feast day of their patron saint, 'to maintain the guild light and to supervise the income and expenditure of the guild in maintaining and staffing the [guild's] chapel' in the parish church.[37] The primary function of the guild was to maintain a light or candle in its chapel, and to procure prayers and alms from all members for the repose of the souls of deceased members.[38] Members were obliged to meet together on the

---

34 Ibid., p. 78. 35 Jefferies, 'The visitation of the parishes in Armagh *inter Hibernicos*, 1546' in Dillon and Jefferies (eds), *Tyrone: history and society* (2000), pp 163–80. 36 See especially, Colm Lennon, 'The confraternities and cultural duality in Ireland, 1450–1550' in Christopher Black and Pamela Gravestock (eds), *Early modern confraternities in Europe and the Americas* (Aldershot, 2006), pp 35–52, and Empey, 'Layperson in the parish', pp 36–41. Lennon has also highlighted the importance of confraternities in Dublin during the Tudor reformations: idem, 'The chantries in the Irish Reformation: the case of St Anne's guild, Dublin, 1550–1630' in R.V. Comerford, M. Cullen, J.R. Hill and C. Lennon (eds), *Religion, conflict and coexistence in Ireland: essays in honour of Monsignor Patrick J. Corish* (Dublin, 1989). 37 Empey, 'Layperson in the parish', p. 37. 38 Ibid., pp 37–8.

patronal feast day for a Mass, the annual guild dinner and the election of officials, and they were expected to attend the funerals of fellow guild members and to provide alms for families of members in times of hardship.

Lennon has highlighted the existence of sixty-two separate confraternities in forty-five towns and villages in Ireland, three quarters of them in the Pale (twelve of them in Dublin alone), and the remainder located principally in the larger outlying boroughs, and one in Sligo, an urban centre which was independent of English control.[39] Empey has pointed out that the membership of craft and trade guilds 'secured the same spiritual benefits and system of mutual support as a religious guild'.[40] He observed that, 'nothing better illustrates the close ties between the craft guilds and the Church than their participation in the annual Corpus Christi pageant', as outlined in the regulations drawn up in the Chain Book of Dublin in 1496. The pageant was a major civic occasion regulated by Dublin's ruling body, which also sponsored the religious fraternity of St George, and it clearly reflected the integration of religion into the life of the entire citizenry.[41]

Lennon sees the confraternities as having played 'an important part in Irish society since the Middle Ages'.[42] They fostered a heightened religious commitment among their members centred on the parish church (or, at least, a chapel therein).[43] Lennon suggested that the surge in fraternity foundations after 1450 could be seen as a vital adjunct to the contemporaneous assertion of colonial separatism.[44] I am more inclined to see it as another manifestation of the increase in lay involvement in and commitment to the Church and religion in the later Middle Ages, contemporaneous with the wide-scale establishment of the office of churchwarden in parishes in the lordship and the massive lay investment in their parish churches and chapels. Lennon opined that some of the confraternal impulse in Gaelic and gaelicised parishes may have channelled into the Franciscan Third Order Secular, which enjoyed 'a huge vogue among lay men and women throughout Gaelic Ireland on the eve of the Reformation'.[45] That is interesting in showing how a general impulse among lay people towards greater participation in the life of the Church was able to manifest itself in different ways in different environments.

There remains the question of the significance of the confraternities for the religious history of Ireland. Lennon proposed that the doctrinal conservatism of the population of English descent in Ireland 'was buttressed by a strong sense of religious corporatism, deriving at least in part from the shared experience of fraternal and collegiate foundations', while the counter-reformation endeavours of the mendicant orders in Gaelic Ireland 'found ready hearers among their lay associates, most notably the tertiaries'.[46] I would hesitate before ascribing a major

39 Lennon, 'The confraternities', p. 36. 40 Empey, 'Layperson in the parish', pp 40–1.
41 Lennon, 'The confraternities', p. 40. 42 Ibid., p. 35. 43 Ibid., p. 38. 44 Ibid., p. 40.
45 Ibid., p. 38, citing Ó Clabaigh, *Franciscans in Ireland*, pp 80–105. 46 Lennon, 'The

role to the religious confraternities in thwarting the Tudor reformations in Ireland: not only is there no clear evidence of their actively resisting Protestantism, but there is also the fact that the strength of religious corporatism in Ireland, as reflected in the tiny number of known religious guilds, paled into virtual insignificance when compared with the estimated 30,000 religious guilds in Britain.[47] Even though some of the Irish confraternities survived into the seventeenth century (their number is unknown), it is difficult to imagine that they exerted greater religious influence than did their vastly more numerous counterparts across the Irish Sea.

PRIESTS AND PEOPLE

In the Armagh registers of the sixteenth century, there are records of only two financial disputes between clerics and lay people, and one of them certainly does not bear out the traditional interpretation about anticlericalism: in a dispute about their liability to pay butter tithes, the parishioners of Carlingford were happy to have the president of the consistory court of Armagh and the archdeacon of Armagh act as arbitrators between themselves and their vicar.[48] In a suit wherein two curates sued some parishioners for non-payment of dues, it emerged in the consistory court that the true defendant was the prioress of Termonfeckin, whose orders the parishioners were obeying by diverting their dues to the curate based at the convent in Callystown.[49] These rare instances of financial disputes are not examples of anti-clericalism.

One may speculate that there was some degree of lay resentment at the fees charged by the parish clergy for the rites of passage. Primate Dowdall's abolition of such fees in the important provincial synod of 1553 may reflect his anxiety to remove a source of tension between the priests and the laity in the ecclesiastical province of Armagh.[50] There was certainly resentment against the fees charged for the rites of passage, and for the 'canonical portions', expressed by several of the juries who made presentments in south-eastern Ireland in 1537.[51] My assessment is that while the relative poverty of the generality of the Irish clergy obliged them to insist on the payment of fees for the rites of passage, their manifestly modest lifestyles may have dulled some of the resentment roused by the imposition of fees. Demonstrating that as fact is impossible for want of documentation, but the gifts bequeathed by many humble men and women to priests in their wills suggest a positive relationship.[52]

There are no fewer than six records of clergymen in Armagh *inter Anglicos* (in

confraternities', p. 43.   **47** Felicity Heal, *Reformation in Britain and Ireland* (Oxford, 2005), p. 89.   **48** Jefferies, 'Role of the laity', p. 78.   **49** Ibid., pp 78–9.   **50** Dowdall's register, pp 99–106 (85), Art. 9.   **51** SP 60/5/60, 60/5/64, 60/5/78, 60/5/85; 60/5/74, no. xv; 60/5/76, no. lv; 60/5/85, no. liv.   **52** Empey, 'Layperson in the parish', p. 46.

effect, County Louth) claiming to have been assaulted by laymen within the relatively short time covered by the incomplete act book of the consistory court of Armagh in 1518–22. However, one needs to be cautious in drawing conclusions from this (alleged) violence. My judgment is that the hostility encountered by the priests was not directed randomly at the clerical estate, but arose from specific circumstances in which the individual priests are likely to have been at least partly to blame.[53]

It is not being argued here that the parish clergy in late medieval Ireland did not stand in need of reform. Yet it seems clear, as shown for example by the suits presented to Armagh's consistory court by parishioners in Crowmartin and Termonfeckin,[54] that contemporary parishioners preferred to have each of their local churches or chapels served by one of the available priests rather than have a less numerous, if better educated and salaried, priesthood. They wanted priests for their sacramental functions rather than for their oratory.

LAY PEOPLE'S WILLS

It is difficult to define the disposition of the laity to the pre-Reformation Church and clergy with very great precision. The surviving wills processed by the church court in Armagh *inter Anglicos* in the early years of the sixteenth century suggest that strong lay piety was fairly general, at least among the middling townspeople who made wills.[55] A couple of mid-fifteenth-century wills from Cork conform to this pattern of lay benevolence to the Church and clergy.[56] The so-called 'register' of Archbishops Tregury (1449–71) and Walton (1473–83) of Dublin is particularly useful in preserving the wills of a significant number of rural parishioners.[57]

In terms of their disposition towards the parish church and clergy, it is interesting to note that thirty of the thirty-four rural male testators in the Dublin register made specific bequests to their local churches or priests. The fact that four did not do so shows that such bequests were not obligatory. Only four of the male testators left money to the poor.[58] Only one of the thirty-four male testators wished to be buried at a friary rather than in his parish, and he made generous bequests to his parish church and appointed its vicar as the executor of his will.[59]

In many cases male testators left sums of between 12*d*. and 20*d*. for priests, though two left more.[60] However, the number of male testators who made no

---

53 For a strikingly similar situation elsewhere, see Christopher Haigh, *Reformation and resistance in Tudor Lancashire* (Cambridge, 1975), pp 46–66.   54 Jefferies, 'Role of the laity', p. 80.   55 Ibid., p. 80.   56 Jefferies, *Cork: historical perspectives*, p. 103.   57 Berry, *Register of wills*, passim.   58 Ibid., pp 81–3, 94–9.   59 Ibid., pp 41–5.   60 Ibid., pp 151–3, 83–5.

specific bequests to priests comprises more than half of the wills in the Dublin 'register'. That may serve to warn against impressions of an exaggeratedly close relationship between lay people and their priests. Nonetheless, these qualifications must be borne in mind: the parish priest would have been paid to celebrate the funeral Mass and any other obsequies for their deceased parishioners, and they would have shared in the food and drink which were commonly provided after funerals. John Palmer, who owed many debts, made no specific bequests to his parish church or priest, but made reference to his 'burial expenses'.[61] The mendicant friars attracted bequests from ten of the thirty-four male testators in the Dublin 'register', and in only two instances were those bequests to the exclusion of the parish clergy. Interestingly, only one man and no woman in the Dublin 'register' wished to be buried in a friary or its cemetery.[62]

In general, it will be noted that the gifts made by female rural testators to their parish church and clergy were modest in size, with three exceptions.[63] Thirteen of the twenty-one female testators made a specific gift to their parish church or priest. One woman left 12*d.* to a monk and a friar. No woman in the Dublin 'register' left money to a parish fraternity, and only three left money to friars. Significantly, wealthier women made very similar bequests as men, though the gifts of copes and robes for statues, and the gifts for the priests' mothers show a distinctly feminine sensitivity.

There was a general concern reflected in the Dublin wills with being buried in the most efficacious place one could afford, with obituarial Masses and prayers, with burning candles before the images of preferred saints, and sometimes with posthumous almsgiving that would have been typical of lay piety across western Europe. Unfortunately, the scale of the losses of late medieval Irish records is such that there are no comparable collections of wills outside of Dublin diocese prior to the Tudor reformations, and one can only speculate that the concerns reflected in Dublin were not atypical of those of lay men and women elsewhere in Ireland.

POPULAR PIETY

The sources available for the study of lay piety in late medieval Ireland are very scarce. The volume of surviving religious imagery in glass and wall paintings is extremely small indeed because of the upheavals in early modern Ireland. Salvador Ryan reckons that the bardic poems are, 'by far the most useful texts for peeling back the layers that enwrap the devotional concerns of the Gaelic Irish laity', though they have proven to be more difficult to interpret that one

---

61 Ibid., pp 34–6.   62 Interestingly too, three of the ten men who left money to the mendicants gave bequests to all four orders of friars in Drogheda.   63 Ibid., pp 55–6, 63–4, 102–3.

might have thought.[64] Ryan's close study of Máire Ní Mháille's 'Book of piety', which was compiled by a scribe on Tory Island in 1513, provides 'a rare snapshot of piety in practice'.[65] Máire's book shows her devotion to Patrick and Colmcille, but also 'reveals a concern for some of the most popular elements of late medieval western European spirituality'.[66]

Rachel Moss reminds us that religious imagery 'paid a pivotal role in the lay piety of the late Middle Ages in Ireland'.[67] On the eve of the Reformation, there was a growing trend to install tombs with elaborate imagery in churches, which very often depicted the patrons (male and female) in their worldly finery, along with a range of religious images which, though drawing on a stock range of readily recognisable iconography, reflected the personal piety of the patrons. Such tombs were durable statements of both piety and social and dynastic importance.[68] The main drawback in using such impressive monuments to study late medieval piety, is their socially unrepresentative character. On the other hand, those monuments were designed with a wide audience in mind, to encourage them to pray for the souls of the patrons, and they do reflect a wider religious sensitivity than simply that of individuals of the propertied classes.

The cult of St Francis seems to have been particularly popular in late medieval Ireland.[69] The cult of the Virgin Mary was even more popular, and appealed especially to women. She was represented with her son in a range of motifs in sculpture, art and poetry from across Ireland, and the rosary was well-established in Ireland.[70] As Clodagh Tait observed, 'her traditional centrality in the Catholic message made her the ideal conduit for the updated ideas and devotions that promoted the dogmas of the Council of Trent'.[71] More local devotions related to Irish saints and holy wells also served to link medieval religious practices to the reinvigorated Catholicism associated with Trent.

Éamonn McEneaney used Waterford's *Great parchment book*, the register of the chantry of St Saviour, a rent roll of Waterford's cathedral, Mayor James Rice's tomb in the cathedral, several surviving statues, Dean Collyn's will and a remarkable set of late fifteenth-century high Mass vestments from Waterford as the bases of a richly textured study of religious devotion in late medieval Waterford.[72] His study shows the 'symbiotic relationship between civic and religious life' in Waterford and how the 'civic and Church authorities collaborated to ensure that religion remained central to everyday life in the city'.[73]

---

64 Salvador Ryan, 'Windows on late medieval devotional practice: Máire Ní Mháille's "Book of piety" (1513) and the world behind the texts' in Moss, Ó Clabaigh and Ryan, *Art and devotion*, pp 1, 11. 65 Ibid., passim. 66 Ibid., p. 2. 67 Moss, 'Permanent expressions of piety: the secular and the sacred in later medieval stone sculpture' in Moss, Ó Clabaigh and Ryan, *Art and devotion*, p. 89. 68 Ibid., p. 86. 69 Colmán Ó Clabaigh, 'The other Christ: the cult of St Francis in late medieval Ireland' in Moss, Ó Clabaigh and Ryan, *Art and devotion*. 70 Clodagh Tait, 'Art and the cult of the Virgin Mary in Ireland, c.1500–1660' in Moss, Ó Clabaigh and Ryan, *Art and devotion*, pp 164–70, 172. 71 Ibid., p. 183. 72 Éamonn McEneaney, 'Politics and the art of devotion in late fifteenth-century Waterford' in Moss, Ó Clabaigh and Ryan, *Art and devotion*, pp 33–49. 73 Ibid., pp 38, 49.

William Neely declared that the 'whole culture' of Kilkenny was religiously orientated before the Reformation.[74] The life of the town was consciously synchronised with the Church's calendar, and civic days and fairs were held on holy days. On the feast of Corpus Christi the craft guilds of Kilkenny came together to stage the mystery plays, one of the great occasions of the civic year. Every Sunday, the sovereign and great twelve of Kilkenny processed in their scarlet robes to their seats in St Canice's Cathedral.[75] Though Colm Lennon's study of the lords of Dublin is focused on the period after 1548, it reveals the same symbiotic relationship between the religious and secular aspects of life in Dublin. The confraternity of St Anne in the city was so dominated by aldermen that Lennon likened it to the corporation at prayer.[76] Devotions associated with the holy wells in and around Dublin knew no social boundaries.[77] In fact, where evidence survives, it shows that religious culture was infused into the general life of the late medieval Irish cities and towns.

Raymond Gillespie, in a study of religious relics, reliquaries and hagiography, showed that in the very different socio-economic environment in southern Ulster in 1450–1550, 'spiritual realities were deeply embedded in daily life' and 'spiritual objects were also political and social ones'.[78] Incidentally, Cormac Bourke has revealed something of the number of significant religious relics and reliquaries that survived in southern Ulster into relatively modern times.[79] There is clearly a great deal more evidence available for the study of late medieval piety in Ireland than has yet received scholarly attention, but recent work has revealed a richness and strength to popular religious culture in Ireland.

CONCLUSIONS

The massive investment of the laity in building new parish churches and chapels, in refurbishing and/or extending and embellishing older churches, together with the surviving wills, point towards a generally positive relationship between the laity and the diocesan Church and clergy up to the eve of the reformations. The widespread establishment of churchwardens is another striking demonstration of lay concern with and active involvement in the life of the Church in their parishes. The lay confraternities, and the religious activities of the trade and craft guilds, give further proof of the depth of many lay people's commitment to their Church and religion on the eve of Henry VIII's reformation.

74 Neely, *Kilkenny*, p. 35. **75** Ibid. **76** Colm Lennon, *The lords of Dublin in the age of Reformation* (Dublin, 1989), pp 34, 130, 147. **77** Ibid., p. 149. **78** Raymond Gillespie, 'Relics, reliquaries and hagiography in south Ulster, 1450–1550' in Moss, Ó Clabaigh and Ryan, *Art and devotion*, pp 200–1. **79** Cormac Bourke, 'Medieval ecclesiastical metalwork from the diocese of Clogher' in Jefferies (ed.), *History of the diocese of Clogher*.

Work on the pre-Reformation parishioners serves as a warning against the lazy assumptions often made about the laity in Ireland during the course of the Tudor reformations: they were not mindless masses waiting to be moulded by preaching clergymen of any denomination. Many of them held strong Catholic convictions, as the physical manifestations of their faith in parchment, stone, wood and other media still testify. Their religious beliefs and practices, of which the cults of the Virgin Mary and St Francis are only partial manifestations, permeated many people's lives and culture. The challenge for the Protestant reformers was to wean them away from their often deeply held convictions and somehow convince them of the veracity of the new creed, and that was no easy challenge.

PART II

The early Tudor reformations

4

Henry VIII's reformation

The course of the Tudor reformations in Ireland was shaped significantly by the strong general attachment to Catholicism among the clergy and laity, which is reflected in evidence from all across Ireland. Yet, that is not to suggest that the failure of the Tudor reformations in Ireland was somehow inevitable. England's experiences of the Tudor reformations suggest, by analogy, that a popular attachment to Catholic beliefs and practices was not, in itself, sufficient to guarantee the survival of Catholicism as the religion of the people in Ireland.[1] The end results of the Tudor reformations in Ireland and England were not predestined.

EARLY DEVELOPMENTS

The secular and religious élites in Ireland were not unaware of developments surrounding Henry VIII's 'great matter'. From 1529 to 1532, Garret Fitzgerald, 9th earl of Kildare, the leading nobleman of the Pale and oft-time lord deputy, was detained at the English royal court and witnessed at first hand the escalating campaign waged in support of the king's divorce proceedings, and signed a petition along with the lords of England to the pope on Henry VIII's behalf.[2] When the king charged the English clergy with breaching the statute of praemunire in 1531, John Alen, archbishop of Dublin, was charged along with them and fined.[3] George Cromer, archbishop of Armagh, was in England for about two years from October 1530, and witnessed there the early stages of king's rift with Rome. In his next diocesan synod, he launched a programme of reform to strengthen the Church in Armagh before it was confronted by the maelstrom which was engulfing the Church in England.[4] From the first half of 1533, the possibility of Irish resistance to Henry's escalating Reformation campaign was

---

1 H.A. Jefferies, 'The early Tudor reformations in the Irish Pale', *JEH*, 52 (2001), p. 40.
2 S.G. Ellis, *Tudor Ireland: crown, community and the conflict of cultures, 1470–1603* (London and New York, 1985), pp 118–22. In Kildare's library was a copy of Henry VIII's book in defence of the seven sacraments against Luther. 3 Murray, 'Archbishop Alen', pp 11–12. 4 H.A. Jefferies, 'Diocesan synods and convocations in Armagh on the eve of the Tudor reformations', *SAM*, 16 (1995), pp 124–5.

being discussed in imperial circles.[5] The English provincial of the Observant Franciscan friars planned to visit Ireland in 1534 to encourage adherence to the papacy.[6]

Henry VIII planned to send a new deputy to Dublin in 1534 with a programme for government that required him to terminate the pope's jurisdiction over the Church in Ireland.[7] However, on 11 June 1534, Lord Thomas Fitzgerald, vice-deputy of Ireland and son of the earl of Kildare, dramatically renounced his allegiance to the English monarch and launched a major rebellion.[8] Cromwell soon received a letter from Ireland informing him that Kildare's son and affinity boasted that 'they were of the pope's sect and band, and him will they serve against the king and all his partakers'.[9] The rebels declared that Henry VIII was 'accursed'. The Kildare revolt did not accord with the pattern of medieval rebellions, or the Pilgrimage of Grace, wherein protest was combined with protestations of loyalty to the king.[10] It was an attempt at revolution. Kildare's son denied Henry's title to the lordship of Ireland, and insisted that all men in Ireland take an oath of allegiance to the pope, the emperor and to himself – an interesting adaptation of the crown's imposition of oaths in favour of the royal supremacy in England.[11]

The Kildare revolt was no 'accident',[12] or 'gesture of protest' that escalated into rebellion only when the earl of Kildare was arrested.[13] Cromwell received a letter from Ireland written a week or more *before* the arrival in Ireland of news of Kildare's arrest reporting the rebels' avowed allegiance to the pope against the 'accursed' Henry VIII.[14] The letter to Cromwell was amply confirmed by subsequent reports. On 7 July 1534, the imperial ambassador informed the emperor that Lord Offaly had gathered an army together, seized some of the king's ordnance and had 'done many other things equally offensive' to Henry VIII.[15] For that news to reach the ambassador in London by 7 July, a messenger would

5 Micheál Ó Siochrú, 'Foreign involvement in the revolt of Silken Thomas', *PRIA*, 96C2 (1996), pp 49–66 at 51–2; *L&P*, vi, 541.   6 R.D. Edwards, *Church and state in Tudor Ireland: a history of penal laws against Irish Catholics* (London, 1935), p. 53.   7 SP 60/2/63.   8 Bradshaw, 'Cromwellian reform', pp 69–93; Steven Ellis, 'The Kildare rebellion and the early Henrician reformation', *HJ*, 19 (1976), pp 807–30; Laurence McCorristine, *The revolt of Silken Thomas: a challenge to Henry VIII* (Dublin, 1987). See now Jefferies, 'The Kildare revolt: accident or design?', *JCKAHS*, 19 (2004–5).   9 SP 60/2/47.   10 Michael Bush, *The pilgrimage of grace: a study of the rebel armies of October 1536* (Manchester and New York, 1996), pp 7–12, 407–16.   11 *Cal. SP Spain*, v/1, no. 86; SP 60/2/78; Ellis, 'The Kildare rebellion', p. 813.   12 Ciarán Brady, *The chief governors: the rise and fall of reform government in Tudor Ireland, 1536–1588* (Cambridge, 1994), p. 1.   13 McCorristine, *The revolt of Silken Thomas*, pp 65–6; Bradshaw, 'Cromwellian reform', pp 69–93; Ellis, 'Kildare rebellion', pp 497–519; Steven Ellis, *Tudor frontiers and noble power: the making of the British state* (Oxford, 1995), pp 207–32. This interpretation was reiterated in two more recent books: Steven Ellis' magisterial, *Ireland in the age of the Tudors* (Harlow, Essex, 1998), p. 136, and in Mary Ann Lyons, *Gearóid Óg Fitzgerald* (Dundalk, 1998), pp 63–4.   14 *L&P*, vii, 915; *StP*, ii, 197; LPL, MS 602, fo. 139v; *Cal. Carew MSS, 1515–74*, no. 84. As a rough rule of thumb, it may be stated that it took about a week for news from Dublin to reach London and vice versa.   15 *Cal. SP Spain*, v/1, no. 70.

have had to leave Ireland at the start of July at the latest, several days before news of Kildare's arrest could have reached Ireland. Chapuys' letter serves to confirm the report about the rebels being active in June.

The Kildare revolt was characterised throughout by the strong personal hostility directed against the king by Lord Offaly. Henry VIII came to read some of Offaly's letters 'in which besides the injurious and opprobious vituperations he heaps on him [Henry], he threatens to expel him from his kingdom'.[16] Chapuys observed that the king was extremely upset at being personally abused in such a manner. The Act of attainder against the rebel leader was to specifi-cally condemn his 'reviling of his grace with the most shameful and detestable infamies'.[17] Edmund Campion, while in Dublin a generation later, learned of Offaly's use of many 'slanderous and foul terms' against the king which, out of regard for Elizabeth, Henry and Anne Boleyn's daughter, he could not bring himself to repeat. Also, according to Campion, Offaly condemned the king for his 'heresy, lechery and tyranny, wherein the age to come may score him among ancient princes of most abominable and hateful memory. ... adding to his shameful oration many other slanderous and foul terms'.[18] If Offaly had ever sought simply to wrest concessions from Henry, he would never have abused the king personally. His words and actions from the very outset of his rebellion are not consistent with the prevailing view that he intended no more than 'a public relations exercise'.

Indeed, on receiving a message from his father in May 1534, Offaly had travelled to south-western Ireland to discuss his plans with Thomas Fitzgerald, earl of Desmond, and Conor O'Brien, lord of Thomond.[19] A letter to the warden of the collegiate church at Youghal from his brothers on 17 May 1534 indicates the nature of the discussions as it referred to Offaly as a 'traitor' – almost a month before the rebellion began.[20] Within a couple of weeks of Lord Offaly's meeting with Desmond and O'Brien, an English agent noted the departure of three imperial agents from Toledo on 8 June, one of them, he suspected, being destined for Ireland.[21] Chapuys reckoned that the agent appointed to go to Ireland must have landed there by late June.[22] William Wise, mayor of Waterford, wrote to Cromwell on 12 July 1534, reporting the vicar of Dungarvan as saying that the emperor had sent letters to the earl of Desmond 'to win [over] the Geraldines and O'Briens, and that the emperor intends shortly to send an army to invade the cities and towns by the sea coasts of this land'.[23]

---

16 *Cal. SP Spain*, v/1, no. 87.   17 *Stat. Ire., 28 Henry VIII*, ch. 1.   18 Edmund Campion, *A history of Ireland, written in the year 1571* (Dublin, 1809), pp 175–6. The source is, admittedly, late but still of a time when such information could have been gathered from eye-witnesses to the tumultuous events of 1534/5.   19 *L&P*, vii, 681.   20 Ibid.   21 *L&P*, vii, 945; BL, Titus, MS B.X.I., fo. 409; LPL, MS 602, fo. 44; *StP*, ii, 198, 201.   22 *Cal. SP Spain*, v/1, no. 70. 23 *L&P*, vi, no. 815; *StP*, ii, 198–9. Ó Siochrú has shown that this letter was mistakenly dated a year too early in *Letters and papers of Henry VIII*: 'Foreign involvement', p. 54.

Desmond and O'Brien sent letters to Charles V offering to recognise him as their overlord in return for military aid.[24] That would account for the rebels' boast of the imminent arrival of 12,000 Spanish soldiers as reported by Chapuys.[25]

At the start of the rebellion, Lord Offaly's forces ravaged the area around Dublin, a tactic intended to compel the local gentry to submit to his authority.[26] Campion referred to Offaly taking oaths from the gentlemen of the shires.[27] Contemporary sources indicate that oaths of fealty to the pope, the emperor and to Offaly himself were imposed on the townsmen who came under his authority.[28]

Religion may not have been the central motivating cause of the Kildare rebellion, but it was a key aspect of the rebel leader's strategic planning for the rebellion, both for maximising its support within Ireland and for attracting crucial help from mainland Europe.[29] The council established by the earl of Kildare to advise his son several months before the rebellion, included a number of clerical stalwarts of the Catholic Church.[30] They were motivated by a desire to preserve the Catholic faith in Ireland from Henry VIII, and the initial success of the rebellion owed something to the wide appeal of the war in defence of religion.[31] Steven Ellis showed that the local clergy throughout the Pale played an active and vital part in rousing support for the revolt.[32]

The Kildare insurrection demonstrated something of the widespread hostility towards the planned extension of Henry VIII's religious programme to Ireland. However, the revolt is significant primarily in revealing that a considerable proportion of people in Ireland – the size of the proportion is now indeterminable – was willing to transfer their allegiance from the English monarchy to the Holy Roman emperor, ostensibly for religious reasons. Henry VIII's subsequent appointees as deputy in Ireland did not attempt to enforce the Henrician reformation in Ireland, even in the Pale, as rigorously as it was enforced in England, for fear of making the lordship ungovernable. There was no attempt to compel all men in Ireland to take oaths acknowledging the royal supremacy, as was done in England. On the other hand, the elimination of several of the leading opponents of the Reformation weakened the Catholic cause in the English lordship. So too did the realisation that no help would be forthcoming from mainland Europe. In the immediate aftermath of the Kildare rebellion, there was a large garrison of English troops quartered in the Pale, a guarantee that the crown's wishes could not be ignored. Hence, while there was still widespread dissent from the king's ecclesiastical policies, it was not likely to be expressed forcibly.

---

24 *L&P*, vi, no. 999.   25 *Cal. SP Spain*, v/1, no. 70.   26 *L&P*, vii, 915; *StP*, ii, 197. He was still burning and destroying pockets of resistance in the countryside in early August; LPL, MS 602, fo. 44; *L&P*, vii, 1045; *StP*, ii, 201.   27 Campion, *History of Ireland*, p. 176.   28 *L&P*, vii, 1095.   29 Jefferies, 'The Kildare revolt', pp 449, 456.   30 Ibid., p. 449.   31 SP 60/3/59.   32 Ellis, 'Kildare rebellion', pp 815–16.

THE REFORMATION PARLIAMENT OF 1536–7

The Irish Reformation parliament was convened on 1 May 1536 and, as Brendan Bradshaw demonstrated, within a month the lords and commons had endorsed the bills concerning the royal supremacy.[33] However, the crown's legislation programme ran into insuperable opposition in the Convocation House, the third house within the Irish parliament.[34] Therein, the lower clergy of the lordship were represented by six or seven proctors.[35] As early as 17 May 1536, Brabazon complained that the Convocation House refused to endorse the key ecclesiastical bills put before them: 'Loath they are', he wrote, 'that the king's grace should be supreme head of the Church'.[36] A year later, the proctors were still being criticised as 'froward and obstinate', and 'in nothing conformable'. It seemed to Lords Grey and Brabazon that the clerical proctors were engaged in a strategy devised by themselves and 'their masters the bishops' to block the Henrician religious changes.[37] Significantly, perhaps, the Act for the submission of the clergy was not imposed on Ireland. In May 1537, the spiritual peers and clerical proctors stone-walled proceedings in parliament.[38] Their intention was to deny parliamentary sanction to all of the ecclesiastical bills that had not been endorsed by the Convocation House over the previous twelve months. Effectively, they kept the Henrician reformation at bay for an entire year.

The main focus of lay opposition to the ecclesiastical legislation in the Reformation parliament was the bill for the suppression of a small number of monasteries.[39] Patrick Barnewall, MP, the king's serjeant at law in Ireland, was most outspoken in the Commons in his opposition to the dissolution. Cromwell was informed that

> Barnewall ... said openly in the Commons House that he would not grant [acknowledge] that the king as head of the Church had such large power as the bishop of Rome; and that the king's jurisdiction therein was but a spiritual power, to reform or amend the enormities and defaults in religious houses, but not to execute man's laws nor to dissolve abbeys, or to alter the foundation of them to any temporal cause.[40]

That was a very courageous declaration of principle in a very public forum. Nor was he content to limit his opposition to words, he was audacious enough to lead a deputation to the king in person to defend the monasteries. Barnewall's opposition to the dissolution of the monasteries, and that of the commons generally,

33 Ibid., pp 291–2; Lambeth, MS 616, fo. 44. 34 SP 60/4/74. 35 *Alen's register*, p. 300.
36 Lambeth, MS 616, fo. 44. 37 SP 60/4/74. 38 Ibid. 39 Bradshaw, 'Opposition in the Irish Reformation parliament', pp 286, 289–90, 294–7; idem, *Dissolution*, pp 49–61. 40 SP 60/3/154; Bradshaw, *The dissolution*, pp 49–51.

has been dismissed as being motivated by mercenary concerns rather than religious principle.[41] Yet, the suppression bill submitted to the Irish Reformation parliament, and eventually endorsed by it, was directed against eight (and later nine) monasteries in border districts where the Palesmen had few vested interests.[42] For some considerable time after the parliament, there continued to be hope (and there may have been an undertaking from the crown) that there would not be a universal dissolution of the religious houses and, indeed, no universal dissolution was intended at the time. Deputy Grey, undoubtedly yielding to local political pressure, licensed a deputation of friars to visit Henry VIII late in 1538 to persuade the king not to dissolve the friaries.[43] As late as May 1539, the council of Ireland, again one may safely assume at the behest of its local members, appealed to Cromwell to exempt five monasteries and one convent from the general dissolution.[44] The sovereign and council of Wexford had already made a similar plea on behalf of one of their local monasteries.[45] These appeals all fell upon deaf ears, but they show that the community in the English lordship did not readily acquiesce in the dissolution of the monasteries, but made real efforts to rescue what they could of the monastic establishment, with some assistance from the chief governor.

Barnewall did not take any grant of monastic property from the first suppression campaign. Only subsequently, once it was clear that all of the religious communities were doomed, did he secure a grant of the convent at Grace Dieu, but he conveyed the manors of Grace Dieu and Fieldston to six clergymen and a gentleman of Turvey.[46] Among the clergymen was William Hamlin, one of the clerical proctors who resisted the Henrician reformation in parliament. Barnewall and his family supported the community of nuns from Grace Dieu long after the dissolution of their convent by Henry VIII.[47] It seems reasonable to deduce that his opposition to the dissolution of the monasteries was not motivated solely by material self-interest.

To break the impasse in the Reformation parliament, Henry VIII sent four commissioners to Ireland in September 1537. They convened the fourth session of the parliament and read a letter from the king directing the parliamentarians to conform themselves to the king's wishes and warning that 'if anyone will not, we shall so look upon them with our princely eye as his ingratitude therein shall be little to his comfort'.[48] This threat, from a king with so much blood already on his hands, could hardly be ignored. There may have been another factor involved, however. In early summer 1537, Lord Deputy Grey had a conference with Archdeacon Roth, Primate Cromer's chief subordinate.[49] No record of the

41 Bradshaw, 'Opposition in the Irish Reformation parliament', pp 295–8.   42 Bradshaw, *The dissolution*, pp 47–9.   43 SP 60/7/152.   44 SP 60/8/33; Jefferies, *Priests and prelates*, p. 39.   45 SP 60/4/180.   46 *CPCRI*, i, Patent roll 33 Henry VIII, m. 6.   47 Lennon, *Lords of Dublin*, p. 143; Bradshaw, *The dissolution*, p. 128.   48 *Letters and papers*, xii (ii), no. 388.   49 *CPCR*, i, Patent roll 27/28 Henry VIII, m. 25.

meeting survives, but one may surmise that the archdeacon acted as an interme-
diary for the primate and the Catholic opponents in the Reformation parliament.
It can hardly be a coincidence that on 31 July 1537, a general pardon was issued
to all of those involved in the Kildare revolt.[50] The king's commissioners came
to the Irish parliament with a bill confirming the royal pardon, a valuable incentive to ensure the compliance of the Palesmen.[51] As well as the pardon, Grey may
have given an informal undertaking not to enforce the Henrician reformation too
vigorously.

The final session of the parliament went as the king desired. The
Convocation House was formally declared to have no power in the making of
parliamentary legislation.[52] The suppression bill and the remainder of the
Reformation programme were endorsed by the Commons and House of Lords.
Significantly, the justification for the king's supremacy over the Irish Church
was political rather than religious: 'like as the king's majesty justly and rightly is
and ought to be supreme head of the Church of England, and so is recognised
by the clergy, and authorised by an Act of parliament made and established in
the said realm: so in like manner of wise, forasmuch as this land of Ireland is
depending and belonging justly and rightfully to the imperial crown of
England'. It was an argument that side-stepped the controversial theological
underpinning of the Henrician supremacy to appeal directly to the political
loyalties of the élites in the lordship of Ireland.

THE DISSOLUTION OF THE MONASTERIES

The first wave of monastic dissolutions in Ireland, in 1537, was very limited in
scale.[53] Nonetheless, the dissolutions generated an atmosphere of great uncertainty and rumours abounded.[54] Religious communities were demoralised,
including the Observant friars.[55] It was reported in November 1538 that,
whereas the Observants used to have twenty friars in each friary, by then they
had but four through desperation and the withdrawal of popular support.[56] This
report is interesting in revealing how developments in England helped to
psychologically prepare people in the English lordship to acquiesce in religious
change.

Following the enactment of the English monasteries act to dissolve all of the
religious houses in April 1539, an Irish suppression commission was issued for
the same purpose. Within twelve months, 'the medieval edifice of monasticism
in the crown territories [in Ireland] had been dismantled'.[57] Altogether, about 55

---

50 *CPCRI*, i, Patent roll 27/28 Henry VIII, dorso, m. 3.   **51** Bradshaw, 'Opposition in the Irish
Reformation parliament', p. 302.   **52** SP 60/5/131.   **53** Bradshaw, *The dissolution*, p. 77.
54 SP 60/6/129, 60/7/13.   **55** Lambeth, MS 602, fo. 104; SP 60/6/88; 60/6/127; 60/7/152.
56 SP 60/7/152.   **57** Bradshaw, *The dissolution*, pp 110–12.

per cent of Ireland's 140 or so monasteries were dissolved under Henry VIII, with the suppression campaign in the English lordship 'as near totally effective as makes no difference'.[58] The mendicant communities in the English lordship were also dissolved, encompassing about eighty of Ireland's 200 or so friaries.[59]

Despite Henry VIII's avowed intention to 'reform' the Church, the opportunity was lost to deploy even a fraction of the monastic windfall to address the problems of clerical poverty, education or training. A bill to ensure that all parishes that had been appropriated to monasteries were endowed with a benefice proved abortive in 1541. Furthermore, no stipulations were ever laid down among the terms of leases or bills of sale of former monastic possessions regarding the stipends payable to the unbeneficed priests who served most of the parishes in the English lordship, and many beyond it. The church courts, which had formerly taken action to ensure that monastic appropriators paid a decent stipend to the priests who served parish cures, evidently were not able to act effectively against the English crown or other holders of parish revenues following the dissolution. The church courts were similarly powerless when confronted with lay appropriators who failed to maintain the chancels of the churches they held impropriate, and there was a growing problem with chancels and, indeed, entire church buildings falling into ruin.

ENFORCING THE REFORMATION

The massive efforts of the crown to secure support for, or at least acquiescence in, its various religious policies in England are now reasonably well understood.[60] However, the enforcement of the Henrician reformation in the Pale contrasted sharply with that in England. There was practically no propaganda campaign, and such Reformation preaching as there was depended largely on the efforts of one individual: George Browne, the newly appointed archbishop of Dublin (1536–54). Browne arrived in Dublin in July 1536 to spearhead the Reformation campaign in Ireland.[61] However, the rearguard action of the clerical proctors in parliament and the lack of a royal commission left the archbishop feeling unable to promote religious change for an entire year, prompting Henry VIII to rebuke him in July 1537, together with Bishop Staples of Meath, for failing to give himself to 'the instruction of the people in the word of God nor framing himself to stand us in any stead for the furtherance of our affairs' in Ireland.[62]

58 Ibid., pp 206–7. 59 Ibid. 60 G.R. Elton, *Police and policy: the enforcement of the reformation in the age of Thomas Cromwell* (Cambridge, 1972), passim; Haigh, *English reformations: religion, politics and society under the Tudors* (Oxford, 1993), pp 130–202, 235–50, 268–84; Eamon Duffy, *The stripping of the altars: traditional religion in England, 1400–1580* (New Haven and London, 1992), pp 379–477. 61 Brendan Bradshaw, 'George Browne, first Reformation archbishop of Dublin, 1536–1554', *JEH*, 21 (1970), p. 310. 62 SP 60/4/186; Bradshaw,

Browne found that the pope's authority was 'a thing not a little rooted among the inhabitants here'.[63] He complained that of the twenty-eight most senior clergymen in his diocese, there was 'scarce one' who favoured the Reformation. He admitted that

> neither by gentle exhortation, evangelical instruction, neither by oaths of them solemnly taken nor yet by threats of sharp correction, can I persuade any, either religious or secular [priests], since my coming over, once to preach the word of God, or the just title of our most illustrious prince ... [though previously] they would very often, even till the right Christians were weary of them, preach after the old sort and fashion, [but now] will not once open their lips in any pulpit for the manifestation of the same, but in corners and in such company as them like and they can full earnestly utter their opinions, and so much as in them lies, hinder and pluck back amongst the people the labour that I do take in that behalf.[64]

He encountered even more virulent hostility from the Observant friars.[65] Spurred into action, Archbishop Browne set about imposing the oaths of supremacy and succession on the diocesan and regular clergy of his diocese late in 1537. It seems clear that the oaths were sworn by virtually all of the senior churchmen and women they were proffered to (though not the Observant friars who, as an order exempt from episcopal jurisdiction, refused to recognise the archbishop's authority over them), with the notable exception of James Humphrey, a canon of St Patrick's Cathedral, Dublin, who refused the oath and encouraged others to do likewise. Interestingly, no action was taken against Humphrey at that time, despite the fact that the statute book stipulated the death penalty for anyone who refused the oaths.[66]

Lord Butler and Thomas Agard commended Archbishop Browne to Henry VIII and Cromwell respectively for setting forth the word of God.[67] His new-found enthusiasm for the Reformation was not universally appreciated. In April 1538, the archbishop complained that Staples had called him a 'heretic and beggar' following his Lenten sermon, and warned a congregation to

> beware of seditious and false preachers which move questions of scripture for I tell you, all misery, wretchedness and also death come

---

'George Browne', p. 312. **63** Ibid. **64** Lambeth, MS 602, fos 104, 123. **65** Lambeth, MS 602, fo. 104, SP 60/6/88; 60/6/127; 60/7/152. **66** James Murray, 'Ecclesiastical justice and the enforcement of the Reformation: the case of Archbishop Browne and the clergy in Dublin' in A. Ford, J. McGuire and K. Milne (eds), *As by law established: the Church of Ireland since the Reformation* (Dublin, 1995), p. 39. **67** SP 60/6/77; 60/6/88.

> by moving of a question; for they that move questions of scripture do preach now this way, now that way, and be inconsistent.[68]

Yet Browne's enthusiasm for scriptural questions appeared concurrently as scriptural expositions were being promoted in England. Bradshaw has shown that Browne was always careful to keep within the bounds set down by the state-sponsored religious programmes, and his actions faithfully reflected changes authorised by the king or his vicegerent, Thomas Cromwell.[69]

By early April 1538, Archbishop Browne had revised the 'Form of the beads' to promote the royal supremacy in the parishes. These bidding prayers bade congregations to pray for the 'Church of England and Ireland' and for the 'supreme head on Earth, immediate under God, of the said Church', for Prince Edward, his son, for the bishops and clergy, 'especially for all that preach the word of God purely and sincerely', for the governing authorities and all of the laity, and for the souls of the departed. About the same time, Browne issued a series of injunctions that he had drawn up at the king's command 'for the reform of certain enormities and abuses amongst the clergy'.[70] The eighteen articles included a number of traditional disciplinary concerns, such as the clergy visiting common taverns or ale-houses. The bulk of the articles, however, were concerned with promoting the royal supremacy, though they were otherwise rather conservative doctrinally. It directed that the 'Form of the beads' be read after the Gospel at Mass on Sundays and holydays. It directed the clergy to teach their congregations the Our Father and creed in English, and to explain to them the true meaning of holy communion. James Murray has characterised the injunctions as being, 'in effect, a handbook for Henry VIII's new model Irish clergy'.[71]

Only one Dublin clergyman is known to have defied Browne's injunctions. In May 1538, Canon Humphrey of St Patrick's Cathedral celebrated Mass in St Audoen's Church, Dublin, but deliberately omitted to read the 'Form of the beads'. When Humphrey was presented to Archbishop Browne by some of his parishioners, he was arrested and put in the episcopal gaol. However, Deputy Grey released Humphrey from the gaol, and one is left to speculate as to whether there were other dissidents who were emboldened by Humphrey's experiences. Browne complained bitterly that the deputy's action had so undermined his authority that he was no more esteemed than a holy water clerk.[72]

---

68 SP 60/6/100; *State papers of Henry VIII*, iii, part 3, no. ccxlvi. 69 Bradshaw, 'George Browne', pp 312–14. 70 Browne's articles are printed in J. Payne Collier (ed.), *The Egerton papers: a collection of public and private documents* (Camden Society, London, 1840), pp 7–10. In an earlier study, I adopted James Murray's characterisation of this episode as a 'primary visitation' by Archbishop Browne: Jefferies, 'The early Tudor reformations', pp 51–2, citing Murray, 'Ecclesiastical justice', pp 40–2. Now I would suggest that the evidence is too limited and ambiguous to sustain confidence in the characterisation. 71 Murray, 'Ecclesiastical justice', p. 44. 72 Jefferies, 'Early Tudor reformations', p. 53.

Certainly, Archbishop Browne's efforts were undermined by Bishop Staples. Not only did the latter publicly preach against Browne's scriptural expositions and correspond with Humphrey, he also played a part in giving currency to the widespread rumour in June 1538 that Browne 'does abhor the Mass'.[73] Yet, Staples' chief grievance with the archbishop appears to have been jurisdictional rather than theological. In June 1538, he complained that the archbishop sought to rule all of the clergy in the English lordship – though Meath was outside of the archbishop's ecclesiastical province.[74] Indeed, Browne had in the previous month arrested Staples' suffragan bishop for praying for the pope and the Holy Roman emperor as well as for Henry VIII.[75]

Browne's injunctions were superseded by Cromwell's second set of injunctions, which were issued in October 1538. They were published by the council of Ireland early in 1539, not only in Dublin, but throughout south-eastern Ireland; at Carlow, Kilkenny, New Ross, Wexford, Waterford and Clonmel.[76] Archbishop Browne preached to sizeable congregations in several of those towns before presenting papers with the injunctions, together with English translations of the Our Father and Hail Mary, the ten commandments and the creed to local bishops and other senior churchmen with instructions to disseminate them throughout their jurisdictions. At Clonmel, the council and Browne met with two archbishops, those of Cashel and Tuam, and eight other bishops (mostly from Munster) and tendered them the oath of supremacy.[77] Whether his sermons had any lasting effect must be doubted, but the injunctions certainly made some impact far and wide across southern Ireland.

The injunctions' decree to pluck down 'any notable images or relics' was widely carried out. The annalist of the monastery at Lough Key wrote that 'there was not a holy cross, a statue of Mary nor a venerable image within their jurisdiction that they (i.e. the English) did not destroy'.[78] Certainly, in Dublin and Meath, the dioceses of Browne and Staples, many shrines were despoiled and destroyed. Yet in the diocese of Armagh, only one shrine is known to have suffered, that of St Richard in St Nicholas' Church, Dundalk, probably at the hands of Deputy Grey.[79]

In February 1539, a royal commission was established in Ireland to oversee the rigorous implementation of Henry VIII's religious decrees.[80] However, before the commission became effective, the 'Six articles' were promulgated by

---

73 Lambeth, MS 602, l.131. ccxxxiii. 74 Ibid. 75 SP 60/6/127. 76 SP 60/8/1. 77 SP 60/8/1; 60/8/9. 78 McNeill (ed.), 'Accounts of sums realised', p. 12; Bradshaw, *The dissolution*, p. 110; Duffy, *Stripping of the altars*, p. 407; William Hennessy (ed.), *The annals of Loch Cé: a chronicle of Irish affairs, 1014–1590* (London, 1871), *s.a.* 1538 (recte 1539). 79 McNeill (ed.), 'Accounts of sums realised', p. 12; White (ed.), *Extents of Irish monastic possessions*, p. 249. Eamon Duffy has shown that in England too the intensity and scope of the enforcement of the injunctions varied from diocese to diocese; Duffy, *Stripping of the altars*, pp 415, 431–42. 80 *CPCRI*, i, Patent roll 30, 31 Henry VIII, m. 1.

the king on 10 June 1539. These articles endorsed most traditional Catholic doctrines and ceremonies – except those relating to purgatory, images and the cult of saints. They even upheld the obligation of clerical celibacy in Henry VIII's Church. The royal supremacy was maintained as stoutly as ever and, indeed, was extended geographically across most of Ireland in subsequent years. However, the years of doctrinal turmoil came to a (temporary) end within the English lordship.

IMPACT OF THE REFORMATION

Traditionally, historians assessing the impact of the Henrician reformation in Ireland ventured little further than Archbishop Browne's series of melancholy reports to Henry VIII and Cromwell dated between September 1537 and May 1539. These suggested that the Cromwellian phase of the Reformation had failed to 'make an impact', even in Dublin, where it was most vigorously promoted.[81] However, my study based upon the Armagh registers revealed a more complex situation, in which those elements of the Henrician reformation which had the sanction of parliamentary statute had a real impact, though some of the statutes were enforced in a moderated fashion in the Pale compared with England, while the doctrinal and liturgical aspects of the Reformation, which were chiefly advanced by means of injunctions and proclamations rather than by parliamentary legislation, were more effectively blocked by the diocesan clergy.

The dissolution of the monasteries was the most dramatic feature of the Henrician reformation in Ireland.[82] It was significant in closing down some hospitals and schools in the English lordship. In terms of pastoral care, the suppression of the mendicant orders impoverished the spiritual lives of the people in a direct fashion.[83] Yet, the most important impact of the dissolution of the monasteries was the secularisation of the bulk of the revenues of the parishes, which had been impropriated to religious houses, and the transfer of the rights of patronage to benefices and curacies to the English crown. If Henry VIII had been inspired by a desire to reform the Church in Ireland, the dissolution of the monasteries gave him an unprecedented opportunity to transform the institution. However, he failed to do so.

The success of Irish priests in securing benefices from the English crown during the 1540s suggests that there may have been increasing difficulty in securing local priests of English descent for promotion. That coincided with a collapse in the numbers of men offering themselves for ordination across England.[84] The small number of former monks who became parish priests may

81 Murray, 'Ecclesiastical justice', p. 51.   82 Bradshaw, *The dissolution*, cited above.   83 Ibid., pp 8–16.   84 Margaret Bowker, 'The Henrician reformation and the parish clergy' in Haigh,

have helped to meet a real need in staffing the parishes.[85] Nonetheless, it is clear that the crown's power to re-constitute the parish ministry in Ireland was greatly curtailed by the lack of Protestant-inclined priests available for promotion to its parishes.

A further problem was that the failure of the English authorities to establish a university in Ireland, or a training college for the ministers of the Henrician Church, meant that the parish clergy throughout the period of the early Tudor reformations were educated and trained in the late medieval manner, by an 'apprenticeship' with older and, in all probability, conservative priests. After a small influx of former religious into parish cures following the dissolution of the monasteries, it appears that there was very little change in the parish clergy in terms of their training and professional backgrounds. Continuity, rather than change, characterised the clergy of Ireland, despite the Henrician reformation.

The Act for presenting priests to benefices was widely enforced in the Pale. Inquisitions were held regularly to identify Gaelic Irish men who were appointed to benefices in contravention of the statute.[86] However, such clergymen as were identified were able to purchase charters of English denizenship to overcome the legal impediment of their Irish blood. The clause in the Act requiring parish priests to conduct schools for teaching English created difficulties for rather more of the clergy.[87] Since it was rigorously enforced, it seems safe to conclude that those in authority in the Pale – in particular the gentry – supported this cultural aspect of the Henrician reformation in Ireland. The significance of this, that the government's will could be imposed with local assistance, is that it shows that the structures existed through which the entire Henrician reformation programme could have been enforced, if it had enjoyed support from among the secular élites in the Pale.

In 1538, the values of the parochial benefices in the English lordship in Ireland were recorded in the *Valor in Hibernia* by royal commissioners, for the purposes of levying the first fruits and the twentieth tax.[88] Yet, the twentieth took the place of clerical subsidies which had been levied by the crown at about the same rate in the later Middle Ages, and the unbeneficed parish clergy never paid the twentieth tax, nor the subsidy before it.[89]

The Act of faculties had an effect in that it can be shown that some couples from the English lordship sought dispensations from Canterbury for consanguinity, though (at least in the late 1530s) others preferred to travel beyond the lordship to secure a dispensation from a non-schismatic bishop.[90] The Act against the pope's authority led to the arrest of a small number of clergymen,

English reformation revised, pp 75–93, and especially pp 78–84. 85 Jefferies, *Priests and prelates*, p. 139. 86 NAI, Exchequer inquisitions, Dublin, III, Inq. 133, fo. 492. 87 Ibid., Inq. 143 (1543), fo. 503; Inq. 148 (1544), fo. 509; Inq. 149 (1545), fo. 510. 88 Jefferies, *Priests and prelates*, pp 26–8, 141–2; Ellis, 'Economic problems', pp 244–57. 89 Jefferies, 'Diocesan synods', pp 127–30. 90 Jefferies, *Priests and prelates*, p. 144.

though it seems that prosecutions were very rare if, indeed, there were any at all.[91]

English evidence shows that 'the intensity and scope of the Henrician assault on popular religion would vary greatly from region to region, from diocese to diocese'.[92] It is difficult to see what happened in Ireland's dioceses. However, Armagh's synodal records show that instead of using their annual synods to promote the Henrician reformation, Primates Cromer and Dowdall employed them to promote traditional reformist goals.[93] They may have helped to thwart the Reformation in Armagh by largely ignoring it, and by maintaining a high level of continuity with the pre-Reformation period in terms of the format of the assemblies and of the agendas they presented to the parochial clergy. The *acta* which survive for the visitation of parishes in Armagh *inter Hibernicos* in 1546, confirm Dowdall's very conservative religious disposition.[94] While he was prepared to accept the king as head of the Church, he worked to promote traditional reform – not Reformation – in his archdiocese.

There is no doubt that the conservative diocesan clergy hampered the progress of the Reformation in Ireland, but the reason why their opposition to religious change was so much more effective than that of their English counterparts was political. Deputy Grey calculated that the political costs of rigorously enforcing the king's religious programme in Ireland were impracticably high. Archbishop Browne complained more than once that the local élites, both religious and secular, were generally hostile to Henry VIII's reformation. John Alen, master of the rolls, concurred in condemning the lawyers of the Pale as 'Papists, hypocrites and worshippers of idols'.[95] Robert Cowley complained to Cromwell of the 'papistical sect springing up and spread abroad, infecting the land pestiferously'.[96]

Deputy Grey treated the unpopular archbishop of Dublin (a 'polshorne knave friar', he called him) with open contempt.[97] He released Canon Humphrey, the only open Catholic dissident among the clergy of Dublin, from the prison to which Archbishop Browne had condemned him.[98] He also released Dean Art O'Gallagher of Derry, a Catholic dissident who had been arrested with papal bulls in his possession.[99]

On another occasion, Deputy Grey 'heard three or four masses' in an ostentatious display of devotion before Our Lady's statue at Trim, County Meath, while the suffragan bishop of Meath, whom Browne had arrested, together with a number of friars, were being tried in the town for breaching the statute against

---

91 SP 60/6/127; 60/7/147; 60/9/152, articles 29, 68, 71.   92 Duffy, *Stripping of the altars*, pp 413–15.   93 Ibid., 8 (7), 36 (31), 38 (32), 92 (78).   94 Aubrey Gwynn (ed.), 'Documents relating to the medieval diocese of Armagh', *Archivium Hibernicum*, 12 (1947), pp 26–9; Jefferies, 'The visitation of the parishes of Armagh *inter Hibernicos* in 1546' in Jefferies and Dillon, *Tyrone: history and society* (2000).   95 SP 60/7/147.   96 Lambeth, MS 602.l.iii.   97 SP 60/9/62.   98 SP 60/6/127.   99 SP 60/9/152, articles 29, 68, 71.

the pope's authority. [1] Grey's piety may, conceivably, have reflected his personal religious disposition, but such a public action conveyed a powerful political message. It undoubtedly encouraged the jury not to indict the clergymen on trial in Trim, which was, presumably, the intended effect. The actions of the deputy, whether from personal or political motives or a combination of both, accorded with the wishes of the élites in the English lordship who did not want religious change.

The advent of Anthony St Leger as the king's deputy in Ireland in July 1540 served to confirm his predecessors' policy of avoiding religious controversy as far as possible. St Leger took advantage of the partial reversal of the king's policy in the 'Six Articles' of 1539 to promote the royal supremacy in Ireland shorn of doctrinal or liturgical innovation. [2] The royal supremacy was extended widely into Gaelic and gaelicised regions in tandem with Deputy St Leger's 'surrender and regrant' programme in the 1540s. The pan-Irish Geraldine League, which had committed itself to war in 1539–40 against Henry VIII, 'a heretic against the faith', dissipated as great Irish lords like the earl of Desmond, and the newly created earls of Clanrickard and Tyrone, and many others, acknowledged Henry's sovereignty and the royal supremacy, and the bishops in their lordships generally did likewise.

Yet, while the English crown was able to secure the acquiescence of the secular élites and the Church authorities across much of Ireland to the royal supremacy and the dissolution of the religious orders, the impact of the Henrician reformation on religious belief and practice was very limited, most especially beyond the Pale. That lack of impact clearly reflected the wishes of the conservative population in Ireland, clergy and laity, Irish and English, but it was facilitated by Deputies Grey and St Leger who, from a mix of personal and political motives, did not enforce the doctrinal aspects of the king's religious programmes with any vigour or enthusiasm.

The remaining years of Henry VIII's reign saw no further attempts to alter the religion of the peoples of Ireland. In return for their acknowledgment of the moderated supremacy, St Leger offered bishops and clergy across the south and west of Ireland not only continued tenure of office but also practical assistance with problems such as unwarranted lordly interference in the finances and appointments in the Church. [3] It was a strategy that worked well and won wide acceptance for a schismatic if essentially Catholic religious settlement. [4] A great many of the lordship's élites, senior clergymen, urban oligarchs and landowners

1 SP 60/6/127; 60/7/147. 2 Haigh, *English reformations*, pp 152–67; Brendan Bradshaw, *The Irish constitutional revolution of the sixteenth century* (Cambridge, 1979), pp 245–9. 3 See, for instance, St Leger's major commitments to the churchmen in the ecclesiastical provinces of Cashel and Tuam in *Cal. Carew MSS, i, 1515–74*, nos 157, 158, 170, 180, 185, 188, 193. 4 Murray now accepts that that was true even in Dublin: Murray, 'Tudor diocese of Dublin', p. 106; idem, *Enforcing the English Reformation in Ireland* (Cambridge, 2009), pp 135–6.

of English descent, were prepared to turn their backs on papal authority as long as they could retain their Catholic religion and practices.

Murray revealed a staggering scale of asset-stripping that was carried out in Dublin diocese by Archbishop Browne with the 'active support and collaboration of the cathedral chapters'.[5] When Deputy St Leger dissolved St Patrick's Cathedral, Dublin, in 1547, not only was there no demur from the cathedral clergy, but several of the former canons acted as feoffees to uses in a land conveyance transaction for the deputy.[6] One looks in vain for evidence of a '*Laudabiliter*-inspired canonical ethos' in the words or actions of Dublin's clerical élites.[7] Their true motives were much more mundane and hard-headed.

CONCLUSIONS

Recent studies of the pre-Reformation Church in England and Ireland have argued that there was nothing inevitable about the ultimate outcomes of the Tudor reformations on either side of the Irish Sea.[8] The subsequently different experiences of England and Ireland suggest that one critical factor determining the progress of the early Tudor reformations was the English crown's ability to impose them upon unwilling congregations, because in the Pale where the crown's capacity to secure the co-operation of the secular and ecclesiastical authorities was weaker than in England and Wales (though not altogether inconsiderable), the Tudor reformations were imposed to much less effect.[9] The Kildare rebellion, although it was not primarily religious in motivation, may have been of profound importance as a lesson to Grey and St Leger of the potential risks involved in enforcing religious changes in a disturbed borderland with virtually no local support.

In Armagh, the diocesan Church seems to have come through Henry VIII's reformation relatively unscathed – at least on the surface. James Murray declared that the Henrician reformation failed to make 'an impact' in Dublin.[10] Mary Ann Lyons reckoned that the dissolution of the monasteries was 'the only element of the Henrician reformation which had a real impact' in County Kildare.[11] Brendan Scott reached a similar judgment about Meath diocese because its bishop, Staples, 'seemed more interested in undermining Browne than in promoting reform'.[12]

5 Ibid., pp 170–85. 6 Murray, 'Tudor diocese of Dublin', p. 153. 7 For my views on this see Jefferies, 'Early Tudor reformations in the Pale', passim; H.A. Jefferies, review of Murray, *Enforcing the English Reformation*, *History Ireland*, 17:3 (May/June 2009), p. 61. 8 Jefferies, 'Early Tudor reformations', op. cit. 9 For a less than convinced perspective on the revisionist thesis, see David Loades, *Revolution in religion: the English Reformation, 1530–1570* (Cardiff, 1992), pp 3–5. 10 Murray, 'Ecclesiastical justice', pp 50–1. 11 Lyons, *Church and society*, p. 184. 12 Scott, *Tudor diocese of Meath*, p. 46.

On the other hand, Henry VIII had largely succeeded in displacing the papacy's jurisdiction over the Church in the Pale and over wider parts of Ireland where the royal writ ran effectively. When the first Jesuit mission arrived in Ireland in 1542, they formed a very bleak impression of the prospects for the Catholic Church there.[13] Lords and bishops across Ireland seemed to accept the royal supremacy over the Irish Church. With hindsight, it is clear that the Jesuits were unduly pessimistic. Nonetheless, as long as the senior clergy and secular élites were prepared to acquiesce in the Tudors' royal supremacy over the Church, there remained a possibility that the Reformation might eventually succeed, especially in the most 'English' part of Ireland.

13 Aubrey Gwynn, *The medieval province of Armagh* (Dundalk, 1946), pp 248–53.

5

Edward VI's reformation

Early in Edward VI's reign, before he had an inkling of the religious radicalism that was to follow, Archbishop Browne of Dublin travelled to London to submit a 'device' petitioning for the foundation of a university in Ireland.[1] He proposed that St Patrick's Cathedral, Dublin, which had only recently been suppressed, and the residences of the former cathedral staff in its vicinity, be transformed into a 'large' university of 200 students,

> as well for the increase of God's divine service as the king's majesty's immortal fame and the unspeakable reformation of that realm and for the education of students and youth, which may … grow as well in the knowledge of God, author of all goodness, without whom the knowledge of the king [and] the obedience of his laws shall never be had there …

He proposed that lectors in Latin, Greek, civil law and divinity be employed by the chancellor of the new university college for £40 *per annum* from a fund comprising the revenues of a number of rectories (all outside of his diocese), though he also suggested that the archdeacon of Meath, and the archdeacons of Dublin and Glendalough (once the latter offices were restored as he requested), could each support a lector too. He suggested that the king write letters to the nobility and bishops of Ireland to elicit further endowments for the university, and he recommended that the chantries in Ireland be dissolved and their assets be made available for the support of the university's staff and students. His suggestion that free schools might be erected from the proceeds of the dissolution of the chantries, collegiate churches and free chapels was erased from the 'device' for some reason. Embedded in the 'device' is his request that the dean, dignitaries and prebendaries of Christ Church be translated to the former cathedral of St Patrick, 'there to continue with their livings forever for the better maintenance of God's divine service there'. Browne's 'device' was drawn up, not because of his belated realisation of the utility of an Irish university, but as a

1 E.P. Shirley (ed.), *Original letters and papers … of the Church in Ireland under Edward VI, Mary and Elizabeth* (London, 1851), no. ii. His proposal for the assets of St Patrick's Cathedral was written in England. It was dated to an unspecified time in 1547, but a date early in Edward's reign seems most probable if he was to have any chance of influencing the crown's plans for the insti-

desperate attempt to reverse the secularisation of St Patrick's Cathedral – the best-endowed church in his diocese.[2]

Brendan Bradshaw observed that 'It is difficult to understand, in view of the document which he submitted to the London government at that time how scholars could suggest that Browne was initially hostile, or at least apathetic, to the Edwardian programme'.[3] Browne asked for a commission to be established to deal with ecclesiastical causes in Ireland, to discourage people from resorting to 'the Popish trade', to swear Irish bishops and priests to obedience to the supreme head of the Church, and for the execution of the king's ecclesiastical programme 'according [to] the order used in England'. He called for three bishops to be sent to Ireland 'now immediately' to 'most diligently and earnestly travail in setting forth to the people by an uniform doctrine the words of God and the Christian proceedings of the king's majesty as it is here in England'. That is a clear indication that he had not, at the start of the new reign, abandoned his reformist ideals. However, it must be noted that in 1547 it was not yet clear how radical Edward VI's reformation was to become.

Archbishop Browne's university proposal fell on deaf ears.[4] Thereafter he fell silent – was he, perhaps, disquieted by the increasingly radical direction of the crown's religious policies? In the winter of 1548, he was accused by Chancellor John Alen of having failed to 'set out, or cause to be set out, the king's injunctions or homilies'.[5] He was also accused of having failed to preach any sermon whatsoever from November 1547 until September 1548. Interestingly, no correspondence from him has survived from those months either. It is as though Browne adopted silence, as his Irish clerical opponents had done in the late 1530s, as his response to religious changes he did not support.

In September 1548, Browne broke his silence to deliver a formal sermon against a Scottish preacher in Dublin whom he compared to Luther for condemning the Mass and 'other our ceremonies', and for speaking against good works. The archbishop declared that whoever supported or concurred with the Scot's preaching was not the king's true subject. That conservative sermon is very significant in that Browne can have had no doubt that the Scot reflected the crown's latest religious thinking: England was awash with printed tracts attacking the Mass in 1548. The same Scottish preacher had already delivered a sermon before Deputy Bellingham, the council of Ireland and the archbishop himself at Kilmainham, 'setting forth the gospel, the prince's authority and condemning the abuse of the bishop of Rome's Masses and ceremonies', and he had preached again 'against the former abuses' before the archbishop in Christ Church Cathedral at the request of its dean, without prompting any complaint from him.[6] Yet, in his highly publicised sermon, Browne spoke out strongly

tution. 2 This is also the view of Murray ('Ecclesiastical justice'). 3 Brendan Bradshaw, 'The Edwardian reformation in Ireland', *Archivium Hibernicum*, 34 (1976–7), p. 83. 4 Shirley, *Original letters*, no. i. 5 Ibid., no. v.

against the latest developments in the Edwardian reformation. Among those especially invited to the sermon was William Hamlin, vicar of St Peter's, Drogheda, who was one of the clerical proctors who defied Henry VIII in the Irish Reformation parliament in 1536–7, and Rector Luttrell, who would be deprived for opposing the Elizabethan religious settlement.[7] That sermon may provide a reflection of the archbishop's personal convictions – and he was later to offer Cardinal Pole written testimony from others of his adherence to the Catholic doctrine of the Mass. Nevertheless, true to form, Browne bowed to pressures exerted on him by the state and he became an active proponent of religious change from November 1548.

DEPUTY BELLINGHAM

During the uncertain early months of Edward VI's reign, Sir Anthony St Leger remained as lord deputy in Ireland. No one in London thought of sending him explicit instructions regarding the crown's changing religious policies, and no one in Ireland thought to anticipate unwelcome religious directives from London. However, in May 1548, St Leger was replaced as deputy by Sir Edward Bellingham, the commander-general of the crown's army in Ireland. Bellingham's more bellicose style was reflected in his military campaigns in the Irish midlands, and in his sponsorship of a robustly Protestant preacher in Dublin – Walter Palatyne, presumably the same Walter the Scot whose criticisms of the Mass prompted Archbishop Browne's uncharacteristically conservative sermon.

Once Archbishop Browne had been persuaded to embrace the more conservative stage of Edward VI's reformation, Palatyne worked with him in drawing up a 'book of reformation'. On 23 November 1548, Palatyne wrote to the lord deputy informing him that the archbishop had already circulated copies of the book to the suffragan bishops of his ecclesiastical province.[8] The contents of the 'book of reformation' must remain a matter for speculation but, according to a letter from Bellingham, it established 'godly and true order' in the Church 'grounded upon holy writ; the king's majesty's injunctions being consonant thereunto'.[9] The 'book of reformation' probably incorporated the reasonably moderate royal injunctions of 1547 as well as some of the more radical decrees that followed, directed against all religious images, sacramentals and pilgrimages and all expressions of veneration for saints or sacred objects, and (at least some of) the homilies whose neglect Browne was criticised for.[10]

6 Ibid. The fact that the radical preacher was invited to preach in the cathedral by the dean should serve as a warning against exaggerated claims about the hostility of Dublin's cathedral clergy to the Tudor reformations.   7 Jefferies, *Priests and prelates*, pp 137–8, 158.   8 SP 61/1/133: Bradshaw, 'Edwardian reformation', p. 84.   9 Shirley, *Original letters*, no. x.

The 'book of reformation' was certainly put into effect in the more anglicised parishes in Dublin, as shown by Bellingham's rebuke to the former treasurer of St Patrick's Cathedral, Dublin, for infringing the same and for trying to 'incite' and 'stir' others against it.[11] It may also have been imposed in at least some of the more anglicised parishes of the Pale. Interestingly, Palatyne, in his letter to Bellingham in November 1548, made reference to a Mr Stephens, who had expected to be appointed to a benefice by the bishop of Ferns until the dean and chapter of the diocese dissuaded the bishop against appointing him.[12] This incident, though very poorly documented, probably reflects not only the opposition of the local clergy to Edward VI's reformation, but also Bellingham's interest in promoting the Reformation across Leinster.

In northern Leinster, the deputy encountered determined opposition from George Dowdall, archbishop of Armagh. Bellingham appealed to Dowdall to be 'circumspect' in his actions and to set forth 'the plain, simple and naked truth'. He directed the primate to meet him on his return to Dublin for a consultation for the 'better setting forth [of] the truth and obedience' among the king's loving subjects.[13] What transpired at that consultation cannot be determined, but Dowdall continued to resist the Edwardian reformation resolutely: as late as 1551, he was charged with failing to implement even the most elementary of the Edwardian reforms concerning 'holy water, Candlemas candles and such like'.[14] A hint, perhaps, of the reason for Bellingham's failure to tackle Dowdall's audacious obstinacy lies in his reference to the primate's 'reputation among the people' (reminiscent of Thomas Cusack's characterisation of him ten years earlier as a 'papistical fellow being able to corrupt a whole country').[15]

There is no evidence that Bishop Staples was any more active than Browne in promoting the Edwardian reformation before November 1548, the same time as Browne was galvanised into supporting Protestantism.[16] Staple's first Protestant sermon, delivered in Dublin, came as a tremendous shock for many people in his diocese. It seems clear that they had no prior inkling of Staple's sudden espousal of Protestant doctrines. His letter to Bellingham's secretary describing reactions in Meath to his sermon is worth quoting *in extenso* for the insights it offers into religious sentiments among the social élite[17] in the rural heart of the Pale:[18]

> You have not heard such rumour as is here all the country over against me as my friends do show me. One gentlewoman to whom I did christen a man child which bears my name came in great council to a friend of mine desiring how she might find means to change her

10 Ibid., no. v; Bradshaw, 'Edwardian reformation', p. 84.   11 Shirley, *Original letters*, no. x.
12 SP 61/1/133.   13 SP 61/1/162; Jefferies, *Priests and prelates*, p. 158.   14 SP 61/3/45;
Bradshaw, 'Edwardian reformation', p. 85; Jefferies, *Priests and prelates*, p. 159; Scott, *Tudor diocese of Meath*, p. 55.   15 SP 60/3/112.   16 Bradshaw, 'Edwardian reformation', p. 85; Scott, *Tudor diocese of Meath*, p. 49.   17 Their social class may be inferred from their easy familiarity with the bishop, or his friends.   18 Shirley, *Original letters*, no. vii.

child's name, and he asked her why? And she said, 'because I would not have him bear the name of a heretic'. A gentleman dwelling nigh unto me forbade his wife which would have sent her child to be confirmed by me, to do so, saying his child should not be confirmed by him that denied the sacrament of the altar. A friend of mine rehearsing [i.e. announcing] at the markets that I would preach this next Sunday at Navan, diverse [people] answered they would not come thereat lest they should learn to be heretics. One of our lawyers declared to a multitude that it was great pity that I was not burned for I preached heresy ...A beneficed man of my own promotion came unto me weeping ... 'My lord', said he, 'before you went to Dublin you were the best beloved man in your diocese that ever came in it, and now you are the worst beloved that ever came here'. I asked why. 'Why', said he, 'for you have taken open part with the Scot, that false heretic, and preached against the sacrament of the altar and deny saints, and will make us worsethan Jews. ...' and [he] besought me to take heed of myself for he feared more than he did tell me. He said, 'You have more curses than you have hairs on your head. And I advise you for Christ's sake not to preach at Navan as I hear you will do'.

Staples confessed in the letter that he feared for his life in 'diverse ways'. There is no record of what transpired subsequently, though one suspects that Staples may have become more circumspect. The only other reference to his preaching comes from an observation by St Leger that when the bishop preached at a fort he was treated with 'so little reverence' that he showed 'no great haste' to repeat the experience.[19] Brendan Scott opined that 'the available evidence ... points to the possibility that Staples was, perhaps, not quite the enthusiastic reformer he has been supposed to be'.[20] With Browne and Staples spearheading the Edwardian reformation in Ireland, it is hardly surprising that it made so little positive impression.

   In December 1548, Bellingham, in a letter to Protector Somerset's secretary, highlighted the 'great need' for Protestant pastors in Ireland; 'good shepherds ... to illuminate the hearts of the flock of Christ with his most true and infallible word'.[21] He asked that no bishop be promoted in Ireland without his being consulted beforehand.[22] When conservative bishops did not oblige him by dying, Bellingham secured the protector's permission, some months later, to 'take the resignations of such ... bishops as will voluntarily resign' and nominate their successors.[23] He nominated an English Protestant, Thomas Lancaster, for Kildare diocese in 1549.

---

19 Ibid., no. xvii.   20 Scott, *Tudor diocese of Meath*, p. 51.   21 Shirley, *Original letters*, no. viii.
22 Ibid.

In January 1549, the Act of uniformity was enacted by the English parliament. It decreed that the *Book of Common Prayer*, a somewhat ambiguously Protestant service book, was to take the place of all Catholic liturgical books from 9 June 1549.[24] The Act did not explicitly refer to Ireland, but it is likely that Deputy Bellingham imposed it on parts of the English lordship in Ireland regardless, though the evidence is inconclusive. In April 1549, the sovereign of Kilkenny wrote to Bellingham to inform him that he had 'warned' the priests whom Anthony Colcough had 'named specially' (except for the dean of Kilkenny, who lay ill in Waterford), together with 'the rest of [the] priests' of Kilkenny, to appear before the deputy and council when they visited the town.[25] This suggests that they may have been disobedient to the crown's religious decrees, and that the deputy intended to remedy their disobedience in person. Yet the letter cannot be read as clear evidence of the deputy's preparations for the impending implementation of the Act of uniformity from June 1549. Significantly, the summons was not extended to clergymen beyond the Anglophone town. It seems a safe assumption (though definite evidence is lacking) that the first *Book of Common Prayer* was widely introduced in Anglophone parishes in Archbishop Browne's ecclesiastical province, with the acquiescence of the local secular élites. The same is likely to have been the case in Bishop Staples' diocese of Meath – but not in the diocese of Armagh, where Archbishop Dowdall was as obstreperously conservative as ever.

In June 1549, Bellingham and the council of Ireland authorised the attorney general and the king's surveyor to exercise 'ecclesiastical jurisdiction' wherever they travelled in the ecclesiastical province of Cashel, for 'abolishing idolatry, papistry and the Mass sacrament and the like'.[26] This has been read as evidence of the enforcement of the first Act of uniformity and the propagation of the first *Book of Common Prayer* in the south,[27] but the absence of any subsequent report as to its progress makes it impossible to draw any definite safe conclusions. One might have presumed that any efforts they made on behalf of the Reformation were confined to the Anglophone towns; it is difficult to conceive of what might have been achieved in the Irish-speaking countryside. Yet, intriguingly, the archbishop of Cashel conducted a metropolitan visitation with eleven articles later in 1549, and he deprived a number of clergymen of their benefices in rural parishes of his diocese.[28] One can only speculate as to the grounds on which they were deprived of their benefices.[29] Intriguingly, though, there was a spate of clergymen removed from their benefices across the Ormond lordship ostensibly because of being Irish, and a spate of requests by Irish clergymen in the region seeking grants of English denizenship. It is as though the pernicious system of

23 Ibid., no. xiii. 24 SP 61/1/155. 25 Shirley, *Original letters*, no. xii. 26 SP 61/2/47; Shirley, *Original letters*, no. xiv; Bradshaw, 'Edwardian reformation', p. 86. 27 Bradshaw, 'Edwardian reformation', pp 85–6. 28 *CPCRI*, pp 195, 237; *Fiants*, Edward VI, 681, 760. 29 Bradshaw, 'Edwardian reformation', p. 98, n. 36.

delating beneficed clergymen for their benefices at Rome had been replaced with
an equally pernicious system of suing Irish clergy in royal courts on the grounds
of their nationality. Whatever the case, the extension of Edward's government's
authority over the Church in the Ormond territories was significant. However,
it is not at all clear if the doctrinal aspects of the Edwardian reformation made
any real impact. Bradshaw characterised the early Tudor reformations in the
south and west as 'haphazard' and 'spasmodic', with no attempt at evangelisation, polemic or even explanation.[30]

Bellingham was recalled to England in December 1549, his demotion
coinciding with the fall of Protector Somerset. It was written of him that 'there
was never [a] deputy in the realm that went the right way as he does both for the
setting forth of God's word to his honour, and to the wealth of the king's
highness' subjects'.[31] On the other hand, St Leger's (admittedly not entirely
disinterested) assessment of 'the advancement of religion' a year later was that
'although it has been much talked of these two or three years past, yet it has been
smally set forth in deed'.[32]

With Bellingham's departure, the government of Ireland was entrusted to a
series of short-lived caretaker administrations and it is highly probable that the
momentum that the deputy had injected into the Edwardian reformation was
lost. The early months of 1550 saw a French ambassador visit the lords of Ulster
with letters from the king of France. At the same time, Archbishop Wauchop,
the papal appointee to Armagh, stayed in Derry and tried to whip up support for
a war against the heretical English régime.[33] It was not a favourable time to
impose religious change on a conservatively inclined population.

ST LEGER'S SECOND TERM

Evidently it proved difficult to find a suitable and willing replacement for
Bellingham. In July 1550, Sir Anthony St Leger was re-appointed as lord deputy
of Ireland. He was directed by the king and English council to

> set forth God's service ... as largely as he may according to our
> ordinances and proceedings in the English tongue in all places where
> the inhabitants, or a convenient number of them, understand the
> English tongue. And where the inhabitants understand not the
> English tongue, they cause the English to be translated truly into the
> Irish tongue unto such time as the people may be brought to under-
> stand the English.[34]

---

30 Bradshaw, 'Reformation in the cities', pp 454, 456, 459.   31 M.V. Ronan, *The Reformation in Dublin, 1536–1558* (Dublin, 1926), p. 356.   32 Shirley, *Original letters*, no. xix.   33 Ibid., no. xv.

St Leger himself remained conservatively inclined in religion, and he let it be known to the English privy council that he would prefer to fight in a war against Spain, 'or any other place where the king should have cause to make war', than be responsible for religious change in Ireland.[35] Nonetheless, he accepted office on the king's terms and he repeatedly showed himself anxious to reassure the government in London that he was doing his best to promote Edward VI's reformation.[36]

One of St Leger's first acts on returning to Ireland was to meet with Archbishop Dowdall of Armagh to persuade him to conform to the crown's religious programme – unsuccessfully.[37] St Leger advised the primate to amend his ways, but allowed him to return to his diocese without further ado. The deputy issued a proclamation ('to content the outward appearance of the world' according to Archbishop Browne) setting forth the Edwardian reformation. However, St Leger failed to address the primate's open and continuing rejection of the Edwardian 'reforms' nor, according to Browne, did he cause anyone else who contravened the Edwardian religious decrees to be punished or corrected. St Leger's failure to act against Dowdall, in particular, led to heated clashes in the council of Ireland.

St Leger explained to Cecil that regarding the Edwardian reformation, 'if the disposition of men here were thoroughly known it would be thought a thing not easy to be brought to pass'.[38] A few weeks later, in January 1551, he informed Cecil that 'although it be hard to plant in men's minds here, yet I trust I am not slack to do what I can to advance the same'.[39] In particular, he referred to his promotion of the Reformation in Limerick city, where he sent 'books' to unidentified individuals who 'most gladly have condescended to embrace the same with all effect, although the bishop there, who is both old and blind, be most against it'.[40] Bishop Quinn of Limerick (1522–51) was obliged to retire on 'health grounds' soon afterwards, though it seems clear that the real reason for his resignation was his opposition to the *Prayer Book*.[41] The retirement of Nicholas Comin, bishop of Waterford & Lismore (1519–51), also on 'health grounds', took place at about the same time, probably for the same reason.[42] Comin had earlier offered Henry VIII to resign in favour of one Balthazer Butler, whom he asked the king to commend to the pope – implying a lack on engagement with the Tudor reformations.[43] The new appointees to the sees of Limerick and Waterford were both local men who were willing to accept the Edwardian reformation.[44]

---

34 Ibid., no. xvi. 35 Ibid., no. xxvi. 36 Ibid., nos xviii, xix, xx. 37 SP 61/3/45; Jefferies, *Priests and prelates*, p. 159. 38 Shirley, *Original letters*, no. xix. 39 Ibid., no. xx. 40 Ibid. 41 *CPCR*, i, 233 (226); *Works of Ware*, i, p. 510; Edwards, *Church and state*, p. 143. Quinn resigned on 9 April 1551. 42 Comin's letter of resignation commended a suitable successor to the king and asked that a papal provision be sought. 43 *Cal. Carew MSS*, i, p. 485; Edwards, *Church and state*, p. 143. 44 William Casey, a local cleric, was recommended to the king by the

It has been assumed that the 'books' which St Leger sent to Limerick *ante* 19 January 1551 were hand-written copies of a Latin translation of the communion service of the first *Book of Common Prayer*, yet the letter referring to the 'books' is very ambiguous.[45] I would suggest that the 'books' were copies of the first *Book of Common Prayer* in English, whose introduction would have had the support of Edmund Sexton, a Limerick merchant with strong Protestant convictions.[46] In February 1551, St Leger was able to inform Protector Somerset that the Lord Chancellor of Ireland and the Master of the Rolls had recently been to Limerick and Galway and 'had established the king's majesty's orders for religion in such sort as there is great assurance the same shall be duly observed, so as I trust those parts be without suspicion of adhering to any foreign power [i.e. the papacy]'.[47]

St Leger's Latin translation of the communion service (presumably that in the first *Book of Common Prayer*) seems, to judge by his letter to Cecil of January 1551, to have been made on his own initiative. He informed Cecil that the translation was soon to be printed, yet he asked for the king's 'express commandment not only to me, to put his pleasure in use, but also to all his subjects to follow and observe the same'.[48] It is not clear whether St Leger was seeking a retrospective sanction for his Latin communion service. His instructions of July 1550 had clearly directed him to have Church services translated into Irish (not Latin) for use in parishes where English was not understood.

Interestingly, there is no evidence to show that St Leger's Latin communion service was, in fact, printed. The first book known to have been printed in Ireland was an English-language edition of the first *Book of Common Prayer*; its publication was authorised by St Leger, though he had been removed from the office of deputy before its actual printing. That authorisation reflected St Leger's compliance in carrying out his religious responsibilities to Edward VI's régime. The fact that Deputy Croft's instructions of 1551 repeated those to St Leger to propagate religious services in English, or Irish where English was not understood, suggests that the Latin communion service did not find favour at the royal court in Edward's reign.[49]

St Leger's commitment to religious change was queried by Archbishop Browne. Early in February 1551, St Leger gave five books to Browne that

---

earl of Desmond: *CPCR*, i, 244 (91). He was condemned for his Protestant convictions by Ignatius of Loyola, presumably on information provided by David Wolfe, SJ, who had been dean of Limerick: 'Wolfe', T.J. Morrisey, *ODNB*; Colm Lennon, *An Irish prisoner of conscience of the Tudor era: Archbishop Richard Creagh, 1523–86* (Dublin, 2000), pp 40–1. Patrick Walsh, dean of Waterford, was promoted as bishop on the recommendation of his chapter: *CPCR*, i, 244 (92, 93). **45** Bradshaw, 'Edwardian reformation', pp 90–1. It seems that Bradshaw inadvertently conflated two separate actions of St Leger; the translation of the communion service into Latin, and the sending of books to Limerick: Shirley, *Original letters*, no. xx. **46** Colm Lennon, 'The urban patriciates of early modern Ireland: a case-study of Limerick', *The 26th O'Donnell Lecture* (Dublin, 1999), p. 5. **47** Shirley, *Original letters*, no. xxi. **48** Ibid., no. xx. **49** Ibid., p. 39.

summarised the bases of the Catholic doctrine of transubstantiation. The archbishop had a copy of the books sent to Protector Warwick in England.[50] It is impossible to demonstrate whether that episode led to St Leger's recall from Ireland, but within weeks of Browne's letter reaching Warwick, a new deputy, Sir James Croft, was appointed to take his place.

In August 1551, Archbishop Browne made further allegations against the former deputy.[51] He pointed to St Leger's persistent failure to tackle Primate Dowdall's adamant refusal to introduce Edward VI's 'reforms' in Armagh diocese and he quoted the former deputy as commending the obstreperous primate to the earl of Tyrone as 'that good father, sage senator and godly bishop'. More grievously, Browne alleged that on one occasion when he challenged the deputy to deal with Dowdall's defiance, St Leger is said to have retorted, 'Go to/go to, your matters of religion will mar all'. That was an allegation the Edwardian régime insisted on investigating further. Browne failed, in the event, to persuade witnesses to confirm his allegations against St Leger. The allegation about St Leger's anti-Reformation retort was not made until after the deputy was recalled from office and played no part in the decision to recall him – but one must suspect that St Leger's lack of enthusiasm for religious change played some role in the decision to replace him with a Protestant viceroy. Certainly his toleration of Primate Dowdall's intransigence was problematical. Soon after St Leger's departure from Ireland, Dowdall fled the country, declaring in a letter to Lord Chancellor Cusack, his cousin, that 'he would never be bishop where the holy Mass (as he called it) was abolished'.[52]

It is very difficult to assess how much progress was achieved by the Edwardian reformation in Ireland during St Leger's abbreviated term of office. Evidently, Archbishop Browne had overcome his earlier scruples about the Edwardian assault on the Mass and, to judge from his letter of August 1551, he replaced the Catholic Mass and other ceremonials with the first *Book of Common Prayer* in the more anglicised parishes of Dublin diocese, and probably directed his suffragans to do the same in the more anglicised parishes (chiefly in urban areas) in the outlying dioceses of his province. Bishop Staples of Meath may have done the same.[53] St Leger himself pointed more than once to the progress of the Reformation in Limerick. In that city, as in Waterford, a new bishop was promoted who was local-born but favourably disposed to the first *Book of*

---

50 Ibid., no. xxiii. Ronan plausibly identified Browne's copy of St Leger's books with the 'Book out of Ireland' preserved among the Marian state papers: Ronan, *Reformation in Dublin*, p. 368.
51 Shirley, *Original letters*, no. xxiii. Among the charges made by Browne was that on St Leger's return to Ireland he offered to the chief altar in Christ Church, Dublin, 'after the old sort ... to the comfort of his too many like Papists, and the discomfort of the professors of God's word'.
52 Ibid.   53 There is no evidence to corroborate this suggestion – apart from the fact that Staples was not criticised by Archbishop Browne, as Dowdall was, for failing to abolish the Mass, Candlemas and other such ceremonies.

Common Prayer. The first *Book of Common Prayer* was also imposed in Galway with the co-operation of the local bishop, Christopher Bodkin, archbishop of Tuam. It is evident then that the first *Book of Common Prayer* displaced the Mass in churches in many of the most anglicised parishes in Ireland, except for those in the diocese of Armagh *inter Anglicos*. On the other hand, the great majority of the clergy across Ireland, and most clergy even in the Pale, could not read the *Book of Common Prayer* and must have continued to use the Latin ceremonials of Rome as before.

DEPUTY CROFT

Croft's instructions on the Reformation were little different to those of St Leger: he was to see that the first *Book of Common Prayer* was used in parishes where English was understood, and an Irish translation where it was not, but he was also directed to 'give good regard that the bishops and the clergy of that realm give good example in this behalf'.[54] Browne was very complimentary towards the new deputy, and Croft himself stated that he imposed the Protestant service book in 'every place' he travelled.[55]

However, despite the fact that since his arrival in Ireland, he 'daily' appealed to have men promoted to the vacant dioceses of Armagh, Cashel and Ossory, and wrote directly to the lord protector in November 1551, none was promoted before 1553.[56] For Armagh, Croft suggested that an Englishman with financial support from England be promoted who could act as a royal commissioner in that area. For Cashel and Ossory, neighbouring dioceses in 'the more quieter country' in the south-east, Croft could recommend no suitable man except Thomas Leverous, a man he commended for his 'learning, discretion and (in outward appearance) for good living', and for being able to preach well in English and Irish: Croft remarked that, 'I heard him preach such a sermon as in my simple opinion I heard not in many years'.[57] Leverous was not promoted in the reign of Edward VI, and it is not clear whether this was because his Catholic sympathies were unacceptable to the English crown or because of his own scruples. Another suggestion of Croft, that the English bishop of Kildare, Thomas Lancaster, be promoted to Ossory, was not given effect either. It seems that as the Edwardian reformation in England lurched from Lutheranism to Zwinglianism, Ireland was relegated to being an after-thought at the English royal court.

Meanwhile, the Edwardian reformation in Ireland stalled. Croft complained in a letter to Cecil in March 1552 that 'through the negligence of the bishops and other spiritual ministers it is so barely looked into as the old ceremonies yet

54 SP 61/3/32. 55 SP 61/3/45. 56 Shirley, *Original letters*, no. xxiv. 57 Ibid.

remain in many places'. He condemned the bishops in Ireland – and they included Browne and Staples, and the Edwardian appointees to Kildare, Leighlin, Waterford & Lismore and Limerick – as 'negligent and few learned, and none of any good zeal'. He asked again that some 'learned men' be sent from England to be bishops of the vacant Irish dioceses and 'to preach and set forth the king's proceedings' or, if that were not possible, for a learned man to be sent to advise him, by whose counsel he might 'the better direct the blind and obstinate bishops'.[58] No such adviser was sent to counsel Croft.

Croft's negative assessment of the zeal of the Edwardian bishops was amply confirmed by John Bale, the fiery Protestant bishop of Ossory (1553) whose *Vocacyon* preserves a unique insight into the progress of Edward VI's reformation in its final phase.[59] Bale landed in Waterford with his wife and a servant on 23 January 1553, having finally been persuaded to overcome his antipathy to becoming a bishop in Ireland.[60] He found that the communion service being celebrated in the city, though derived from the first *Book of Common Prayer*, 'was there altogether used like a Popish Mass with the old apish toys of Antichrist, with bowings and beckonings, kneelings and knockings'.[61] He complained that 'many abominable idolatries' were maintained by the priests in Waterford, and he was shocked to encounter keening at a local funeral (with 'prodigious howlings and patterings'), accompanied by the traditional Catholic rites associated with death. He declared that 'such horrible blasphemies' showed that Christ had no bishop in Waterford, nor the king a mayor in the city.[62] While it was not easy to match Bale's exacting expectations, one gets the impression that the bishop and mayor of Waterford contented themselves with a very superficial conformity to the rubrics of the first *Book of Common Prayer* and gave no thought to conversion or convictions.

To judge from Bale's *Vocacyon*, the situation in Dublin may not have been very different. The first *Book of Common Prayer* was in use in the city, but Bale noted that Archbishop Browne seemed not 'much exercised' in the use of the Edwardian communion service.[63] Certainly, Browne made no effort to convert anyone to Protestantism. In fact, according to Bale, he was accustomed to preach only two sermons a year:

> of the ploughman in winter by *exit qui seminat*, and of the shepherd in summer by *ego sum pastor bonus*; [which] are now so well known by rote of every gossip in Dublin that before he comes up into the pulpit they can tell his sermon.[64]

58 SP 61/4/28. 59 Bale, 'Vocacyon', passim. See also Katherine Walsh, 'Deliberate provocation or reforming zeal? John Bale as first Church of Ireland bishop of Ossory (1552/3–1563)' in Ciarán Brady (ed.), *Worsted in the game: losers in Irish history* (Mullingar, 1989), pp 49–55. 60 Bale, 'Vocacyon', p. 446. 61 Ibid. 62 Ibid., p. 447. 63 Ibid.

Since Browne did not preach at all for almost a year earlier in Edward VI's reign, this colourful tale is actually quite plausible. Certainly the impression created is that outward conformity rather than inner conversion was all that was required by the archbishop ... Bale dismissed Browne as 'a dissembling proselyte and a very pernicious Papist'.[65]

Bale's personal experiences in Kilkenny throw fascinating light upon the Edwardian reformation in Ireland. It was not until early 1553 that Bale arrived in Ireland, about the same time as Hugh Goodacre, the royal nominee for the diocese of Armagh.[66] He and Goodacre were to be consecrated as bishops in Christ Church Cathedral, Dublin, by the archbishop of Dublin and the bishops of Kildare and Down & Connor, though the archbishop (according to Bale) delayed the consecration in order to secure another instalment of the revenues of Ossory diocese. The ceremony itself did not take place until 25 March 1553. It proved to be contentious, as Bale insisted on being consecrated according to the rites laid down in the very Protestant second *Book of Common Prayer* despite the strong opposition of the dean of Christ Church, Thomas Lockwood ('Blockhead he might well be called', quipped Bale), who objected to the new ordinal on the grounds that its use was not authorised by the Irish parliament, and that it could prove to be 'an occasion of tumult'.[67] The consecrations passed off without tumult, but Goodacre died in Dublin shortly afterwards; according to Bale he was 'poisoned at the procurement of certain priests of his diocese'.[68] In Kilkenny, Bale was unable to persuade or compel the clergy to adopt the second *Book of Common Prayer* in place of the first.[69] They too pointed out that its use was not authorised by an Irish parliament, or by their metropolitan, the archbishop of Dublin, and in any case there were no copies of the second Prayer Book available in the town. Bale complained that, 'helpers I found none among my prebendaries and clergy, but adversaries a great many'.[70] Undoubtedly, Bale's abrasive style and extremist views antagonised the clergy in Kilkenny. He declared onto them

> among other [things], that the white gods of their making, such as they offered to the people to be worshipped, were no gods but idols; and that their prayers for the dead procured no redemption for the souls departed ... I added that their office, by Christ's straight commandment, was chiefly to preach and instruct the people in the doctrine and ways of God, and not to occupy so much time in chanting, [organ] piping and singing.[71]

---

64 Ibid., p. 455.   65 Ibid.   66 Ibid., p. 446.   67 Ibid., p. 447.   68 Ibid., p. 449.   69 Ibid.
70 Ibid., p. 448.   71 Ibid.

This kind of talk caused 'much-ado' among the priests, and there were 'angers, slanders, conspiracies and, in the end, slaughter of men'. The latter reference relates to the killing of five of the bishop's servants, and an attempt on his own life, for which he held the clergy of Kilkenny, and in particular the treasurer of St Canice's Cathedral, Richard Roth, responsible to no small degree.[72] When, about 25 July 1553, news of the death of Edward VI reached them, the priests of the town 'went by heaps from tavern to tavern' in Kilkenny to celebrate the end of his reformation.[73]

Yet the more remarkable feature of Bale's ministry in Kilkenny is the following he built up among people in the town.[74] On the occasion of the attempt on his life, he was rescued by Robert Shea, the sovereign of Kilkenny (a man described by Bale as 'sober, wise and godly'[75]), leading a contingent of one hundred horsemen and 300 footmen from the town; 'the young men singing psalms and other godly songs all the way in rejoice of my deliverance'. More strikingly, he recorded that 'as we came to the town, the people, in great number, stood on both sides of the way, within the gates and without, with lighted candles in their hands, shouting out praise to God for delivering me from the hands of those murderers'.[76] In another telling episode, Bale recounts how, on the day that Mary Tudor's accession as queen was proclaimed in Kilkenny, some young men of the town under his direction staged two plays at the market cross, with music and songs, a tragedy called 'God's promises' in the forenoon and a comedy called 'John the Baptist's preachings' in the afternoon, 'to the small contention of the priests and other Papists there'.[77] Anyone who presumes that the Edwardian reformation was doomed to inevitable failure in Ireland need only read Bishop Bale's *Vocacyon* to realise the contrary.

Nonetheless, with Mary's accession, time ran out for Bishop Bale in Kilkenny. Once the queen's proclamation was read in the town to the effect that 'they who would hear Mass should be suffered to do so, and they that would not should not thereunto be compelled', the Edwardian reformation was swept away. The local clergy 'suddenly set up all the altars and images in the cathedral church'.[78] Bale remained in the town a little longer, but on hearing mutterings that another attempt was to be made on his life, and there being no English deputy in place in Ireland, he left Kilkenny forever.

CONCLUSIONS

Ireland's experience of Edward VI's reformation reveals that popular attachment to Catholic beliefs and practices remained very strong. Yet it suggests too that the

---

72 Ibid., pp 452–3. 73 Ibid., p. 449. 74 Steven Ellis, 'John Bale, bishop of Ossory, 1552–3', *Journal of the Butler Society*, 2:3 (1984), p. 288. 75 Bale, 'Vocacyon', p. 451. 76 Ibid., p. 453. 77 Ibid., p. 450. 78 Ibid., p. 454.

ultimate failure of the Tudor reformations in Ireland was not inevitable. John Bale, in his *Vocacyon*, noted that in Dublin 'much of the people did greatly rejoice at our coming thither, thinking by our preaching the pope's superstitions would diminish and the true Christian religion increase'.[79] Yet some months later he was obliged to don 'mariner's apparel' to escape the wrath of Catholics in the city.[80] People in Dublin were evidently divided in their dispositions towards Edward VI's reformation, as indeed, one might expect, though who exactly welcomed Bale in Dublin, and how numerous they were, is impossible to determine. It may well be that he was welcomed mainly by office-holders motivated by political considerations and by English immigrants (Bale himself remarked that those who were 'bred and born' in Ireland tended to oppose Protestantism, though not all of them), but I think it likely that, given its frequent intercourse with England, some Protestant ideas were adopted by at least some citizens of Dublin by the mid-sixteenth century. Colm Lennon, though, reckons that as late as 1553, Protestantism had gained little currency in the city beyond 'a small official group and its supporters'.[81]

Beyond the capital, one may point to a couple of persons, including Edmund Sexton of Limerick and Robert Shea of Kilkenny, who gave support to the Edwardian reformation but, certainly in Sexton's case and probably in most others, those who became Protestant were isolated individuals who were unrepresentative of the communities they lived in.[82] At the same time, Bishop Bale's success in inspiring support for Protestantism in Kilkenny, especially among the young men of the town, shows what could be achieved by zealous Protestant preaching in an Anglophone community, even in the face of fierce hostility from the local clergy. Bale's success, however short-lived, suggests that the failure of the Tudor reformation in Ireland was by no means inevitable.[83]

Generally, it is striking how successful the English crown was in imposing the first *Book of Common Prayer* on Anglophone parishes across Ireland. Archbishop Browne's reforming activities appear to have encountered very little open resistance from the clergy of Dublin, especially after Deputy Bellingham chastised the former treasurer of St Patrick's Cathedral for trying to foment opposition to the archbishop's 'book of reformation'.[84] Even in Kilkenny, despite their passionate hostility to Protestantism, the local clergy conformed to Bishop Bale's directives.[85] Brendan Bradshaw observed that

> For the moment, anything short of outright rejection of the religious changes ... could be regarded as a potential victory. It held out the

79 Ibid., p. 447. 80 Ibid., pp 439–40. 81 Lennon, *Lords of Dublin*, pp 128, 130. 82 Lennon, 'The urban patriciates', pp 5, 16; Clodagh Tait, *Death, burial and commemoration in Ireland, 1550–1650* (Basingstoke, Hampshire and New York, 2002), pp 93–4. 83 Having written that, I must acknowledge Brendan Scott's admonition to me to beware of investing too much confidence in Bale's estimation of his own success in Kilkenny in his *Vocacyon*. 84 Shirley, *Original letters*, no. x. 85 Shirley, *Original letters*, no. xii.

possibility that the state, by bending all its resources of persuasion and education to the task could in time create a favourable climate of opinion towards religious change.[86]

Yet, though outward conformity seems to have been general in Anglophone areas, it is not apparent that the Edwardian reformation in Ireland made significant progress in terms of winning hearts and souls.

Apart from Bishop Bale's short-lived ministry in Kilkenny, in Edward's reign we are confronted with the spectacle of a Reformation without reformers. In the key dioceses of the Pale, there appears to have been no Protestant preachers, except for Walter Palatyne, whose collaboration with Browne on the 'book of reformation' in November 1548 was his last known contribution to the Edwardian reformation. Browne himself failed to preach in favour of religious change. Bishop Staples received such a hostile reaction to his first Protestant sermon that it seems unlikely that he made many others.[87] Hugh Goodacre, the Edwardian archbishop of Armagh, may never have seen his diocese.[88] Thomas Lancaster, the Edwardian bishop of Kildare, would have made little impact in terms of preaching Protestantism in his Gaelic-speaking diocese.[89] Therefore, while priests in many Anglophone parishes were compelled to use the first *Book of Common Prayer* (often in a very traditional guise), their congregations were not exposed to Protestant preaching and were not persuaded to become Protestants.

Outward conformity remained the norm in the Anglophone areas in Edward's reign – though one can only speculate about the actual degree of conformity – despite the increasingly Protestant character of those policies, and it was still possible to find men willing to take up benefices in the outlying parishes of the former English lordship in the gift of Edward VI.[90] Nonetheless, without Protestant preachers to propagate a positive message, the outward conformity to Edward VI's religion would avail nothing positive, and probably alienated many people with Catholic convictions. There could be no certainty, though, about the ultimate outcomes of the Tudor reformations at that point.

86 Bradshaw, 'Edwardian reformation', p. 96. 87 Shirley, *Original letters*, no. xvii. Indeed, the manner in which Staples advertised the fact that he was about to preach in his own diocese of Meath in November 1548 would indicate that his delivery of a sermon was something of a rare event. 88 Jefferies, *Priests and prelates*, p. 160. 89 See the experiences of Alexander Craik, the Elizabethan bishop of Kildare, who complained several times that he could not make himself understood in Kildare diocese: M.V. Ronan, *The Reformation in Ireland under Elizabeth* (London, 1930), p. 54. 90 Bradshaw, 'Edwardian reformation', p. 87.

6

Mary's restoration

Mary's accession to the throne was greeted in Dublin with 'general shouts and acclamations', and in Kilkenny there were processions and banquets in celebration.[1] It seems safe to assume that the news would have been greeted with similar enthusiasm in the English-speaking towns across Ireland. Mary's accession was everywhere expected to result in the official restoration of Catholicism wherever it had been suppressed under Edward VI. In a great many parishes, the Catholic liturgy was restored spontaneously, and where it was not, for fear of the authorities, then Mary's proclamation of early September 1553, declaring toleration of the Mass, cleared the way for a complete restoration of Catholic worship across England and Wales, and wherever it had been displaced by Edwardian services in Ireland.[2] Bishop Bale of Ossory has left us with a very vivid account of the joy with which the clergy of Kilkenny availed of the proclamation to reinstall all of the traditional ecclesiastical paraphernalia in St Canice's Cathedral and restore the Catholic liturgy.[3] It is highly probable that, in the absence of so determined a Protestant prelate as Bale, Catholic restoration had already taken place elsewhere in Ireland.

Since the Edwardian reformation had been imposed in Ireland by virtue of the royal supremacy only, Mary used the same authority to undo it – though she did so without the official approval of the Catholic Church. On appointing Sir Anthony St Leger as her lord deputy in Ireland, she directed him, together with the council of Ireland, to restore the old religion as far as possible.[4]

With advice from the deputy, lord chancellor and the council of Ireland, Mary began to reconstitute the Irish episcopate.[5] Ossory received attention early on, possibly because of Bishop Bale's influence there. The diocese was declared to be vacant on Bale's flight into exile and, on 14 October, John Thonery, BD, a native of Kilkenny, was promoted in his place.[6] Thonery had himself consecrated in the dissolved priory of Inistioge – a gesture clearly intended to symbolise his commitment to the old order.[7] Also on 14 October 1553, Mary nominated Roland Baron Fitzgerald as archbishop of the vacant see of Cashel.[8]

1 Ware, 'Annals', s.a. 1553 in Works of Ware, i; Bale, 'Vocacyon', p. 450.   2 Proclamations, ii, 390.
3 Bale, 'Vocacyon', p. 454.   4 James Morrin (ed.), Calender of the patent and close rolls of Ireland, Henry VIII–Elizabeth, i (Dublin, 1861), Patent roll 1 Mary, no. 2.   5 CPCR, i, Patent Roll 1 Mary, no. 77.   6 Ibid., no. 79.   7 Ware, 'Annals', s.a. 1553.   8 CPCR, i, Patent Roll 1 Mary, no. 77.

In her letter of nomination, the queen referred to Fitzgerald's 'good learning and integrity of life', but he had not been her first choice: Richard Creagh of Limerick had earlier been approached but had declined the honour.[9] Creagh was subsequently compelled by the pope to become the Catholic archbishop of Armagh.[10] Interestingly, Mary directed that Thonery and Fitzgerald be consecrated and installed 'according to the order of our realm of Ireland heretofore accustomed' – a vague phrase which I presume to mean according to Catholic rites, though that would not have been possible in England at that time.[11]

Mary also restored to office George Dowdall of Armagh who had been deprived after he fled to mainland Europe in the summer of 1551, declaring that 'he would never be bishop where the holy Mass (as he called it) was abolished'.[12] He had taken refuge in the monastery at Centre in the Netherlands.[13] He received a papal provision to the see of Armagh in March 1553.[14] It may have been on Cardinal Pole's recommendation that Queen Mary restored Dowdall to the see of Armagh in October 1553, and persuaded her to grant him the revenues of his former hospital at Ardee.[15] The title of 'primate of all-Ireland', which had been granted to Archbishop Browne of Dublin by Edward VI in 1551, was restored to the archbishop of Armagh on 12 March 1554.[16]

DOWDALL'S PROVINCIAL SYNOD OF 1553

Archbishop Dowdall's first recorded action following his return from exile was the convening of a provincial synod in St Peter's Church, Drogheda, to restore and revitalise the Catholic religion throughout the ecclesiastical province of Armagh.[17] The synodal articles are listed in no clear order. They addressed issues of immediate concern in the province of Armagh, *inter Anglicos* and *inter Hibernicos*, and they should be viewed within the context of Armagh's synodal tradition.

The provincial synod ordered the clergy and laity to restore all of the ancient rites, religious practices, feasts, customs, sacraments and sacrifices to which they had been accustomed (Art. 7). Provision was made for the reconciliation of those clergymen who had, under compulsion, celebrated the Mass or administered the sacraments according to heretical rites, or given it approval in their sermons (Art. 6). Clergymen with concubines and those who had presumed to marry

9 Ware, 'Annals', *s.a.* 1553. 10 Lennon, *Archbishop Creagh*. 11 *CPCR*, i, Patent roll Mary 1, no. 77. 12 *CPCR*, i, 1 Mary, no. 4; Jefferies, *Priests and prelates*, pp 138–67; idem, 'Primate George Dowdall and the Marian restoration', *Seanchas Ard Mhacha*, 17 (1998), pp 1–6. 13 Ware, 'Annals', *s.a.* 1558. 14 Brady, *Episcopal succession*, i, p. 218. It was Pole's personal friend, Cardinal Morone, who promoted Dowdall's cause before the Roman curia. 15 *CPCR*, i, 1 Mary, no. 4. 16 *CPCR*, i, Patent Roll 1 Mary, nos 4, 65. 17 Dowdall's register, pp 99–106 (85).

during the period of schism were to be deprived of their office and would be prohibited from exercising a cure of souls or administering the sacraments without a dispensation (Art. 1). The appointment of metropolitan and diocesan inquisitors was authorised to identify and to prosecute persons expressing heretical opinions. Parish priests were ordered to identify any such persons known to them or face suspension from office (Art. 8). Heretical books were to be burned (Art. 18).

Several decrees were of a traditional character; insisting on traditional standards of clerical dress (Art. 10), reiterating the long-standing obligations of the laity concerning the repair of their parish churches (Art. 11), a decree against simony (Art. 4), and another against persons securing papal provisions through deceit (Art. 5). It was decreed that parish priests who did not know how to preach were to commission a preacher to deliver their quarterly sermons (Art. 17), which was not a new requirement, but it was probably given a greater emphasis at a time of theological debate.

The decree enjoining moderation in the exaction of burial fees from widows and orphans (Art. 12) was not new but, when combined with the novel decree against exacting fees for the administration of the sacraments, especially extreme unction (Art. 9), it seems clear that Archbishop Dowdall was making a great effort to defuse one of the most obvious sources of tension between the Catholic laity and their priests. Archbishop Dowdall had yet to turn his attention to the question of clerical training: but he had decided to end the system whereby the fruits of benefices might be enjoyed by men who were not ordained, even if they gave an undertaking to seek ordination within the customary year allowed (Art. 2).

Within the archdiocese of Armagh, the work of restoration was quickly carried out. By the time that Primate Dowdall presided over his first diocesan synod of the clergy of Armagh *inter Anglicos* since his restoration, on 3 July 1554, the traditional pattern of things had been well restored.[18] Dowdall celebrated Mass dressed in full pontificals and there was the customary procession to Drogheda's town cross and back. There was a sermon to inspire the assembled priests, as usual. Dowdall exhorted the priests in the synod to strive to reform themselves and their parishioners. Similar exhortations were made at other synods in the remaining years of Primate Dowdall's episcopate.[19] Though the calls for reform may have been made more earnestly than ever, the statutes endorsed by Armagh's diocesan synods were wholly traditional.

Armagh's 1554 diocesan synod decreed that priests who exercised a cure of souls without having been admitted by the ordinary were to be suspended, priests who failed to pay their procurations were to be suspended and, finally, any parish whose church's chancel was ill-maintained was to have its revenues

---

18 Dowdall's register, pp 97–8 (82).   19 Ibid., pp 98–9 (83), pp 99–101 (84).

sequestrated and its priest suspended. The same statutes were reiterated in the synod of 1556.[20] The synod of 1556 also re-enacted existing legislation about the obligation on parish priests to register wills with the church court officers within a month of a parishioner's decease, or face suspension. It seems clear that, after the initial urgency on his return, Primate Dowdall could feel satisfied that the work of restoration was well advanced and the problems needing attention were generally those which had been features of the late medieval period. The difficulties with defective chancels, admissions to parish cures and the payment of procurations did not constitute moral or religious problems, but financial. Protestantism, clerical negligence or immorality in Armagh *inter Anglicos* presented no problem in the primate's eyes. This impression of good order and stability seems to be confirmed by the business of Dowdall's provincial synod of 1556, which did no more than to confirm a number of feast days as holy days of obligation, though agricultural labourers were not forbidden to work on those days.[21]

A 'DOWDALL PROGRAMME' FOR DUBLIN?

James Murray proposed that Archbishop Dowdall framed the legislation of Armagh's provincial synod 'with the English Pale in view rather than his own predominantly Gaelic province', as they were 'more relevant to the Church in English Ireland, including the diocese of Dublin and its suffragan sees'.[22] However, canon law did not countenance a synod of one ecclesiastical province legislating for another and there is no evidence in Dowdall's register, or in any other document(s) associated with him, that lends credence to the assertion that he devised or implemented a 'programme' for Dublin.

According to Murray, the implementation of Dowdall's programme for Dublin began early in 1554 with the operation of a royal commission to remove married clergymen from their benefices.[23] He stated that it was 'instituted ... to advance Dowdall's strategy' – but, in fact, it was simply an extension to Ireland of similar commissions established in England and Wales on the queen's initiative. With Archbishop Browne deprived because of being married, Dowdall was supposed to have proceeded to the 'second vital step in the implementation of his counter-reformation ... the appointment of a suitable successor to Browne'.[24] Murray asserted that Queen Mary appointed Hugh Curwen as the archbishop of Dublin because he possessed the credentials for the job 'as specified by Dowdall and the ex-prebendaries [of St Patrick's cathedral]'.[25] Yet there

20 Ibid., pp 99–101 (84). 21 Ibid., p. 107 (86). 22 Murray, 'Tudor diocese of Dublin', p. 174. Also, idem, *Enforcing the English Reformation in Ireland*, p. 220. 23 Murray, 'Tudor diocese of Dublin', p. 176. 24 Ibid., p. 179. 25 Ibid., pp 181–2. Also, idem, *Enforcing the English Reformation*, p. 226.

is not a single shred of evidence to show that Dowdall influenced in any way the queen's appointment of Curwen to Dublin. Curwen, in fact, was one of the queen's chaplains, and it can be safely assumed that his expertise in law commended him to her for the post of chancellor of Ireland. There is no evidence to sustain Murray's assertion that he was appointed 'with the express purpose of implementing Dowdall's strategy'.[26] Murray claimed that it is 'certainly known' that the delegation of former prebendaries of St Patrick's Cathedral who attended upon the queen in 1554, 'operated under the aegis and direction of Archbishop Dowdall' – but in truth it is not even known who they were or what they said.[27] Murray variously characterised them as 'Dowdall's negotiators', his 'cohorts' (twice), and his 'negotiating team' whom he 'fully briefed' – but there is absolutely no evidence at all to show that those men operated under Dowdall's direction.[28] According to Murray, Dowdall placed 'the restoration of St Patrick's at the very heart of his strategy for restoring the old religion in English Ireland',[29] but yet again there is no evidence whatsoever to sustain the contention that Dowdall was involved in any way whatsoever with Mary's restoration of St Patrick's Cathedral. Again, the assertion that Dowdall played a key role in originating the idea of seeking papal confirmation for the kingly title is not supported by any evidence whatsoever.[30] In fact, Nicholas Ormanetto, a former associate of Cardinal Pole, stated that the initiative originated solely with the queen.[31] Again and again, speculation about Archbishop Dowdall is presented as fact without the evidence to sustain it.

My judgment is that Archbishop Dowdall of Armagh never had a 'programme' for Dublin. Not only is there an inherent improbability about an archbishop imposing a programme on the metropolitan see of another province, but without credible evidence, the supposed 'Dowdall programme for Dublin' must be rejected as baseless conjecture. I do not accept the characterisation of Dowdall as being 'as much an architect of Catholic restoration in the English Pale as the queen and cardinal had been in England'.[32] In fact, the queen and the cardinal were the key architects of the Marian restoration in Ireland, as in England.

CARDINAL POLE

Mary's accession was welcomed as a miracle in Rome, and Pope Julius III moved quickly to appoint Cardinal Reginald Pole as his papal legate with comprehen-

---

26 Murray, *Enforcing the English Reformation*, p. 244.   27 Murray, 'Tudor diocese of Dublin', p. 180.   28 Ibid., pp 179, 180, 184, 185, 186, 181. Also, idem, *Enforcing the English Reformation*, p. 229.   29 Murray, 'Tudor diocese of Dublin', p. 188. Also, idem, *Enforcing the English Reformation*, p. 232.   30 Murray, 'Tudor diocese of Dublin', p. 185. Also, idem, *Enforcing the English Reformation*, p. 215.   31 *CSP Rome*, ii, pp 240–1; Murray, 'Tudor diocese of Dublin', p. 168.   32 Murray, *Enforcing the English Reformation*, p. 253.

sive powers to reconcile England to the Catholic Church.[33] Born in 1500, of royal blood, Pole looked destined for high office in the English Church until his opposition to Henry VIII's first divorce obliged him to go into exile in 1532.[34] His personal sanctity and his prominence as an aristocratic English Catholic cleric won him favour in Rome and he was made a cardinal in 1536.[35] In 1545, Pope Paul III appointed him as one of the three cardinals who presided over the Council of Trent.[36] When Mary Tudor succeeded her Protestant half-brother to the throne, Pole seemed the obvious choice to take responsibility for the Catholic mission to England.

However, Pole's mission was delayed by two key factors: the strong opposition from many to the operation of a papal legate in England, and his own insistence on the complete restoration of obedience to the papacy (and he saw the restoration of the medieval monastic establishment as integral to the restoration of obedience) before he would countenance the deployment of his legatine faculties.[37] Pole was out of touch with the profound changes that had been wrought in England in his absence.[38] He wrote to the queen on 2 October 1553, stating that she should expect trouble only from a tiny minority.[39] She knew differently, however, and had to warn him that his life might be endangered as a legate in England.[40] Nothing less than the Church's recognition of the possessors' titles to former churchlands would suffice to ameliorate her parliament's opposition to the restoration of the pope's spiritual jurisdiction, but for eighteen months, Pole remained inflexibly adamant in insisting on the restoration of monastic properties to the Church.[41]

Meanwhile, Mary did what she could to restore Catholicism in England and Ireland, and did so with a sense of urgency that Pole lacked.[42] The cardinal told the queen that her restoration of the Mass before the restoration of papal obedience constituted a damnable schismatic offence.[43] It was a characteristic declaration of Pole's – legalistic but unrealistic. Mary could hardly have presided over the continued use of the *Book of Common Prayer* in the parishes – The queen was anxious to remove Protestant bishops and other clergymen from office and to have Catholic bishops and priests appointed in their places.[44] She secured an Act of parliament to depose married clergymen. Royal commissions were established in England and Wales to give effect to the act. She was keen to promote Catholic prelates as the 'best remedy' for England's religious travails,[45] and she wrote to Pole to learn how she might promote Catholic clergy before

33 Loades, *Mary Tudor*, p. 124. 34 'Reginald Pole', T.F. Meyer, *ODNB*; T.F. Mayer, *Reginald Pole: prince and prophet* (Cambridge, 2000). 35 Loades, *Mary Tudor*, p. 122. 36 Ibid., p. 122; Thomas Mayer, *Prince and prophet*, pp 203, 205; idem, *The correspondence of Reginald Pole, 1500–1558* (Aldershot, 2002, *et seq.*), nos 684, 691. 37 *CRP*, no. 746; Mayer, *Prince and prophet*, pp 205–8. 38 Peter Marshall, *Reformation England, 1480–1642* (London, 2003), pp 94–5. 39 *CRP*, no. 719. 40 Ibid., no. 757. 41 Loades, *Mary Tudor*, pp 126, 128, 262–5. 42 Ibid., p. 126. 43 Mayer, *Prince and prophet*, p. 210; *CRP*, no. 765. 44 *CRP*, no. 831. 45 Ibid., no. 831.

'Catholic and apostolic obedience' had been restored without infringing the pope's authority.[46] He, however, failed to respond and she had to push hard to make him consider what she ought to do, both about the schismatic bishops who wished to be reconciled to the Catholic Church and about the dozen or so men she nominated for episcopal office.[47] Pope Julius III himself wrote to Pole to tell him to stop being exaggeratedly scrupulous.[48] In the end, it was the sheer necessity of having Catholic bishops in the House of Lords for Mary's second parliament that made Pole relent and agree to grant temporary legatine provisions to the queen's nominees little more than a fortnight before the parliament was due to meet on 2 April 1554.[49]

In April 1554, the queen authorised a royal commission, similar to those she had already established in England and Wales, headed by Archbishop Dowdall and Dr William Walsh, to remove bishops and other clergymen in Ireland who had presumed to marry during her half-brother's reign.[50] It was a crude but effective means of weeding out priests and bishops who, she stated, had 'sown heresies and schisms away from the true Catholic faith'.[51] The bishops of Dublin, Meath, Kildare, Leighlin and Limerick, together with a couple of lesser clergymen, were deprived of their offices for being married.[52] Nonetheless, as in England, clerics who were prepared to put their wives away and do penance for their sin were generally allowed to seek benefices elsewhere. Thus, Browne of Dublin ended his days as a canon of St Patrick's Cathedral, Dublin.[53] Edward Staples, despite an understanding reached with Cardinal Pole, received no new office and suffered impoverishment as a result. He subsequently complained about the verbal abuse directed against him by Catholic clergymen, presumably for his role in the early Tudor reformations.[54] It is not possible to determine what number of clergymen had been married in *facie ecclesia* in Ireland by 1553, but it seems to have been extremely small.

With the married bishops deprived, the way was clear to reconstitute the episcopal bench in the Pale, as in England. William Walsh was nominated to the see of Meath on 18 October 1554.[55] He hesitated to accept it without a papal provision, but Pole granted him a legatine provision on condition that he secured a papal provision within a year.[56] Walsh was a Cistercian monk from County Meath who, following the dissolution of the monasteries, had gone to Italy and became one of Pole's chaplains.[57] He must have played an important role in

---

46 Ibid., no. 794.   **47** Ibid., nos 808, 831; Mayer, *Prince and prophet*, p. 212.   **48** Ibid., no. 822.
49 Mayer, *Prince and prophet*, p. 214.   **50** Ware, 'Annals', s.a 1554; *CPCR*, i, 1 & 2 Mary & Philip, no. 59; TCD MS F.I.18, fo. 2; Jefferies, 'Primate George Dowdall', p. 10.   **51** *CPCR*, i, Patent roll 1 & 2 Mary & Philip, no. 3.   **52** Ware, 'Annals', *s.a.* 1554; *CPCR*, i, Patent roll 1 & 2 Mary & Philip, nos 3, 4, 5, 13, 14.   **53** Bradshaw, 'George Browne', p. 323.   **54** Shirley, *Original letters*, no. xxxi.   **55** *CRP*, no. 962.   **56** *CPCR*, 1 & 2 Philip and Mary, i, no. 59; Brady, *Episcopal succession*, i, p. 235. David Edwards reckoned that Walsh secured a papal provision, despite the doubts expressed on the matter: 'William Walsh', David Edwards, *ODNB*.   **57** 'William Walsh', David Edwards, *ODNB*.

shaping the cardinal's thoughts about the Irish Church. On the other hand, I get the definite impression from Cardinal Pole's correspondence that he gave very little thought to Ireland throughout his career.[58]

In any event, by the close of 1554, Cardinal Pole was finally resigned to the loss of the former churchlands – except for those still in the crown's possession – and, on that understanding, he was finally allowed to enter England. On 30 November 1554, he stood before England's assembled parliamentarians and granted them, and the people whom they represented, absolution and reconciled them to the Roman Catholic Church.[59]

LEGATINE ACTS

With England formally reconciled, Pole embarked on a period of intense labour to reconstruct the Church in Mary's dominions.[60] Bishops and priests who had gained office irregularly during the schism were told to supplicate for dispensations, and absolutions were offered to all who repented. From January 1555 to the end of June 1557, there were more than 1,500 acts recorded in Pole's legatine register.[61] One-hundred-and-seventy-five acts, or about 15 per cent of the total, related to Ireland.[62] Seventy-eight of that number, or 45 per cent of the Irish acts, concerned dispensations for marriage (often regularising dispensations gotten from the 'schismatic' court of faculties in Canterbury), compared with 30 per cent for England. The concern with marriage reflects its importance for the inheritance of property in areas under English jurisdiction, and the greater prevalence of marriage within the prohibited degrees of consanguinity in Ireland compared with England. Thomas Mayer, the editor of Pole's correspondence, observed that 'as in England, the total number of clerical acts [for Ireland] is tiny, numbering about 86'.[63] Of those, he calculated that only twenty-three related to the recent schism. Those statistics represented a remarkably small proportion of Ireland's clergy at the time.

Pole's register includes an absolution granted in May 1555 to Roland Fitzgerald, Mary's appointee as archbishop of Cashel, for an invalid dispensation from Archbishop Cranmer for being illegitimate, and for being consecrated by schismatic bishops.[64] In May 1555, Patrick Walsh, Edwardian bishop of Waterford & Lismore, was absolved for becoming a bishop by schismatic

---

58 See *CRP*, vols 1–3, passim. Pole seems to have given little thought to the north of England either. He commented to Bishop Gardiner that 'almost all' of the people in England lived in the ecclesiastical province of Canterbury [*CRP*, no. 1054], and he may have forgotten to summon the northern convocation of the English Church to the legatine synod of London [Mayer, *Prince and prophet*, p. 236]. At the same time, he was aware that the people in the north of England and Cornwall were the most obedient Catholics in England, and the least heretical: *CRP*, no. 815.
59 Loades, *Mary Tudor*, p. 80.   60 Mayer, *Prince and prophet*, p. 225.   61 Ibid., pp 254–68.
62 Ibid., p. 268.   63 Ibid., p. 271.   64 *CRP*, no. 1208.

authority, and he was dispensed to hold a canonry in Ossory diocese *in commendam*.[65] In June 1555, Alexander Devereux, Edwardian bishop of Ferns, was absolved for becoming a secular cleric after his monastery was dissolved by Henry VIII, for accepting promotion to the see of Ferns by schismatic authority, and for being consecrated with a non-Catholic rite.[66] On 3 October, Christopher Bodkin was absolved for accepting the schism after his provision as bishop of Kilmacduagh, despite his 'constancy' in the Catholic faith.[67] Following an investigation conducted in Lambeth Palace in September 1555, Pole resolved the conflicting claims of Bodkin, citing schismatic authority, and Art O'Friel, citing a papal provision, to the see of Tuam.[68] Pole regularised the situation with a compromise: the *status quo* was acquiesced in for the moment, with Bodkin remaining in place *de facto* with the right of succession to Archbishop O'Friel *de jure*.

Most of the other clerical acts pertaining to Ireland were comprised of absolutions for having taken orders and/or receiving benefices by schismatic authority. A review of the acts reveals that Cardinal Pole's legatine mission in Ireland was largely reactive, in the sense that he responded to individual supplications and did not initiate a proactive programme of renewal. It also shows the tiny scale of the legatine reconciliations among the lower clergy. Pole did delegate faculties to Archbishop Dowdall and the dean and chapter of Armagh to reconcile on 19 March 1555, and there are no (surviving) acts of reconciliation in Pole's register for the diocese of Armagh, but it is not clear whether he delegated his powers more widely because Archbishop Bodkin of Tuam is the only other Irish prelate who certainly received such faculties from the cardinal.[69]

As well as the Act granting absolution for schism to George Browne, the former archbishop of Dublin, on 12 March 1555, the only clerical acts for Dublin diocese that survive in Pole's register include a dispensation for illegitimacy granted to a man wishing to take holy orders, a dispensation to an acolyte from Dublin who was studying at Oxford University and who wished to take orders, and separate absolutions granted to three former Augustinian canons for becoming diocesan clergy after Christ Church in Dublin had been transformed into a secular cathedral, and for accepting benefices by the crown's schismatic authority.[70] Mayer was struck by the fact that the last two absolutions sought by the former Augustinian canons came two years after the first, and he noticed a general pattern wherein former members of religious orders across England and Ireland were tardy in seeking absolutions from the papal legate.[71] Indeed, Mayer

65 Ibid., nos 1229, 1230. 66 Ibid., no. 1236. 67 Ibid., no. 1390. 68 P.F. Moran, *History of the Catholic archbishops of Dublin since the Reformation*, i (Dublin, 1864), pp 53–4. 69 *CRP*, nos 1136, 1398. From the same time there are copies in Dowdall's register of dispensations granted by Pole to two couples in Armagh diocese who had secured faculties from Canterbury during the time of schism to allow them to marry despite the impediment of consanguinity: Dowdall's register, pp 83–8 (74, 75). 70 *CRP*, nos 1431c, 1915d, 1304, 1959, 1960. 71 Mayer, *Prince and*

expressed surprise that so very few of the former religious sought them at all.[72] I suspect that the former religious may have hesitated to seek absolutions because they often stipulated that they must resume life in a religious community once the opportunity to do so materialised. Perhaps too they waited for their former monastery to be restored before jeopardising their current pensions or incomes. In any event, the tiny number of acts relating to Dublin diocese, and the dearth of supplications from diocesan clergy after almost two decades of schism, suggests a certain lack of engagement with Pole's mission. On the other hand, only one of the Dublin acts, drawn up for John Haklott, a layman, absolved for heresy.[73]

In the neighbouring diocese of Meath, there was a similar story. A former Augustinian canon from Dublin sought absolution for being promoted to a rectory in Meath without a papal dispensation.[74] One man sought a dispensation for having taken holy orders despite being the illegitimate son of an Augustinian canon.[75] Three other men secured absolutions for accepting benefices in Meath diocese by schismatic authority, despite being illegitimate – including Robert Luttrell, the archdeacon of Meath who would distinguish himself in 1560 by rejecting the Elizabethan religious settlement.[76] Another sought absolution for holding incompatible benefices in Meath and in Dublin dioceses by schismatic authority.[77] Altogether, this is a tiny tally from the 200 or so parishes in Meath diocese after almost twenty years of schism.

The archdeacon of Kildare secured a dispensation for becoming a diocesan clergymen after the dissolution of the monastery at Connall, of which he was the last prior, and for accepting his new office without papal authority.[78] The chancellor of Kildare's cathedral, a former Dominican, did likewise, as did another former Dominican who held a rectory.[79] All three of these men waited until 1557 before supplicating for absolution. Otherwise, there was one supplication for absolution for schism and for receiving orders by 'another rite' – one of only a couple of references to the use of an Edwardian ordinal in Ireland.[80] There was one supplication for absolution for holding two incompatible benefices by schismatic authority.[81] Otherwise, the clerical acts from Kildare only include dispensations for two scholars to take holy orders in the future, despite being illegitimate, and another for a man seeking holy orders, despite some unspecified irregularity – acts which had nothing to do with the time of schism.[82]

Five clergymen in Ossory diocese secured absolution for proceeding to holy orders without a Catholic dispensation for illegitimacy, of whom four were absolved for holding a benefice by schismatic authority also.[83] Two others were

prophet, p. 271. See his note to *CRP*, no. 1959. 72 Mayer, *Prince and prophet*, p. 261. 73 *CRP*, no. 1445. 74 Ibid., no. 1950. 75 Ibid., no. 1334a. 76 Ibid., nos 1255, 1271 (repeated in 1328), no. 1284. 77 Ibid., no. 1217. 78 Ibid., no. 1952. 79 Ibid., nos 1842, 1848. 80 Ibid., no. 1311. 81 Ibid., no. 1951. 82 Ibid., nos 1954b, 1954c, 1933a. 83 Ibid., nos 1176a, 1625a,

absolved simply for taking benefices by schismatic authority, one of them a pluralist.[84] In Emly diocese, three clergymen were absolved for illegitimacy, one of whom was absolved for holding a benefice by schismatic authority also.[85] Two others had taken a second benefice by schismatic authority,[86] and another sought a dispensation to secure another benefice.[87] Two clergymen sought absolution for schism,[88] but one sought absolution for having married during the schism, a most exceptional occurrence in Ireland.[89]

In Limerick diocese, three men were absolved for holding benefices by schismatic authority.[90] There were three such men in Cork & Cloyne, one of them a pluralist.[91] There were two such men in Tuam, and one in Waterford & Lismore.[92] Two priests were absolved for illegitimacy in Limerick, one in Cork & Cloyne, one in Tuam and three in Waterford.[93] A striking feature of the Waterford acts is the number of men who sought dispensations from Cardinal Pole to take orders in the future, six of them for illegitimacy, two of them in order to receive holy orders faster than usual and one from an acolyte looking for extra time before his ordination.[94]

Thomas Mayer calculated that about a quarter of the acts in Pole's legatine register have been lost. There may be stray records of some of those elsewhere. On 12 December 1555, Pole authorised Dominic Tirrey, bishop of Cork & Cloyne, to absolve the precentor of Cork for having accepted his office at the hands of Henry VIII.[95] Nonetheless, the large number and high proportion of the surviving records provide a representative sample of Pole's work. The overall impression is that Pole was supplicated by only a tiny minority of the clergy in those dioceses in Ireland whose bishop had been schismatic or Protestant during the early Tudor reformations. The supplicants generally sought to regularise their status as priests or benefice-holders in canon law. Why so few supplicated for absolutions is impossible to determine, though the high proportion of clergymen seeking absolutions or dispensations because of illegitimacy may, conceivably, reflect an increased concern with sexual incontinence in Mary's reign. Interestingly, the diocesan synod convened in 1557 by Hugh O'Carrollan, bishop of Clogher, was strikingly strict in condemning clerical concubinage, partly reflecting the strong tone of the northern provincial synod of 1553, but maybe also reflecting a greater insistence on more rigorous adherence to canon law.[96]

As regards doctrinal deviancy in Ireland, there is very little evidence in Pole's

---

1625b, 1625c, 1992. **84** Ibid., nos 1374, 1733. **85** Ibid., nos 1143, 1178, 2050a. **86** Ibid., nos 1173, 1175. **87** Ibid., no. 1606. **88** Ibid., nos 1276, 1609. **89** Ibid., no. 1314. **90** Ibid., nos 1234, 1277, 1634. **91** Ibid., nos 1409, 1417, 1433. **92** Ibid., nos 1394, 1399, 1138. **93** Ibid., nos 1176, 1209a, 1644, 1400, 1301, 1324, 1332. **94** Ibid., nos 1192a, 1192b, 1192c, 1204a, 1204b, 1332, 1994b. **95** Evelyn Bolster, *A history of the diocese of Cork from the reformation to the penal era* (Cork, 1982), pp 44–7. **96** William O'Sullivan, 'Two Clogher constitutions', *CR*, 15 (1996), pp 153–5.

legatine register. A layman from Dublin was the only supplicant for an absolution for heresy.[97] Only two clergymen sought absolution for receiving orders by 'another rite'; a priest of Ross diocese ordained by Bishop Walsh of Waterford & Lismore, and a priest of Kildare diocese.[98] The dean of Limerick supplicated for absolution for having celebrated the Mass improperly, while the archdeacon of Limerick sought absolution for obeying schismatic laws while the Protestant bishop, William Casey, held the see – possible references to the use of Edwardian rites or rituals.[99] Otherwise, one gets no sense of a great need in Ireland for a formal reconciliation of the lesser clergy, nor of any general anxiety to secure one. The legatine court responded to supplications as best it could, but did not and could not insist that all clergymen who had been ordained or appointed to benefices in the time of schism be reconciled individually. Its operation was neither comprehensive nor systematic.

RENEWAL

It was Queen Mary rather than Cardinal Pole who showed the greater sense of urgency in addressing the needs of the Irish Church. Once England was formally reconciled to Rome, the queen turned some of her attention to Ireland. On 18 February 1555, Mary directed the dean and chapter of Christ Church, Dublin, to elect Dr Hugh Curwen as the new archbishop of Dublin.[1] Significantly, Curwen was the only English-born man promoted to the Irish episcopal bench in Mary's reign; Irish clergymen seemed to be less contaminated by heresy. He may not have been appointed for his pastoral qualities, but for his legal expertise: on 12 September 1555, prior to his departure for Ireland, he was appointed as the lord chancellor of Ireland, the revenues of both of his offices combined to provide him with an income worthy of his status. It proved to be a costly decision for Mary's religious programme for Curwen, 'a complier in all reigns', was to conform readily to the Elizabethan settlement.[2] Nonetheless, in 1555, the queen could reasonably have expected her chaplain to fully support the revival of Catholicism in Ireland. Shortly after his arrival in Ireland in October 1555, Curwen convened a synod for the ecclesiastical province of Dublin 'in which there were many things instituted touching ecclesiastical rites'.[3] The queen nominated Thomas Leverous to the see of Kildare on 1 March 1555, and he received his papal provision on 30 August.[4] Unlike Curwen, Leverous had been a stalwart of the Catholic Church during the early Tudor reformations, and would continue to be so after Mary's death.[5] Curwen, by contrast, had to

97 *CRP*, no. 1445. 98 Ibid., nos 1374, 1311. 99 Ibid., nos 1277, 1634. 1 'Curwen', Helen Coburn Walshe, *ODNB*. 2 Jefferies, 'Irish parliament of 1560', pp 137, 139–40. 3 Ware, 'Annals', *s.a.* 1555. 4 Brady, *Episcopal succession*, i, p. 351. 5 Jefferies, 'Irish parliament of

supplicate for a dispensation for schism and heresy from Cardinal Pole but, significantly, perhaps, he avoided swearing an oath to the pope.[6]

From the outset, Pole had exerted enormous pressure on Mary to restore to the Church all of 'God's own property' that had been taken from it since the schism began.[7] From early in 1555, the queen and king returned significant properties to the Church in both England and Ireland, including St Patrick's Cathedral on 25 March.[8] Leverous, who had spent some time in Pole's household, was appointed as dean, presumably on the cardinal's recommendation.[9] George Browne, the former archbishop of Dublin, was given a prebend in the cathedral. Archbishop Dowdall was made a canon of the cathedral, which would have afforded him with a residence in the capital whenever he was called there on state business.[10] The restoration of St Patrick's arose from the queen's and king's commitment to Cardinal Pole to restore all Church properties in their possession to the Church.[11]

On 10 March 1555, Cardinal Pole wrote to Pope Julius III that Mary and Philip wished for papal confirmation of Ireland's status as a kingdom.[12] According to the direct testimony of one of Pole's most senior officers, the request originated directly with the queen herself.[13] Julius' successor, Pope Paul IV, duly recognised Ireland as a kingdom in July of that year, thereby regularising its status following the Act for the kingly title of 1541, and formally extended Pole's legatine authority to the 'new' kingdom.[14] In 1556, the English and Irish legations were re-united for administrative convenience.

When Mary appointed Lord Fitzwalter as her deputy in Ireland on 17 April 1556, she instructed him to advance the Catholic religion and to help the bishops to root out heresy. He was directed to prepare for a parliament that would underpin the work of Catholic restoration in Ireland. He was directed too to afford every facility to the legatine commission through which Cardinal Pole intended to conduct a visitation of the Irish Church.[15] It is not possible to state what effects a legatine commission might have had on the Irish Church. Pole may not have been entirely sure himself: he informed Pope Paul IV, in a letter dated the day after Fitzwalter's appointment as deputy, that he intended to do 'something' about Ireland, but gave no indication as to what he had in mind.[16]

1560', pp 129, 137–8. **6** *CRP*, no. 1099. **7** See *CRP*, no. 1009, for example. Mayer, *Prince and prophet*, pp 217–21. **8** *CPCR*, i, 1 & 2 Philip & Mary, nos 33–8. **9** Moran, *Archbishops of Dublin*, pp 52, 58; *CPCR*, i, 1 & 2 Philip & Mary, nos 34, 35, 38; Ware, 'Annals', *s.a.* 1555. **10** *CPCR*, i, 1 & 2 Philip & Mary, nos 34, 38. Dowdall would certainly have approved of Leverous' promotion as dean since he held him in very high regard, having invited him to preach at the synod of the clergy of Armagh *inter Anglicos* in 1554. However, that does not prove that the archbishop was responsible for the dean's appointment by the queen. **11** Dowdall's register, pp 97–8 (82). **12** *CRP*, no. 1109. **13** *CSP Rome*, ii, pp 240–1. **14** *CRP*, nos 1376, 1377, 1378; J. Hogan, 'Miscellanea Vaticano-Hibernica, 1520–1631', *Archivium Hibernicum*, 4 (1915), p. 217; Edwards, *Church and state*, p. 164, quoting Quirini, *Epistolarum Reginaldi Poli*, v, pp 5, 41. **15** SP 62/1/22. **16** *CRP*, no. 1544.

As it happened, the cardinal's visitation of the Irish Church was not conducted before he was stripped of his legatine authority in April 1557.

Pole had experienced an overwhelming personal crisis of faith at Trent.[17] Theological discussion, he had learnt to his cost, led to confusion and doubt. Preaching he distrusted as a two-edged sword.[18] The path to salvation, he now believed, lay with complete obedience to the authority of the Catholic Church, and of the pope in particular. He believed that in the short term, Catholicism could best be promoted through the revival of traditional practices of worship conducted with order and ceremonial.[19] To restore the 'beauty of holiness' in Catholic liturgies priests had to recover any vestments or ornaments that had been confiscated during the Edwardian period. To that end, royal commissions were established in Ireland on 3 December 1557, as they had already been in England and Wales, to enquire as to the location of all chalices and ornaments, bells, houses and lands belonging to parish churches and chapels, with the aim of restoring any items that had been confiscated by the crown under Edward VI and his father to the use of the Church. The commission for County Louth included Archbishop Dowdall, the dean of Armagh, Vicar Hamlin, Lord Louth and the mayor of Drogheda.[20] The Irish commissions were issued later than the English ones, possibly because the losses sustained in Edward's reign were less than in England. However, the inclusion of Hamlyn's name on the Louth commission suggests that the issuing of the commissions may simply have been delayed, as the vicar had been succeeded to his benefice by another (following Hamlyn's death doubtless) by August 1556.[21] It is not possible to determine how effective the royal commissions were, though it seems unlikely that the Irish Church had been as badly affected as its English counterpart. Even in Kilkenny, despite the attentions of the zealous Bishop Bale, the Catholic clergy managed to preserve their vestments and ornaments from destruction, and were able to bring them back into use in Mary's reign.[22] Even the chantries survived destruction.[23] There was certainly no need for the 'Herculean efforts' required in England to reconstruct the ritual and sacramental framework of the Catholic religion.[24]

For the longer term, Cardinal Pole hoped to have the Church re-endowed with some, at least, of its former possessions and to use those assets for a planned assault on clerical poverty.[25] He reckoned that impoverished benefices were

17 Dermot Fenlon, *Heresy and obedience in Tridentine Italy: Cardinal Pole and the counter-reformation* (Cambridge, 1972), pp 125–6, 161–2, 165, 254–6. 18 R.H. Pogson, 'Reginald Pole and the priorities of government in Mary Tudor's church', *HJ*, 18:1 (1975), pp 6–7, 13, 16, 17. 19 Pogson, 'Reginald Pole', p. 11; Loades, *Mary Tudor*, p. 82. 20 *Fiants of Philip & Mary*, no. 181. 21 Jefferies, 'Primate George Dowdall and the Marian restoration', *SAM*, 17 (1998), p. 13. 22 Bale, 'Vocacyon', p. 454. 23 Laurence Murray, 'Ancient chantries of County Louth', *CLAHJ*, 9 (1939), passim; see especially Lennon, *Lords of Dublin*. 24 Duffy, *Stripping of the altars*, pp 526–8. 25 R.H. Pogson, 'Revival and reform in Mary Tudor's church: a question of money' in Christopher Haigh (ed.), *The English reformation revised* (Cambridge, 1988), pp

unlikely to appeal to well-educated pastors, while poor pastors were unlikely to enjoy the respect they were entitled to. He wanted to establish diocesan seminaries to educate and train an exemplary priesthood.[26] Such far-reaching plans needed finance to be made available by parliament.

Mary's Irish parliament met, not on 21 January 1557 as originally scheduled, but on 1 June 1557. Before the parliament was convened, the lord deputy received through Cardinal Pole a bull from Pope Paul IV promising pardon and forgiveness to the clergy and laity in Ireland who had swerved from allegiance to the apostolic see and entered into schism. This bull, 'having been delivered by the lord deputy to the lord chancellor, Archbishop Curwen, was by him devoutly and reverently received and read upon his knees, in open parliament deliberately and distinctly, in a high voice. And the lords spiritual and temporal, and the commons, in the name of themselves particularly, and also of the whole body of the realm, hearing the same, embraced it right reverently and humbly kneeling upon their knees, being repentant; and yielding thanks, had the *Te Deum* solemnly sung'. Thus declared the preamble of the Act repealing all statutes and proclamations made against the papacy in Ireland since 1534 [c.8]. By this act, the queen formally renounced her claim to the royal supremacy and all papal bulls and dispensations not prejudicial to the crown's authority in Ireland were allowed to be given effect. The same Act contained a provision guaranteeing the ownership of suppressed religious houses to their grantees, though it also contained an exhortation to such grantees to make restitution of former ecclesiastical properties for the sake of their souls.

An Act was passed whereby the crown renounced its claim to the payment of first fruits and twentieths, to tithes, glebes and advowsons – except those revenues that had been granted away by letters patent [c.10]. This was a strikingly generous Act that, as in England, Cardinal Pole hoped to use as the basis for a concerted assault on clerical poverty. Unfortunately for the clergy, there was insufficient time for the planning and administration required before Mary's successor rescinded her half-sister's benefaction. Another of Mary's major donations to the Church was also revoked by Elizabeth; the resurrection of the hospital of St John of Jerusalem at Kilmainham, County Dublin. This institution had property to the value of £426 *per annum* restored to it, but it was all clawed back by the crown after Mary's death.[27]

In August 1558, while visiting the queen, Primate Dowdall secured her consent to restore his former hospital at Ardee 'for the better relief of poor and sick people'. The queen directed the lord deputy to fund the erection of a new friary for the Carmelite community at Ardee.[28] There may have been an intention to re-found the Cistercian monastery at Mellifont,[29] and perhaps the

140–52. 26 Pogson, 'Reginald Pole', p. 16; Loades, *Mary Tudor*, p. 82. 27 Loades, *Mary Tudor*, p. 413; Ware, 'Annals', *s.a.* 1557, 1559; Parliament of 2 Elizabeth, c. 7. 28 SP 62/2/9. 29 *CSPI*, Mary, i, no. 62.

Franciscan house at Trim.[30] However, Mary was not in a position to contemplate the complete reversal of her father's dissolution of the monasteries. A petition to Queen Mary and Cardinal Pole by the Observant Franciscans of Kilcullen, County Kildare, soon after the English reconciliation, asked that they write to the deputy and chancellor of Ireland 'firmly ordering them' to restore the friaries at Kilcullen, Enniscorthy, Trim and Multyfarnham to the friars who had been obliged to live in the mountains since their suppression.[31] The latter, interestingly, was held by Sir Thomas Cusack, the previous lord chancellor, and he expressed a willingness to restore it to the friars in return for some small compensation. In the event, the friars recovered their house at Multyfarnham and held on to it until the end of the sixteenth century under the patronage of Baron Delvin.[32]

The secular peers were not generally inclined to make significant restitution to the Church. James, earl of Desmond, stood apart from the others. He had played a key role in preserving several monasteries and friaries in his sphere of influence from dissolution. He purchased the Dominican friary in Limerick for £96 in order to save it from the crown and he restored it to the friars on Mary's accession to the throne.[33] In 1557, the earl of Desmond supported the Dominican prior in Youghal in pleading, in vain, for the restoration of the dissolved Dominican friary in Cork.[34] One of the earl's chaplains, Robert Remon, petitioned the queen unsuccessfully for the restoration of the Augustinian priory at Waterford to which he had been appointed as prior.[35] From Desmond's stronghold of Kilmallock in County Limerick, the queen was petitioned by the proctor and vicars of St Peter's Collegiate Church for a license permitting them to receive grants and donations offered to them by several townsfolk to an annual value of £20 – a request to which Mary acceded. All in all, by the time of the queen's death, only a fraction of the former monastic possessions had been returned to the Church, yet there had been little time to achieve significantly more by means of restitution. The queen herself had set a fine example by surrendering the spiritualities in her possession, in reviving the hospital at Kilmainham and in restoring St Patrick's Cathedral, Dublin.

Among the remaining acts of Mary's Irish parliament was one to revive the three medieval statutes for the suppression of heresy [c.9]. One cannot say for certain what action, if any, was taken against Protestants in Ireland under this legislation. Six English-born counsellors and five other Englishmen were granted pardons *inter alia* for heresy. This suggests that there was no persecution of Protestants in Ireland.

30 Ibid., no. 42. 31 *CRP*, no. 1020. 32 Scott, *Tudor diocese of Meath*, p. 109. 33 Bradshaw, *The dissolution*, pp 151, 163–9. 34 *CSPI*, Mary, i, nos 58, 59. 35 *CSPI*, Mary, i, nos 66, 65.

CONCLUSIONS

Queen Mary, with the belated support of Cardinal Pole, was the driving force behind the Catholic restoration in Ireland as in England. She authorised the restoration of Catholic ceremonies in Ireland, ordered the deprivation of married clergy and promoted bishops in Ireland even before Pole finally reconciled her kingdom with the Catholic Church at the end of 1554. She restored St Patrick's Cathedral, Dublin, and the hospital at Kilmainham, and she ordered the restoration of a couple of lesser religious establishments. She sought, through Pole, the papal bull by which the papacy recognised Ireland as a kingdom, and the bull which absolved the Irish clergy and laity who had forsaken their allegiance to Rome during the early reformations.

Pole's role in the Marian restoration in Ireland was one of promise rather than achievement. The ecclesiastical legislation of Mary's Irish parliament, including the crown's renunciation of its claim to the first fruits, twentieths, etc., bore witness to his influence. The legatine visitation that he planned for Ireland was to parallel that which he conducted in England and Wales and would probably have provided the information base for some significant reforms. However, Pole was preoccupied with the demands of Church and state in England,[36] and gave little sustained attention to Ireland. His legatine register records his responses to scores of supplications for absolutions and dispensations from Ireland, but gives no sense of a systematic approach to the challenges confronting the Irish Church. It may have been fortuitous that Protestantism presented no threat in Ireland, but that may have encouraged Pole, if he needed such encouragement, to leave Ireland on the long finger. With Mary's death, and the accession of Elizabeth, Pole's intentions for the Irish Church, addressing the poverty among the clergy and establishing seminaries to train priests did not materialise, though his plans for seminaries were to be adopted at the Council of Trent with a tremendous effect on the future of the Catholic Church.

Archbishop Dowdall was no programmatic reformer. The agendas of his annual diocesan synods were very traditional, and when he purchased lands from the queen for the erection of a college, he showed himself to have been a man of the later Middle Ages rather than the counter-reformation: the college was to be a chantry staffed by a number of priests 'for the maintaining of God's divine service'.[37] He failed to see an opportunity to establish a diocesan school or seminary. In any event, the college was never founded. Dowdall died in London on 15 August 1558, possibly of the same influenza as was shortly afterwards to end the lives of Cardinal Pole and Queen Mary herself.[38] Yet, though he did not anticipate the counter-reformation, through his ministry he laid foundations

36 Mayer, *Prince and prophet*, p. 232. 37 SP 62/2/64. 38 Dowdall's register, pp 217–18 (115).

that helped to some degree to ensure that the counter-reformation would find receptive congregations during Elizabeth's reign.[39] There is no evidence to suggest that there was already a general commitment to counter-reformation Catholicism in Ireland in Mary's reign. Her years as queen offered a short reprieve from religious controversy in Ireland, but it left open the question of what would happen next.

39 Jefferies, *Priests and prelates*, pp 165–73.

PART III

The Elizabethan reformation

7

Elizabeth's reformation: initial reception

Elizabeth's Irish Reformation parliament was convened in Christ Church Cathedral, Dublin, on 12 January 1560 and sat until 1 February.[1] Nine acts subsequently entered the statute books. By the first act, the queen was duly acknowledged as supreme governor of the realm, and of all her dominions and countries, in all spiritual or ecclesiastical things or causes as well as temporal. All officeholders in Church and state were required to take an oath acknowledging the same. The second statute, the Act of uniformity, imposed a reformed, vernacular liturgy on the Irish Church, but it declared that 'in every such church or place where the common minister or priest had not the use or knowledge of the English tongue, he might say and use the matins, evensong, celebration of the Lord's Supper and administration of each of the sacraments, and all their common and open prayer, in the Latin tongue, in the order and form mentioned and set forth in the book established by this act'. The retention of Latin in Church of Ireland services was a concession to the conservative members of the Irish parliament, and one which could appeal to laymen and clergy alike.[2]

Furthermore, the Elizabethan Act of uniformity and the *Book of Common Prayer* stipulated that the ornaments of the Church and clergy as used in the second year of Edward VI's reign were to be retained in the Elizabethan Church.[3] In effect, the paraphernalia of medieval Christian worship was to be retained in the 'reformed' Church of Ireland, and her clergy were to continue wearing the traditional Mass vestments for Church services. The fact that the act of uniformity authorised relatively little change in the outward form of Christian worship in Ireland may have been significant in facilitating its endorsement by the parliament.

It had been expected that the ecclesiastical measures would encounter strong opposition in the Irish parliament 'by reason of the clergy there is so addicted to Rome'.[4] Yet there is evidence that the Elizabethan religious settlement had at least three important advocates among the bishops in the House of Lords. Fr Strange, guardian of the Franciscans in Ireland, authoritatively reported that

1 Jefferies, 'Irish parliament of 1560', p. 132. 2 William Haugaard, *Elizabeth and the English reformation* (Cambridge, 1970), pp 112–19. 3 *Stat. Ire.*, i, 284–90; *The prayer book of Queen Elizabeth, 1559* (London, 1890), p. 41. 4 'The device for alteration of religion', quoted in Henry Gee, *The Elizabethan prayer book and ornaments* (London, 1902), p. 196.

Patrick Walsh, a Catholic bishop by election and consecration, a man
of learning and of great repute throughout the kingdom for his gifts
of teaching and preaching, in so much that in parliament all the
bishops of Ireland spoke *ad nutum ejus* and stood firm while he stood
firm, but when he fell all fell with him save only the bishop of Kildare.
Not content with taking the oath, he married and had sons ... Walsh
died a confirmed heretic.[5]

Walsh had been consecrated as bishop of Waterford & Lismore on 23 October
1551 on the mandate of Edward VI.[6] He is known to have embraced 'heresy' in
Elizabeth's reign. His son Nicholas was to become Church of Ireland bishop of
Ossory. Unfortunately, with the paucity of contemporary materials, we cannot
confirm whether Bishop Walsh's support for the ecclesiastical bills was as
decisive as Strange believed.

However, Archbishop Curwen of Dublin, as the senior Irish prelate in 1560,
certainly played a key role in securing the lords' assent for the ecclesiastical bills.
Thomas O'Fihilly, bishop of Leighlin, also endorsed the religious reforms with
alacrity. He renounced papal authority on his own volition on 28 May 1559.[7]
Soon after the parliament, O'Fihilly was praised for 'his good conformity in
matters of religion'.[8]

Opposition to the ecclesiastical bills was limited. Three bishops were
summoned before a commission to take the oath of supremacy on 4 February
1560.[9] Of these, Archbishop Bodkin of Tuam subscribed to the oath, while
Bishop William Walsh of Meath and Bishop Thomas Leverous of Kildare
refused. Leverous, it seems, refused the oath on the grounds that women were
by nature excluded from any authority in the Church. He was consequently
deposed and he retired to Limerick diocese where he became a teacher.[10]

Bishop Walsh was deprived by May 1560;[11] his deprivation probably dates
from the time of his refusal of the oath in February. He openly opposed the
religious changes after the 1560 parliament and Brendan Scott has credited him
with a critical role in actively disrupting and retarding the progress of the
Elizabethan reformation in Meath diocese.[12] He was arrested and imprisoned in
July 1565, released in 1569, but arrested again in 1572 for his persistent opposition to the reformation. He escaped later that year and, after a short ministry in
Ireland, retired to Alcala in Spain, where he died in 1577.

5 *Wadding papers, 1614–38*, ed. Brendan Jennings (Dublin, 1953), p. 319. 6 *Works of Ware*, i,
p. 537. Archivio Segreto Vaticano, Nunziatura di Portogallo, ii, fo. 408v, quoted in Bolster, *Diocese
of Cork*, ii, p. 77. 7 *CSPI, 1509–73*, p. 154. 8 *Cal. Carew MSS*, no. 225.
9 *Fiants, Ire., Eliz.*, nos 198, 199. 10 David Rothe, *Analecta et de processu martyriali*, ed. P.F.
Moran (London, 1884), pp 447–55. 11 John Bruce and T. Perowne (eds), *Correspondence of
Mathew Parker* (Cambridge, 1853), Letter lxxxi, p. 117. 12 Scott, *Tudor diocese of Meath*, pp
19, 55–6.

In England, the crown had adopted the strategy of deposing the most recalcitrant Marian bishops in the hope of persuading the remainder to conform.[13] Hence, it seems likely that the three Irish bishops summoned before the commission of 4 February 1560 were those who had distinguished themselves by opposing the religious measures. Conformity, tacit or otherwise, appears to have been general among the remaining prelates. From Limerick on 12 October 1561, David Wolfe, SJ, reported to Cardinal Moroni that the archbishop of Tuam and the bishop of Clonfert were both 'adherents of the queen as, I have already informed you, are all the rest in Munster'.[14] I interpret this to mean that they were loyal to Elizabeth and not necessarily as an indication that they subscribed to the oath of supremacy. Regrettably, the letter referred to here has been lost and it is not clear how far the conformity of the southern bishops extended at that early stage.[15] In 1562, the bishop of Limerick, Hugh Lacey, was described by Sussex as 'a stubborn and disobedient man in causes of religion, and has committed offences whereby he has, by the laws of the realm, forfeited his bishopric'.[16] He actively supported the papal commissary, David Wolfe, SJ, and Richard Creagh. Yet none of Lacey's fellow prelates summoned to the 1560 parliament were quite so defiant.

By June 1564, no fewer than eight bishops of Mary's reign had been appointed to ecclesiastical commissions which demanded subscription to the oath of supremacy, including the archbishops of Dublin and Tuam, the bishops of Clonfert & Elphin, Leighlin, Ossory, Waterford & Lismore, Cork & Cloyne, and Limerick.[17] The archbishop of Cashel and the bishops of Down & Connor and of Emly all died in office within two years of the parliament, while Bishop Devereux of Ferns continued in office until his death in 1566.[18] Only the bishops of Meath and Kildare were deprived for refusing the oath of supremacy. In contrast with the situation in England, the Elizabethan religious settlement appears to have enjoyed a surprising degree of acceptance or at least acquiescence, however unenthusiastic, among the bishops who attended the Irish parliament of 1560.

The Act of uniformity came into effect in Ireland on 23 June 1560, and gave juridical authorisation for liturgical change throughout the Irish Church. In practice, however, change could be imposed only where the efforts of a favourably disposed bishop were complemented by English royal authority. Yet in Ireland, there were very few supporters of the ecclesiastical revolution initiated in 1560.

13 Haugaard, *Elizabeth and the Reformation*, pp 36–42. 14 *CSP Rome, 1558–71*, no. 108. 15 Edmund Hogan (ed.), *Ibernia Ignatiana, 1540–1607* (Dublin, 1880), p. 13. 16 *Cal. Carew MSS*, no. 237. 17 *Fiants, Ire., Eliz.*, nos 221, 666, 667, 668. 18 Brendan Bradshaw, J.G. Simms and C.J. Woods, 'Bishops of the Church of Ireland from 1534' in *A new history of Ireland*, ix (Oxford, 1984), pp 400, 411, 417, 425.

INITIAL ENFORCEMENT

The speedy endorsement of the Elizabethan religious settlement by the Irish parliament might seem to have augured well for its prospects, at least in the more anglicised regions of Ireland. Crown officials moved quickly to consolidate the settlement. On 3 February 1560, a royal commission was established to administer the Elizabethan oath of supremacy to the archbishop of Tuam, and the bishops of Meath and Kildare.[19] The two latter prelates refused the oath and were deprived. There are unclear references among the state papers that suggest that the Marian bishops of Ossory and Limerick did not take the oath either. The diocese of Ossory was stated to be vacant early in 1562,[20] though Bishop Thonery was to die in office in 1565. A report of 1562 observed that 'Limerick may be void by deprivation',[21] but Bishop Lacey, who actively supported leading Catholic dissidents in his diocese, was not finally obliged to retire until 1571.[22] The Marian nominee for Cork & Cloyne, Roger Skiddy, was not consecrated until 1564, presumably because of his reluctance to take the oath, and his continuing conservatism following his belated promotion was instrumental in causing him to be removed from office by Deputy Sidney in 1567.[23] The critical problem facing the crown was the sheer lack of suitable candidates to promote to the highest offices in the Irish Church. Rigorous imposition of the oath of supremacy would only have served to underline the tenuous nature of the consent secured for the Elizabethan settlement in the Irish parliament of 1560.

On 17 February 1560, a commission was established to tender the oath to Archbishop Curwen of Dublin and the clergy of Dublin's two cathedrals.[24] On the following day, a certificate was issued to the effect that Curwen, Robert Wesseley, archdeacon of Dublin, Robert Nangill, chancellor of St Patrick's and Thomas Crief, precentor of St Patrick's, had taken the oath, as well as Christopher More, a prebendary of Christ Church, but it had been refused by the chancellor, the treasurer and the precentor of Christ Church, and by one of the prebendaries. Thomas Lockwood, dean of Christ Church, took the oath before a separate commission about the same time.[25] Intriguingly, the certificate recording the submission of Curwen and some others indicates that the oath was not tendered to the rest of the cathedral clergy at Christ Church, and it is not clear whether it was tendered to the remainder of the cathedral clergy in St Patrick's either. One might be tempted to assume that they were tendered the oath on a subsequent occasion, but there is no evidence to show if that actually occurred. There is no record of any further certificate being issued, nor do I know of any other clergymen being deprived for refusing the oath, as one would expect if the oath had been tendered more widely given the strong opposition

19 *Fiants, Ire., Eliz.*, nos 198, 199.   20 Shirley, *Original letters*, no. xxxvii.   21 Ibid., no. xliii; *Cal. Carew MSS*, no. 237.   22 Brady, *Episcopal succession*, ii, pp 139–40.   23 Bolster, *Diocese of Cork*, pp 59–60.   24 *Fiants, Ire., Eliz.*, nos 225, 226.   25 *Fiants, Ire., Eliz.*, nos 222, 227.

demonstrated towards it, particularly in Christ Church. My own suspicion is that, having had the oath refused by so many of the most senior clergymen in Christ Church, the commissioners may well have decided not to insist on a universal subscription lest Dublin's cathedrals be left bereft of staff. Several of St Patrick's canons continued to draw their salaries but absented themselves from the Protestant services in subsequent years. In January 1565, Bishop Brady of Meath complained that the clergy of St Patrick's were all 'disguised dissemblers';[26] apparently they told the Protestant prelate that 'they be old bottles and cannot away with this new wine [of Protestantism]'.

The Elizabethan oath of supremacy is known to have been tendered to Robert Luttrell, archdeacon of Meath, but he refused to take it and was deprived of his office on 25 March 1560.[27] He was the only clergyman in Meath diocese known to have been tendered the oath, other than its bishop, who had already been deprived. There are no records of commissions being established to take the oath from the clergy of Armagh or Kildare dioceses, let alone from clergymen beyond the Pale at that time. The circumspection of the crown officials in tendering the oath of supremacy to the Irish clergy reflects the very strong hostility they encountered.

Commissions to tender the oath of supremacy to secular officers of the crown were established at the same time as those for clergymen. Certificates issued following the establishment of commissions on 17 February 1560 indicate that subscription was general among the most senior officers of the crown, who were mainly but not exclusively English-born, though no certificate exists to indicate which of the six mainly Irish-born officials tendered the oath by another commission actually subscribed.[28] A commission to tender oaths to all of the justices of the peace with their clerks and ministers, and to all town officers and their ministers in County Kildare succeeded in taking oaths from only three JPs, and from only one town officer, the sovereign of Naas, and one gets the definite impression that a decision was taken not to force consciences in the county.[29] A similar commission for County Meath has left no record at all of its proceedings. There is no record extant of commissions being established for Dublin city or county, or for County Louth. While it seems safe to assume that commissions were established for those counties, it seems no less safe to assume that subscription to the oath was not insisted upon. Significantly, it was not until 9 June 1564 that commissions were established to tender the oath of supremacy in Counties Kilkenny, Carlow, Tipperary, Waterford, Cork, Limerick and Kerry.[30] A commission established for Connacht and Thomond in 1564 directed that the oath be tendered to all persons 'as may seem good to them' – a clear indication of the circumspection employed in tendering the oath.[31]

26 Shirley, *Original letters*, no. lxii. 27 *Fiants, Ire., Eliz.*, no. 236; Scott, *Tudor diocese of Meath*, p. 55. 28 *Fiants, Ire., Eliz.*, nos 222, 227, 223, 221. 29 Ibid., nos 223, 224. 30 Ibid., no. 666. 31 Ibid., no. 668.

The overall impression is that the crown officials encountered so much resist-ance to the imposition of the oath of supremacy, from clergymen and secular officials, that they were obliged to be very circumspect in tendering the oath for fear of undermining the operation of the Church and state at local levels. A remarkable contrast is evident, therefore, between the initial responses to the Elizabethan religious settlement in England, where the Elizabethan oath was generally accepted by secular office-holders and the great majority of the beneficed clergymen, and that in Ireland, where the crown's officers hesitated to tender the oath, or to punish those who would not subscribe to it, in the face of more general opposition.

There is no actual record to show if the mayor of Dublin was tendered the oath of supremacy in 1560. Alderman Nicholas Penteney, who was elected as mayor of Dublin for the term 1560–61, was fined an incredible £200, apparently for refusing to subscribe to the oath.[32] Colm Lennon reckons that Penteney's replacement was 'unlikely' to have been presented with the oath. He observed that 'there were very few incidents of Dublin priests or lay people being punished for non-conformity throughout the period of the queen's reign. Refusals of the oath of supremacy by municipal officials are not recorded for the reason that the oath was not tendered to them'.[33]

Lennon found evidence of there being only a couple of Protestant families among Dublin's oligarchy. The 'lords of Dublin' remained, predominantly, Catholics. They resisted the temptation to liquidate the assets of the city's religious guilds, as was quite common in England in pre-emptive moves to avoid royal confiscations, even when faced with the need to raise finance to fund a school for the city in 1561/2. Lennon has emphasised the role of the guild of St Anne, in particular, in helping to maintain the Catholic religion in Dublin.[34] I have to point out, however, that there is no explicit evidence that the chantry priests of St Anne's, or any other religious guild, played an active role in sustaining Catholic beliefs in the city. I suspect that they made use of the *Book of Common Prayer*, most likely the requiem service in the Latin edition – since celebrating the Mass would have invited their dissolution. I am inclined to believe that the chantries and religious guilds were more significant as symbols of the Catholic sentiments of Dublin's oligarchs than as active instruments for maintaining Catholicism in the capital.

In 1563, the mayor and council of Dublin compelled two of the city's trade guilds, the butchers and the fishmongers, to restore some traditional Catholic customs that they had abandoned since Elizabeth's accession to the throne.[35] It is both interesting and significant that at least two of Dublin's trade guilds had followed the example of their English counterparts in abandoning traditional customs with religious associations without being directed to do so. That may

32 Ibid.   33 Lennon, *Lords of Dublin*, p. 134.   34 Ibid., pp 146–9.   35 Ibid., pp 133–4.

suggest that there was a constituency in Dublin whose commitment to the old order was not inviolable. It hints at the possibility that the Reformation could have made differential progress within different social classes within Dublin's citizenry – but there is no evidence to show that religious divisions actually emerged in Dublin along the social cleavages in the city. On the other hand, the insistence of the city's mayor and council that the traditional customs be reinstated points to a fundamental weakness in the enforcement of the Elizabethan religious settlement in Dublin. In England, the successful imposition of religious change depended on the co-operation of the secular élites in the towns and countryside with the Church authorities. In Dublin, and across Ireland generally, the social élites were not so co-operative.

A REFORMATION WITHOUT REFORMERS?

With Dowdall of Armagh dead, and Walsh of Meath and Leverous of Kildare deprived, Hugh Curwen, the English-born archbishop of Dublin, was the only remaining bishop in the Pale from early February 1560. James Murray claimed that 'Archbishop Curwen and his diocesan administration consciously set out to subvert the 1560 settlement from day one', and he referred to the archbishop's 'staunch defence of the Catholic religion' – but his claim is not substantiated by the available evidence.[36] Murray associated Curwen with two supposed amendments to the Irish act of uniformity but, in fact, the regulations concerning clerical dress did not constitute an amendment (being identical with the text of the earlier English act), and there is no evidence whatsoever to support the contention that Curwen may have sponsored the provision of a Latin edition of the *Book of Common Prayer*. Murray's characterisation of Curwen is flawed.

Sir Thomas Wrothe and Sir Nicholas Arnold, commissioners for Ireland, described Archbishop Curwen in a letter of March 1564 as 'civil and conformable and will do as he seems what authority shall command'.[37] Curwen himself pointed out to Elizabeth that he was 'always contented to be ordered as shall please' the crown,[38] and he pointed out to Cecil that he was the bishop who had 'surliest stood to the crown either in England or Ireland' – a reference to his decision to embrace the Elizabethan settlement though his Marian colleagues in England and Wales rejected it almost to a man.[39] Curwen was certainly not a 'staunch' Catholic. On the eve of his translation from Dublin to Oxford, he confessed that his service was not as good as it ought to have been, 'yet', he declared, 'was it done with all my heart, to the best of my power'.[40] It was, he wrote, 'sickness not age' that hindered him.[41] As early as November 1560, he was

---

36 Murray, 'Tudor diocese of Dublin', pp 220, 222. 37 SP 63/10/34; Shirley, *Original letters*, no. liv. 38 Shirley, *Original letters*, no. lv. 39 Ibid., no. xxxiv. 40 Ibid., no. lxxxiv. 41 Ibid.,

beseeching Cecil, via the lord lieutenant, to be translated to an English diocese, where he knew he would be expected to oversee the rigorous imposition of the Elizabethan settlement.[42] A 'staunch' Catholic would not have been quite so keen to serve as a bishop in the Elizabethan Church of England.

According to Strype, Archbishop Loftus wrote to Archbishop Parker of Canterbury in 1562 condemning Archbishop Curwen as 'a known enemy' and accused him of 'labouring under open crimes'; what those were Loftus declined to put on paper, but Curwen subsequently defended himself against allegations of corruption.[43] Bishop Brady of Meath complained in March 1564 that Curwen only preached 'now and then',[44] and in a letter to Cecil in January 1565 he characterised Curwen and the clergy of St Patrick's Cathedral, Dublin, 'from bishop to petty canon, none but disguised dissemblers'.[45] With such an 'old unprofitable workman' (as Brady called him), occupying the most senior position in the Church in Dublin diocese, it is not to be wondered that the Elizabethan reformation made little progress there during Curwen's episcopate.

It is virtually certain that Curwen oversaw the introduction of the Elizabethan *Book of Common Prayer* in the more anglicised parishes in his diocese: Christ Church Cathedral, Dublin, was whitewashed and prepared for the new liturgy weeks in advance of its formal introduction and, although the rood screen before the cathedral's chancel was still in place in 1564, the rood itself had earlier been removed.[46] In all probability, the reformation of Christ Church was mirrored in churches throughout those parishes where the archbishop exercised effective jurisdiction, yet at the same time, it is no less probable that Curwen organised no campaign to evangelise on behalf of the reformed religion.

The first Protestant bishop appointed to Ireland in Elizabeth's reign was Alexander Craik, a Scotsman, who was appointed as bishop of Kildare and dean of St Patrick's Cathedral, Dublin, on 21 August 1560.[47] His was neither a happy nor a fruitful appointment. He fell ill on arriving in Ireland, and never fully recovered.[48] He very soon regretted his appointment and wrote to Lord Robert Dudley, his patron, 'diverse and sundry times' to be relieved of his office – without a response.[49] He complained that he was in a diocese 'where neither can I preach unto the people nor the people understand me'; one wonders whether

nos xlvii, lv, lvi, lxxxii, lxxxiv, lxxxviii.   42 Ibid., no. xxxiv.   43 John Strype, *The life and acts of Matthew Parker, the first archbishop of Canterbury in the reign of Queen Elizabeth*, i (London, 1711), p. 221; Ronan, *The Reformation in Ireland*, p. 106. Curwen's rebuttal may be read in Shirley, *Original letters*, nos lv, lvi. He was confident that the lord lieutenant and commissioners would vindicate him.   44 SP 63/10/30; Shirley, *Original letters*, no. liii.   45 SP 63/12/7; Shirley, *Original letters*, no. lxii. Brady did have a vested interest in that he wished to see a university founded in place of St Patrick's, but his letter is credible enough.   46 *Loftus' Annals, s.a.* 1560; Raymond Gillespie, 'The shaping of reform, 1558–1625' in Kenneth Milne (ed.), *Christ Church Cathedral, Dublin: a history* (Dublin, 2000), p. 175.   47 *CPCRI*, Eliz., i, 435.   48 Shirley, *Original letters*, nos xxxv, xxxviii, xxxix, xli, xlii.   49 Ibid., no. xxxv.

the inhabitants of Kildare diocese really were so completely ignorant of the English language (or was it Craik's Scottish accent that baffled them?), or whether they just pretended complete ignorance. Craik pleaded repeatedly for preachers to be sent from England to the 'rude realm of Ireland', but he never received a reply.[50]

Craik employed Adam Loftus as his chaplain, but Loftus, ever keen on advancement, soon abandoned Craik and became the lord lieutenant's chaplain instead.[51] Craik succeeded in persuading an acquaintance of his, a rector from Winchester diocese, to go to Ireland – but the minister was sued for non-residence by his bishop and seems to have returned to England.[52] Craik begged Cecil to be allowed to go to England for the sake of his health – but he was obliged to remain in Ireland to die.[53] There was simply no one available to take his place in Kildare. Meanwhile he was beset with crushing financial levies by the crown's administration in Dublin, in the form of demands for first fruits and the payment of the twentieth tax on the benefices in his diocese. Lord Lieutenant Sussex ordered that the claims against Bishop Craik be cancelled, but when Sussex left Ireland in 1562 the bishop was sued by the baron of the exchequer for the first fruits, and by William Basnett, son of an earlier dean of St Patrick's, for the deanery, for which he claimed to possess a lease granted by Henry VIII.[54] Though he desperately sold off parts of Kildare's diocesan assets to meet the financial demands imposed on him, he was imprisoned for debt in the Marshalsea in Dublin, from whence he wrote his last known letter in August 1563.[55] As he feared, his financial troubles did 'abbreviate' his days and he died within a few weeks.[56] His ministry in Kildare seems to have been absolutely fruitless, and his tenure as dean of St Patrick's Cathedral, Dublin, made no discernible impression.

Ever since Dowdall died, Sussex tried to get someone to take his place as archbishop of Armagh, but 'could get none', until he nominated his young chaplain, Adam Loftus, in 1561.[57] He commended Loftus to the queen as someone with 'a vehement zeal in religion, good understanding in the scripture, doctrines and other kinds of learning, continued study, good conversation of life and a bountiful gift of God in utterance'. On 30 October 1561, Elizabeth directed the dean and chapter of Armagh to elect him as archbishop, and she directed Archbishop Curwen to consecrate him.[58] However, Terence O'Donnelly, dean of Armagh, reported that he was unable to get the chapter to assemble at Armagh and indicated that some of the canons were clients of Shane O'Neill, lord of Tyrone.[59] O'Neill was bound to have been hostile to the promotion of an Englishman to Armagh, and that may explain why Elizabeth

---

50 Ibid., nos xxxvii, xxxviii, xxxix, xlii. 51 'Adam Loftus', Helga Robinson-Hammerstein, *ODNB*. 52 Shirley, *Original letters*, no. xli. 53 Ibid., nos xxxviii, xxxix, xli. 54 Ibid., no. xxxix. 55 Ibid., no. xlvi. 56 Ibid., nos xxxix, cxxviii. 57 Ibid., nos xxxvi, xxxvii. 58 Ibid., p. 98. 59 Ibid., no. xlv.

subsequently 'froze' Loftus' appointment to the see. It was not until a year later, on 11 October 1562, that she granted Loftus the revenues of the archdiocese of Armagh and a commission for ecclesiastical causes there, on the recommendation of the lord lieutenant and council of Ireland.[60] Yet, in August 1563, Cecil considered promoting O'Donnelly as the archbishop of Armagh and appointing Loftus to Craik's places as bishop of Kildare and dean of St Patrick's Cathedral, Dublin, while in October 1563, the queen informed Sussex of her intention to promote O'Donnelly as archbishop, while transferring Loftus to Dublin in place of Archbishop Curwen, who would be recalled to England 'as he has oftentimes desired, and as his great years require'.[61] In fact, Loftus had to wait until 1567 for Curwen to be translated, finally, to Oxford, before he was promoted to Dublin.

Meanwhile, on the eve of his translation, Loftus informed Cecil that nothing remained of the diocesan estates of Armagh 'but the bare house and four score acres of ground at Termonfeckin', worth about stg£20 per annum he reckoned. 'Neither is it worth anything to me', he declared, 'nor I able to do any good in it for altogether it lies among the Irish'.[62] It seems clear that Loftus had stripped the archdiocese of Armagh of the greater part of its fixed assets *inter Anglicos*, and that during his episcopate, the Elizabethan reformation made no progress in the most northerly shire of the Pale.

Meath, the most populous diocese in Ireland, was left without a bishop for three years following William Walsh's deprivation in January 1560. Its archdeacon was deprived for non-conformity and was replaced in March 1560 by John Garvey, who subsequently combined that office with that of dean of Christ Church, Dublin, where he chose to reside primarily. It is very difficult to conceive how Dean Garvey would have been able to impose the *Book of Common Prayer* on the parishes in Meath diocese from his deanery in Dublin, without the support of a cathedral chapter (Meath had no chapter), and faced with the challenge of a popular Catholic bishop who actively and openly organised resistance to Protestantism.[63] In 1565, Archbishop Loftus complained about the tremendous influence which Dr Walsh exerted over the people in the Pale in favour of Catholicism.[64] Brendan Scott has reckoned that Walsh played a decisive role in thwarting the Elizabethan reformation in Meath.[65]

An insurmountable problem for the Church of Ireland was the sheer lack of suitable candidates for the episcopal bench. A list of five supposedly eligible clerics for the vacant dioceses of Armagh, Cashel and Ossory in 1561/2 included the pathetically incapable Craik, bishop of Kildare, the almost-dead Bale, former bishop of Ossory, an Oxford-educated dean of Kilkenny whose non-promotion

60 Ibid.   61 Ibid., no. xlvii.   62 Ibid., no. cii.   63 Brian McCabe, 'An Elizabethan prelate: John Garvey (1527–1596)', *Breifne*, 26 (1988), p. 596; Scott, *Tudor diocese of Meath*, pp 55–7; 'Garvey', K.W. Nicholls, *ODNB*.   64 SP 63/14/22.   65 Scott, *Tudor diocese of Meath*, pp 56–7.

reflected his Catholic disposition, someone called Mr Dethick and, remarkably, Thomas Leverous, who had only recently been deprived as bishop of Kildare for refusing the oath of supremacy.[66] On Christmas Day 1561, Bishop Craik was told by Sussex that the queen intended to translate him to Meath, despite his desperate pleading to be allowed to go to England for the sake of his health.[67] That translation did not take place. In the summer of 1562, the number of vacant Irish dioceses was so great, and the number of eligible candidates so few, that a decision was taken to leave Thonery in place in Ossory and Lacey in Limerick, though neither seems to have been prepared to conform to the Elizabethan settlement, and to promote Roger Skiddy, the Marian nominee to Cork & Cloyne, though he was so conservative in religion that Deputy Sidney would oblige him to retire in 1567.[68]

As late as August 1563, Cecil was still contemplating translating Craik to Meath (where someone might understand him), translating Loftus into Craik's places, promoting Terence O'Donnelly as archbishop of Armagh, and promoting the precentor of Armagh in O'Donnelly's place.[69] However, by that time Craik, had been imprisoned for his failure to pay his first fruits – £316, an impossible sum for him to pay – and he was to die within a few weeks afterwards. On 15 October 1563, Elizabeth informed Sussex of her intention to translate Loftus to Dublin, and promote O'Donnelly in Loftus' place, but she failed to translate her intentions into actions.[70] However, a breakthrough of sorts was achieved when she was able to nominate for Meath diocese 'an honest, learned man of that country named Brady, whose learning and sufficiency is here so well recommended upon proof'.[71] Hugh Brady was a native of Meath, an Oxford graduate and professor of divinity, able to preach in English and Irish. Yet Brady's lack of pastoral experience or familiarity with diocesan administration may have hampered his mission to make Meath Protestant: he had been parish priest of Aldermary, London, for just a couple of years prior to his promotion to Meath.[72] He arrived in Dublin on 3 December 1563, and great things were expected of him.[73] However, already by March 1564, he was writing to Cecil that 'being a bishop [in Ireland] is more of a burden than an honour'.[74]

Bishop Brady informed Cecil that outside his diocese of Meath, Archbishop Loftus of Armagh preached 'diligently', Archbishop Curwen of Dublin preached 'now and then', but otherwise there was only one Protestant preacher in Ireland, Mr Beard, vicar of Greenwich, 'a good helper in this business'.[75] Brady and Loftus recommended that Beard be promoted to Kildare in place of the late Bishop Craik, but that never happened and Beard disappears from Irish

66 Shirley, *Original letters*, no. xxxvii.   67 Ibid., no. xxxviii.   68 Ibid., no. xlii.   69 Ibid., no. xlvii.   70 Ibid.   71 Shirley, *Original letters*, no. xlvii.   72 Helen Coburn Walshe, 'The life and career of Hugh Brady, bishop of Meath, 1563–84: ecclesiastical and secular roles in the life of an Irish Elizabethan bishop' (MA, NUIM, 1985), pp 1–11; Scott, *Tudor diocese of Meath*, pp 57–8. 73 Shirley, *Original letters*, no. l.   74 Ibid., no. liii.   75 Ibid., nos lii, liii.

records.[76] Two days after Brady's letter was written, the queen's commissioners for Ireland confirmed that the only Protestant preachers in Ireland were the archbishop of Armagh and the bishop of Meath, 'their diligence in preaching worthy to be commended, especially [Brady of] Meath, ... also one Beard, a preacher who seems honest and preaches well', and the 'civil and conformable' Archbishop Curwen (about whose preaching no comment was made).

It is quite remarkable that more than four years after the Elizabethan religious settlement had been endorsed by the Irish parliament, it was being promoted only by two Protestant bishops, a conformist bishop, and a visiting vicar from England. On that basis alone, the prospects for a Protestant breakthrough must be reckoned to have been slight indeed. The absence of any Protestant preachers in Ireland reflected the complete absence of an indigenous community of Protestants from whence a Protestant ministry could have been recruited. Having said that, with the promotion of Robert Daly, an Irish-born graduate of Oxford and Paris, to the see of Kildare in August 1564, the tally of Protestant bishops in Ireland rose to three, albeit nearly six years since Elizabeth's accession.[77] The failure of the Elizabethan reformation in Ireland may not have been inevitable, but the probability of failure was already high very early in the queen's reign.

RESISTANCE AND ENFORCEMENT

The Elizabethan reformation in Ireland was stymied, not only by an extraordinary lack of Protestant preachers, but also by popular resistance. Brady's letter to Cecil in March 1564 offers real insights into the challenges facing a Protestant bishop in early Elizabethan Ireland:[78]

> O, what a sea of troubles have I entered into; storms rising on every side, the ungodly lawyers are not only sworn enemies of the truth but also for lack of due execution of the law the out-throwers of the country; the ragged clergy are stubborn and ignorantly blind, so as there is little hope of their amendment; the simple multitude is through continual ignorance hardly to be won so, as I find, troubles everywhere.

In simple terms, Brady found himself charged with leading a body of poor clergymen who would not be persuaded to embrace his (Protestant) vision for them, responsible for converting a 'simple multitude' who were 'hardly to be won' to his (Protestant) faith, and confronted with a confident, highly educated

76 Ibid., no. lii.   77 Ibid., p. 149.   78 Ibid., no. liii.

body of noblemen and gentry who were extremely hostile to the Reformation ('sworn enemies to the truth'), and who used their positions in the judiciary and the legal system generally to undermine his efforts to impose religious changes upon them, their families and the wider communities they lived in. Brady was pessimistic about his chances of converting the gentry of Meath; 'the malefactors increase and are emboldened, and the chief ministers discouraged and in effect unabled'. His one hope was that 'a great number of the simple people', especially around his native Dunboyne, were 'greedy hearers' and might be won over to the established religion. In fact, even that modest hope was to be disappointed. Try as he undoubtedly did, Brady was not able to persuade people in any part of his extensive diocese to become Protestants. The absence of a significant number of Protestant preachers clearly hampered the progress of Elizabethan reformation in Ireland, but one should not assume that, had they existed in any significant numbers, Protestant preachers would automatically have achieved conversions: Brady's experiences suggest otherwise.

Bishop Brady was an assiduous preacher, but one preacher could not single-handedly evangelise an entire diocese of more than 200 parishes – it would have taken him more than four years to deliver one sermon in each parish if he visited a different parish each week, not that even that modest tally was actually feasible in practice. Without Protestant ministers, it was not possible to organise preaching tours to counteract the preaching of the friars – but there is no evidence that such tours were ever conceived of, even when there was a sufficient number of Protestant preachers available in later years to make them feasible. Even in Dublin, where the rich cathedral prebends of Christ Church and St Patrick's Cathedrals were remunerative enough to satisfy the expectations of most graduate clergymen, there were no evangelical campaigns.

Brady's concern about the lack of enforcement of the Elizabeth's religious statutes was shared by the queen herself. On 20 October 1563, she sent secret instructions to Sir Thomas Wrothe and Sir Nicholas Arnold, her commissioners for Ireland, directing them to enquire 'in what sorts our laws are there observed for the orders of religion, and what disorders you find therein, and by what causes the same do arise, and to note well who be of our nobility and council therein conformable, and who not'.[79] One must suspect that Sussex had been lax in imposing the queen's religious settlement, probably because of his over-riding pre-occupation with political problems.[80] It is interesting to note that Bishop Craik, who did very little to advance the Reformation, could declare in January 1561 that without Sussex's consent, he did nothing 'as touching the setting forth of God's holy word and the queen's majesty's proceedings'.[81] In April 1564, Archbishop Curwen, who was not very active as an evangelist either, asked the

---

79 *Cal. Carew MSS*, no. 241. 80 His willingness to embrace Protestantism is suggested by his employing Loftus as his chaplain. 81 Shirley, *Original letters*, no. xxxvii.

queen and Cecil to enquire of Sussex for a positive assessment of his tepid ministry in Dublin.[82] Bishop Brady was clear in his letter of 14 March 1564 that there was little or no enforcement of the religious laws.[83]

The queen's commissioners' tardy response on 16 March 1564 to her enquiries of the previous October confirmed Brady's lament about the lack of enforcement, though they were (naively?) more optimistic than he was about the prospects for future progress.[84] Rather than provide the queen with a detailed report about how the religious laws were being enforced, they informed her that 'those we have to do with we find conformable to laws' – presumably a reference to the men in authority in the Dublin administration – while the judges and other lawyers in the Pale seemed to them 'ready' to enforce the religious laws in the future (whatever about the past), 'and accordingly have promised us *now* in the assizes and sessions to enquire specially of defaulters against those laws of religion'. Yet the scale of non-conformity was such that officials were directed to 'meddle not with the simple multitude now at first, but with one or two boasting Mass men in every shire – that it may be seen that the punishment of such men in meant'. The significance of the commissioners' report has been lost on most modern commentators: it points to the extreme difficulty faced by the English crown in imposing the Elizabethan religious settlement effectively in the face of the hostility of some determined and confident recusants (the 'boasting Mass men'), and the hostility or disinclination of the 'simple multitude'. The queen's commissioners reported to her that there were only two 'good' bishops in Ireland, Brady and Loftus, and the 'civil and conformable' Curwen, but otherwise 'the rest of the bishops, as we hear, be all Irish – *we need say no more*'.

Elizabeth was anxious, nonetheless, to extend her reformation beyond the Pale, and to strengthen its enforcement within the Pale itself. On 9 June 1564, she established a commission to exercise her ecclesiastical jurisdiction in Counties Carlow, Kilkenny, Waterford, Cork, Kerry, Limerick and Tipperary, with power to correct heresies and other offences and to tender the oath of supremacy to all persons there 'as may seem good to them' (in other words, circumspectly).[85] A similar commission was established for Connacht and Thomond.[86] These commissions probably made little impression in their respective spheres of operation.

On 6 October 1564, the queen informed Sussex of her intention to establish an Ecclesiastical High Commission for the ordering of all ecclesiastical causes in Ireland under the chairmanship of the Church of Ireland primate, Archbishop Loftus of Armagh, and comprising also of Bishops Brady of Meath, O'Fihilly of Leighlin and Daly of Kildare, Terence O'Donnelly, dean of Armagh, the earl of Kildare, and the lay members of the council of Ireland as commissioners.

---

82 Ibid., nos lv, lvi. 83 Ibid., no. liii. 84 Ibid., no. liv. 85 *Fiants, Ire., Eliz.*, no. 666.
86 Ibid., nos 667–8.

This body reflected the queen's new determination to advance her reformation, particularly in the Pale.[87] It was directed to

> enquire into any heretical opinions, seditious books, conspiracies, false rumours, tales, slanderous words or sayings, published or invented by any person or persons against her majesty or the laws and statutes of the realm ...; of any disturbance or misbehaviour committed in any church or chapel, or against divine service; and to enquire, order, correct all such persons as should obstinately absent themselves from church and divine services as by law established; authorising them to visit, reform and redress in all places, all errors, heresies, schisms, spiritual or ecclesiastical by censure or ecclesiastical deprivation, for the increase of virtue, the pleasure of God, the preservation of peace and the unity of the realm.

The queen's commissioners were empowered to hear and determine a range of ecclesiastical causes and were to

> devise politic ways and means for the performance of this duty, and upon due proof to award such punishment, by fine or imprisonment as to them shall seem expedient ... and as there are still in the realm diverse perverse and obstinate persons who refuse to acknowledge her majesty's prerogative and to observe the ceremonies and rites in [the] divine service established by law, her majesty directs the commissioners to cause all archbishops, bishops and other ecclesiastical officers or ministers to subscribe the oath contained in the statute ... and if any ... refuse to take the oath, their refusal is to be certified into chancery without delay.

Loftus took the initiative and had the Ecclesiastical High Commission summon juries from 'all of the several parishes within the English Pale' to make presentments regarding 'all manner disorders and offences' committed against the queen's laws and injunctions concerning 'causes ecclesiastical'.[88] Loftus sent a report of their findings to Elizabeth in May 1565 (telling her that the other commissioners were 'contented to put the chief care and, in a manner, the whole burden on me'). A careful reading of Loftus' letter should dispel the prevailing misapprehension that the general response to the Elizabethan reformation in anglicised Ireland is best characterised as 'church papistry'.

Loftus informed the queen that he discovered, 'by their own confessions', that the 'greater part ... the greatest part' of the nobility and other landowners

---

87 SP 63/9/51. 88 SP 63/10/42; Shirley, *Original letters*, no. lxx.

of the Pale had 'continually' frequented the Mass and other Catholic services
over the past five years since the Irish parliament of 1560, while 'very few of
them' had ever attended Protestant Church services or received holy
communion according to the rites of the Elizabethan Church of Ireland. This is
not a reflection of 'church papistry', but of recusancy on a scale unknown
anywhere in contemporary England or Wales. Nor was the problem confined to
the social élites, for Loftus' survey found other 'many and great offences'
committed by the lower orders too.

Loftus explained to the queen that the scale of non-conformity in the Pale
was such, particularly among the nobility and leading gentlemen who, he
informed her, 'condemned your majesty's most godly laws and proceedings more
manifestly than the rest', that 'we shall never be able to correct them by the
ordinary course of the statute'. He proposed that 'a good round fine and sum of
money' be taken from the leading men as recognizances for future conformity,
and suggested that 'their example should be a great cause to bring the rest and
meaner sort to a godly reformation', but he held back from taking any action
without first knowing the queen's pleasure. In fact, it is not likely that she would
have considered Loftus' call for permission to deal 'sharply' with the Catholic
nobility and gentry as the 'politic ways and means' she had in mind to enforce
conformity to the Church of Ireland. Loftus beseeched Cecil in July 1565 for
some response from the queen regarding what he should do about the lords and
gentlemen of the Pale.[89] He received no known response from the queen.

Meanwhile, the Ecclesiastical High Commission took action against those
who were more vulnerable to its operations. Robert Daly, who had been
appointed as the bishop of Kildare in August 1564, informed Cecil in July 1565
that a controversy concerning the use of vestments in the Church of England
had emboldened Catholics in Ireland so much that the Ecclesiastical
Commissioners 'dare not be so bold in executing the said commission as we have
been unto this time'.[90] He asked Cecil for reassurance to 'confirm the wavering
hearts of the doubtful and also suppress the stout brags of the sturdy and proud
Papists'. Daly's reference to the 'wavering hearts' may reflect some tentative
progress in imposing conformity, but there was clearly very strong opposition
being offered by determined and confident Catholics. Brady of Meath lamented
that 'all things waxeth rather worse than otherwise and, as I said before, I fear
me, without some speedy redress, the whole body will be so sick as it shall with
difficulty recover, so frowardly be men here disposed'.[91] No doubt he was
encountering increased hostility because of the operation of the Ecclesiastical
High Commission.

On 13 July 1565, the Ecclesiastical Commission imprisoned Dr William
Walsh, Catholic bishop of Meath, in Dublin Castle, because he refused to

89 Shirley, *Original letters*, no. lxxi.   90 Ibid., no. lxxiii.   91 Ibid.

subscribe to the oath of supremacy yet again. Archbishop Loftus informed Cecil that 'he openly protested before all the people the same day he was before us that he would never communicate or be present (by his will) where the [Protestant] service should be ministered, for it was against his conscience and (as he thought) against God's word'. Loftus beseeched Cecil for directions as to what to do with Walsh, for he was a man 'of great credit amongst his countrymen'.[92] He suggested that Walsh be sent to England, where some Protestant bishops might be able to persuade him to 'some conformity'. In fact, Walsh was not sent to England, nor persuaded to conform. Instead, he remained imprisoned until 1569, when he resumed his campaign against the Reformation.

A memorandum among the *State papers* reflects the crown's concern to 'cause the people to resort to *Common Prayer*'.[93] In 1563, a fine seems to have been instituted on the heads of any households in Dublin who refused to attend the Elizabethan service in their parish church on Sundays.[94] The existence of churchwardens in many parishes in Dublin and throughout the inner Pale no doubt facilitated that compulsion in the initial stages of the Elizabethan reformation, though at some point during the Tudor reformations, the office of churchwarden ceased to exist in most parishes outside of Dublin and some larger towns.

For want of evidence, one cannot even guess at the number of parishes, even in the Pale, in which the secular and ecclesiastical authorities were able to compel people to attend their local parish church or chapel after the displacement of the Catholic liturgies by the Elizabethan *Book of Common Prayer*. Yet it seems that strong antipathy among many of those compelled to attend Protestant services reflected itself in disrespectful and disruptive behaviour during services. Sussex himself, no less, complained to Cecil that that the clergymen who conformed to the Elizabethan Church were held 'in contempt', and that the people who attended church services 'come to divine service as to a May game'[95] – I presume that their disruptiveness reflected their resentment at being forced to attend the Protestant services under duress. Sussex declared that 'our religion is so abused as the Papists rejoice'. He observed that the problem was so great that no commission would be sufficient to tackle it and he proposed that parliamentary legislation be enacted to set down requisite 'limits in religion and discipline', with 'such severe orders for punishment of the breakers thereof as men may fear to go beyond or come short'. When establishing the Irish Ecclesiastical High Commission in 1564, Elizabeth directed it to tackle both those who 'obstinately absent themselves from Church and divine service as by law established', and those responsible for 'any disturbance or misbehaviour committed or perpetrated in any church or chapel, or against divine service'.[96] Clearly, the problems

92 Ibid., no. lxxvii.   93 Ronan, *Reformation in Ireland*, p. 138.   94 Loftus' annals, *s.a.* 1563.
95 Shirley, *Original letters*, no. xliv.   96 *PCRI, Eliz.*, i, pp 489–90.

of absence from Church of Ireland services, and recalcitrant disruptions by those forced to attend its services, were persistent and considerable.

The open and strong hostility that characterised the reaction to the Elizabethan religious settlement, even in the Pale, was not simply a reflection of the limited enforcement of the settlement – the enforcement was limited because the leaders of society even in the most anglicised parts of Ireland (the 'ungodly lawyers') were hostile to the queen's religious settlement. The corollary of that is that popular attachment to Catholicism remained strong across Ireland, and the people were generally immune to the appeal of Protestantism. The queen's commissioners in March 1564 declared that it was 'hard to persuade willingness to hear the truth soberly taught'.[97] Deputy Sidney observed in 1566 that the Elizabethan reformation progressed but slowly, because of 'the former errors and superstitions inveterated and leavened in the people's hearts'.[98]

AN IRISH UNIVERSITY

Bishop Brady quickly reached the conclusion that he would not be able to deploy his 'stubborn and ignorantly blind' clergy to convert their parishioners.[99] Instead, he hoped to create a Protestant ministry in Meath *de novo* and he made the fateful assumption that it could only be formed through an education in an *Irish* university. The prospects for an Irish university seemed promising early in Elizabeth's reign. In October 1563, the queen herself informed the commissioners who governed Ireland in her name of her intention to erect some public schools in Dublin, and she directed them to consider how St Patrick's Cathedral, Dublin, might be converted into a university.[1] The commissioners invested considerable energy in the project, but they made little progress. They informed Cecil that they doubted that the proposal would be well-received for, even in the central government, 'there be amongst us few earnest favourers of religion but [John Parker] the Master of the Rolls'. Nonetheless, they compiled a survey of the assets of the cathedral, and Wrothe personally addressed the English privy council on the subject – but nothing materialised.[2] Consequently, the commissioners waited for further instructions from the queen as to how best to proceed on the university question.

Archbishop Curwen, for his part, was adamant in his opposition to the proposal to dissolve St Patrick's, and offered ecclesiastical and political reasons for that opposition.[3] He declared that 'a university will be but of small profit [in Ireland] for here be no promotions to bestow upon clerics when they be learned'. He argued that were the dissolution of St Patrick's to proceed, the archbishop

97 Shirley, *Original letters*, no. liv.   98 Ibid., no. lxxxii.   99 Shirley, *Original letters*, no. liii.
1 *Cal. Carew MSS*, no. 241.   2 Shirley, *Original letters*, no. lxxxii.   3 Ibid., no. lviii.

'shall not be able to have one learned man to preach the word of God in his diocese', for want of a benefice sufficiently endowed to support one. He pointed out that the prebends of the senior cathedral clergy consisted of parochial benefices that ought to be staffed by mature clergymen, and not be given over to young scholars. He also pointed out that while the price of corn in the Pale was high at that time, and so too were tithes in consequence, the value of the prebends would fall if the price of corn fell back, with implications for the viability of the university project. He also argued that

> the Irish enemy under colour of study [in the proposed university] would send their friends hither who would learn the secrets of the country, and advertise them thereof, so that the Irish rebels would by them know the privacy of the Pale, whereof we are likely to grow no small hurt.

It is not clear how much weight the queen attached to Curwen's arguments, but the university proposal was not advanced for a time. It seems clear to me that the fundamental problem hampering the university project was simply a lack of finance: the idea of converting the assets of St Patrick's Cathedral to the endowment of a university was deceptively appealing, but once provision had been made for the staffing of the many parish churches impropriated to the cathedral, and for the maintenance of their chancels, as well as providing pensions for the many well-salaried staff of the cathedral who would be made redundant, only a fraction of the cathedral's assets would be left available for endowing the proposed university. The parsimonious queen was never likely to make good the sizeable shortfall, so the project inevitably languished.

In the absence of an Irish university, the advocates of the Elizabethan reformation in Ireland floundered. They could only think in terms of applying the English Reformation model, with universities educating a Protestant graduate ministry for the parishes, to Ireland. They seem not to have considered the validity of Curwen's (very well-founded) doubts as to whether the Elizabethan Church of Ireland was capable of supporting the financial expectations of a graduate ministry in the mid-sixteenth century.

The advocates of Elizabeth's reformation in Ireland seem not to have realised that distance from a university, by itself, was not the greatest obstacle to Irish students acquiring an education in a Protestant university: even in the earliest years of Elizabeth's reign, there were Irish students travelling considerable distances overseas to Catholic universities on mainland Europe, particularly those at Louvain and Paris. Given the choice, a greater proportion of young Irishmen, and their families, opted for Catholic rather than Protestant universities in Elizabeth's reign, regardless of the distances involved. The advocates of the Elizabethan reformation in Ireland seem not to have considered the options of sponsoring or at least partially subsiding Irish students who might attend England's universities (though some bursaries were made available to Irish students in continental colleges by the pope and Holy Roman emperor). In any case, it would be wrong to automatically assume that an Irish student in a Protestant school or university would inevitably embrace Protestantism – though several Irish Protestant clergymen were, in fact, educated in England's universities. Thus, it remained the case that there was a severe lack of Irish Protestant graduate clergymen available for promotion in the Elizabethan Church of Ireland, fewer even than the number of benefices available that were rich enough to support such graduates' lifestyle aspirations.

The advocates of the Elizabethan reformation failed to devise an alternative strategy for creating a Protestant ministry in Ireland, or for evangelisation, without an Irish university. They made no discernible efforts to convert their clergymen or, if they made such efforts, they soon resigned themselves to failure. They seem to have accepted that nothing more was to be expected of the parish clergy than a nominal conformity; that they read the *Book of Common Prayer* in Latin in their churches and a 'blind eye' was turned to the discreet celebration of Catholic sacraments for layfolk by priests who literally could not afford to ignore the wishes of their parishioners. There was no provision of even a basic minister's manual with a basic outline of the knowledge and standards required of Elizabeth's clergy. The Protestant catechism of John O'Kearney of 1571 was an eclectic mix of materials, hardly likely to inspire many conversions to 'true religion', and in any case it was printed in numbers too small to be distributed even to all of the Irish-speaking clergymen of the Pale.[4]

In the absence of an Irish university, a more humble training institute for the clergy of the Elizabethan Church, a seminary of some kind, modelled on the friary schools for training their members, or even the traditional *studia particularia*, would have been relatively inexpensive to operate and yet would have been pastorally effective – as the friars demonstrated. Of course, Bishop Brady operated a free school in his diocese, but the purpose of such schools was not to train clergymen, though it may have provided a grounding in Latin grammar, which a clerical student would find helpful subsequently – if any local student had been drawn to a career in the Elizabethan Church of Ireland.

In sum, the fixation with establishing an Irish university, despite the obvious ongoing problems of having one established and financed, distracted the minuscule number of Protestant reformers in Ireland from considering alternative options, and ensured that in the absence of an Irish university or of many Irish graduates from England's universities, there remained a severe dearth of Protestant preachers to promote the Elizabethan reformation in Ireland

4 Brian Ó Cuív (ed.), *Aibidil Gaoidheilge & caiticiosma: Seaán Ó Cearnaigh's Irish primer of religion published in 1571* (Dublin, 1994).

throughout the later sixteenth century. In their steads, the Elizabethan Church of Ireland had generally to make do with priests who were Catholic by background, education, training and disposition. Arguably, by the time an Irish university was eventually founded in 1592, it was too late to affect the outcome of the Elizabethan reformation in Ireland.

CATHOLIC MISSION

By contrast with its counterpart in lowland England, the Catholic Church in Ireland did not experience a catastrophic collapse following the parliamentary enactment of the Elizabethan settlement. In fact, the papacy was relatively quick to appoint a new Catholic primate in succession to Archbishop Dowdall, and a papal commissary to spearhead a *counter*-reformation in Ireland. In terms of human and physical resources, the Catholic mission was initially very modest indeed, but it was able to harness a continuing commitment to Catholicism among many of the clergy and lay men and women in Ireland, across social and geographical divides, and a more general popular sympathy among those who may have been less committed. Some of its key figures, including David Wolfe, SJ, and Richard Creagh, were undoubtedly remarkable figures in themselves, but one must observe that a key reason why they were so much more effective in the battle for souls than their Protestant counterparts is that they preached a message that their Catholic fellow countrymen were well-disposed to hear.

On 7 January 1560, Pope Pius IV appointed Donat O'Taig, a priest of Limerick diocese, as the archbishop of Armagh and primate of all Ireland in succession to Primate Dowdall.[5] O'Taig seems to have been consecrated in Rome before travelling to Ireland and exercising his ministry. He was active in his diocese and ecclesiastical province during his short episcopate.[6]

In August 1560, Pius IV appointed David Wolfe, SJ, another Limerick man, as papal commissary in Ireland, and charged him with responsibility for encouraging the nobles and bishops of Ireland to remain loyal to the Catholic faith, for reforming the clergy and maintaining ecclesiastical discipline, for proposing suitable candidates to Rome for bishoprics and other greater benefices and for providing them with testimonials, for reorganising some of the religious houses and hospitals, for erecting colleges and academies for the youth in Ireland, and for absolving all persons in all cases, especially in cases of heresy and schism.[7] It was, needless to say, an impossibly ambitious remit, given the extent of English

5 W.P. O'Brien, 'Two sixteenth-century Munster primates: Donnchadh O Taidhg (1560–2) and Richard Creagh (1564–85)', *SAM*, 14 (1990), pp 37–41. 6 Brady, *Episcopal succession*, i, p. 219; O'Brien, 'Two Munster primates', p. 40. 7 Wolfe was once dean of Limerick, but he joined the Society of Jesus in 1554: Moran, *Archbishops of Dublin*, pp 78–9; 'Wolfe', Thomas J. Morrisey, *ODNB*.

power in Ireland, and the political fragmentation that characterised most of the country. Nonetheless, Wolfe came highly recommended by the General of the Jesuits, and he proved to be extremely able and energetic in Ireland.[8] He was able to exercise a significant influence on the Church throughout Ireland, including the Pale, where he was active both in person and through his deputy, a Dublin priest named Thady Newman.

It is very difficult to know what actually was expected of Wolfe: my own interpretation is that his was a 'holding mission', to confirm Irish Catholics in their faith until such time as Elizabeth 'returned' to the Catholic Church. Of course, the assumption that Elizabeth could have become a Catholic was naïve and unrealistic, but that illusory possibility was nourished at Rome throughout the first decade of her reign. Wolfe was not authorised nor directed to establish a parallel Church organisation to that of the Elizabethan establishment – he was to maintain the *status quo* as far as possible. Interestingly, as late as 1565, when Elizabeth clashed with some of her more Protestant clergy about the ornamentation of the royal chapel, it was interpreted in Ireland as a sign of her impending 'return' to Rome.[9]

David Wolfe landed in Cork on 20 January 1561. He found the people of southern Ireland much given to vice (in terms of infringing the Church's sexual regulations) but free from heresy.[10] He made his way to his home city of Limerick, where he had familial support and also the support of the bishop, Hugh Lacey. The papal commissary established his primary base in Limerick, though he travelled far and wide. He stated that 'no one, either heretic or Catholic', was unaware of his mission, since he had it publicised 'in every part of the country'.[11]

Wolfe sent a report to Rome detailing the condition of the Church in Munster in 1561 but, unfortunately, it has not survived. In it, he reported that all of the bishops in the southern province were 'adherents of the queen'.[12] Given the bishop of Limerick's active support for his mission, I believe that that phrase of Wolfe's refers to a political adherence and not a doctrinal allegiance. Wolfe visited Archbishop Bodkin of Tuam and, in October 1561, he forwarded a positive assessment of the archbishop to Rome, despite Bodkin's subscription to the Elizabethan oath of supremacy.[13] He reported that Bodkin became archbishop by royal authority, and established himself through force of arms, and that he recovered Tuam Cathedral for the Church

> by force and at great personal risk, and rededicated it to its proper uses; and where of yore there were but horses and other beasts, now Mass is sung and said, and he himself is daily in the choir ... He is in

8 'Wolfe', T.J. Morrisey, *ODNB.* 9 Shirley, *Original letters*, no. lxxiii. 10 Hogan, *Ibernia Ignatiana*, pp 10–13; Ronan, *Reformation in Ireland*, p. 41. 11 Ronan, *Reformation in Ireland*, p. 91. 12 *CSP Rome, 1558–71*, no. 108. 13 Ibid.

good repute with all, even with his enemies, the former possessors of the church.

Wolfe recommended to Rome that Bodkin be recognised as the legitimate Catholic archbishop of Tuam, because 'he is a man that knows how to govern, and is in good repute with the magnates of the country'. Already, Wolfe treated Bodkin as a Catholic bishop: he had Bodkin summon a canon of Kilmacduagh to appear before him, and swear an oath on the gospels to help resolve a dispute concerning the authenticity of alleged papal dispensations.[14] In 1563, Hugh O'Carollan, bishop of Clogher, appealed to Rome to appoint Wolfe, or his deputy/deputies, to decide in his suit against one Cornelius McArdle who had procured a papal provision and employed temporal support to take the bishop's place.[15]

Wolfe was instrumental in having a number of Catholic bishops appointed in Ireland. Late in 1561, he nominated Eugene O'Harte, a Dominican friar, to Achonry as one who was likely by his good life and the support of his friends to recover Achonry Cathedral for the Church, as Bodkin had done at at Tuam.[16] He nominated Andrew O'Crean, another Dominican, to Elphin.[17] Thomas O'Herlihy, a diocesan priest, was nominated to Ross diocese, and Dónal McCongail, also a diocesan priest and a trusted associate of the papal commissary, was nominated to Raphoe.[18] Bishops O'Harte, O'Herlihy and McCongail attended the final session of the Council of Trent in 1562.[19] They participated in a number of the discussions in the council. During the eighteen months they spent there, they subsisted on a small pension from the pope. On their return to Ireland, there is some fragmentary evidence to show that they strove to give effect to the decrees of the Council of Trent. The bishops of Achonry, Elphin and Killala convened a synod for the ecclesiastical province of Tuam in 1566, which endorsed the Tridentine decrees.[20] A synod for the ecclesiastical province of Armagh promulgated the Tridentine decrees in 1568.[21] Evidence for the introduction of the Tridentine decrees elsewhere is wanting, but one may safely assume that it proved to be a protracted process to enforce general compliance to the novel decrees of Trent without the support of a centralised government, especially in the face of some hostility from the English crown.

Wolfe's mission was not confined to the south, west and north of Ireland. In a letter of 1572, he could claim to know the nobility and other gentlemen of

14 Moran, *Archbishops of Dublin*, p. 86.   15 Ronan, *Reformation in Ireland*, pp 91–2.
16 Hogan, *Ibernia Ignatiana*, pp 12–13; Brady, *Episcopal succession*, ii, p. 187; Flynn, *The Dominicans*, pp 57–9.   17 Brady, *Episcopal succession*, ii, pp 200–1.   18 Moran, *Archbishops of Dublin*, p. 88.   19 Ibid., p. 77.   20 Brady, 'Ireland and the Council of Trent', p. 193; Flynn, *The Dominicans*, p. 60.   21 Edward Rogan, *Synods and catechesis in Ireland, c.445–1962* (Rome, 1987), p. 27; S.A. Meigs, *The reformations in Ireland: tradition and confessionalism, 1400–1690* (London and New York, 1997), p. 75.

Meath, and their religious dispositions, extremely well. In a commission of 7 December 1563, he deputed to Thady Newman, a priest of Dublin diocese, the power to absolve in all cases of schism and heresy in Leinster, where Wolfe himself would be in greatest danger of arrest.[22] Already William Walsh, the deposed bishop of Meath, was actively promoting resistance to Protestantism. Archbishop Loftus wrote in 1565 that ever since the 1560 parliament, Walsh had 'manifestly condemned and openly showed himself to be a misliker of all the queen's majesty's proceedings'.[23] Loftus stated that 'he is one of great credit amongst his countrymen, and upon whom (touching causes of religion) they wholly depend'. The fact that the nobility and gentry of the Pale enjoyed 'continual' provision of the Mass and other Catholic services, according to the survey conducted by Loftus under the aegis of the Ecclesiastical High Commission in 1565, may even suggest the possibility that Walsh had been involved in organising a Catholic pastoral network in the Pale to parallel that of the established Church wherever the *Book of Common Prayer* was used in the parish churches or chapels.

It is not clear from Loftus' summary of the High Commission's findings in 1565 who precisely celebrated the Mass and other Catholic services throughout the Pale. One might suspect that some such services were celebrated by at least some of the Catholic priests who outwardly conformed to the Elizabethan religious settlement (and there is certainly clear evidence from the 1570s of conforming priests in Meath diocese doing just that).[24] However, there were also English Catholic priests who came to Ireland after the establishment of the Elizabethan Church of England, and one suspects that some of them may have found employment as chaplains in the homes of wealthy landowners or merchants.[25] There were also Irish Catholic priests who chose not to conform to the new religious establishment. In 1563, Lord Lieutenant Sussex felt obliged to issue a proclamation forbidding Catholic priests and friars from convening meetings within Dublin, or residing within its walls – a striking reflection of the continuing strength of the Catholic Church within the capital itself.[26] A community of Observant Franciscan friars is known to have maintained an existence at Multyfarnham, and a community of Dominican friars appear to have maintained an existence at Mullingar, throughout Elizabeth's reign.[27] From such bases, just outside the inner Pale, the friars could operate extensive preaching tours reaching into the very heart of the Pale itself – and there were many other mendicant communities operating elsewhere in Ireland.

The role of the friars in resisting the Elizabethan reformation has often been commented on, if not always understood. One of their primary contributions to the survival of Catholicism was their provision of effective preachers, who could

---

22 Shirley, *Original letters*, no. xlix. 23 Ibid., no. lxxvii. 24 W.M. Brady (ed.), *State papers concerning the Irish Church* (London, 1868), no. xi. 25 SP 63/2/9. 26 Loftus' annals, *s.a.* 1563. 27 Bradshaw, *The dissolution*, p. 141; Scott, *Tudor diocese of Meath*, pp 109–11.

appeal directly to receptive audiences, and operate at a fraction of the cost of educating, training and waging their preaching counterparts in the Elizabethan Church of Ireland. Too many modern historians tend to explain the failure of the Elizabethan reformation in Ireland by reference to a supposed lack of resources to educate and employ Protestant preachers. The Irish mendicant communities showed what could be achieved with very limited resources, and a lot of religious zeal. However, one must take care not to give the friars an exaggerated importance in the immediate aftermath of the 1560 parliament. Not until the 1570s are they identified as a major obstacle to the Elizabethan reformation in Ireland, though the 1563 proclamation issued in Dublin shows that they were already active in sustaining a popular attachment to Catholicism. It is unclear whether the increased references to the friars in the 1570s reflected an upsurge in mendicant numbers and activities at that time – or simply that the crown authorities were receiving better intelligence – I think that both possibilities are probable, with the likelihood that the increased information reaching the authorities on the activities of the friars tended to exaggerate a real increase in mendicant activity at a later date. Nonetheless, it does seem that there was a revival of some kind in the fortunes of several mendicant communities in the second half of the sixteenth century, following a nadir that coincided with the crown-sponsored dissolution of religious houses under Henry VIII and Edward VI, but also a wider collapse in confidence that affected houses beyond the crown's reach.[28]

Another group of clergymen who were destined to play a critical role in the survival of the Catholic Church in Ireland were the continentally trained priests. By the later 1570s, they were relatively numerous, particularly in the south, but they were already a cause of great concern in government circles by 1564.[29] Evidently it came to the attention of the crown's administration in Dublin that Thady Newman, Wolfe's deputy in Leinster, had been recruiting priests and aspirant priests for Catholic colleges overseas. Memoranda among the Irish state papers in August 1564 directed that Newman be questioned on the matter, and an enquiry was to be made at Waterford of Denis McVard, to secure information about priests being shipped to Antwerp for the university of Louvain.[30] The master of the ordnance was directed to apprehend Malachy Quinn and Sir Richard, the clerk of Wicklow Church, who were on their way to Waterford: Newman and another priest named Edmund Quinn (who was probably the same person as Turlough Luineach O'Neill's chaplain and secretary at a later date, and possibly a relative of Malachy Quinn) had undertaken to provide money for the journey and for the education of the student. Enquiry was also to be made about a 'Thomas Fitzgerald [who] had written unto his brother Sir Peter Fitzgerald

28 Flynn, *The Dominicans*, pp 44–71. 29 SP 63/11/81; Ronan, *Reformation in Ireland*, pp 113–14. 30 SP 63/11/81.

who is in Paris' (the designation of 'Sir' probably denotes that Peter was a priest), and about an Oliver Fitzgerald who was to be sent to Peter in Paris. It was also to be asked 'who is the archdeacon that provides for John White, scholar at Louvain, [and] that provides for James White'. The memoranda mention a James Comerford at Waterford who had written to his brother Nicholas who was at Louvain on 14 August and identified himself as being 'of the old religion'.

These memoranda offer a very rare insight into how the Catholic Church was organising itself against the Elizabethan reformation. They point to the existence of some kind of network for the education of Irish Catholics, of both Gaelic Irish and English descent, in Catholic colleges overseas soon after the 1560 parliament. The papal commissary's deputy, Newman, was directly involved, physically and financially, in supporting priests and clerical students going to continental colleges for further study, and Denis McVard was obviously heavily involved also. The memoranda point to the critical role of families in sponsoring the priests/clerical students in their studies at Louvain and Paris, and also the role of some clergymen as sponsors, including the archdeacon whom the crown's officials were keen to identify.

Richard Creagh, one of the best-known Irish scholars to study at Louvain, well exemplifies the pattern reflected in the state papers.[31] Creagh was from a strongly Catholic family in Limerick. In 1549, as the Edwardian reformation began to be imposed on Ireland in earnest, he entered the university at Louvain.[32] He was exempted from matriculation fees and other expenses on account of his poverty, and he was awarded a bursary by the almoner of the Holy Roman emperor, Charles V. He was also supported by his family: on one occasion his brother travelled to Louvain with £32 for Creagh, but the money was confiscated by the 'searcher at Dover'.[33] Among the other students who matriculated with Creagh in February 1549 was an Irishman named John Nilannus (O'Neill?), and another named Morgan from Kildare.[34] Another contemporary student at Louvain was Dermot O'Hurley, the future archbishop of Cashel, who was to be executed in 1584.[35] According to Creagh, David Wolfe, another Limerick man, had been seven years in Rome before being sent back to Ireland by the pope in 1560.[36] That suggests that he decided to go overseas and become a Jesuit in response to Edward VI's reformation – paralleling Creagh's decision to embrace the counter-reformation.

Creagh impressed the Jesuit general, Ignatius of Loyola, sufficiently for him to recommend him to Cardinal Pole as a worthy candidate for the see of Limerick once William Casey, 'a public Lutheran', had been deposed under Queen Mary for having been married – but Creagh refused the cardinal's offer of promotion.[37] He returned to Limerick instead *c.*1557 and established a school

31 Lennon, *Archbishop Creagh*. 32 Ibid., pp 37–8. 33 Ibid., pp 38–9. 34 Ibid., p. 38.
35 Ibid. 36 Shirley, *Original letters*, no. lxiv.

in the former Dominican friary in the city under the patronage of the earl of Desmond.[38] He was joined by Thomas Leverous, the deposed bishop of Kildare, in 1560. Together, these men provided a decidedly Catholic education in south-western Ireland. Creagh produced a book entitled *Epitome officii hominis Christiani*, a catechism in Irish and English, with Latin explanations, encapsulating the decrees of the first two sessions of the Council of Trent.[39] Here is definite evidence of the early propagation of the counter-reformation in Ireland.

Dr Peter White operated a similar academy in Kilkenny, combining high quality teaching with zealous Catholic faith.[40] Among the progeny of such Catholic schools were to number many scholars who went on to study in Catholic colleges overseas, as well as laymen who were committed to the Catholic religion. White's academy has been credited as 'the single most positive and most effective incident responsible for the failure of the Reformation in Waterford city', while it has also been credited with a most important role in maintaining the Catholic faith throughout the Ormond territories.[41] One may reasonably suspect that the communities of Franciscan and Dominican friars who operated from Waterford in the 1560s were also important in shaping the local (strongly negative) responses to the Elizabethan reformation.[42] Nonetheless, the Catholic schools were certainly critically important in ensuring that commitment to the Catholic religion was inculcated in the next generation.

Richard Creagh left Ireland for Rome in August 1562 on the directions of David Wolfe, who obliged him to go under the terms of an oath that Creagh had sworn to obey the pope while at Louvain.[43] Wolfe recommended Creagh as 'a man exceedingly renowned for his life and learning', and suitable to be made an archbishop.[44] Wolfe provided Creagh with forty crowns for his journey, Bishop Lacey of Limerick gave him twelve marks, while Creagh had twenty crowns of his own.[45] Creagh was supported by the pope during his sojourn in Rome.

In March 1564, Pope Pius VI appointed Creagh as the archbishop of Armagh in succession to Donat O'Tadhg, who had been arrested by the English and who died shortly afterwards. Creagh was given a commission for himself, as the primate of all Ireland, and for David Wolfe, as papal nuncio, which insisted on the enforcement of the decrees of Trent, but which also reflected some of the realities facing the commissioners in Ireland.[46] They were directed to promulgate the decrees of the Council of Trent in Ireland, and they were to proceed

37 Lennon, *Archbishop Creagh*, pp 40–1. 38 Ibid., p. 42. 39 Lennon suggests that it may have been based on a catechism published in Louvain in 1556: Lennon, *Archbishop Creagh*, pp 44–5. 40 Colm Lennon, 'Pedagogy and reform: the influence of Peter White on Irish scholarship in the Renaissance' in Thomas Herron and Michael Potterton (eds), *Ireland in the Renaissance, c.1540–1660* (Dublin, 2007), pp 43–51; Colm Lennon, *Richard Stanihurst: the Dubliner, 1547–1618* (Dublin, 1981), pp 24–6. 41 Byrne, 'Reformation in Tudor Waterford', p. 31. 42 W.M. Brady, *The Irish reformation* (London, 1867), p. 179; Byrne, 'Reformation in Tudor Waterford', p. 30. 43 Shirley, *Original letters*, no. lxiv. 44 Lennon, *Archbishop Creagh*, pp 48–9. 45 Shirley, *Original letters*, no. lxiv.

against all churchmen, including bishops or archbishops, who were tainted with simony, the open keeping of concubines or with the unlawful usurpation of ecclesiastical benefices, and also against regulars of dissolute and scandalous life, regardless of which mendicant order they belonged to, according to the canons of the Council of Trent, and other canonical regulations. They were to prohibit the practice of 'Rome-running' for benefices, but instead provide testimonials for those they considered fit for promotion. There was also a dispensation made available for those who could not gain access to fish during times of fasting, such as Lent, allowing them to eat dairy produce instead.

However, in view of the difficult circumstances in which the Catholic Church was obliged to minister in Elizabethan Ireland, the pope granted his commissioners the authority to unite vacant dioceses to the sees of neighbouring bishops as they saw fit, on condition that they kept Rome notified of their intentions, and set aside sufficient revenues for the maintenance of the cathedral church of the vacant see, and its ornaments. They were authorised to transfer cathedras from any cathedral church 'oppressed by heretics' to churches in neighbouring towns or any other places where Catholic services could be celebrated more conveniently. They were empowered to delegate to bishops the power to authorise priests to use portable altars in suitable places whenever it was not possible to celebrate Catholic services inside churches for 'fear of the heretics'. Archbishop Creagh was also directed to report to Rome as to when and where outside church buildings he may be able to celebrate Mass, what saints' relics may be granted to him, and what arrangements could be made for transporting holy oil from Rome to Ireland. The papal nuncio had his existing powers in matrimonial causes amplified to dispense existing impediments to marriages of the fourth degree of consanguinity or affinity (an impediment that was widely breached in Ireland). Altogether, this papal commission was ambitious, yet more realistic too in terms of its recognition of the need to circumvent the effects of the enforcement of the Elizabethan reformation over much of the east of Ireland.

However, very shortly after Archbishop Creagh arrived in Ireland in December 1564, he was arrested while celebrating Mass at a Franciscan friary in the archdiocese of Armagh and, after three weeks of imprisonment in Dublin, he was transferred to the Tower of London, where he was interrogated.[47] Under interrogation on 22 February 1565, Creagh mentioned meeting in Rome Muirchertach and Donagh O'Brien, Diarmaid O'Mady, Knoghour Óg, one Muires, and other scholars whose names he said he could not remember. The O'Briens were probably from Thomond and may possibly have attended Creagh's academy in Limerick, as some of the others may also have done. He also mentioned meeting 'some young Irish scholars at Louvain'. During a subsequent interrogation, he mentioned William Moiryrtagh or Morgan, Brian

46 *CSP Rome, 1558–71*, no. 313.   47 Lennon, *Archbishop Creagh*, pp 60–1.

Tadhg Richiblican or Kiblican, Domigha fr Rikard, Croeun Diarmaid Mady, Richard Ardur (or so) and Moiris Derby, 'of which some were handsomely learned, also beyond seas, whose names I did not remember ... with many others of diverse parts of Ireland; of which aforenamed three or four had of the pope exhibition for themselves and their servants' (that reference to papal bursaries is interesting).[48] The definite impression given is of a significant body of Irish clerical students (with Irish as well as Anglo-Irish surnames) engaged in studies overseas – from the very start of the Elizabethan reformation in Ireland.

Back in March 1564, Archbishop Creagh had been granted a papal bull, at his own request, which authorised the setting up of colleges and at least one university in Ireland under pontifical regulation on the lines of those at Louvain and Paris.[49] Colm Lennon has pointed out that the decree envisaged the introduction of clerical educators and trainers from teaching orders such as the Jesuits, though under interrogation, Creagh stated that 'as for [the] erection of any university, I am not so ignorant but that I know it cannot be done without the aid and authority of the queen's majesty'.[50] In fact, the prospects for the establishment of a Catholic university anywhere in Ireland in the later sixteenth century were very slight indeed, however much the operation of Catholic schools was tolerated beyond the Pale – unless the queen had become a Catholic. Yet Creagh was not the only Catholic in the sixteenth century who believed in miracles.

CONCLUSIONS

By the summer of 1565, the Elizabethan reformation had manifestly failed to gain acceptance in Ireland. It was widely resisted in the Pale, most particularly by the nobility and gentlemen, who generally refused to attend Church of Ireland services, but participated in Catholic services instead. Many of the Catholics of the Pale who were compelled to attend services in their local churches were openly and persistently disruptive, and they proved to be resistant to Protestant sermons. Beyond the Pale, David Wolfe, as papal nuncio, played an extraordinary role in maintaining allegiance to Rome and in exercising a supervisory jurisdiction over most of the Church in Ireland in the pope's name, and he was able to exert considerable influence even in the Pale itself. Recusant priests and friars operated openly even in Dublin as late as 1563 (and later, if one may doubt the efficacy of Sussex's proclamation against them).

Nonetheless, Wolfe's mission was predicated on the unsustainable assumption that Elizabeth's reformation would be short-lived: the papacy did not finally

---

48 Shirley, *Original letters*, no. 176.   49 P.F. Moran (ed.), *Spicilegium Ossoriense: being a collection of original letters and papers illustrative of the history of the Irish Church from the Reformation to the year 1800*, i (Dublin, 1874), pp 32–8; Lennon, *Archbishop Creagh*, p. 54.   50 Lennon, *Archbishop Creagh*, p. 54; Shirley, *Original letters*, no. lxiii.

abandon its hope that she would 'return' to the Catholic Church until 1570. The Catholic mission depended much upon a lack of political will to enforce the Elizabethan reformation on Ireland in the earliest years of the régime. Once the English crown decided to enforce compliance to its religious statutes and injunctions within the Pale with greater rigour, and to extend its ecclesiastical jurisdiction beyond the Pale, the Catholic mission would be confronted with challenges that it was ill-prepared to face. The establishment of the Irish Ecclesiastical High Commission in 1564, and its activities within the Pale (including the arrest and imprisonment of Bishop Walsh of Meath), and the commissions established to extend the Elizabethan reformation to Munster and southern Connacht did not augur well for the continuance of the Catholic mission.

8

Elizabeth's reformation: the Sidney years

The years encompassed by Sidney's terms as lord deputy, intermittently from 1565 to 1578, saw the Elizabethan Church of Ireland transformed from a legal fiction into an institution with a semblance of reality across much of Ireland. Within the dioceses of the Pale, and in the larger outlying boroughs, the *Book of Common Prayer* displaced the Catholic service books for the liturgy publicly celebrated in the parish churches. Across most of Ireland, Marian bishops were progressively replaced as they died or retired, with bishops who owed their promotion to Elizabeth rather than the pope and, though they were generally conservative rather than Protestant by inclination, they represented a real extension of the Elizabethan Church of Ireland across the country. However, the greater insistence on conformity to Elizabeth's reformation in the Pale and in the larger towns, and the extension of the Reformation into regions where royal authority was being extended in a radical fashion, worsened a growing alienation from the crown and its representatives in Ireland. The secular grievances that accompanied the religious upheavals were varied and manifold, and have been much discussed by historians – but religious disaffection provided the glue that gave cohesion to the disparate elements that began to gel into a coherent sense of alienation from the state and its (increasingly English-born) officials, and religious dissent was a key factor in fomenting that alienation in its own right.

THE QUEEN'S RELIGIOUS PROGRAMME

In July 1565, Elizabeth had instructions drawn up for the new viceroy in Ireland. These began with the declaration that

> the principal and first care which her majesty committed to the said lieutenant and council is that they have regard to the due and reverent observation of all good laws and ordinances established in that realm for the maintenance of Christian faith and religion, and that all means be used ... that devotion and godliness may increase ... and errors and evil opinions may be restrained, suppressed and abolished.

Responsibility for advancing the Elizabethan reformation was devolved on Sir Henry Sidney, who was appointed as lord deputy on 13 October 1565. Ciarán Brady observed that the 'Instructions' given to Sidney 'constituted "not a programme of striking originality", but an excellent summary of the conventional wisdom of the day'.[1] He stated that 'though they are replete with the rhetoric of change, they emerge on examination to be nothing more than a recapitulation of the principal reforms deemed by Sussex [Sidney's predecessor] to be immediately necessary for Ireland'.[2] That was true also of the religious instructions among them.

It was the queen, or Cecil acting on her behalf, who identified religion as 'the principal and first care' of the government of Ireland.[3] The 'Instructions' directed the deputy and council of Ireland to enquire into the state of the clergy, and propose ways by which they might be improved because, it was observed, a well-instituted clergy was 'one of the principal means' to advance religion. The queen's 'Instructions' directed that consideration be given to the union of the dioceses of Cashel and Ossory, 'because these two livings are very meanly endowed'. The 'Instructions' referred to the queen's previous order to Wrothe and Arnold for the conversion of St Patrick's Cathedral, Dublin, into a university, and indicated her strong desire to see that conversion carried out. She directed that the clergy should not be allowed to diminish the revenues of their benefices through alienations or impropriations. The 'Instructions' referred to the Ecclesiastical High Commission that the queen had recently established in Ireland and reiterated her determination that 'open' breaches of her religious laws ('as is reported') would no longer be tolerated in the Pale and 'would be from henceforth more severely reformed'. She directed that the bishops and other ordinaries should visit parish cures, without demanding procurations, to see that the ecclesiastical laws and injunctions were duly observed.

Sidney offered his 'opinions upon the minute of Instructions devised for him'.[4] He indicated his willingness to enquire into the state of the clergy, to have any of their defects certified, and to have remedies proposed, but he ventured his personal opinion that 'the only way is by sending learned pastors from hence [England] and by giving them competent livings there [Ireland]'. He indicated that he saw value in the suggestion to unite the dioceses of Cashel and Ossory in order to attract the service of an English pastor as bishop there. Sidney considered the queen's instructions for the conversion of St Patrick's Cathedral as 'very good', and indicated his willingness to advance the project 'as near as I can'. He wrote that he would consult with the judges about preventing alienations and impropriations of ecclesiastical benefices, but he thought that it would be 'impossible' to prevent their occurrence without parliamentary sanction. He

---

1 Brady, *The chief governors*, p. 118. 2 Ibid., p. 117. 3 Shirley, *Original letters*, no. lxxiv.
4 Ibid., no. lxxv.

asked for a copy of the commission issued to the Ecclesiastical High Commission and committed himself to supporting its execution 'as it shall seem expedient unto me' – a somewhat qualified commitment.

The first progress report sent to the queen by Deputy Sidney and the council of Ireland during his viceroyalty, dated 15 April 1566, relegated religion to the very end of their report – actually referring to the religious clauses of her 'Instructions' as the '*residue*', a clear reflection of Sidney's priorities.[5] The report adhered very closely to the agenda set down in the queen's 'Instructions'. In response to her direction that they enquire into the state of the clergy, they declared that the archbishops of Dublin and Armagh, and the bishop of Meath were

> diligent in the function of their pastoral offices, as well in often and fruitful preaching and setting forth of God's glory and true Christian religion themselves, as also in the earnest calling on and looking to the other pastors and ministers within their provinces and dioceses to do the like.

They affirmed that they were committed to 'maintain and further the same ... throughout all this realm universally', yet they confessed that

> It goes slowly forward, both within their said three dioceses ... and out of their said dioceses, the remote parts of Munster, Connacht and other the Irish countries and borders thereof (saving the commissioners for the ecclesiastical causes have travailed with some of the bishops and other [of] their ministers residing in the civil and nearer parts), [but] order cannot yet so well be taken with the residue until the countries be first brought into more civil and dutiful obedience.

In other words, the Elizabethan reformation was still largely confined to the Pale, and even there it was progressing 'slowly'.

To explain the lack of progress, the report of Sidney and the council referred to 'the former errors and superstitions inveterated and leavened in the people's hearts'. They also pointed to the lack of parochial benefices or livings sufficiently well endowed to support 'well chosen and learned curates' because the parish livings were, for the most part

> appropriated benefices in the queen's majesty's possessions [and] are let by lease unto farmers with allowance or reservation of very small stipends or entertainments for the vicars or curates, besides the decay

5 Ibid., no. lxxxii.

of the chancels, and also of the churches universally in ruin, and some
wholly down.

Sidney informed the queen that he had

> given charge to the said bishops to make diligent search, and to certify
> me in the next term of every the said decayed chancels and churches
> in their dioceses, and also of the want and vacancy of curates, upon
> which certificate the parties faulty therein shall be called before us,
> and straight order taken with them for the re-edifying of them, and
> also for the supply of want and vacancy of curates, and so (as we may)
> we shall proceed for the rest of the realm.

Interestingly, Archbishop Bodkin of Tuam recorded the results of a visitation in
the dioceses of Tuam, Kilmacduagh and Clonfert about that time, which
outlined something of the sorry state of the Church in much of southern
Connacht, with 10 per cent of parishes reported to be 'wasted'.[6] Time was to
show that Sidney's assumption that 'straight order' would suffice to have the
churches restored and the parishes staffed with clergy was extremely naïve.

In response to the queen's 'Instructions' regarding St Patrick's Cathedral, it
was pointed out that Wrothe and Arnold had already conducted a survey of the
assets of the cathedral and that Wrothe had personally forwarded it to the lords
of the English privy council, together with his opinions about how the conversion into a university might best be achieved. Meanwhile, Archbishop Curwen
affirmed that, in keeping with instructions given to him, he had made no new
appointments to the cathedral chapter. He and Archbishop Loftus and Bishop
Brady had interviewed the cathedral clergy and found them willing to surrender
their offices on receipt of pensions. However, the council of Ireland had taken
no further action on the matter, but waited for further instructions from the
queen.

To the next ecclesiastical instruction, Sidney and the council of Ireland
responded by declaring that they did not know 'as yet' of many alienations
committed by the clergy, apart from those made by Alexander Devereux, bishop
of Ferns, who had alienated most of the assets of his diocese to his bastard sons'
benefits. That was a disingenuous statement, given the extent of the alienations
of diocesan estates effected by Bishop Craik in Kildare and Archbishop Loftus
in Armagh *inter Anglicos*.

To the final instruction, they answered that the commissioners for ecclesiastical causes 'do (as they may) proceed therein, howbeit slowly for the causes

---

6 K.W. Nicholls, 'Visitations of the dioceses of Clonfert, Tuam and Kilmacduagh, *c.*1565–67',
Analecta Hibernica, 26 (1970), pp 144–58.

aforesaid', that is to say, the resistance of the people to religious change. One must conclude that, almost a year since the first draft of the queen's 'Instructions' were drawn up, there was very little real progress achieved in terms of advancing the Elizabethan reformation in Ireland.

ECCLESIASTICAL HIGH COMMISSION

It may be significant that so little was written about the Ecclesiastical High Commission in the report of April 1566, certainly in comparison with the detailed consideration given to the problems posed by the leasing of impropriated benefices, and the same strong emphasis on the problems of impropriations is evident again in Sidney's report on the state of the Church of Ireland in 1576.[7] The latter report was based to no small degree upon information supplied by Bishop Brady of Meath and it seems that Sidney's religious policy was greatly influenced by Brady, a bishop whom he warmly commended to Cecil in 1566, 'both for his sufficiency in preaching, wherein he is equal to the best of the bishops here, and for his grave judgment in council, wherein he far exceeds the rest; neither is he inferior to any in good example of life, and maintenance of hospitality'.[8] Ten years later, Sidney commended Brady to Elizabeth herself as 'the honest, zealous and learned bishop ... a godly minister for the gospel and a good servant to your highness'.[9] By contrast, Sidney made a slighting reference to Loftus' concern with money.[10]

Brady counselled in favour of less coercion than Loftus advocated. Just before he left Ireland for England to recover his health in 1566, Loftus let it be known that he intended to 'complain of [the] small assistance he had in executing his commission for ecclesiastical causes'.[11] Apparently, Loftus held Brady chiefly to blame for the slackened support enjoyed by the Commission, doubtless through his influence in the council of Ireland. Brady responded by declaring that 'if he say that I have drawn backward I only say that he has drawn too fast forward, as the circumstances shall well declare'.[12]

How much of Loftus' hostility towards Brady was the result of 'private quarrels or causes', as suggested by Brady,[13] and how much reflected the disagreement about strategy, is impossible to define at this stage. In any event, Loftus sought to 'procure to himself a more absolute authority' within the Ecclesiastical Commission – which he was not given.[14] On the contrary, on his translation from Armagh, the primatial see in the Irish Church, to Dublin in the summer of 1567, Loftus' position as *ex officio* chairman of the Ecclesiastical Commission was allowed to lapse. My suspicion is that Deputy Sidney ensured

7 Brady (ed.), *State papers*, no. xi.   8 Shirley, *Original letters*, no. lxxxiii.   9 Brady, *State papers*, no. xi.   10 Shirley, *Original letters*, no. lxxxiii.   11 Ibid., no. xcix.   12 Ibid., no. xcix.   13 Ibid., no. xcix.   14 Ibid.

that Loftus was not empowered to proceed with the kind of draconian measures he advocated in 1565 to enforce conformity to the queen's religious settlement. He probably reckoned that the political costs would have been unacceptably great. The new Ecclesiastical Commission authorised in June 1568 was presided over by Dr Robert Weston, an English lawyer with extensive experience as a church court judge.[15] Yet Weston was already an old man when he was appointed as chancellor of Ireland, and he was to suffer from repeated bouts of illness.[16] His secular responsibilities would have prevented him from concentrating his undivided attention on the Church of Ireland, which raises questions about the queen's commitment to her reformation in Ireland.

It is impossible, for want of evidence, to determine the effectiveness of the Ecclesiastical Commission under Weston's presidency. Its register was destroyed in the Irish Public Records Office in 1922.[17] Apparently, the main form of punishment it used was the levying of monetary fines. James Murray calculated that fines totalling Ir£442 7s. 4d. were levied throughout Ireland in the five-year period between Michaelmas 1568 and Michaelmas 1573, but 58 per cent of those fines were still outstanding at the end of that period.[18] Murray reckons that the figures show that the Commission 'exercised a far from draconian policy of enforcement' in Weston's lifetime.[19] I think he is correct, though the figures are very difficult to interpret with any degree of precision. There is no way now of telling the size of the individual fines, or their chronological spread, which undermines any attempt at analysis. If, as one suspects, the fines were levied in a socially selective manner, at the middling classes – rather than the destitute poor who could not afford the fines or the social élites whose support the crown depended upon – then the number of heads of households fined could have run into several hundred, albeit over a period of years (though one cannot assume that there was no 'repeat-offending'). On the other hand, it could be that a smaller number of wealthy householders was fined significant sums of money, bearing in mind the queen's commissioners' earlier advice not to proceed against the 'simple multitude',[20] and that many of them had the confidence to refuse to pay their arrears. One can only guess as to who was fined, and the answer to that question would skew our understanding of the figures very considerably. The absence of chronological detail precludes the possibility of discerning whether the Commission applied steady pressure on the populace to conform over a number of years, or (as I suspect) exerted more pressure at some times than others, or whether an initial campaign by the commission achieved general

15 SP 63/21/6, 10; SP 63/42/76; Shirley, *Original letters*, no. cxii; 'Weston', Andrew Lyall, *ODNB*; Murray, *Enforcing the English Reformation*, p. 265.   16 'Weston', Lyall, *ODNB*; Murray, 'Tudor diocese of Dublin', pp 255–6; idem, *Enforcing the English Reformation*, pp 285–6. 17 Murray, 'Tudor diocese of Dublin', p. 249.   18 Murray, 'Tudor diocese of Dublin', p. 251; idem, *Enforcing the English Reformation*, p. 282.   19 Murray, 'Tudor diocese of Dublin', p. 252; idem, *Enforcing the English Reformation*, p. 282.   20 Shirley, *Original letters*, no. liv.

conformity thereafter – or whether the campaign was simply unsustainable over time.

James Murray has tabulated the arrears of fines owed to the Ecclesiastical Commission in 1582, and his figures suggest that 37% of the arrears were owing from Dublin city and county, 28% for Meath and a further 3% from Westmeath, 14% for County Kildare and 11% from Drogheda and County Louth. It seems a reasonable assumption that the geographical distribution of arrears bore some relationship to the geographical spread of the fines levied. That being the case two facts above all are striking: firstly, it is very interesting that the Ecclesiastical High Commission as late as 1582 largely confined its attentions on the Pale (only 7% of the arrears were due from beyond the Pale), and secondly, Dublin city (which accounted for no less than 24% of all arrears in 1582) suffered disproportionately from the attentions of the Commission, as did Drogheda (5%).

In his report from Lisbon, dated 24 March 1574, David Wolfe, SJ, noted that although 'almost all' of the citizens of Dublin were Catholics, 'especially the natives of the city', they went 'perforce to the communion and sermons of the heretics'.[21] The reference to the native Dubliners points to the existence of the growing community of immigrant English in the capital of Ireland. The people of Drogheda, 'all Catholics' according to Wolfe, were also compelled to 'hear the Koran of the heretics'. That constitutes credible evidence to show that conformity was general in the cities in the Pale in 1574. However, it is not clear whether such conformity extended to the congregations in small towns or rural parishes (in which the bulk of the people of the Pale lived), or among the propertied classes in the Pale. Wolfe declared that among the barons, lords and nobles of the diocese of Meath, whom he claimed to know 'not only personally' but also 'their very frame of mind', he knew of no heretic except for Viscount Gormanstown. This statement may not be very much of an exaggeration, in the light of Loftus' findings in the survey of the parishes of the Pale in 1565 and the general recusancy that is known to have prevailed among the landowners of the Pale in the mid-1580s. In any case, the figures for Dublin city (and Drogheda) may reflect the Ecclesiastical Commission's greater ability to enforce conformity to the Elizabethan religious settlement in the cities than in the countryside – or they might reflect a not inconsiderable degree of persistent dissent in the cities.

EPISCOPAL APPOINTMENTS

Meanwhile, Deputy Sidney knew that forcing congregations into churches would serve very little purpose unless they were catechised. In a letter to Cecil

21 Wolfe's report is printed in J. Begley, *The diocese of Limerick in the sixteenth and seventeenth centuries* (London, 1927), pp 494–515, with the best translation printed in Ronan, *The Reformation in Ireland*, pp 473–89.

on 19 August 1566, he complained about the 'pitiful estate [of] the ecclesiastical causes in this realm' because apart from Loftus and Brady, he found 'few or none [of the bishops] either worthily to walk in his function, willing to reform their clergy, or able either to teach any wholesome doctrine or to serve their country or commonwealth as magistrates'.[22] Archbishop Loftus concurred; he criticised the previous episcopal appointees for their 'inability and untowardness' and asked the privy council that 'by your means unto the queen, her majesty, such bishops hereafter … may be sent [to Ireland] as for their learning and zeal in God's holy word may be bishops indeed'.[23] It is interesting that Robert Daly, the Protestant bishop of Kildare (1564–83), whose letter to Cecil in 1565 showed such zeal for Protestantism, was not numbered with Brady and Loftus as an effective bishop. Why that was is not clear, but I would suggest that Sidney's dependence on the earl of Kildare obliged Bishop Daly to be circumspect in his enforcement of religious change in Kildare diocese.[24] One indication of Daly's isolation is the fact that he was robbed and expelled from his house on three separate occasions, the last occasion probably contributing to his death in 1583.[25]

Sidney appealed in writing 'sundry times' for the granting of Archbishop Curwen's fervent wish to be translated from Dublin to an English diocese.[26] Despite Curwen's increasingly desperate pleas to be repatriated, however, he was not allowed to leave Ireland until August 1567, when he was 'a very weak and impotent man through the palsey'.[27] With Curwen's departure imminent, Sidney was keen to see Bishop Brady translated to Dublin. He warmly commended Brady as 'fittest to succeed' by reason of his fine preaching and outstanding judgment.[28] Yet Brady's standing at court was undermined by Loftus,[29] who took the opportunity while in England in the autumn of 1566 to canvass for Curwen's speedy replacement with a 'zealous and learned' man.[30] Sidney, realising that Brady's prospects of promotion were not good, recommended Christopher Goodman instead.[31] However, Loftus' assiduous promotion of himself paid off, and in a letter of 11 March 1567, Sidney informed him that the queen had decided to translate him to Dublin.[32] In his letter, Sidney expressed his pleasure that 'by this means I am in hope that as the city of Dublin is the chief place within this realm, and most open for any good example; so it will grow (by your good and careful order) to reformation in religion'. In a postscript, the deputy wrote, 'Now comes the hour for the reform

---

22 Shirley, *Original letters*, no. xcvi. 23 Ibid., no. xci. 24 Ibid., no. lxxiii. 25 Ibid., p. 149, quoting Ware's, 'Bishops'. 26 Shirley, *Original letters*, nos xlxxxix, lxxxiv, lxxxviii, cxii, cxiii. 27 Ibid., p. 304. 28 Ibid., no. lxxxiii. 29 Ibid., nos xcviii, xcix, cxvii. 30 Ibid., nos xci, xcii, c, cvii. 31 Ibid., no. cv. An interesting reflection of the crown's priorities regarding Ireland is the fact that Sidney's request that Goodman be made the dean of St Patrick's Cathedral, Dublin, if Loftus were appointed as bishop of Dublin, was ignored and the deanery was awarded instead to a layman to supplement his income from the chancellorship. 32 Shirley, *Original letters*, no. cix.

of the Church' – an interesting indictment on the progress of the Reformation in Ireland to that point.

Little evidence survives for Loftus' routine diocesan administration, though it seems that he was content to delegate much of the work to his new official principal, John Ball, a layman.[33] Despite his earlier advocacy of the conversion of St Patrick's Cathedral into a university, as archbishop of Dublin Loftus, decided to hold onto the rich source of ecclesiastical patronage. In April 1569, Chancellor Weston, in his capacity as dean (though he was a layman like Ball, his nephew), initiated a visitation of St Patrick's Cathedral. During the course of his visitation, Weston was given reason to suspect that Thomas Creef, precentor of St Patrick's and Ball's predecessor as official principal and vicar general of Dublin diocese, had been guilty of adultery. As Murray observes, 'it does seem an unusual allegation given that the precentor was in or around 70 years of age at the time', and he suggests that it was 'politically motivated' to embarrass a senior conservative in the cathedral chapter.[34] Creef, in fact, survived the drive made against him, but several other prebendaries were deprived of their prebends for non-residence.[35] None was deprived for doctrinal reasons.

In place of the absentees, Ball, despite being a layman, was made the archdeacon of Glendalough, John O'Kearney, an Irish graduate of Cambridge University and soon-to-be author of the first Protestant catechism in Irish, was made the treasurer of the cathedral, and another Cambridge graduate was given the prebend of Swords.[36] Yet, in a letter to Burghley on 26 September 1571, Archbishop Loftus complained that 'all the old prebendaries [are] ignorant papists' and he referred to a 'popish faction' in the cathedral chapter.[37] I would suggest caution in interpreting the archbishop's remarks as signifying anything more than a conservative disposition among a number of the older cathedral clergy in 1571. The archbishop's reference to the lack of vicars in the cathedral parish itself and in seven prebendal parishes within about five miles of Dublin, is more significant in that it suggests a poor provision of pastoral care in several of the parishes impropriated to the cathedral. Chancellor Weston ameliorated that problem just a little by endowing three vicarages from the revenues of the deanery of St Patrick's Cathedral.[38]

Loftus summoned a synod for the ecclesiastical province of Dublin in February 1570, but no record of its deliberations has survived.[39] The synod was followed by a metropolitan visitation but, again, there is a lack of evidence about

---

33 Murray, 'Tudor diocese of Dublin', pp 232–3; idem, *Enforcing the English Reformation*, p. 268.
34 Murray, 'Tudor diocese of Dublin', p. 238; idem, *Enforcing the English Reformation*, p. 272.
35 Murray, 'Tudor diocese of Dublin', pp 240–1; idem, *Enforcing the English Reformation*, pp 273–4. 36 Murray, 'Tudor diocese of Dublin', p. 241; idem, *Enforcing the English Reformation*, p. 274. 37 SP 60/34/13; Ronan, *Reformation in Ireland*, p. 359. 38 Murray, *Enforcing the English Reformation*, pp 265–6. 39 *Registrum Dublinensis*, pp 34–5; Murray, 'Tudor diocese of Dublin', pp 242–3.

its proceedings.[40] Significantly, Loftus did not take the opportunity to promote the Reformation in person across his ecclesiastical province. Instead, he operated through commissaries, such as Daniel Kavanagh, bishop of Leighlin, and David Clere, dean of Waterford, who visited Kavanagh's own diocese.[41] The value of the latter exercise must be doubted. Even more tellingly, Loftus appointed Ball as his commissary to visit his own diocese of Dublin, rather than involve himself directly in its conduct. Shortly after the visitation had been completed, Christopher Browne, prebendary of Wicklow, complained of Ball 'having any rich man of the country in the censures of the Church for fornicating, adultery or any like offence' would absolve them 'for money … with the pope's absolution, *Absolvo te* … and has been seen and heard giving that absolution on horseback in the fields, the penitent kneeling before him'.[42] I presume that when it came to selling absolutions, a Catholic rite commanded a greater market value in Ireland than one based on the *Book of Common Prayer*.

To take Loftus' place in Armagh diocese, the queen initially decided to promote Terence O'Donnelly, dean of Armagh, as archbishop.[43] However, with the death of Shane O'Neill in 1567, the dean's political value fell sharply. Instead, Thomas Lancaster, the Edwardian bishop of Kildare (1550–4), who accompanied Deputy Sidney in Ireland, was promoted as archbishop of Armagh in 1569.[44] Thus, nine years after the enactment of the Elizabethan religious settlement by the Irish parliament, the four dioceses of the Pale were finally entrusted to committed Protestant bishops.

The deaths of a series of Marian bishops during his first term of office gave Sidney the opportunity to appoint conformable candidates to sees in south Leinster and east Munster. On 18 May 1566, Sidney wrote to the privy council recommending Daniel Kavanagh as bishop of Leighlin in place of the late Thomas O'Fihilly, and forwarded commendations for his candidate from Archbishops Curwen and Loftus, and Bishop Brady.[45] He commended Kavanagh to Cecil in November 1566, and again in March 1567, 'as an apt man for his alliance in the diocese, to be a minister of justice, and not uncommended for his learning and conformity in religion'.[46] The reference to Kavanagh's political utility should be noted, and also the qualified commendation of his 'learning and conformity in religion'. Kavanagh was promoted by the queen on 10 April 1567 and was consecrated by Archbishop Curwen – almost a year following Sidney's original recommendation.[47]

40 Murray, 'Tudor diocese of Dublin', p. 244.   41 *Registrum Dublinensis*, pp 35–5; Murray, 'Tudor diocese of Dublin', p. 244.   42 SP 63/71/10; Murray, 'Tudor diocese of Dublin', p. 244; idem, *Enforcing the English Reformation*, pp 287–8.   43 Shirley, *Original letters*, no. xlvii. Sir Nicholas Wrothe commended the dean by observing that he 'would promise to do much with Shane O'Neill and some think he could perform it': ibid., p. 124.   44 SP 63/21/70; 63/23/86; 'Lancaster', Jefferies, *ODNB*.   45 Shirley, *Original letters*, no. lxxxvii.   46 Ibid., no. cviii. That was hardly a resounding endorsement of Cavanagh's academic qualifications, or evangelical zeal. 47 Shirley, *Original letters*, no. cxi; M.V. Ronan, *The Reformation in Ireland under Elizabeth*,

On 8 June 1566, Sidney recommended Christopher Gaffney, a prebendary of St Patrick's Cathedral, Dublin, for the diocese of Ossory, and he attached letters of commendation from Archbishop Curwen and Bishop Brady.[48] He mentioned in his letter that it was his custom to consult with the bishops (presumably the three bishops in the Council of Ireland) before recommending any candidate. Archbishop Loftus wrote directly to Cecil, recommending Gaffney 'for the place is Irish, and none of his country birth (that I know) are more meter than he'.[49] Again, almost a year elapsed since Sidney's recommendation before the new bishop was consecrated in May 1567. One might be tempted to assume that the delays in promoting bishops were motivated by a desire to exploit the temporalities of the vacant dioceses for a time. However, delay and procrastination also characterised the choice of Curwen's replacement in Dublin.[50]

On 19 August 1566, Sidney wrote to Cecil recommending John Devereux, dean of Ferns, to be bishop of the diocese, with a commendation from Bishop Brady for his 'learning and sufficiency ... for besides that he is a gentleman of the best house in the county of Wexford, and brought up in the university of England, [and] I find him of good discretion and judgment, and able in causes of justice to do her majesty and this country very good service'.[51] He was consecrated as bishop later that year, despite strong opposition from Loftus, who informed Cecil that 'an unfitter man [there] cannot be; he is now of late deprived of his deanery for confessed whoredom'.[52] Devereux was, in fact, allowed to hold the deanery of Ferns for the first five years of his episcopate; a testament of the political priorities of the crown.

David Wolfe, SJ, in his 'Description of Ireland' in 1574, observed that the five bishops in the ecclesiastical province of Dublin were 'heretics or schismatics', but he knew 'some of them would much rather be Catholics but that they would lose their sees'.[53] Bishop Gaffney of Ossory was probably one of the latter. He is known to have employed a Catholic bishop to ordain priests in his diocese.[54] The geographical spread of the fines imposed by the Ecclesiastical Commission shows that it was largely inactive beyond the Pale and it seems a safe assumption that beneath a superficial veneer of conformity in southern Leinster, religious life in the parishes was little affected by Protestantism.

The veneer of conformity in Waterford was remarkably thin. Diego Ortiz, writing from Waterford in the early 1560s, reported that English was not used in the liturgy celebrated in Waterford's churches.[55] A report from 1577 indicates that even then the churches of Waterford were still being used for Catholic services, albeit very early on Sunday mornings, and they were still decorated

1558–1580 (London, 1926), p. 181. **48** Shirley, *Original letters*, no. xc. **49** Ibid., no. xciii. **50** Almost four years elapsed between the decision to translate Curwen from Dublin and his actual departure. Shirley, *Original letters*, no. xlvii. **51** Shirley, *Original letters*, no. xcvi. **52** Ibid., no. xcviii. **53** Ronan, *Reformation in Ireland*, pp 473–89. **54** Brady, *State papers*, nos xviii, xix. **55** Byrne, 'Reformation in Tudor Waterford', p. 30.

with arrays of Catholic images.[56] It seems too that communities of Franciscan and Dominican friars habitually resided in Waterford and in Dungarvan, a significant town in the same diocese.[57]

Waterford's bishop, Patrick Walsh, certainly conformed to the Elizabethan religious settlement, and his son Nicholas became the Elizabethan bishop of Ossory.[58] However, Patrick Walsh did not advance the Elizabethan reformation in Waterford city or diocese to any discernible degree. On the contrary, he presided over a city that was to be a key conduit for the counter-reformation in Ireland.[59] In 1565, he resigned the deanery of Waterford in favour of Peter White, a zealous Catholic whom he commended as 'a man very well learned, past degrees in schools, and of virtuous sober conversation, by whose industry and travail a great part of the youth of both this country and of Dublin have greatly profited in learning and virtuous education'.[60] White was deprived of the deanery in 1570 for refusing to take the oath of supremacy. Walsh's recommendation of such a zealous Catholic is difficult to explain, but it must hint at some continuing attachment to Catholicism on his part. The Jesuit, Edmund Tanner, Catholic bishop of Cork & Cloyne (1574–9), claimed to have reconciled Bishop Walsh to Rome before his death, though in the seventeenth century he was remembered as having died 'a confirmed heretic'.[61] Ambiguity seems to have been the keynote of his episcopate.

It is not clear whether Roger Skiddy, bishop of Cork (1562–7), oversaw the introduction of the Elizabethan *Book of Common Prayer* into the parishes in Cork. Skiddy was a Marian nominee who was not consecrated before Elizabeth's reign.[62] His resignation as bishop about the time of Deputy Sidney's visit to Cork can hardly have been a simple coincidence. Unfortunately, the record of the pardon granted to him in May 1567 does not specify what he was actually pardoned for.[63] Skiddy's resignation is far more likely to have been a consequence of his refusal to commit himself to conform in the future, than as a punishment for previous dissidence, if one may judge from the experience of Hugh Lacey, bishop of Limerick. After his resignation, Skiddy became the warden of the collegiate church at Youghal.[64] The citizens of Youghal would probably have welcomed a conservative clergyman: they supported a Jesuit school in their town at that time.[65]

To take Skiddy's place, Sidney nominated his chaplain, Richard Dixon, an Englishman who had already been promoted as a canon of St Patrick's Cathedral, Dublin, in December 1569.[66] Just prior to Dixon's episcopate, there

56 Brady, *State papers*, no. xv.   57 Byrne, 'Reformation in Waterford', p. 30. 'Nicholas White', N.J.A. Williams, *ODNB*; Ronan, *Reformation in Ireland*, p. 500.   58 Byrne, 'Reformation in Waterford', pp 28–30.   59 Ibid., pp 28–30; Brady, *State papers*, no. xv.   60 *CPCRI, Eliz.*, i, 494.   61 Byrne, 'Reformation in Waterford', p. 44; Bolster, *Diocese of Cork*, ii, p. 77; Jefferies, 'Irish parliament of 1560', p. 137.   62 Bolster, *Diocese of Cork*, pp 59–60.   63 Ibid., p. 60. 64 Ibid.   65 Ibid., pp 73–4.   66 SP 63/29/84.

is definite evidence of there being Protestants in Cork: in 1569, Sir James Fitzmaurice Fitzgerald demanded that all 'Huguenots' in Cork be expelled from the city. It is not clear how many, if any, of those Protestants were native Corkonians as against English refugees from the settlement in Kerrycurrihy that had just been overthrown by Fitzmaurice's men.[67] In any case, Protestants had some kind of presence, however tenuous, in Cork at that time. In his will made in November 1571, Adam Gould made a bequest to Christ Church in the city 'so that the olde faith be set up'.[68]

Yet the Elizabethan reformation suffered an unexpected set-back in Cork when Bishop Dixon was found guilty by the Ecclesiastical High Commission of taking a woman 'of suspected life in the city of Cork as his wife', though he was already married to a woman in England. He was forced to perform an exemplary penance in Christ Church, Dublin – 'though not in such penitent sort as was thought meet',[69] and he was removed from office by the queen. He was replaced by Matthew Sheyne, whom Loftus commended as 'a man in the judgment of the godly there that know him for his sound religion, honest life and good learning most meet for that dignity. I have known him for seven years and think him the fittest man for the place as he is acquainted with the country's language'.[70]

When Sidney visited Limerick in 1567, he was greeted by Bishop Lacey 'in full pontificals and with much ceremony of an entirely Romish character'.[71] It seems, however, that Lacey conformed as a result of the deputy's visit, because Wolfe, who had previously commended Lacey for his steadfast Catholicism in 1568, did not do likewise in his report of 1574.[72] It is not likely that Lacey embraced the Elizabethan *Book of Common Prayer* with anything approaching positive affirmation. He was compelled to resign as bishop in 1571, to make way for William Casey, the Edwardian bishop of Limerick who had been removed from office by a Marian commission in 1554 because he had married.[73]

The archdiocese of Cashel was vacant since the death of Roland Baron Fitzgerald in October 1561. In July 1566, Loftus wrote to Cecil recommending James MacCawell for Cashel.[74] MacCawell was well-commended by the Anglican apologist, John Jewel, bishop of Salisbury. He had been appointed as the queen's bishop of Down & Connor in 1564, but for fear of Shane O'Neill, lord of Tyrone, it was reported that 'he durst not travel to Down, for doubt of bodily harm'.[75] Yet MacCawell was not granted letters patent for his promotion to Cashel until 2 October 1567. His appointment brought the Church over most of Munster under the queen's authority.

Sidney reached the city of Galway in spring 1567. There, he was greeted by Archbishop Bodkin of Tuam 'in his pontificals, accompanied with diverse

67 SP 63/29/8; Jefferies, *Cork: historical perspectives*, p. 111. 68 *Gentlemen's Magazine*, Nov. 1861, p. 501; Jefferies, *Cork: historical perspectives*, p. 111. 69 SP 63/32/10. 70 SP 63/34/30. 71 SP 63/20/66. 72 Ronan, *Reformation in Ireland*, pp 470–3, 473–89. 73 Edwards, *Church and state*, p. 210. 74 Shirley, *Original letters*, no. xcv. 75 Ibid., nos lx, lxix.

priests and clerks in copes singing ... the *Te deum* ... Latin'.[76] The Catholic ceremonial was punctuated, though, by a sermon preached by a former friar – 'a godly lesson', the deputy observed. Wolfe's tally of fifteen Protestants in Galway in 1574, 'young men who to please the Lady Elizabeth embrace that Lutheran novelty', made it the most 'Protestant' city in Ireland.[77] Another Jesuit, Edmund Tanner, having returned to Ireland via Galway on 21 June 1576, reported to Rome that the land was full of heretics and robbers.[78] Christopher Bodkin, archbishop of Tuam (1537–72), and Roland Burke, bishop of Clonfert (1534–80), though conservative in religion, supported the education of a number of clerical students in Dublin and in the English universities with the revenues of some benefices in their dioceses.[79] Whether they realised it or not, that facilitated the protestantisation of at least some of those students. The citizens of Galway, feeling themselves threatened by the earl of Clanrickard's unruly sons, were well-disposed towards the English presidency in Connacht, and the greater order and peace it promised. That combination of local Protestant clergymen and a favourable disposition towards the English crown, created the conditions for Galway to be characterised, albeit very briefly, as a 'second Geneva'.[80]

On the other hand, one ought not to exaggerate the popularity of Protestantism in Galway. In 1572, Franciscan friars from across Ireland held a conference inside Galway and celebrated many Masses and delivered many sermons in the city, which were attended by 'diverse aldermen of the town', among them a recent mayor of Galway.[81] The Protestants of Galway were obliged to maintain a low profile for fear of their fellow citizens. The impression is left of a small and isolated community of Protestants. Other evidence too points to local resistance to Protestantism in the city.[82] The Reformation certainly made some progress in Galway, though not quite so much as some believe.

SCHOOLS AND CHURCHES

Having the queen's appointees in charge of dioceses was only a preliminary stage in the Elizabethan reformation. The work of establishing a Protestant ministry in the parishes, let alone of converting the people of the parishes into Protestants, had hardly begun. By common consent, the conformist clergy in the Church of Ireland's parishes were ill-educated and poorly grounded in theology. Chancellor Weston observed in April 1568, that 'their parsons, vicars and

76 SP 63/20/66.   77 Ronan, *Reformation in Ireland*, p. 485; Canny, 'Why the reformation failed', pp 444–5.   78 Bolster, *Diocese of Cork*, p. 77.   79 Nicholls, 'Visitations', pp 146, 151, 155, 156.   80 Canny, 'Why the reformation failed', p. 444.   81 SP 63/38/52, i.   82 Berry, 'Documents relating to the wardenship', pp 13, 16–18, 34; SP 63/163/6.

curates, some of whom I examined, be so void of knowledge of God and his will that they know not his commandments'.[83] The situation was hardly better in the extensive diocese of Meath in April 1576, when Deputy Sidney observed that only eighteen of the more than one hundred unbeneficed parish priests (who served more than half of the parishes of the diocese) were able to speak English, and characterised the rest as 'Irish priests or rather Irish rogues, having very little Latin, less learning and civility'.[84] Sidney's parliament of 1569–71 intended, *inter alia*, to address those fundamental problems.

Victor Treadwell has observed that Sidney's parliament was not preoccupied with religious issues.[85] Of the twenty bills transmitted from England in July 1568, only three were of ecclesiastical import: a bill to establish free diocesan schools, another for the repair of parish churches and a third empowering the deputy and council to appoint the ecclesiastical dignitaries in Munster and Connacht for a term of ten years.[86] Much of the opposition encountered by the deputy's programme in the parliament of 1569–71 was secular in motivation, but Sidney himself sensed that religious dissent simmered in the assembly and formed a not-insignificant element in the medley of motives that shaped the parliamentarians' reactions to the official legislative programme.[87]

When John Hooker, MP, the solicitor of the English adventurer Sir Peter Carew, introduced the crown's wines bill in the Commons with a speech in which he likened Philip and Mary to Pharaoh, and Irish MPs to 'kerns', he unwittingly conjoined elements of material interests, religious conservatism and anti-English sentiment into a potentially explosive cocktail. Edward Butler, MP, who was directly affected by Carew's predatory adventuring, responded to Hooker's speech by declaring that, 'if these words had been spoken in any other place than in this house, there be a great many here that would rather have died than to have suffered it'.[88] Shortly afterwards, Butler went into open rebellion against the English crown. Nonetheless, what strikes me most strongly about the proceedings of the Irish parliament of 1569–71 was the deputy's failure to consult with the key players in advance of drafting the ecclesiastical bills, thereby allowing the Catholic dissidents to find allies among a number of Elizabethan bishops who were anxious about their jurisdiction being curtailed, and among laymen with vested interests in the *status quo*.

The bill concerning the appointment of dignitaries in Munster and Connacht was passed by the Commons early on, but was blocked in the Lords, presumably by a combination of the bishops from the south and west: the bill was never enacted.[89] The schools bill, which gave the deputy and council of Ireland absolute power to appoint or dismiss teachers, and made the beneficed clergy entirely responsible for the teachers' salaries, was also blocked in the Lords,

83 SP 63/24/2. 84 Brady, *State papers*, no. xi. 85 Victor Treadwell, 'The Irish parliament of 1569–71', *PRIA*, 65C (1966), p. 85. 86 Ibid., p. 63. 87 Ibid., p. 67. 88 Ibid., p. 69. 89 Ibid.

presumably with the bishops in the vanguard again.[90] By contrast, the bill for the repair of parish churches was endorsed by the Lords, but was rejected by the Commons.[91] In any case, it was an anaemic piece of legislation since its vested responsibility for its enforcement on the bishops – at a time when the bishops were clearly incapable of enforcing compliance to it. It, too, was never enacted. Chancellor Weston lamented that 'churches and schools ... found no favour with us, yet the reformation of Ireland must come out of them unless good government may be without God and humanity'.[92]

A new bill for the transfer of the cathedra of Ferns diocese from its location *inter Hibernicos* to Wexford, was endorsed by the Commons but rejected by the Lords.[93] A bill to prosecute non-resident clergymen was also rejected. Bills for uniting the diocese of Clonmacnoise to Meath, and Emly to Cashel, were enacted.[94] A revised schools bill was eventually enacted, which gave the Protestant bishops of the Pale full authority over their own schools, and shared the costs of the teachers' salaries between the holders of appropriated tithes and the beneficed clergy.

The official proposal for a university envisaged the conversion of St Patrick's Cathedral, Dublin. Everyone realised that the endowments of the cathedral alone would not suffice to finance a university, especially when pensions were deducted for its numerous well-paid staff.[95] Sidney's project depended on additional voluntary endowments being forthcoming from within Ireland itself – little or nothing could be expected from Elizabeth.[96] However, the Irish parliamentarians proved unwilling to pay more than lip-service to the project and it lapsed.

Both the deputy and the speaker of the parliament expressed the hope that the schools act would be made effective,[97] though the very fact that they expressed concerns about its implementation suggests that they already saw the writing on the wall. Yet the prognosis for the free schools was not entirely negative, as schools had recently been established in Dublin and Navan, and requests for royal support had recently been sought for a school in Galway. However, Archbishop Lancaster of Armagh struggled in vain for royal support to found a diocesan school at Drogheda.[98] Bishop Brady's school at Navan failed, presumably for want of local support.[99] A school at Waterford failed in 1585, when the children's parents withdrew them following the appointment of a Protestant teacher.[1] Hence, the schools Act failed to bear much fruit.

---

90 Ibid., p. 76. 91 Ibid., p. 74. 92 SP 63/27/48. 93 Treadwell, 'Irish parliament of 1569–71', p. 77. 94 Ibid., p. 73. 95 There is no basis for Ciarán Brady and James Murray's suggestion that the conversion of the cathedral would have generated a surplus large enough to ease 'the burden of the army on the community as a whole': Ciarán Brady and James Murray, 'Sir Henry Sidney and the Reformation in Ireland' in Elizabethane Boran and Crawford Gribben (eds), *Enforcing the Reformation in Ireland and Scotland, 1550–1700* (Aldershot, 2006), p. 31. 96 Treadwell, 'Irish parliament of 1569–71', p. 84. 97 Ibid., p. 85. 98 SP 63/77/29, 63/82/58; 63/83/60. 99 Scott, *Tudor diocese of Meath*, pp 60, 64. 1 SP 63/118/29 i.

The speaker bewailed the failure of the university project in his closing speech in the parliament of 1569–71.[2] Sidney took up the same theme in his valediction. Undoubtedly, it was a significant set-back for the Elizabethan reformation in Ireland, though I do not believe that it was among the most important reasons for the eventual failure of the Reformation. Irish students could have gone to Oxford or Cambridge – as their Welsh counterparts did in Elizabeth's reign – but instead, a great many Irish students chose to attend Catholic colleges on mainland Europe. The lack of Irish Protestant graduate clergymen was more a symptom of the Reformation's failure in Ireland than its cause: there was simply a lack of Irishmen who wished to become Protestant ministers.

The bill to repair the parish churches addressed only one of the symptoms of the failure of the Reformation in Ireland (not very promisingly), and I do not regard its rejection as a decisive factor in the course of events. The churches fell into disrepair, for the most part, because the Elizabethan Church of Ireland did not enjoy the levels of support, financial and otherwise, enjoyed by its Catholic predecessor.[3] In any case, the Catholic Church was to succeed in operating effectively without churches in Ireland for a great many years. The difficulty experienced by the bishops of the Church of Ireland in compelling its clergy to reside in their parishes was another symptom of a deeper, underlying malaise, and the parliament's rejection of the bill intended to remedy that symptom would not have provided committed Protestant ministers in many parishes. Likewise, the utility of the rejected bill to empower the deputy and council to appoint dignitaries in the Church in Munster and Connacht must be doubted in the absence of Protestant clergymen available for promotion.

In sum, the ecclesiastical bills submitted to the Irish parliament of 1569–71 were not likely to have made a decisive contribution to the course of the Elizabethan reformation in Ireland, but the rejection of virtually all but the schools bill emasculated Sidney's ecclesiastical legislative programme. His imminent recall from Ireland early in 1571 was its final *coup de grace*. His successor, Sir William Fitzwilliam, adopted a far less ambitious approach to government, with regards to the Reformation as much as to the strictly political affairs of state. The drive to have more schools established foundered and the parish churches continued to crumble, while the idea of an Irish university languished.

When Sidney was re-appointed as lord deputy in 1575, he found that the Reformation had made virtually no progress during his years of absence. In April 1576, he penned a lengthy indictment of the state of the Church of Ireland, based on his own observations and on detailed information provided by Bishop Brady:[4]

2 Treadwell, 'Irish parliament of 1569–71', p. 85.   3 I recognise that economic difficulties, much of them caused by the political and military upheavals in Elizabethan Ireland, contributed to the poor state of many churches, though the universal scale of the problem of decayed churches suggests that collective decisions were taken to not maintain the buildings.   4 Brady, *State papers*, no. xi.

The ... Church is now so spoiled (as well by the ruins of the temples, as the dissipation and embezzling of patrimony, and most of all for want of sufficient ministers) as so deformed and overthrown a Church there is not, I am sure, in any region where Christ is professed ...

I would not have believed had I not for a great part viewed the same throughout the whole realm, and was advertised of the particular estate of the Church in the bishopric of Meath (being the best inhabited country of all this realm) by the honest, zealous and learned bishop of the same, Mr Hugh Brady, a godly minister for the Gospel and a good servant to your highness, who went from church to church himself and found that there are within his dioceses 224 parish churches, of which number 105 are impropriated to sundry possessions of your highness, and all leased out for years or in fee farm to several farmers [of tithes], and great gain reaped out of them above the rent which your majesty receives. No parson or vicar resident upon any of them, and a very simple or sorry curate, for the most part, appointed to serve therein. Among which number of curates, only eighteen were found to be able to speak English, the rest Irish priests or rather Irish rogues, having very little Latin, less learning and civility. All these live upon the bare altarages, as they term them (which, God knows, are very small) and were wont to live upon the gain of Masses, dirges, shrivings and such like trumpery godly abolished by your majesty. Not one house standing for any of them to dwell in. In many places the very walls of the churches down, very few chancels covered, windows and doors ruined or spoiled. There are 52 other parish churches more in the same diocese who have vicars endowed upon them, better served and maintained than the others, yet but badly. There are 52 parish churches more residue of the first number of 224, which pertain to diverse lords. And these, though in better estate than the rest, commonly are yet far from well. If this be the estate of the churches in the best-peopled diocese, and best-governed country of this your realm (as in truth it is), easy it is for your majesty to conjecture in what case the rest is, where little or no reformation, either of religion or manners, has yet been planted and continued among them.

Sidney's proposed solutions to these problems were, firstly, to seek authorisation from the queen to enquire as to who was responsible for the poor condition of the churches, and 'to compel them speedily' to restore them. He asked that a search be conducted in England's universities for anyone who could speak Irish and would willingly serve as a minister in Ireland (he hoped for 'ten or twelve at the least') or, if there were none or not enough, he suggested that the Scottish regent be approached to remedy the deficiency, since in Scotland 'there are many of the Reformed Church that are of this language'. Meanwhile, Sidney asked that 'three or four grave, learned and venerable personages of the clergy there [of England], be sent hither [to Ireland], who in short space being here would sensibly perceive the enormities of this overthrown Church and easily prescribe orders for the repair and upholding of the same … that your officer here might execute the same'. Three months later Lord Burghley replied to Sidney's proposals for the Irish Church, directing him to consult first with the Council of Ireland and reduce his opinion 'to such heads as the cause will bear', and send over two representatives ('of each nation [English-born and Irish-born] one').[5] Nothing came of Sidney's initiative.

The sorry state of the Church of Ireland in Meath was not simply a result of economic problems. Meath encompassed most of the most productive farmland in the Pale. It included a number of well-endowed benefices: Brendan Scott has calculated that there were ten benefices in Meath diocese that yielded at least £19 *per annum* in 1538–9, while in 1604, partly as a result of inflation, thirty-two benefices yielded more than £30.[6] Over the course of Hugh Brady's twenty-year episcopate, it should have been financially possible to wage a team of Protestant preachers to at least attempt to evangelise the people of Meath diocese – if there had been Protestant preachers available to recruit into the diocese's ministry. The fundamental problem was the absence of a Protestant community from which Protestant clergymen could be recruited.

The generally poor state of the church buildings was a glaring symptom of the absence of popular support, with churches throughout the Pale and beyond it, suffering from severe neglect in Elizabeth's reign. Even by 1566, Deputy Sidney could observe in the dioceses of Armagh, Dublin and Meath, 'the churches universally in ruin (and some wholly down)'.[7] Bishop Nicholas Walsh of Ossory observed of his diocese in 1577, that 'almost all the churches [and] chancels within that diocese were utterly ruined and decayed and that neither the parishioners nor others that are bound to repair them and set them up could by any means be won or induced to do so'.[8] The churches in the neighbouring diocese of Leighlin were generally in ruinous order. Of course, many churches were ruined in the upsurge in violence that swept across extensive parts of Ireland, sometimes repeatedly, in the course of Elizabeth's reign, but the pervasive nature of the ruination of the churches, even in the Pale itself, suggests that it reflected communal hostility towards the Elizabethan reformation, rather than the outcome of mischance.

5 Ibid., no. xiii.   6 Scott, *Tudor diocese of Meath*, pp 68–9, 71.   7 Shirley, *Original letters*, no. lxxxii; Jefferies, *Priests and prelate of Armagh in the age of reformations* (Dublin, 1997), p. 171. 8 RCB Library, Graves Collection, p. 9, cited in Neely, *Kilkenny*, p. 44.

James Murray has shown that Deputy Sidney came to regard Archbishop Loftus, in particular, as an obstacle to the reform of the Church of Ireland.[9] He forced the archbishop to appoint Dr George Acworth, a noted and experienced church lawyer, as the official principal and vicar general of Dublin diocese in place of John Ball who was also removed from the registrarship of the Ecclesiastical High Commission at the same time.[10] Several members of the clergy of St Patrick's Cathedral, Dublin, had earlier charged Ball with leading a 'licentious' life which was 'complained of by many', but it was claimed that Chancellor Weston, his uncle, dean of the cathedral and chairman of the Ecclesiastical High Commission, merely 'winked at' his offences.[11] It was alleged that when any

> woman that is fair and well-favoured comes before him for fornication or the like crime he never hears the cause in open court, but appoints her his chamber for hearing where, for his filthy pleasure gained with her, he absolves her offences, as is well known by the above-named Cicely Fletcher.

Furthermore, Ball was charged with being a drunkard and 'a devilish and detestable briber'. It was claimed that during visitations, he granted absolutions from serious sins for sums of money, using the Catholic formula, '*Absolvo te, et cetera*'. It was alleged that he was 'greatly suspected to be a Papist or else a neuter, which is worse'. Such were the formal allegations made against one of the key officers in Loftus' diocesan administration by his own colleagues. Another of Loftus' key administrators, John Bird, was removed from office as Dublin's diocesan registrar following a church court-case presided over by Acworth.[12] The fact that Loftus appointed such disreputable laymen to the most senior positions in his diocese does not reflect well on his priorities.

Not content with reforming Loftus' diocesan administration, Sidney erected a court of faculties in Ireland on 18 March 1577.[13] He appointed Dr Acworth and Robert Garvey as its judges. This court assumed responsibility for large parts of the bishops' jurisdictions, in visitation rights, testamentary matters and the right to grant dispensations for a wide variety of causes. Sidney intended that the new, independent church court would address the rising tide of corruption within the Church of Ireland. In the summer of 1577, Deputy Sidney dissolved the Ecclesiastical High Commission established by the queen in 1568, and had a new Commission established, which he intended to be more forceful in imposing

9 Murray, 'Tudor diocese of Dublin, pp 269–78; idem, *Enforcing the English Reformation*, pp 296–9. 10 Ibid., pp 269–70. 11 Brady, *State papers*, no. xxiv. 12 Murray, 'Tudor diocese of Dublin', p. 270; idem, *Enforcing the English Reformation*, p. 297. 13 Brady, *State papers*, no. xviii; Murray, 'Dublin diocese', pp 270–1; idem, *Enforcing the English Reformation*, p. 298.

the Elizabethan religious settlement in Ireland.[14] However, Sidney left office in Ireland on 14 September 1578.

Once Sidney was gone, Archbishop Loftus launched a counter-attack on his reformatory schemes.[15] He sacked Acworth.[16] He travelled to England in December 1578, and succeeded in rehabilitating himself. A new commission was issued for the Court of Faculties in May 1579, making Loftus and Garvey its two judges – thus removing the greatest threat to Loftus' archiepiscopal jurisdiction and many of the fees associated with it.[17] Loftus remained the key figure on the Ecclesiastical High Commission, and while he had to accept failure in his efforts to have Ball reappointed as the Commission's registrar and collector of fines, he managed to get John Bird, his former diocesan registrar who was sacked by Acworth, appointed to that office instead.

James Murray has shown that the Ecclesiastical High Commission escalated its activities in Ireland significantly, with an 86 per cent increase in the fines levied over the period 1577–82, compared with the preceding period, 1573–7.[18] Progress was certainly made in compelling outward conformity: Sir Edward Waterhouse informed Walsingham that he found

> that which I never hoped of, namely, that the whole inhabitants being in effect all noted to be obstinate Papists in times past, do now all repair to the church and show themselves obedient in the substance of religion. Most of the nobility (amongst which one has been noted to be a Jesuit) come to sermons and show themselves examples to others.[19]

It is interesting and very significant, though, to note that that conformity was only very recently achieved – but the coercion employed to enforce such conformity was likely to have been highly counter-productive in terms of winning hearts and souls for the Elizabethan Church.

CATHOLIC REACTION

The intensification and extension of the Elizabethan reformation in Ireland began prior to Sidney's appointment, but was promoted more energetically under his auspices. The Spanish ambassador in London informed Philip II in March 1568 that, although Sidney's administration 'dissemble with them

---

14 Murray, 'Tudor diocese of Dublin', p. 280; idem, *Enforcing the English Reformation*, p. 303. 15 Brady, *State papers*, nos xviii, xx; Murray, 'Tudor diocese of Dublin', pp 277–8. 16 *Fiants, Ire., Eliz.*, nos 3510, 3512; Murray, 'Tudor diocese of Dublin', p. 270. 17 Murray, 'Tudor diocese of Dublin', p. 279; idem, *Enforcing the English Reformation*, p. 304. 18 Murray, 'Tudor diocese of Dublin', p. 284; idem, *Enforcing the English Reformation*, p. 308. 19 SP 63/66/66.

[Catholics in Ireland], deeming it expedient so to do for the present in order not to disturb the country, they yet display great vigilance in obstructing any provision that may there be made by bull or ordinance of his holiness'.[20]

In April 1567, Archbishop Creagh was captured and imprisoned in Dublin Castle.[21] Sidney would have had Creagh sent to the Tower of London, but the queen was anxious to make an example of the archbishop in Ireland. He was put on trial in Dublin and, as Sidney feared, he was acquitted by a jury comprised of twelve gentlemen of the Pale.[22] The jurors were themselves imprisoned and fined for their verdict, as they may well have anticipated. That serves as a reminder, if it were needed, of the Pale's élites' continuing commitment to Catholicism. Creagh himself was incarcerated in awful conditions until he eventually died in 1586. As a prisoner of conscience, his steadfast commitment to his faith exerted great influence over the minds of many in Ireland. In 1575, Archbishop Loftus importuned Deputy Fitzwilliam to seek Creagh's transfer from Dublin because, the deputy wrote, the Catholic archbishop 'wonderfully incites this people and hinders the [Protestant] archbishop of Dublin's godly endeavours to promote religion'.[23] Creagh's modern biographer, Colm Lennon, has endorsed the judgment of contemporaries as to the archbishop's profound influence on behalf of Catholicism in Elizabethan times.[24]

The institutional Catholic Church was shown to be extremely vulnerable in the face of the concerted efforts of the English crown to enforce conformity to the Elizabethan reformation in the Pale, and to extend its ecclesiastical jurisdiction beyond the Pale, from 1565. Catholic bishops were replaced on their deaths by a series of bishops who were appointed by the English crown, right across those dioceses that had traditionally been within the English sphere of influence. In the Pale and in the larger outlying towns, the *Book of Common Prayer* was increasingly employed in church services and, in Dublin and Drogheda and in some other places, local congregations were being compelled to attend those services.[25] There was a real possibility that people in Ireland would become inured to Protestantism over time, especially where congregations regularly attended Church of Ireland services. This created the very real possibility of their conversion to Protestantism (as was happening in England at that same time).

There was a real challenge in terms of Catholic catechesis and sacramental ministry, over an increasing number of parishes in areas under effective English

20 *CSP Rome, 1558–71*, no. 525; Ronan, *Reformation in Ireland*, pp 269–70. 21 Lennon, *Archbishop Creagh*, pp 88, 90. 22 Ibid., pp 104–6. 23 SP 63/xlix/65. Denis Molam, a renegade Irish friar who spied on Irish Catholic dissidents on behalf of the English crown, identified Creagh's reputation, along with Sir James Fitzmaurice Fitzgerald and the survival of a number of friaries, as one of three key factors sustaining Catholicism in Ireland; Ronan, *Reformation in Ireland*, p. 572. 24 Lennon, *Archbishop Creagh*, pp 106–48. 25 Ronan, *Reformation in Ireland*, pp 473–89.

authority. The provision of Catholic services could only be achieved by turning a blind eye to the increasingly widespread use of the *Book of Common Prayer* by priests who had been ordained by Catholic rites but who conformed to the Elizabethan Church of Ireland. Those priests were not necessarily ordained prior to the enactment of the Elizabethan religious settlement. There had long been a movement of priests from Ulster and Connacht to take up cures in the Pale, as well as the movement of priests from outlying parts of Leinster, and it is probable that any decline in recruitment to the ranks of the diocesan clergy from within the areas affected by the Reformation had to be compensated for by an even greater recourse to the employment of priests from beyond the Pale.[26] In Meath diocese, there were more than 120 parishes served by unbeneficed priests, of whom only eighteen were capable of speaking English in 1576.[27]

I have no doubt that the clergy of Meath generally used the *Book of Common Prayer* for services under Bishop Brady's direction, with the Latin version predominantly employed by the unbeneficed parish priests, and use of the English version probably confined to the more anglicised eastern parishes served by a rector or vicar – but Sidney acknowledged that many priests still celebrated Catholic rites through sheer financial necessity if not conviction, because of their dependence on altarages. It is clear that the Elizabethan bishops were hamstrung, having no alternative to appointing Catholic priests to parishes that would otherwise have no church services, and obliged to turn a blind eye to the continued celebration of Catholic services by a very high proportion of the clergy. However, that kind of ambivalence could not be sustained indefinitely.

In Ossory diocese, the ordination of clergy by the *Book of Common Prayer* rites was delayed by the fact that the Elizabethan bishop, Christopher Gaffney, conducted no ordinations himself but delegated the task to a Catholic bishop, the ordinary of Killaloe.[28] Nonetheless, as more and more of the bishops in *de facto* control of Irish dioceses were consecrated in services using the *Book of Common Prayer*, the future prospects of being able to maintain a ministry of Catholic priests in parishes, even if one was willing to overlook their conformity to the Elizabethan Church, were not promising.

Edmund Tanner, a former Jesuit, returned to Ireland in June 1576 because he had heard from learned and grave men that, although there were not one hundred heretical Irishmen in Ireland, the people lacked religious instruction and consequently few knew and fewer understood even the Lord's Prayer, the articles of faith or the commandments.[29] Though his informants may have exaggerated the situation, it was doubtless true that the number and quality of Catholic priests in Ireland had suffered as a result of the closure of most of the monastic schools, the probable closure of many of the *studia particularlia* in the

26 Lawlor, 'Liber Ruber', p. 166. 27 Brady, *State papers*, no. xi. 28 Ibid., nos xviii, xix.
29 *CSP Rome, 1558–71*, p. 468; Bolster, *Diocese of Cork*, p. 74.

south, and the fact that the priesthood as a career option was not as appealing as it used to be, because of uncertainty and disruption caused by the Tudor reformations.

The vicissitudes of the Elizabethan Church of Ireland have been highlighted by Helen Coburn-Walshe and Aidan Clarke, but the even greater vicissitudes of the Catholic Church at the same time have been overlooked. The Catholic Church was faced with the loss of all of its benefices. It was not possible yet to conceive of the possibility of two churches co-existing in Ireland; a Protestant established Church with possession of the real estate of the medieval Church and its right to tithes, and a disestablished Catholic Church, which would have to subsist on the voluntary offerings of its congregations.

The role of the mendicant friars has long been recognised as significant in affecting the course of the Tudor reformations in Ireland, but they were never in a position to provide a comprehensive parish ministry. Nonetheless, the survival of a number of mendicant communities in the west and north of Ireland provided the Catholic Church with bodies of expert preachers who were cheap to train and maintain (by contrast with their Protestant graduate counterparts), able to operate far and wide on preaching missions (unlike their Church of Ireland counterparts, who were fettered by legal obligations to reside within the bounds of a single parish), and were counted as being very effective by their friends and foes (by contrast with the Protestant preachers who, according to Archbishop Loftus, laboured in vain).[30] Nonetheless, there was a real problem with the limited numbers of friars available in Ireland over much of the latter half of the sixteenth century, and their very uneven distribution across the country. A remarkable glimpse of the mendicant friars in action was afforded by Edward White, clerk to the earl of Clanrickard and a committed Protestant, in a letter to Deputy Fitzwilliam in November 1572:

> A general council of friars assembled in the abbey [Franciscan friary?] of Galway on St Francis' Day last [4 October 1572], which was attended by Bishop [Donough] O'Gallagher [prior of the Franciscans in Ireland]. The godly can scarcely show their faces as though the kingdom of Antichrist were erected again; speaking words against the state, threatening Spanish inquisition, but also defiances against professors of God's word as it would pity all Christian hearts to hear, so far as anything I can hear there is a foul stink of rebellion breeding in that town. Since which council, the friars, yea of Ulster are so open in Galway as sometimes they go 10, 14, 16, yea 20 in a company and so range abroad in that country, sowing the seed of that wicked doctrine, so as the poor countrymen seeing them so embraced in the

30 SP 63/56/27.

town dare say nothing, not [even] the earl himself. After this council, it was concluded another council should be held at Donegal in O'Donnell's country, where after long conference the same is removed to Adare in Munster, but seven Irish miles from Limerick where the friars will be shortly. ... their devices is all how to subvert the English government and set up their own wickedness once again. They are as bold as though the pope were king of England and Ireland ...

All Hallows last there have been 14 friars in Galway and they preached in the abbey there, whither came unto them diverse aldermen of the town, amongst them one Denis Kirwan, mayor 1570–1; the preacher a friar of Ulster; doctrine rebellious. So daily to Galway where they behave themselves like princes. Out of the council of Donegal three or four friars went into France, and took ship at Galway, and thither came a priest very late out of France named Tadhg O'Farrell. There came from Spain five weeks ago a friar Dominican called Cormac [O'Fergus], appointed in Rome Provincial of the Black Friars [Dominicans] in Ireland. His helping hand with the rest must tend to wickedness; he brought indulgences and the rest from the pope and published the same in Sligo.[31]

The deputy passed White's letter on to Burghley with the comment that it was 'no new thing to have friars gad up and down in Ireland', but he was concerned about the 'time, place and occasion of their meeting' in that particular instance. For the friars to convene their council so publicly within the city of Galway, so soon after the St Bartholomew's Day massacre of Huguenots in France was clearly disturbing. White reported that news of the massacre 'was soon known to all friars and priests in Connacht and openly spread abroad in Ireland': small wonder that the 'godly' in Galway could 'scarcely show their faces'.

White's letter is interesting in showing how active some mendicant friars were, across a broad swathe of Ireland, in the early 1570s. They certainly strike one as part of the counter-reformation movement, with close links to Rome and France, a readiness to see the implications of developments in France and Spain for the situation in Ireland, and a confidence about the future of the religious struggle in Ireland. Only for White's letter, we would never have known of their energy and confidence at so early a date in the course of the Elizabethan reformation in Ireland.

I noted some years ago how the Henrician reformation sapped the support enjoyed by the Irish mendicant orders, and their morale, even before the dissolution of their houses.[32] Thomas Flynn, in his study of the Dominican friars in

---

31 SP 63/38/52, i.   32 SP 60/7/152; H.A. Jefferies, 'The early Tudor reformations in the

Ireland from 1536, noted that even where Dominican friaries were not dissolved in the reign of Henry VIII, their communities often died out, probably through a collapse in morale and an inability to secure young recruits.[33] Friaries were also vulnerable to attack by English military commanders.[34] Fitton, following his appointment as president of Connacht, was assiduous in destroying friaries and monasteries and in uprooting their communities.[35]

Flynn's study of the Dominicans shows that although the order was progressively degraded in Connacht, the remaining friars developed a high degree of contact with Rome and numbers of them were certain harbingers of the counter-reformation.[36] That is reflected in White's letter from Connacht in 1572, and also in the mendicants' ministry in the diocese of Waterford & Lismore.[37] Friars were also active in the Pale, with references to their activities in Dublin in 1563[38] and in Meath in 1577[39] – the latter from Bishop Brady suggesting that they were growing bolder at that time. Unfortunately, though, there is a tremendous lack of evidence with which to define the role of the mendicants during the Sidney years. It seems clear that there was a strong revival in the mendicant communities from the late 1560s/early 1570s, with greatly increased contact with mainland Europe and an imbibing of counter-reformation influences. Nonetheless, the numbers of friars, especially in the east and south of Ireland, was small.

In his letter of 1568, David Wolfe, SJ, seemed dejected at the prospects for the Catholic Church in Ireland.[40] He complained that 'the bishops of Ireland are hirelings and dumb-dogs, and acknowledge the queen of England as supreme head of the Church, all except three, besides the said Bishop Redmond [O'Gallagher], who have been strong bulwarks of the bride of Christ'. In his letter of 1574,[41] he wrote that it was the pope's releasing him from loyalty to Elizabeth that allowed him to advocate her ejection from the crown of Ireland, but it seems to me that he had already given consideration to the necessity of 'régime change' even prior to his arrest and imprisonment in 1567. His letter of 1574 shows that he had already made a careful inventory of the English crown's artillery across Ireland, from Carrickfergus to Dingle, before he had been arrested.

With the benefit of hindsight, it might seem that the hopes of Spanish intervention were always doomed to failure. However, that was very far from being obvious at the time. The new, militant version of counter-reformation Irish Catholicism was personified by Maurice Fitzgibbon, OCist, the papally appointed archbishop of Cashel, in 1567. Fitzgibbon ousted his Church of

Irish Pale', *JEH*, 52 (2001), p. 49.   33 Flynn, *The Dominicans*, p. 45.   34 Ronan, *Reformation in Ireland*, p. 339.   35 Flynn, *The Dominicans*, p. 76.   36 Ibid., pp 57–93.   37 Byrne, 'Reformation in Tudor Waterford', p. 30; Ronan, *Reformation in Ireland*, pp 499–500.
38 'Loftus' annals', *s.a.* 1563.   39 SP 63/58/16.   40 Ronan, *Reformation in Ireland*, pp 470–3.
41 Ibid., pp 473–89.

Ireland counterpart, MacCawell, at the point of a knife, and threatened to have him shipped off to Spain.[42] Archbishop Fitzgibbon then placed himself at the centre of a major Irish Catholic conspiracy against Elizabeth's political and religious policies in Ireland. According to Warham St Leger, the archbishop was regarded 'as though he was a god' by the Irish.[43]

Early in 1569, while Deputy Sidney presided over the first sessions of the parliament in Dublin, Fitzgibbon attended an alternative parliament convened in Munster, which also claimed to be a national assembly.[44] It sent a memorial to Philip II of Spain, purportedly signed by the four archbishops of Ireland and by eight other bishops, six earls and nineteen lords from across the country, asking him to protect them from heresy and offering the crown of Ireland to any blood relation of his who would reside in Ireland (subject to the agreement of the pope).[45] The assembly sent Fitzgibbon and Thomas O'Herlihy, bishop of Ross, as their emissaries with the memorial.[46] In fact, the memorial was disingenuous in that the assembly was very much a regional, rather than a national body.[47] Nonetheless, its convening marked a major new phase in the Catholic reaction to the Elizabethan reformation in Ireland.

It is always difficult to define precisely the relative weight to assign the different factors that motivated individuals in history. In Sir James Fitzmaurice's case, it is clear that his commitment to Catholicism was central to his outlook.[48] Significantly, he was a 'gossip' of the Jesuit, Wolfe,[49] and he had contemplated the religious life for himself until he was persuaded that he might serve God better with a sword.[50] His 1569 espousal of a 'faith and fatherland' ideology was sincere and profound, and it gave the insurgency that bears his name a character that set it apart from more mundane rebellions provoked by Elizabethan rule in Ireland.

Archbishop Fitzgibbon was a zealous advocate for Fitzmaurice's revolt. He wrote to the pope and Philip II of Spain that under Henry VIII and Edward VI, the English had 'plundered and devastated the churches and monasteries of Ireland ... and threw the whole population into the greatest confusion'. Elizabeth, he claimed, 'throughout the whole island has executed the policy of her father and brother with the greatest determination and vigour, sending new preachers and heretical bishops with great stores of heretical books to be circulated among the people'. Yet, he affirmed, the Irish 'all in general detest the

42 Loftus MS, Annals, *s.a.* 1567 [recte 1568].   43 SP 63/xxvii/23.   44 A.M. McCormack, *The earldom of Desmond, 1463–1583: the decline and crisis of a feudal lordship* (Dublin, 2005), pp 131–2.   45 Moran (ed.), *Spicilegium Ossoriense*, i, pp 59–62.   46 D.M. Downey, 'Culture and diplomacy: the Spanish-Habsburg dimension in the Irish counter-reformation movement, *c.*1529–74' (1994), pp 69–80; McCormack, *Earldom of Desmond*, pp 111–12.   47 SP 63/27/23; McCormack, *Earldom of Desmond*, p. 112.   48 Ibid., pp 115–16.   49 For the importance of this relationship, see Fiona Fitzsimons, 'Fosterage and gossiprid in late medieval Ireland: some new evidence' in P.J. Duffy, D. Edwards and E. FitzPatrick (eds), *Gaelic Ireland, c.1250–c.1650: land, lordship and settlement* (Dublin, 2001).   50 Ronan, *Reformation in Ireland*, p. 470.

tyrannous and inconstant yoke of the English state, and still more its heresies'.[51] For Fitzgibbon, patriotism was at least as much an inspiration as religion: he told the laird of Clyshe in 1572 that 'He had rather that any nation be their king, yea, rather the muckle devil, than her majesty'.[52]

Archbishop Fitzgibbon's mission to Philip II, despite promises from the king, proved to be a failure.[53] Yet, Fitzmaurice and McCarthy Mór rebelled regardless and launched an all-out assault on the English settlement in Kerrycurrihy on 16 June 1569.[54] The surviving English settlers took refuge in Cork city. Fitzmaurice demanded that the corporation of Cork expunge 'that old heresy newly raised and invented' and restore Catholic services in the city. He ordered that they expel 'the Huguenots, both men and women' from the city.[55] Meanwhile, he declared that he would destroy all cities and towns loyal to the queen.

On the very day that Fitzmaurice and McCarthy Mór attacked the English colonists in Kerrycurrihy, an emergency meeting of the council of Ireland proclaimed Sirs Edmund, Edward and Piers Butler, the brothers of the earl of Ormond, as 'rebels and traitors'.[56] The earl's siblings had been alienated by Deputy Sidney's 'penchant for high-handed arbitrary rule', and particularly by his sponsorship of Sir Peter Carew's spurious claims to the barony of Idrone, County Carlow.[57] Sir Edmund Butler conspicuously opposed several government measures in the first sessions of the Irish parliament of 1569–71, and spoke passionately against Hooker's slurs in the Commons against Philip and Mary, and against the Irish MPs, before quitting the assembly. He joined Fitzmaurice in open rebellion after what David Edwards termed as 'months of planning'.[58] The Butler brothers, with Fitzmaurice and McCarthy Mór, laid siege to Kilkenny in July 1569, but failed to capture it. Sidney appointed Humphrey Gilbert as colonel and governor of Munster.[59] Gilbert used unrestrained terror and systematic brutality to crush the revolt, but the rebel leader would not surrender and the insurgency continued for over three and a half years in all, with the insurgents seemingly 'oblivious to the impossibility of their position'.[60]

From December 1569, Sir Edward Fitton was president of a new provincial council established for Connacht. He sought to promote the Reformation through a wave of iconoclasm in parish churches, the expelling of friars from their houses and the insistence that parish clergy either 'put away their concubines or else … marry them'.[61] His enthusiastic assaults on local political autonomies and religion was ill-advised, and rebellion spread in resonance with Fitzmaurice's revolt in Munster, with the earl of Thomond, the sons of the earl of Clanrickard and MacWilliam Burkes of Mayo openly defying the crown's

51 Moran (ed.), *Spicilegium Ossoriense*, i, 59.   52 Quoted in Ronan, *Reformation in Ireland*, p. 399.   53 Moran (ed.), *Spicilegium Ossoriense*, i, p. 62; Ronan, *Reformation in Ireland*, p. 334. 54 SP 63/28/35, 36, 37.   55 SP 63/29/8.   56 David Edwards, *The Ormond lordship in County Kilkenny, 1515–1642* (Dublin, 2003), p. 196.   57 Ibid., pp 194–8, 200.   58 Ibid., p. 197. 59 McCormack, *Earldom of Desmond*, pp 118–19.   60 Ibid., p. 124.   61 SP 63/30/4.

officers at various times.[62] Clanrickard's sons were the most defiant: they burned the towns of Athenry and Athlone and menaced Galway. For a time in 1572, Fitton lost control completely in Connacht. It was no coincidence that it was at that juncture, in October 1572, that a national conference of Franciscan friars was held in Galway.[63]

According to Redmond Stackbold, son of the dean of Cashel, the rebels still enjoyed much covert support from the gentlemen of Counties Cork, Limerick and Kerry.[64] A priest and a clerical student, and a horseman, posted a papal bull on one of the gates of Limerick; presumably a copy of the bull that excommunicated Elizabeth.[65] However, Edmund Daniel, SJ, a relative of David Wolfe, SJ, was arrested soon after his arrival in Limerick in 1572 by its mayor, Thomas Arthur, and was handed over to Sir John Perrot, the president of Munster, who had him hanged, drawn and quartered in Cork for treason, having been found in possession of correspondence destined for Fitzmaurice, on 25 October 1572.[66] According to Wolfe, his death edified not only Catholics but heretics also.

Finally, wearied of the unending revolt, the English crown agreed to terms with the earl of Desmond on 21 January 1573.[67] With Desmond restored and no prospect of Spanish or French aid forthcoming, Fitzmaurice sued for peace.[68] Perrot rather naïvely hoped that Fitzmaurice would become 'a second St Paul' among the Irish.[69] According to the Four Masters, though, Desmond ordained that 'the Church and men of science should be restored to the possession of their privileges; and he re-established the orders to the law of the pope'.[70] Hugh Lacey was restored as bishop of Limerick in place of William Casey, Elizabeth's appointee. The precentor of Limerick who had been deprived by the Ecclesiastical Commission was also restored to his former office. Adare friary was restored to the Franciscans.[71]

Morgan O'Brien Arra, Elizabeth's bishop-designate of Killaloe,[72] wrote on 22 December 1573 that the earl of Desmond intended to meet with the earl of Clanrickard and with Tadhg McMurrough O'Brien, and to send messengers to seek aid of Philip II of Spain.[73] Matthew Sheyne, the Elizabethan bishop of Cork & Cloyne, reported in October 1573 that David Wolfe had departed for Spain from Desmond's lordship accompanied by a priest named Richard Corbally and one of Sir James Fitzmaurice's sons.[74] There is no evidence to show whether Wolfe went to Spain as an emissary of the earl, yet the coincidence in timing of Wolfe's departure accompanied by Fitzmaurice's son, Desmond's

62 Lennon, *Sixteenth-century Ireland: the incomplete conquest* (Dublin, 2005), pp 244–6. 63 SP 63/38/52. 64 SP 63/34/32, i, ii. 65 SP 63/34/32. 66 Hogan, *Ibernia Ignatiana*, p. 20; Ronan, *Reformation in Ireland*, pp 418–19. 67 McCormack, *Earldom of Desmond*, p. 124. 68 Perrot believed that it was Desmond's impending return to Ireland which convinced Fitzmaurice to capitulate: SP 63/40/19. See also, McCormack, *Earldom of Desmond*, pp 124–5. 69 SP 63/39/40, i; 63/50/11. 70 *AFM* s.a. 1573. 71 SP 63/42/88; 63/43/5. 72 SP 63/29/85; *CPCRI*, Eliz., i, p. 539. 73 SP 63/44/3, i. 74 SP 63/42/49.

belligerent displays of commitment to Catholicism, and the information communicated by O'Brien Arra about Desmond's conspiracy, is certainly intriguing.

Wolfe's lengthy 'Description of Ireland' was written in about March of 1574 to persuade Philip II to send military aid to the Catholics in Ireland. It concluded in the name of Fitzmaurice.[75] The earl of Desmond and his brother (Sir John of Desmond, presumably) were given pride of place in the 'Description' and both were characterised as 'excellent Catholics', along with Fitzmaurice, while the earl of Clanrickard and his wife were characterised as 'well-conditioned Catholics'. In the following month, Philip II sent a military envoy to Ireland to reconnoitre the situation – an indication of the seriousness with which he was considering the matter.[76] The envoy landed at Dungarvan on 3 May 1574, and visited Waterford and Cork and parts of the interior. He found the people he met 'all Catholics, but exposed to disability in the exercise of their religion wherever the English had power'. He reported that they were forbidden to celebrate Mass in their parish churches but assembled for Mass instead in private houses – an interesting early reference to this practice outside the Pale. The envoy concluded that the Irish 'hated the English and longed for the arrival of the Spanish'. I do not doubt that the Spanish envoy was only introduced to and spoke to zealous Catholics while in southern Ireland and not to a representative sample of the general population. However, an Englishman named Henry Ackworth observed about the same time that among the citizens of Waterford 'there are conspiracies among them, partly because they are Papists and partly through hatred of the English government'.[77] Deputy Sidney, having toured Munster in 1575, observed that the people of that province were 'for the most part, all Papists, and that of the malicioust degree'.[78] It seems that the Elizabethan reformation undermined the loyalty of many people in Ireland whose communities had traditionally given their allegiance to the English crown.

Philip II's envoy, though very assuring about the Catholic commitment he encountered in southern Ireland, did not persuade his king of the viability of a military expedition there. Wolfe considered leaving Spain, when he got 'no speedy answer' to his call for support until the papal nuncio in Spain persuaded him to stay longer.[79] Wolfe was joined by Archbishop Fitzgibbon of Cashel, Bishop MacBrien of Emly, Bishop O'Gallagher of Killala and Patrick O'Hely, OFM, and future bishop of Mayo, in lobbying Philip II to send a military expedition to Ireland.[80] O'Hely enjoyed the best access to the king and laid before him the rebels' plans for a papally sponsored Spanish expedition to Ireland in support of Irish Catholics willing to fight to free their country of

75 *CSP Rome, 1572–78*, no. 29; J. Begley, *The diocese of Limerick in the sixteenth and seventeenth centuries* (Dublin, 1927), appendix, pp 494–515.   76 Ronan, *Reformation in Ireland*, pp 499–500. 77 SP 63/47/22.   78 *Cal. Carew MSS, 1575–88*, p. 352.   79 *CSP Rome, 1572–78*, no. 370; Ronan, *Reformation in Ireland*, p. 497.   80 Ronan, *Reformation in Ireland*, pp 501, 507, 518–20.

Elizabeth's heretical governance. Sir James Fitzmaurice Fitzgerald slipped out of Ireland in March 1575 with his wife, and the seneschal of Imokilly. According to the confession of one of Fitzmaurice's men in June 1575, his master had had secret conferences with Sir John, the earl of Desmond's brother, and the seneschal of Imokilly before his departure – but he confessed to no certain knowledge of the earl himself having spoken with Fitzmaurice before his departure, though he referred to rumours to that effect.[81]

Fitzmaurice was favourably entertained by the king of France, but realised in time that no French military support would be forthcoming.[82] The Catholic churchmen in exile, however, continued to lobby at Rome and Madrid.[83] Persistence paid off eventually, and in February 1577, Fitzmaurice received authorisation from Pope Gregory XIII to rebel in Ireland.[84] That news may have reached Catholics in Ireland very quickly, because Bishop Brady of Meath, writing on 12 May 1577, reported that over the previous 'quarter of a year' the people of his diocese in the Pale had grown bolder in religion.[85] He sensed that something significant was afoot. Many clergymen travelled to Armagh for some kind of clerical conference yet, tellingly, no one would tell Brady what was happening. Irish clergymen from the continental colleges were directed to travel to Ireland to support the Catholic cause, and prepare the way for the coming rebellion.[86] Sander, a key supporter of Fitzmaurice, particularly canvassed for Dr Nicholas Comerford, a Waterford man who was a teacher at Louvain, to be sent to Ireland.[87] Drury reported the effects of Comerford's return to the south-east of Ireland in 1577.[88]

In the event, the rebellion in Ireland was delayed by the Spanish king's continuing indecision, and by misfortune. A papal expeditionary force of one thousand swordsmen was eventually assembled early in 1578, but it was annihilated after joining the king of Portugal's ill-fated expedition to Morocco in August 1578.[89] The fiasco exhausted the pope's enthusiasm for large-scale military intervention in Ireland. Fitzmaurice, encouraged by letters from O'Donnell and Desmond, decided to return home anyway and launch a rebellion in the hope that military success in Ireland would demonstrate Irish commitment and capabilities to a sceptical Spanish king and encourage him to support their cause.[90] In July 1579, Fitzmaurice, with Dr Nicholas Sander and sixty Italian and Spanish soldiers, set sail for Ireland.[91] The prevailing view

81 SP 63/52/25. 82 SP 63/51/27, i, ii; *CSP Rome*, no. 475; Ronan, *Reformation in Ireland*, pp 509–11. 83 Ronan, *Reformation in Ireland*, p. 564. 84 Ibid., pp 560–1. 85 SP 63/58/16. 86 Ronan, *Reformation in Ireland*, p. 580. 87 *CSP Rome, 1572–78*, no. 939; Ronan, *Reformation in Ireland*, p. 590. 88 Brady, *State papers*, no. xv. 89 Ronan, *Reformation in Ireland*, pp 577–80. 90 *CSP Rome, 1572–8*, no. 714. I see no reason to question the reliability of this letter from Fitzmaurice to Sander. The two men were very close associates and confidants at that stage and both were willing to die as Catholic martyrs if need be. 91 Ronan, *Reformation in Ireland*, p. 610.

among historians is that it was a forlorn mission – yet Fitzmaurice may have had more than his faith in God to assure him that success was attainable.

THE STATE OF RELIGION

Dublin and the Pale

On 25 January 1568, Archbishop Loftus declared to Cecil that 'the daily service used in both my cathedral churches … and elsewhere in my diocese will report no other form of prayer or administration of sacraments is used than such as is allowed and appointed by the statutes and injunctions usually throughout all England'.[92] Taken at face-value, this implies that the *Book of Common Prayer* was used in services throughout Dublin diocese, but the use of word 'elsewhere' is ambiguous.

James Murray, citing evidence from the 1580s, reckons that it was the Latin version of the *Book of Common Prayer* that was generally used in the Pale throughout this period.[93] The unbeneficed parish priests in the Pale, who were overwhelmingly Irish-speakers, probably used the Latin version,[94] though the beneficed clergy, who included more English-speakers in their ranks, were more likely to use the English version. In either case, its efficacy as an evangelical instrument may be doubted, as there remained the problem that the parish clergy were generally untrained in the art of preaching. Congregations could be forced to attend Church of Ireland services, conducted in English in some places but more often in Latin, but they were given very little explicit doctrinal instruction, even in most parishes in Dublin.

In June 1566, prior to his translation from Armagh to Dublin, Archbishop Loftus lamented that parishioners in Ireland were 'much fleeced and nothing at all fed'.[95] In July 1570, after he had been the archbishop of Dublin for almost three years, Loftus reported that it was 'pitiful to see how the poor people give their tithes to be instructed and for want thereof continue in ignorance'.[96] In September 1571, Loftus wrote again of the people of his own diocese being 'sheep without a shepherd, without any doctrine and preaching of God's word'.[97] Chancellor Weston, writing in April 1568, confirmed Loftus' characterisation of the situation in dramatic terms:

> blinded through corruption of nature, evil bringing up, continual acquaintance and custom of sin, not only void of all knowledge of God like heathenish people, but drowned in idolatry and superstition with disobedience to their prince … a great number of them want all

92 SP 63/24/29.   93 Murray, 'Tudor diocese of Dublin', p. 245.   94 Brady, *State papers*, no. xi.   95 SP 63/18/13; Shirley, *Original letters*, no. xcii.   96 SP 63/30/64.   97 SP 63/34/13.

sense and sealing of sin. Ignorance, the mother and nurse of those foul babes, they have no instruction; their parsons, vicars and curates, some of whom I examined, be so void of knowledge of God and his will that they know not his commandments, no marvel if this blind people led by those blind guides, and being of nature given to sin and bred continually in the same, with no instruction or knowledge, should fall into the ditches or rather into the gulf of infidelity.[98]

Deputy Fitzwilliam referred in 1571 to the 'lamentable ignorance of the people of Ireland. In diverse counties not one preacher'.[99] For historians struggling to explain why the Reformation failed in Ireland, the absence of Protestant preachers must surely form a key component of their overall explanation. However, that does not mean that the provision of preachers would automatically have resulted in mass conversions to Protestantism. Loftus, after serving as a bishop for eleven 'troublesome' years in Ireland, asked in 1574 to be translated to an English diocese where his ministry might be

more profitable to the Church of God amongst the well-affected people of England than the rest of my time has been here amongst this stubborn and obstinate generation where men of far greater perfection than myself have long and vainly employed both doctrine and good examples.[1]

This is a fascinating insight into Loftus' mind: an uncharacteristic *cri de coeur*. What he indicated was that the progress of the Elizabethan reformation, in Dublin and further afield, was greatly impeded by a deep-rooted resistance to Protestantism, and that all efforts at preaching Protestant 'doctrine' and 'good examples' were in vain. Loftus complained in January 1568 that 'this miserable realm [is] overwhelmed with idolatry'.[2] A couple of months later, Chancellor Weston complained that the people of Ireland were 'drowned in idolatry and superstition'.[3] In 1574, shortly after Loftus had appealed to be translated to an English diocese, Deputy Fitzwilliam wrote that Richard Creagh, the Catholic archbishop of Armagh who had languished in prison for some years, 'wonderfully incites this people and hinders the archbishop of Dublin's godly endeavours to promote religion, which has enforced him to be importune unto me for the sending of him away'.[4]

In his essay on 'Why the Reformation failed in Ireland', Nicholas Canny proposed that it is 'likely that in Dublin, where a determined effort was made to promote "true" religion, many converts were won and retained'.[5] He suggested

98 SP 63/24/2. 99 SP 63/32/65. 1 SP 63/56/27; 63/lv/59. 2 SP 63/23/18. 3 SP 63/24/2. 4 SP 63/49/65. 5 Canny, 'Why the reformation failed', p. 432.

that the 'wealthier elements who had constant social and business dealings with the English civil and religious officials', and those who had regular trading contacts with London, might have become Protestant – but could offer no evidence to confirm these suggestions other than references to Rowland White and the Ussher family, and to Andrew Trollope's observation in 1587 that compared to other towns in Leinster the situation in Dublin was 'somewhat better than the rest, but nothing dutiful for the repair to [i.e. attendance at] churches there ... in respect of the number of inhabitants'.[6] In fact, there is no evidence extant to support the contention that 'many converts were won and retained' in Dublin. The claim runs directly counter to the recorded observations of contemporaries. Indeed, it was observed in 1599 that only twenty Irish-born householders in Dublin attended Church of Ireland services, and only four of them received communion.[7] What Canny termed the 'native Protestant tradition' in Dublin was very tenuous indeed.[8]

Colm Lennon reckoned that there were only 'half a dozen or so' families in Dublin that manifested strong leanings towards Protestantism in the 1560s – in a city of between 5,000 and 10,000 inhabitants.[9] David Wolfe, writing in 1574, observed of Dublin: 'The citizens are almost all Catholics, especially the natives of the city, though they go perforce to the communion and sermons of the heretics'.[10] In Drogheda, he wrote that the people were 'all Catholics, though perforce they go to hear the Koran of the heretics'.[11] As was indicated above, the Irish Ecclesiastical High Commission levied a very disproportionate share of its fines on householders in Dublin and Drogheda to compel attendance at Church of Ireland services, and did so over several years, presumably in the face of persistent recalcitrance. Archbishop Loftus, writing in 1574, confirmed that he, and other Protestant preachers, were confronted with 'stubborn and obstinate' people who rendered the preachers' labours in vain.[12] Barnaby Rich, writing in 1589, remarked that in Dublin, Drogheda and Waterford, 'the word of God has been for many years most plentifully preached, but to such a froward and obstinate people that wilfully resisting the truth can rend no other reason, the most of them, but that they will do as their fathers have done before them and that their uncles, their aunts, their cousins and their kindred do thus believe'.[13] Wolfe wrote in 1574 that the inhabitants of Cork were 'all Catholics, though they have a heretic for a bishop who preaches ever the Lutheran heresy to the people, but by God's grace to no purpose, though they are constrained to go to his sermons and other ceremonies that he performs'. Such remarks tell against simplistic assumptions that the only thing needed for the Reformation to succeed in Ireland was more preaching.

6 SP 63/131/64. 7 SP 63/207, pt.6/126. One must suspect that the non-communicants attended the Protestant services for career reasons rather than through Protestant convictions. 8 Canny, 'Why the reformation failed', p. 440. 9 Lennon, *Lords of Dublin*, pp 135, 31. 10 Ronan, *Reformation in Ireland*, pp 473–89. 11 Ibid. 12 SP 63/56/27; 63/lv/59. 13 SP 63/144/35; Canny, 'Why the reformation failed', p. 433.

Lennon found that during the first two or three decades of Elizabeth's reign, there was strong continuity in the religious life of Dublin beneath a veil of outward conformity to the queen's religious settlement. Catholic institutions, including chantries and religious confraternities, continued to function, and many traditional religious devotions remained very popular.[14] The citizens of Dublin supported many non-conforming priests, either as chaplains or tutors, or as peripatetic pastors.[15] He highlighted the key role played by women in succouring recusant priests, especially when the crown's persecution of Catholic clergy escalated.[16] He also suggested that the parish clergy who conformed to the Elizabethan Church were 'as important an agency in maintaining a continuous pastoral service in the older mode as they were in Elizabethan England'.[17] However, by contrast with England where the Catholic ministry atrophied over time as the Catholic-ordained priests either embraced the resonant liturgies of the *Book of Common Prayer* or died, the Catholic community in Dublin and elsewhere was able to communicate its faith to the next generations to remarkable effect. Lennon uncovered a veritable network of Catholic schools run by priests in Dublin city and county from the earliest years of Elizabeth's reign.[18] He plausibly speculated that the first generation of Jesuits and seminary priests who spear-headed the counter-reformation in Dublin had graduated from academies run by priest-teachers.[19] The significance of the network of Catholic chaplains and priest-tutors cannot be exaggerated. It gave the Catholic religion a resilience that it would not otherwise have been able to maintain, and it ensured that the generations that reached maturity in Dublin during Elizabeth's reign were, overwhelmingly, Catholic. Historians have tried to find a time-specific political explanation for unequivocal recusancy among the Dubliners and Palesmen in the 1580s,[20] but it was largely the fruit of the decision taken by so many of the local élites in the 1560s and 1570s to ensure that their children received an unambiguously Catholic education.

Reference was made earlier to Loftus' finding in 1565 that the landowners of the Pale had collectively disengaged from the Established Church following the enactment of the Elizabethan religious settlement. Clodagh Tait stated that Sir John Cusack's will 'indicates that in his part of County Meath in 1571 Catholic services were going on, seemingly as normal, in the local churches'.[21] In 1574,

---

14 Lennon, *Lords of Dublin*, pp 130, 145–7, 149, 150–1, 163, 186, 215. 15 Ibid., pp 142, 143, 147, 149, 150. 16 Ibid., pp 156, 157, 213–14. 17 Ibid., pp 134, 141, 142. 18 Ibid., pp 142–3, 146, 150; Lennon, 'Mass in the manor house: the counter-reformation in Dublin, 1560–1630' in James Kelly and Daire Keogh (eds), *History of the diocese of Dublin* (Dublin, 2000), pp 117–18. 19 Lennon, *Lords of Dublin*, p. 143; idem, 'Mass in the manor house', p. 118. 20 See especially Ciarán Brady, 'Conservative subversives: the community of the Pale and the Dublin administration, 1556–86' in Patrick Corish (ed.), *Radicals, rebels and establishments* (Historical Studies, xv, Belfast, 1985), pp 233–62; Lennon, *Lords of Dublin*, pp 151–8. 21 Clodagh Tait, '"As legacie upon my soul": the wills of the Irish Catholic community, c.1550–c.1660' in Robert Armstrong and Tadhg Ó hAnnrachain (eds), *Community in early modern Ireland* (Dublin, 2006), p. 188.

Wolfe reported about Meath, which encompassed the greater part of the Pale, that 'I can affirm with truth that among so many barons, lords, knights and gentlemen I know (thanks to God) no heretic except Viscount Gormanstown'.[22] The correspondence of Bishop Brady supports the Jesuit's claim. In 1570, Brady commended Baron Robert Cusack as 'the only man in his profession that favours religion in this land ... The number of lawyers is great and bear no less sway. So are they, for the most part, nay, I might say all, thwarters and hinderers of matters that should tend to the reformation of religion'.[23] The lawyers were representative of the landholding classes of the Pale, and Brady was clear that they actively hampered his efforts to enforce compliance to the Elizabethan religious settlement. In May 1577, Bishop Brady wrote to Sidney that 'I find great boldness generally, as well by word as action, against the received religion. Masses be rife, little less than openly said, friars show themselves openly'.[24] In his judgment, the people were growing more defiant 'in matters of papistry and lewd superstition'. In July 1580, Lord Justice Pelham remarked that

> A settled hatred and a general contrariety in religion settled, saving in some few whose love to her majesty, favour of the court, or English education, or office or reputation here holds in all appearance of conformity with us.[25]

He reckoned that if foreign military aid were to arrive in Ireland, 'few would stick to her majesty'. Modern historians have preferred for some strange reason to overlook evidence of disloyalty among the Pale élites, though Viscount Gormanstown, a leading nobleman of the Pale, observed in 1580 that support for Viscount Baltinglass' Catholic rebellion in the Pale was greater 'than could well be judged of'.[26] Another Palesman, named Eustace, implicated 'many of good living in the Pale' in the rebellion.[27] According to yet another source, most of the families in the Pale were 'touched with' the conspiracy.[28] Throughout Sidney's terms of office, there was persistent hostility to the Elizabethan reformation in the Pale. There was certainly some conformity for a time, but very, very few conversions. Indeed, the corrupt operation of the Irish Ecclesiastical High Commission was such that one cannot be sure how much conformity there really was among those wealthy enough to persuade the commissioners to turn a blind eye to Catholic practices.

Nicholas Canny identified six men who conformed to the Church of Ireland, as well as Bishop Brady – the tiny number itself speaks volumes.[29] He observed that 'It would seem, however, that few if any converts to the state religion were being won in the Pale during Elizabeth's reign, which would mean that those

---

22 Ronan, *Reformation in Ireland*, pp 473–89.   23 Brady, *State papers*, no. v.   24 SP 63/58/16.
25 SP 63/74/75.   26 SP 63/75/121.   27 SP 63/77/31.   28 SP 63/86/55.   29 Canny, 'Why the reformation failed', p. 431.

who remained loyal were becoming increasingly isolated among their fellow countrymen, while still considered doubtful by English officials'.[30] Pelham's remarks on Irish-born individuals conforming to the established Church 'in all appearance', neatly confirms Canny's observation on the doubts of the English officials. Yet it seems that the English may have had grounds for being doubtful. At least three of the six laymen identified by Canny as having never 'faltered' in their 'allegiance to the state religion' were Catholic in sympathy, and died in the Catholic faith. Sir Thomas Cusack, a leading Irish-born councillor and lord chancellor for several years, seemed conformable in religion, but his will of 1571 reveals him to have been a Catholic who, *inter alia*, left money for memorial Masses for his soul, and for various artefacts to be purchased for a number of churches in his locality.[31] His eldest son and heir, Edward, was a leading Catholic recusant and was condemned to death for participating in the Nugent conspiracy in 1580.[32] Sir Lucas Dillon, chief baron of the exchequer, after some years of conformity, became a notorious recusant, as was lamented by Archbishop Loftus in 1592.[33] Sir Nicholas Walsh, speaker of the Irish parliament of 1585 and chief justice of Munster, who was commended by Archbishop Loftus in 1582 for his 'soundness of religion (a rare thing or not to be found in any other lawyer of this country birth)',[34] attended the ceremony held to purify Waterford Cathedral from the taint of Protestantism and to re-dedicate it for Catholic use in March 1603.[35] Sir Nicholas White, another prominent conformist, was father to a virulent recusant who was numbered among the most dangerous men in the Pale in the eyes of the crown's officials.[36] Another of Canny's Protestants, Robert Dillon, chief justice of Ireland, was commended for 'love and zeal of religion' by Loftus in 1581,[37] but was later removed from office with suspicions of his partiality to the rebel earl of Tyrone.[38] It is not my intention here to deny that there were any Protestants in Ireland – that would be preposterous. However, it is remarkable that even among the very few Irish-born *apparently* Protestant government officials identified by Canny, there is very good reason in many cases to question their Protestant credentials.

Lennon identified other Irish-born government officials who 'were compliant with the state Church in their public careers while maintaining private Catholic devotions'.[39] Sir John Plunkett of Dunsoghly, chief justice of the queen's bench for many years before his death in 1582, was praised for his loyalty by Church and state officials, yet a study of his private chapel in Dunsoghly Castle, with its

---

30 Ibid., p. 432.   31 Tait, '"As legacie upon my soul"', pp 182–5, 188; Scott, *Tudor diocese of Meath*, p. 137.   32 Scott, *Tudor diocese of Meath*, pp 127, 131–3.   33 SP 63/154/37; Scott, *Tudor diocese of Meath*, p. 123.   34 SP 63/95/36. Cited in Canny, 'Why the reformation failed', p. 431.   35 Byrne, 'Waterford', pp 95–6.   36 SP 63/154/35.   37 SP 63/82/11. Cited in Canny, 'Why the reformation failed', p. 431.   38 Graham Kew, *The Irish sections of Fynes Morysons's unpublished Itinerary* (Dublin, 1998), p. 43. See also, Tait, '"As legacie upon my soul"', p. 185.   39 Lennon, 'Mass in the manor house', p. 117.

funerary sculpture, reveals many of the features of Catholic iconography of the late sixteenth century. James Stanihurst of Corduff, speaker of the Irish Commons on a number of occasions and a trusted official until his death in 1573 was, according to his son, Richard, 'very Catholic' and refused the lord chancellorship on that account. James Bathe of Drumcondra, chief baron of the exchequer until he died in 1570, provided his son with an education that inspired him to become a Jesuit. Fynes Moryson cited the 'general opinion' of the last years of Elizabeth's reign that the Irish-born members of the Council of Ireland, and the judiciary, were

> generally ... Papists, and if some of them, upon hypocritical dispensation went to Church, commonly their parents, children, kinsmen and servants were open and obstinate Papists in profession. Tell me any one of them who did according to the duty of their place, publicly commend or command to the people use of the *Common Prayer* book, or the frequenting of our churches.[40]

The examples cited above suggest that historians have been imprudent to dismiss such criticisms from New English commentators as self-serving and unfounded. The truth is that there was a number of crown officials who conformed to the Elizabethan Church of Ireland for career reasons. The number of Irish-born people who became Protestant through any sense of religious conviction in Elizabeth's reign is indeterminable. It seems that the kind of person most likely to become a Protestant in Ireland in Elizabeth's reign was a student who spent time in an English university, and not even most of such students returned to Ireland as Protestants. Irish-born women, who had little opportunity to leave Ireland, were even less likely than their men-folk to embrace Protestantism.

The south-east

William Neely suggested that 'the most significant man in Kilkenny for its religious future' was the priest-teacher, Peter White, whose school helped significantly in maintaining the sons of Kilkenny's leading families in the Catholic faith.[41] He was obliged to resign as dean of Waterford in 1570 because of his unwillingness to conform to the Church of Ireland, and yet was made a canon of Kilkenny Cathedral.[42] His school attracted boys from the chief families of Kilkenny and Waterford, and even some from Dublin.[43] Neely, echoing Colm Lennon's discussion of the role of priest-teachers, concluded that

---

40 Kew, *Fynes Moryson's*, p. 43.   41 Neely, *Kilkenny*, p. 43. See also Lennon, 'Pedagogy and reform', pp 43–51.   42 Byrne, 'Reformation in Tudor Waterford', p. 38.   43 Neely, *Kilkenny*, pp 43–4.

White's academy in Kilkenny was a 'seed-bed for the beliefs of the counter-reformation'.[44]

In April 1577, Sir William Drury, president of Munster, informed Walsingham that there were four 'principal prelates' from the college at Louvain operating in the south east of Ireland:[45]

> The first is called John White, who is worshipped like a god between Kilkenny, Waterford and Clonmel. He suborns all the dwellers of those parts to detest the true religion established by her majesty. He is a chief preacher to the contrary, an arrogant enemy of the gospel, and one that denies all duties to her majesty. ... The second is James Archer of Kilkenny, a detestable enemy to the word of God. He did swear against her majesty's jurisdiction in Louvain, and to read not in no English book. He arrived the last March and came then out of Louvain. The third is Dr Comerford of Waterford, also of late come out of Louvain. He and all the rest taught all the way between Rye and Bristol against the religion, and caused a number to despair. The fourth is Precentor Walsh [of Waterford], one who has procured dispensation of the pope to use the English service, to receive benefits of the same, and to abjure himself without hurting his conscience. He came over last March. He preached praying to saints and going on pilgrimages.

When Nicholas Walsh, newly appointed bishop of Ossory, arrived in Kilkenny later in 1577, he found that

> not only the chiefest men of the town (as for the most part they are bent to Popery) refused obstinately to come to church, and that they could by no means be brought to hear the divine service there with their wives and families (as they are by her majesty's injunctions bound to do) but that almost all the churches, chapels, chancels within that diocese were utterly ruined and decayed and that neither the parishioners nor others that are bound to repair them and set them up could by any means be won or induced to do so.[46]

Walsh took advantage of Lord Justice Drury's presence to force people in Kilkenny to attend Church of Ireland services: 'we bound the chief men of the town in recognisance of £40 sterling apiece but they or their wives should duly every Sunday and holyday frequent their church and hear divine service therein', and 'there remain during the time of the service'.[47] With that massive fine

---

44 Ibid., p. 43. **45** Brady, *State papers*, no. xv. **46** RCB Library, Graves Collection, p. 9. Cited in Neely, *Kilkenny*, p. 44.

hanging over their heads, Bishop Walsh probably secured some attendance in church by the leading townsmen of Kilkenny, at least for a time, but one may doubt its efficacy on sullen and resentful individuals under such coercion.

In an analysis of over one hundred sixteenth-century funeral monuments in Kilkenny city and county, Paul Cockerham and Amy Louise Harris traced the persistence of traditional religious influences, and the emergence of counter-reformation and Renaissance influences in the region.[48] The designs and iconography on the funeral monuments 'remained distinctly Catholic' throughout the century.[49] It says a great deal about the lack of Reformation influences that more altar tombs in Kilkenny city and county can be dated to Elizabeth's reign than before it. Ecclesiastical Latin inscriptions were almost invariably used throughout because 'it was the language of the Catholic Church and complemented the religious symbolism found as much on the tombs and ledgers as at Mass'.[50] Clodagh Tait noticed the same association between the retention of Latin inscriptions on Irish funerary monuments and the persisting attachment to Catholicism in her wider overview of funerary practices.[51] Tait noted too that the erection of wayside crosses eliciting intercessory prayers reflected the same attachment to Catholic beliefs surrounding the dead across the east of Ireland.[52]

Waterford had been a conduit for Irish students travelling to continental colleges from the very first years of Elizabeth's reign. Drury observed in April 1577 that there was 'a great number' of students from Waterford in Louvain, 'at the charge of their friends and fathers'.[53] According to Drury, through the efforts of the Catholic clergy, the inhabitants of Waterford were 'cankered in Popery, undutiful to her majesty, slandering the gospel publicly as well this side [of] the [Irish] Sea as beyond in England'. They had

> their altars, painted images and candlesticks, in derision of the gospel, every day in their synagogues … Masses infinite they have in their several churches every morning, without any fear. I have spied them, for I chanced to arrive last Sunday at five in the clock in the morning and saw them resort out of the churches by heaps. This is shameful in a reformed city.

Lord Justice Pelham condemned the citizens of Waterford in December 1579 as the 'most arrogant Papists that live within this state'.[54] Marmaduke Middleton, Protestant bishop of Waterford & Lismore, was effusive in his criticisms of the

---

47 Brady, *State papers*, no. xvii.   48 Paul Cockerham and Amy Louise Harris, 'Kilkenny funeral monuments, 1500–1600: a statistical and analytical account', *PRIA*, 101C5 (2001), pp 135–88. 49 Cockerham and Harris, 'Funeral monuments', p. 173.   50 Ibid., p. 160.   51 Tait, *Death, burial and commemoration*, pp 109–10.   52 Ibid., p. 140.   53 Shirley, *Original letters*, no. xv. 54 Ibid., no. xxiii.

'stiff-necked, stubborn, papistical and incorrigible people of the city of Waterford':

> All things are done contrary to the sacred word and blessed will of the Lord, and also her majesty's most godly proceedings in causes spiritual. The gospel of God utterly abhorred, the church in time of divine service of all hands eschewed (*nisi a paucis et id forma tantum*). The [Protestant] sacraments condemned and refused. Massing in every corner. No burial of the dead according to the *Book of Common Prayer*, but buried in their houses with dirges and after cast into the ground like dogs. Rome-runners and friars maintained amongst them. Public wearing of beads and praying upon the same. Worshipping of images, and setting them openly in their street doors with ornaments and deckings. Ringing of bells and praying for the dead, and dressing their graves diverse times in the year with flower pots and wax candles. No marriage agreeing with God's law and her majesty's proceedings, for either they marry in houses with Masses or else before two or three laymen without any minister taking of hands … The windows and the walls of the churches full of images. They will not deface them, and I dare not for fear of a tumult. None of the women do come either to service or sermons.[55]

He identified Sir Patrick Walsh, mayor of the city in the previous year, as the 'greatest supporter' of that state of affairs.

Drury's and Middleton's detailed accounts of the state of religion in Waterford leave no doubt that the Catholic religion had not only survived the initial impacts of the reformations intact, but had already taken on a counter-reformation aspect within two decades of the 1560 parliament. Though Patrick Walsh, bishop of Waterford & Lismore (1554–78), voted in favour of the Elizabethan religious bills in the parliament of 1560, he clearly made no effective effort to promote Protestantism in his diocese. According to Bishop Middleton, the clergy and laity of Waterford had conspired to alienate the assets of the diocese (he stated that the see of Waterford & Lismore was worth only £30 in 1580) to prevent Protestant clergymen being established in its benefices. The practice of asset-stripping has been traced in some detail in Waterford by Niall Byrne,[56] and in Connacht by Thomas Connors, who declares that it was done to discourage English Protestant clergymen from becoming established there.[57] In any case, it is clear that Waterford had already become a counter-reformation city before 1580. At the same time, such was the regionalised nature of Ireland that

55 Brady, *State papers*, no. xxv.   56 Byrne, 'Reformation in Tudor Waterford', p. 33.   57 Thomas Connors, 'Religion and the laity in early modern Galway' in Moran and Gillespie (eds), *Galway: history and society* (1996), pp 133–4.

Pelham recommended that Bishop Middleton be transferred to Ferns, which was presumably still more conformable at that time.[58]

Cork

It was not until 29 October 1562 that Elizabeth confirmed her sister's appointment of Roger Skiddy, dean of Limerick and a member of Cork's élite, as bishop of Cork & Cloyne.[59] Henry Cotton stated that he was consecrated *papali ritu*.[60] He did not embrace Protestantism and his resignation as bishop on 18 March 1567 probably had something to do with his failure to promote the queen's religion.[61] In February 1568, the papacy provided Nicholas Landes as the Catholic bishop of Cork, but he failed to become established in the diocese.[62] His successor, a Jesuit named Edmund Tanner, was provided in November 1574.[63] Tanner arrived in Ireland in 1576 but was soon detained. He was released in 1577 after agreeing not to enter the city of Cork. Instead, he exercised his ministry far and wide across southern Ireland. He died in Upper Ossory in 1579.

Wolfe claimed in 1574 that everyone in Cork was Catholic,[64] but four years earlier, Sir James Fitzmaurice Fitzgerald had demanded of the mayor and corporation of Cork that they banish from the city all Protestants (whom he denoted by the French term 'Huguenots').[65] Whether those Protestants were natives of the city or English folk cannot be determined, though the latter seems likely. Interestingly, Wolfe testified to the zeal of the Elizabethan bishop, Mathew Sheyne, who had been appointed in May 1572. Sheyne publicly burned a venerated statue of St Dominic at the market cross in the city in October 1578, 'to the great grief of the superstitious people of that place'.[66] One cannot rule out the possibility of local support for his iconoclasm, because when Sheyne died in 1582/3 Patrick Galwey, the mayor of Cork, recommended another Protestant, William Lyon, an Englishman, to succeed him.[67] At the same time as the Dominican statue was destroyed, there were inquisitions held in Cork regarding the chantries, whose endowments were subsequently confiscated by the English crown.

Lyon was already bishop of Ross when, in May 1583, Elizabeth directed that he hold Cork & Cloyne *in commendam*.[68] He administered his dioceses with energy. He re-built some churches and furnished them with English bibles, New Testaments and service books. He devoted some attention to education, and

---

58 Brady, *State papers*, no. xxiii.   59 Bolster, *Diocese of Cork*, p. 59.   60 Henry Cotton, *Fasti Ecclesiae Hibernicae* (Dublin, 1848–51), iv, Appendix, p. xxiii; Bolster, *Diocese of Cork*, pp 59–60.
61 Bolster, *Diocese of Cork*, p. 60.   62 Ibid., p. 63.   63 Ibid., pp 73–9.   64 Begley, *Limerick*, pp 473–89.   65 Bradshaw made the point that 'It is possible, of course, that by the time Wolfe wrote in 1574 the reformers had bowed to pressure and left the city': 'Reformation in the cities', p. 475, fn 59. However, Nicholas Pett, Provost Marshall of Munster, left his Protestant service book to his 'friend', Barnaby Daly in his will, dated at Cork on 4 September 1572: *Gentlemen's Magazine*, Feb. 1862, p. 165.   66 *Works of Ware*, i, p. 564.   67 Ibid., p. 565.
68 Ibid.

made an annual inspection of the schools in his dioceses.[69] During the Thanksgiving service after the dispersal of the Spanish Armada in 1588, Lyon preached to a huge congregation in Cork city.

A very short series of twenty-five wills from 1567 to the early 1580s offers tantalising glimpses into the religious outlooks of some wealthier citizens in Cork.[70] Unfortunately, the sample of wills is very small and cannot form the basis of confident assertions. Nonetheless, from a study of the wills, I concluded that they give no grounds for thinking that the Reformation had made significant progress in winning people's adherence in Cork as late as the early 1580s, but it does seem that people's attachment to Catholicism may have been weakened. The wills certainly do not convey an impression of a general religious enthusiasm, even among the generally older age-group represented. The wills seem to show that a small minority of Cork's élites were very committed Catholics, and that Protestantism had very few if any committed adherents (at least among the older age-group most likely to make wills), but the majority of testators (though many were inclined to the religion of their forebears) were willing to conform to the Elizabethan Church establishment. Yet, by 1590, the Catholic counter-reformation had swept all before it in Cork.

Limerick

Limerick enjoyed the pedagogic efforts of learned Catholic stalwarts, most notably its native son, Richard Creagh, whose academy operated in the former Dominican friary in the city even before 1560.[71] Bishop Thomas Leverous subsequently joined Creagh's academy in which he taught for several years. Some time later, up until 1568, there was a Jesuit academy in the city operated by Edmund Daniel, SJ, 'so that he might confirm his fellow countrymen in the path of faith and instruct the Limerick youth in the rudiments of the Catholic faith and the rules of Ciceronian eloquence'. When driven from Limerick under pressure from Sidney, he transferred his academy to Kilmallock and later still to Youghal.[72]

In his 'Description' of 1574, Wolfe stated that the people of Limerick were 'all Catholics, save some seven or eight young men who embrace the Lutheran leprosy rather to please the Lady Elizabeth than for any other cause'.[73] Though that was a very small number of individuals, it is not an implausible one, given the late appointment of a Protestant clergyman in the city, the operation of staunchly Catholic schools since Mary's reign, and the work of Jesuits in the city from 1560. Incidentally, it was larger than the number of Protestants that Wolfe ascribed to Waterford in the same report (though fewer than in Galway). When in 1572 the Jesuit, Daniel, tried to visit Limerick, he was apprehended by the

69 *CSPI, 1596–7*, p. 15.   **70** Jefferies, *Cork: historical perspectives*, pp 111–14.   **71** Bradshaw, 'Reformation in the cities', pp 469, 470–1.   **72** Hogan, *Ibernia Ignatiana*, p. 20; Ronan, *Reformation in Ireland*, p. 418; McCormack, *Earldom of Desmond*, p. 113.   **73** Ronan, *Reformation in Ireland*, pp 473–89.

mayor and handed over to the president of Munster at Cork, where he was tortured and executed. The mayor subsequently wrote to the pope expressing his great regret for his role in the Jesuit's death.[74] The fact that he handed the Jesuit over to the English authorities, though, does not betoken a strong commitment to the Catholic Church, whatever about his subsequent regrets.

In 1571, Bishop Lacey, who had actively supported Wolfe and Creagh in their missions in the early 1560s, was forced to resign in favour of William Casey, his Edwardian predecessor.[75] However, when the earl of Desmond arrived back in his earldom in 1573, he restored Lacey to his see for a time. However, such audacity was no longer tolerated by the English crown's officials and by 1574 the old bishop had been ousted and reduced to taking refuge on an island with friends.[76] Wolfe won the Elizabethan bishop, Casey, back to the Catholic faith prior to his own departure for mainland Europe in 1573.[77] Bishop Casey's wife was subsequently reconciled to the Catholic Church by Bishop Dermot Creagh.[78] It would hardly be surprising then if the Elizabethan reformation made little positive impression on the inhabitants of Limerick. One must suspect that any Limerick-born Protestants must have encountered Protestantism outside the city and diocese, probably through an education in England.

Galway
Nicholas Canny asserted that

> Galway became a Protestant town for a decade or more in the late 1570s and in the 1580s. The term 'Protestant town' is used as it would be applied to an urban centre in continental Europe during the early phases of the reform process. In such situations, the tenets of Protestantism would have been accepted, if but dimly understood, by the ruling hierarchy and the practicing clergy in the particular town, and these would be prepared to support the efforts of zealots from outside to propagate their message to the population at large.[79]

I think Canny was correct in seeing at least the possibility of a Protestant breakthrough among the oligarchs in Galway.

There are no wills from Galway to define religious allegiances in the city – though interestingly the clergy of St Nicholas' Collegiate Church in Galway resorted to legal action to prevent citizens from withholding the monies they had traditionally paid to have commemorative Masses celebrated for deceased family members.[80] I suppose it is possible to interpret that episode as a reflection of

74 Ibid., pp 418–19. 75 *Works of Ware*, i, pp 510–11; Edwards, *Church and state*, p. 210. 76 Ronan, *Reformation in Ireland*, pp 473–89. 77 Brady, *State papers*, no. lxxxvii. 78 SP 63/152/15. 79 Nicholas Canny, 'Galway: from the Reformation to the penal laws' in Diarmuid Ó Cearbhaill (ed.), *Galway: town and gown, 1484–1984* (Dublin, 1984), p. 14.

their loss of faith in prayers for the dead, but I suspect it actually reflected their withdrawal of financial support from a church establishment that no longer met their needs. Edward White's account of Galway in 1572 leaves no doubt that Galway's Protestants were a small and vulnerable minority within the city, while the majority feted the Franciscan friars who convened a council in their city.[81] The evidence highlighted by Canny – the reference to 'the mayor, his brethren and of the towns men and women more orderly repairing to Church than in any town in Ireland', Bingham's expressed hope that Galway might become a 'second Geneva', and Sir Turlough O'Brien's recollection of the city as 'the paradise of Ireland in number of professors of the gospel' – is compelling as an indicator of a level of conformity to the Elizabethan religious settlement in Galway that was greater than that existing in other Irish cities at the time.[82] Yet, that conformity was achieved only through the imposition of fines and punishments. When Deputy Perrot visited Galway in person, he had to direct the mayor of the city to deliver over to him any of those who had been 'deeply fined' for absenting themselves from Protestant services, but defaulted on paying the fines.[83] Galway never became a 'second Geneva', nor was it ever likely to become so.

As evidence of Galway's missionary role, Canny cited the three bishops it gave to the later Elizabethan Church of Ireland: Stephen Kirwan, bishop of Clonfert (1583–1601), Roland Lynch, bishop of Kilmacduagh (1587–1625) and bishop of Clonfert (1601–25), and John Lynch, bishop of Elphin (1584–1611).[84] Kirwan's and John Lynch's Protestantism was attested to by English contemporaries, but Kirwan was subsequently characterised as the 'English Romish bishop'.[85] Thomas Connors found that Roland Lynch, a Cambridge graduate, had a Catholic wife, and his children and his servants were Catholics, and he was persuaded by his Catholic cathedral chapter to alienate his see lands so that no English clergyman (who would inevitably be a Protestant) would accept office there.[86] Connors observed that John Lynch 'accomplished much the same' in Elphin diocese.

Canny observed that 'the white heat of Protestant zeal that seems to have obtained in the Galway of the 1580s cooled quickly'.[87] I suspect it never was quite so intense. Contradictory reports reflect a city community that was divided by the Reformation. I agree with Canny that the period of conformity in Galway must be taken as an indicator that Galway might have been won over to the reformations – but as it happened, there were few converts and many of those who seemed to have embraced Protestantism, including the Galway-born bishops who may have become Protestant while studying at universities in England, seem

80 Berry, 'Documents relating to the wardenship', pp 16–18. 81 SP 63/38/52, i. 82 Canny, 'Why the reformation failed', pp 444–5. 83 Berry, 'Documents relating to the wardenship', p. 34. 84 Canny, 'Why the reformation failed', pp 444–5. 85 Connors, 'Religion and the laity in Galway', p. 133. 86 Ibid. 87 Canny, 'Why the reformation failed', p. 445.

to have lapsed back into Catholicism. An interesting phenomenon that I have noticed is how often even the Irish-born Church of Ireland bishops were married to Catholic wives. It seems that Irish-born women were even less susceptible than Irish-born men to Protestantism, partly no doubt because they were unlikely to have been educated outside of Ireland and were not so constrained by careerism to conform. The role of women in winning their husbands' return to Rome is a subject worthy of serious study.

Gaelic Ireland

Samantha Meigs, drawing mainly on Irish bardic poetry to support her case, argued that the Gaelic *literati* played a pivotal role in the dissemination of a traditional Gaelic religious sensibility, which effectively predetermined the failure of the Reformation in Gaelic Ireland.[88] Marc Caball, however, has warned that the bardic poetry of Elizabeth's reign 'reveals limited engagement with contemporary ecclesiastical issues. This relative indifference probably results from two factors; the initially ineffective course and limited public profile of the Protestant reform movement outside larger urban centres and, secondly, what may have been a traditional bardic reluctance to comment on questions of ecclesiastical remit'.[89] Caball emphasised that the composition of bardic poetry was primarily politically focused, and devotional poetry was 'professionally marginal' to the genre.[90] The 'small number' of bardic compositions that reflect religious dissensions in Elizabeth's reign[91] do not provide sufficient evidence to substantiate Meig's deterministic thesis about the decisive role of the *aos dána* in thwarting the Reformation in Gaelic Ireland, though they may have reinforced a more general antipathy to English-imposed socio-cultural and political changes in Ireland.

Elizabeth herself was not antagonistic to the use of the Irish language to propagate the Reformation in Ireland. Indeed, she paid £66 13*s.* 4*d.* to Archbishop Loftus and Bishop Brady to have the New Testament published in Irish.[92] However, by 1567 she was threatening to demand repayment when nothing materialised, and it was not until 1602 that an Irish Testament was finally printed. No less remarkable is the fact that the *Book of Common Prayer* was not published in Irish until 1608. In the meantime, John O'Kearney's slim catechism was the only book printed in the Irish language to promote the Reformation, and its 200 copies would have made no impact among the vast

---

88 Meigs, *The reformations in Ireland*. 89 Marc Caball, *Poets and politics: continuity and reaction in Irish poetry, 1558–1625* (Cork, 1998). 90 Marc Caball, 'Religion, culture and the bardic élite in early modern Ireland' in Alan Ford and John McCafferty (eds), *The origins of sectarianism in early modern Ireland* (Cambridge, 2005), pp 160–1, 170–1. 91 Caball, 'Religion, culture and the bardic élite', p. 173. 92 Ó Cuív, 'The Irish language in the early modern period' in T.W. Moody, F.X. Martin and F.J. Byrne (eds), *A new history of Ireland* (Oxford, 1976), pp 511–12; idem, *Aibidil Gaoidheilge & caiticiosma*, p. 2.

majority of the thousands of parishes across Ireland.[93] In any case, the catechism was an anaemic affair and was not likely to inspire evangelical zeal in many of its readers. In the absence of any significant number of Irish Protestant preachers (most of the few Protestant preachers in Ireland were Englishmen who could speak no Irish), no vernacular liturgy and almost nothing in print in Irish to promote the Reformation, the general encounter of the Irish-speaking population (who comprised the vast majority of the people in Ireland, even in the Pale) with Protestantism was negative: Sir John Harrington commented in 1605 that it was 'no marvel' that the 'harvest' of souls in Ireland was 'so slender' after forty-four years of Reformation, when it was imposed by 'violent hewing down their crosses, burning and defacing their images, railing in the pulpit on all their saints and ceremonies, feasting on Ash Wednesdays and Good Fridays, going to plough on their Christmas Days, and promising that all their ancestors are damned that did but pray to our Lady, with such like'.[94] The experience of most Irish people of the Elizabethan reformation was mediated through the criticisms of the Catholic clergy who opposed it, or through its physical manifestations, which included ruined religious houses, ruinous church buildings and shocking iconoclasm.

Caball has argued that the small number of bardic poems that reflect something of the religious controversy of the time 'clearly illustrate the degree to which poets interpreted sectarian controversy in socio-cultural as opposed to strictly theological terms'.[95] In terms of religion, the poets articulated a traditional Christian piety that would have been recognisable throughout western Christendom before the Reformation, and they remained faithful to it throughout the sixteenth century.[96] As Caball remarks, the fact that one of the most comprehensive commentaries on Protestantism, 'Grievous my visit to Scotland', was penned by a poet who experienced it first-hand overseas, reflects the Reformation's 'superficial influence' in the Gaelic heartlands of Ireland.[97] The Reformation in Ireland was seen by the poets primarily as an ancillary aspect of the Tudor conquest of Ireland.[98] Eoghan Ó Dubhthaigh's coruscating diatribe against three Irish Protestant bishops, Sheyne of Cork (1572–82/3), Casey of Limerick (1571–91) and Magrath of Cashel (1571–1622), explicitly equated Anglicanism with the English colonial presence in Ireland, and identified the Church of Ireland as an English cultural phenomenon staffed with immigrant clergymen who were characterised by 'corruption'.[99]

The evidence suggests that the Reformation made no positive impression in Gaelic Ireland in Elizabeth's reign, but rather the contrary, as it was often characterised by iconoclasm in the wake of English military actions, unaccompanied by any attempt at explanation or evangelisation. Caball argued that the

93 Ó Cuív, *Aibidil Gaoidheilge & caiticiosma*, p. 2.   94 Quoted in Caball, 'Religion, culture and the bardic élite', p. 181.   95 Caball, 'Religion, culture and the bardic élite', pp 173–4.   96 Ibid., p. 181.   97 Ibid., p. 176.   98 Ibid., pp 174–5, 177–8.   99 Caball, *Poets and politics*, pp 78–9.

ultimate failure of the Reformation in Gaelic Ireland 'was in large part due to the entrenched antipathy of the Established Church to indigenous culture, which was in turn counter-pointed by a systematic campaign on the part of Tridentine Catholicism from the late sixteenth century onwards to invoke Gaelic culture as a complementary social ancillary to Roman Catholicism'.[1] I would not disagree with that judgment, but I would point out that the fundamental reason why no vernacular Bible or liturgy was published in Ireland before the seventeenth century was that no one completed the necessary translations. Unlike Wales and Scotland, there was no one in Ireland to give the work of translating the key Protestant texts into the vernacular the requisite commitment needed to complete the work. Again, that reflects the Irish experience of the Reformation: a Reformation virtually without reformers.

CONCLUSIONS

Through the deployment of an increasing number of officials in Church and state, particularly of the Irish Ecclesiastical High Commission in the Pale and through episcopal authority backed up by civic magistrates in the larger towns beyond the Pale, the Catholic liturgy was displaced by the Elizabethan *Book of Common Prayer* in churches over wide areas by the early 1570s. Conformity was general in the towns, though the lack of evidence precludes any assessment of the degree of conformity imposed in the countryside. It seems that during Sidney's term of office, Church and state officials took care not to pry too deeply into religious dispositions for fear of disturbing a hornet's nest. Bishop Brady's lament in 1577 of the 'infinite' number of Masses being celebrated in Meath, the report that many of the clergy in the Elizabethan Church were regularly providing Catholic sacraments for their parishioners, and the description of friars ministering 'little less than openly', certainly points towards that conclusion. The repeated references to churches falling into ruins in the countryside, even within the Pale, seems to reflect a stark withdrawal of lay support from the established Church in the wake of the reformation. The employment of Catholic priests as chaplains and tutors points to alternative foci for spending on religion.

Ciarán Brady characterised conformity to the Elizabethan Church of Ireland in the Pale as evidence of a general 'complacency', and even 'indifference' in religion.[2] However, the reality was more complex. Conformity was imposed through coercion and intimidation, backed by fines and imprisonment. The disproportionately high share of the fines imposed on people in Dublin (25 per

1 Caball, 'Religion, culture and the bardic élite', p. 162.   2 Brady, 'Conservative subversives', pp 12–13.

cent) and Drogheda (6 per cent) may be interpreted as evidence either of the High Commission's being more rigorous in its efforts to impose conformity in the towns than in rural parishes, or it may reflect more determined resistance to the Commission's efforts to impose conformity in urban compared with rural parishes. Either way, the continual imposition of fines by the High Commission shows that conformity was achieved through coercion. The correspondences of Bishop Brady, Archbishop Loftus and Chancellor Weston are replete with complaints about the stubbornness and obstinacy of the people of the Pale. Deputy Sidney himself had no illusions about the depth of hostility arising from 'the former errors and superstitions inveterated and leavened in the people's hearts'.[3] Close reading of such correspondence does not support claims that the Palesmen or women were complacent or indifferent in religion.

The veneer of conformity to the Elizabethan Church could be remarkably slender, as reported from Waterford. The same was evidently the case in the Pale, though Waterford's ostentatious Catholicism would hardly have survived unscathed the attentions of the Ecclesiastical High Commission in the Pale. I interpret the conformity that occurred as a reflection of the old colonial community's anxiety to mollify the conflicting claims on their loyalties from the English crown and the Catholic Church without offending either. Chancellor Weston recognised that 'there is great fear to offend among this people'.[4]

The period of general conformity of much of the population to the Elizabethan Church of Ireland, at least in urban areas, is interesting as it suggests at least the possibility of an incipient Protestant breakthrough, as Nicholas Canny argued for Galway for about a decade from the late 1570s. At the very least, it provided the Elizabethan Church with captive congregations to preach at. There is tentative evidence from a short series of wills from Cork to suggest that religious commitment may have been weakened for a time by doctrinal controversy, which might possibly have facilitated openness to religious change. Yet Brady and Loftus repeatedly complained about a deep-rooted resistance to Protestant sermons, a phenomenon observed also by Anthony Trollope and David Wolfe, who represented opposing ends of the doctrinal spectrum.

Superficial and grudging conformity did not prove to be a transitional stage towards Protestantism in Ireland. The Elizabethan Church of Ireland was unable to mount a convincing evangelical campaign, even in the cities, because it could not recruit any but a tiny cohort of Protestant preachers. The few Protestant bishops in Ireland, including Brady of Meath and Loftus of Armagh and Dublin, often lacked the kind of administrative experience and expertise that might have prepared them better to deploy the institutional and human resources of their dioceses to full effect to advance the Elizabethan reformation, and they failed to win over congregations to the Reformation, even in those

3 Shirley, *Original letters*, no. lxxxii. 4 Ibid., no. liv.

parishes where the people were systematically forced to attend Protestant church services. That is graphically illustrated in the churchwardens' accounts for St Werburgh's Church in Dublin. By contrast with the pre-Reformation period, when the church was lavished with gifts by parishioners, there were no gifts recorded in the Reformation period and the churchwardens were left to manage a diminishing portfolio of properties given to the parish in the later Middle Ages. By 1605, the church of St Werburgh's was described as 'now down and ruinous'.[5] That shows that even within a stone's throw of Dublin Castle, the people in Dublin had disengaged from their local church as it was protestantised during the Reformation.

The final outcome of the Elizabethan reformation had not yet been decided by 1579/80, but the prospects for a Protestant breakthrough were most unpromising. Years of enforced conformity to the queen's religious settlement in Dublin and elsewhere had not led to significant numbers of conversions to Protestantism, even where Protestant clergymen had made earnest efforts to win converts. There was a communal resistance to Protestantism that proved to be extraordinarily difficult to overcome. Pelham's observation in 1580 about the 'settled hatred and general contrariety in religion settled' was perspicacious. Yet there was no certainty that the Catholic Church would be able to create and maintain a comprehensive pastoral network across Ireland in the face of increasing English military control across more and more of the country.

5 Empey (ed.), *The proctors' accounts of St Werbugh's*, pp 12–13.

9

Elizabeth's reformation: watershed

In the middle years of her reign, Elizabeth's Church of Ireland was beginning to take on the appearance of a substantial institution, at least in districts firmly under English royal authority. However, by the mid-1580s, that semblance of substance was dissipating. In the interval, there were increasingly determined efforts made by the crown's officials to enforce the Elizabethan religious settlement on Ireland, which may well have galvanised further the already considerable commitment to Catholicism among the peoples of Ireland. However, the critical development of those years was the decision by Elizabeth to abrogate the efforts being made to impose Protestantism through coercion because the political costs of doing so were proving to be unacceptably high, while Anglo-Spanish relations were tending towards open war.

RENEWED COERCION

The rebellions that broke out across Ireland in 1579/80 were immediately preceded by renewed drives to force people to conform to the Elizabethan religious settlement. James Murray has pointed to an 86 per cent increase in the fines levied by the Commission in 1577–82 compared with 1573–7 – 'a substantial escalation in the level of the Commission's activity'.[1] The scale of the increase in its activity may not be fully evident in these figures, since the work of the Commission would certainly have been interrupted by the outbreak of the Baltinglass rebellion in 1580 (implying more activity prior to the rebellion than a calculation of annual averages over a five-year period would otherwise suggest), and the figures for the previous period do not explicitly reflect the nadir of the Commission's activity before its re-activation. The targets for the Commission's attention from 1577 appear to have been members of the élites in the Pale who were conspicuously hostile to the queen's religious settlement. James Eustace, son and heir of Viscount Baltinglass, was fined one hundred marks in 1578 for having attended Mass. Deputy Sidney insisted that action be taken against him.[2] He was to serve as an example. Eustace's Catholicism had been steeled by Robert Rochford, SJ, and Dr Nicholas Tanner, priests who were to play key roles in the

1 Murray, 'Tudor diocese of Dublin', p. 284. 2 Ibid., pp 279–80.

rebellions that were to break out in 1579/80, including that headed by Eustace himself once he succeeded his father as Viscount Baltinglass.[3]

Another victim of exemplary punishment was Alderman James Bellew of Dublin who was compelled to renounce his denial of the queen's supremacy over the Church.[4] Margaret Ball, the mother of Alderman Walter Ball, one of the few Protestant oligarchs in Dublin, was imprisoned for her open support for Catholicism about that same time. Her release was secured by a number of aristocrats, but she was re-arrested following her son's appointment to the Ecclesiastical Commission in April 1581, and was left to die in prison *c*.1584.[5] Margaret's incarceration and death at her son's instigation reflected the new intensity of anti-Catholic sentiment among the (mainly English-born) Protestant community in Dublin – but it would have done nothing to win over the Catholic community to the queen's religion.

The work of the Ecclesiastical Commission was reinforced by a directive issued to the lord justice of Ireland in February 1579 to enforce the statutes regarding the erection of schools, repairing churches, appointing curates and compelling noblemen and gentlemen to go to church.[6] The concerted drive for enforcement brought about a result that Secretary Waterhouse, in May 1579, declared was

> that which I never hoped of, namely, that the whole inhabitants, being in effect all noted to be obstinate Papists in times past, do now all repair to the church and show themselves obedient in the substance of religion. Most of the nobility (amongst which one has been noted to be a Jesuit) come to sermons and show themselves examples to others.[7]

William Gerrard, lord chancellor of Ireland and also dean of St Patrick's Cathedral, Dublin (despite being a layman), had pews erected 'for the nobility, for lawyers, for captains and all of the better sort, so as the citizens and all, being under his eye, never dare to be absent'.[8] Waterhouse entertained some naïve hope that the latest efforts at forcing the élites of Dublin and the Pale to sit through Protestant sermons were going to effect Pauline conversions. My own feeling is that the regular ritual of humiliation was more likely to alienate the local élites from the Protestant regime. In July 1580, on the very eve of Viscount Baltinglass' rebellion, Lord Justice Pelham warned about 'a settled hatred and contrariety in religion settled'.[9]

Nor was the drive for conformity confined to the Pale. In 1577, Nicholas Walsh, Elizabethan bishop of Ossory, had Lord Justice Drury force the chief

3 Lennon, *Lords of Dublin*, p. 151. 4 Ibid. 5 Ibid., p. 156. 6 Brady (ed.), *State papers*, no. xxii. 7 SP 63/66/66. 8 Ibid. 9 SP 63/74/75.

men of Kilkenny to attend Church of Ireland services along with their wives, on pain of crippling fines.[10] Drury's discovery in April 1577 that in Waterford, 'Masses infinite they have in their several churches every morning, without any fear', is likely to have been followed by a crack-down on the practice.[11] In December 1579, Marmaduke Midleton, Elizabethan bishop of Waterford & Lismore, complained of Masses 'in every corner' and in houses, which suggests that the Masses were no longer celebrated in the churches, while the Elizabethan services were 'of all hands eschewed' especially by women, none of whom would attend a Protestant service.[12] As Midleton tried to enforce the Reformation in Waterford, its mayor, James Sherlock, countered with criticisms of the bishop's bad life and his allegedly false reports against the citizens: the mayor reported that all of the men of the city (with three or four exceptions) went to Church every Sunday.[13] No mention was made of the women of Waterford. In the event, the bishop was exonerated of the 'slanders' alleged against him, but such was the hostility that he faced in Waterford, that he was soon obliged to leave the city.[14] Indeed, it was claimed that neither a Protestant bishop nor a preacher dared to tarry in Waterford without protection.[15] Cork witnessed the public burning of a statue of St Dominic that was much venerated in the city, and the dissolution of the chantries.[16] Across some of southern Connacht, the Mass was displaced by the Elizabethan *Prayer Book* services at President Malby's insistence.[17]

It is clear, then, that in the months leading up to the Desmond and Baltinglass rebellions, there was a greatly increased insistence on conformity to the Elizabethan religious settlement. The tacit toleration of Catholicism was being ended, without due consideration of the likely reactions to that dramatic shift in the state's religious policy. I do not doubt that the men and women who supported the rebellions of 1579–83 had various motives for doing so – but the religious turmoil generated by the determined drive for conformity in the months immediately prior to the rebellions must surely count as one of the important factors for the outbreak of those rebellions, and for the support and sympathy they garnered over so much of Ireland.

THE SECOND DESMOND REBELLION

The second Desmond rebellion has been comprehensively analysed by Anthony McCormack.[18] In brief, he stated that the rebellion was

---

10 Neely, *Kilkenny*, p. 44; Brady, *State papers*, no. xvii.   11 Brady, *State papers*, no. xv.   12 Ibid., no. xxv.   13 SP 63/78/45.   14 SP 63/84/12; 63/85/33.   15 SP 63/170/44.   16 Jefferies, *Cork: historical perspectives*, p. 110.   17 This is evident from rebels' demands for the restoration of the Mass in 1580: SP 63/77/53, 66; 63/78/41.   18 McCormack, *Earldom of Desmond*, pp 145–92.

one of the most serious military challenges that Elizabeth had to face during her reign. It lasted four and a half years, with fighting spread throughout Munster. Particularly threatening was the fact that Spanish and papal troops intervened on two occasions, the second time to land a force of 600 men, with the possibility of further support for the rebels, who numbered in their thousands.[19]

McCormack played down the role of religion in the rebellion and highlighted instead the role of various local rivalries.[20] Yet religion, and a virulent anti-English sentiment, gave cohesion to the more mundane motivations of the rebels, and religious sentiment helped to sustain the rebellion over several diffi-cult years when simple self-interest would have been far better served by submission to the crown. Also, the rebellion was predicated on the arrival of significant foreign aid on religious grounds, and support for the rebellion waxed and waned depending on news of Spanish preparations. Once that aid failed to materialise on the scale needed for success, most of the rebels submitted.

McCormack argues that it was Sir James Fitzmaurice Fitzgerald's return to Ireland with fifty soldiers (an insignificant number), and the 'increasingly heavy handed' English response to it, that pushed Gerald Fitzgerald, earl of Desmond, into rebellion.[21] However, contemporary evidence shows that the earl of Desmond was directly involved in preparations for a rebellion. Dr Nicholas Sander, the key figure beside Fitzmaurice in the expedition of July 1579, drew up a document sometime around August 1578, in which he referred to a letter that Fitzmaurice had received from Desmond inviting him to return to Ireland, with or without arms.[22] That may or may not have been the same letter to the same effect that Fitzmaurice informed Sander of having received from Desmond at the close of the previous year.[23]

Cornelius Ryan, the Catholic bishop of Killaloe, was informed by an 'intimate friend' of his who had personally spoken directly with Desmond and his brother, Sir John of Desmond, shortly before sailing from Waterford to Lisbon in October 1578, to the effect that the earl and his brother

> asked him to meet Lord James [Fitzmaurice] wherever he might be, and persuade him not to postpone going to Ireland because in all Munster there are no Englishmen, and likewise the people are ready to harbour and aid him; and since the viceroy of Ireland [Sidney] was about to go to England there was now more possibility than hitherto of something being accomplished before more Englishmen should be sent to Ireland.[24]

19 Ibid., p. 145. 20 Ibid., pp 160–7. 21 Ibid., pp 196, 146. 22 *CSP Rome, 1572–78*, no. 943; Ronan, *Reformation in Ireland*, pp 589–91. 23 *CSP Rome, 1572–78*, no. 714; Ronan, *Reformation in Ireland*, p. 599. 24 Quoted in Ronan, *Reformation in Ireland*, p. 600.

Myles Ronan suggested convincingly that the bishop's friend was Seán O'Farrell, a Franciscan friar, who was named in August 1580 by James O'Hea, another Franciscan, as having carried messages from Desmond to Fitzmaurice at Madrid about the time in question.[25] O'Farrell told O'Hea that the earl of Desmond was most anxious for Fitzmaurice's return to Ireland and had sent him to seek out Fitzmaurice to that end, saying that 'if James had found any favour or succour there ... he should bring them over into Ireland: and if he found no favour ... he should come himself'.

A letter, to the same effect, written by William of Danubi at the request of Desmond, his master, was intercepted by the English authorities.[26] The letter beseeched Fitzmaurice

> in the name of God and in my master's name to bring relief soon. ... The flame of war has grown up in many of the men of Ireland against the Saxons, if they but get help. ... Be assured that we cannot tell how much we are in want of you; and though we should like that a host of men should come along with you, we would be exceedingly glad that you yourself should come to our aid ... for we think that the greatest part of the men of Ireland are ready to rise with ourselves, and we would be much better of you. Do not wait for the harvest, for there is danger that the whole affair be set aside by that time.

The consistency of the reports of Sander, Bishop Ryan of Killaloe, O'Farrell and O'Hea, and the letter of William of Danubi, whatever quibbles one might suggest against any one or other of them, compel one towards the conclusion that the earl of Desmond was not innocent of responsibility for the rebellion that ensued.

Historians who are anxious to exonerate the earl of Desmond of responsibility for the second Desmond rebellion may point to the fact that he informed the English administration in Dublin of Fitzmaurice's arrival at Dingle, and surrounded the rebel camp at Smerwick with his own men. However, it seems clear that Desmond was playing for time ... News of Fitzmaurice's return to Ireland was bound to reach Dublin independently of the earl – as was, indeed, the case. Desmond's men may have surrounded the tiny rebel base, but they allowed free passage to Fitzmaurice's messengers to deliver his appeal, 'To the right honourable prelates, princes, lords, estates, citizens and people of Ireland'.[27]

Fitzmaurice appealed to the 'lords, the princes, the leaders and rulers of this our dear country', or their lawful attorneys, to meet at Smerwick (no mention

25 Ronan, *Reformation in Ireland*, p. 601.   26 *Kilkenny Archaeological Journal* (1858–9), pp 360–1; Ronan, *Reformation in Ireland*, pp 602–3.   27 *Kilkenny Archaeological Journal* (1858–9), pp 364–8; Ronan, *Reformation in Ireland*, pp 613–15.

was made of Desmond's men who surrounded Fitzmaurice's camp) 'to the end
that we there make a perpetual peace, league and friendship, first to the utter
destroying of all schism and heresy, and next to the establishing of true love and
amity amongst ourselves. He called on them to show "zeal for God's honour and
their own country". Fitzmaurice reinforced this general appeal with a proclamation on 'the justice of the war which he is waging in Ireland for the faith'.[28] The
proclamation offered two grounds to justify the war; firstly, 'to restore the
outward rite of sacrifice and the visible honour of our holy altars, which heretics
have overturned', and secondly, to defend the people of Ireland 'against the
manifest tyranny of those heretics who … are forcing us, under pain of death, to
forsake our old faith in the primacy of the Roman pontiff, and are constraining
us to accept and profess a new religion which we do not want'.

Fitzmaurice also sent individual letters to certain lords, re-iterating the same
faith and fatherland ideology. His letter to the earl of Desmond is particularly
interesting in that it shows that Fitzmaurice acted as the pope's captain general
in what they conceived of as a 'holy war' – he did not act as Desmond's minion.[29]
His arrival gave Desmond an opportunity to rebel, or not, as he saw fit.
Fitzmaurice's 'Appeal' stated that the pope was confident that the Irish would
need no foreign support in their war. That optimism was not shared in Ireland.
Fr Matthew de Oviedo, who accompanied Fitzmaurice to Ireland, was sent back
to the papal nuncio in Spain in the week after his arrival with the information
that the Irish nobility would only engage in rebellion if the king of Spain was
committed to supporting them.[30]

Edward White, a citizen of Waterford, wrote to the Dublin administration to
warn that 'the state of this realm was never in greater danger than it is at this
instant'. The threat came not from the native Irish he warned, but from
noblemen of English blood who loudly professed their loyalty and yet dissembled, playing a game to overthrow the queen's authority and take the rule of
Ireland into their own hands. Those noblemen would never have rebelled if they
had not 'hope of assistance and aid from other nobles' houses'. He stated that

> If this present action be not well provided for in time, I am afraid you
> shall see the fire in every corner of the realm all our time; for the
> practices and devices of the enemy are great and have their favourers
> in every place, some for the cause of religion, some to shake off the
> government, and such other devices. I speak of knowledge, not of
> guess.[31]

---

28 *Kilkenny Archaeological Journal* (1858–9), pp 368–9; Ronan, *Reformation in Ireland*, pp
619–20. 29 SP 63/77/32. 30 Ronan, *Reformation in Ireland*, pp 621–2. 31 SP 63/68/22;
Ronan, *Reformation in Ireland*, p. 623.

White's 'knowledge' of the nobles who 'dissembled' and of others who offered 'hope of assistance and aid' is intriguing, and it seems to confirm Chancellor Gerrard's and Archbishop Loftus' 'suspicion of a general composition'.[32] Secretary Waterhouse wrote that 'This rebellion is the most perilous that was begun in Ireland, so if foreign help in multitudes, as the rebels give forth, looked for to arrive presently here ... nothing is to be looked for here but a general rebellion'.[33] Lord Justice Drury explained that 'The rebellion of James Fitzmaurice, who has practiced with many foreign princes, is not like other ordinary stirs that have fallen out upon small occasions within this realm for we see great evident appearance of general combination'.[34]

Meanwhile, the earl of Desmond, though his men surrounded the rebel encampment, persisted in taking no action against it, despite the fact that with only fifty or sixty soldiers in the rebels' camp, it could have been overcome very quickly. In fact, on 26 July 1579, Fitzmaurice wrote to the papal nuncio in Spain that 'the chief men amongst them came to us, congratulated us on our arrival ... and placed themselves and their all at our service; owing however to the scarcity of powder, guns, money and arms they could not venture openly to proclaim their adhesion just then ... But it is certain that their hearts are with us and they are ready to obey the Holy See if only we receive reinforcements in good time'.[35] In the absence of those reinforcements, Desmond maintained an ambivalent stance towards the rebels. He ostensibly condemned his brothers' killing of the English commissioners, Davells and Carter, at Tralee on 1 August 1579. He subsequently joined Sir Nicholas Malby, governor of Connacht, in the hunt for Fitzmaurice, which culminated in the latter's death on 18 August 1579 in a skirmish with the Clanwilliam Burkes. However, the English remained doubtful of Desmond's loyalty, and early in October Malby, 'impatient (McCormack observes) at Desmond's prevarication', marched to Askeaton to demand the earl's submission. When Desmond refused, Malby burned the town and abbey.[36] Lord Justice Pelham, however, was keen not to push Desmond into rebellion, and despatched Ormond to him with a set of articles. When Desmond failed to comply, Pelham proclaimed him a traitor on 2 November 1579.[37] In fact, the earl was already in open rebellion since October.[38]

The decisive factor in Desmond's decision to rebel was the assurance that he received from Rome and Madrid of military support. His earlier prevarication is best explained on the assumption that he supported the rebels' aims but was reluctant to commit himself to rebellion without the financial and logistical support necessary for success. Once he received the necessary assurances of foreign support, Desmond openly rebelled.

32 SP 63/68/7, 22. 33 SP 63/67/45. 34 SP 63/67/40. 35 Quoted in Ronan, *Reformation in Ireland*, p. 628. Ronan observes that Fitzmaurice's letter was corroborated by Sander and de Oviedo, and Desmond told a similar story to Philip II and the papal nuncio in Spain on 17 January 1580. 36 McCormack, *Earldom of Desmond*, p. 164. 37 Ibid. 38 SP 63/69/72.

Waterhouse noted on 4 November 1579 that Desmond was expecting support from the pope and Spain, and looked for English Catholics to rebel also.[39] He and his brothers wrote a letter to a number of Irish lords declaring that

> I and my brethren are entered in defence of our Catholic faith and the overthrow of our country by Englishmen, which had overthrown the holy Church and go about to overrun our country, and make it their own, and to make us their bondmen. ... And if you be afraid ... you shall understand that we took this matter in hand with great authority, both from the pope's holiness and from King Philip, who do undertake to further us in our affairs as we shall need.[40]

That Desmond had indeed been assured of military support from Spain and France is confirmed by the fact that envoys from the Spanish and French monarchs complained to Desmond in person in January 1580 that Dr Sander had 'railed and reviled' their two monarchs when the forces they had promised failed to arrive.[41] Nonetheless, the Spanish envoy assured the earl that a force of 30,000 would definitely set sail for Ireland within a month of his return to Spain.

McCormack played down the role of religion as one of the main motives for people supporting the second Desmond rebellion, and highlighted instead the 'personal agendas of the confederate leadership'.[42] He dismissed Desmond's avowed commitment to the Catholic cause and claimed that his 'treasonable diplomacy' was employed simply to restore the *status quo ante bellum*.[43] However, Desmond never asked for the restoration of the *status quo ante*. His letter of November 1579 makes it very plain that he committed himself to a full-scale rebellion for 'faith and fatherland'. The very fact that Fitzmaurice and Desmond couched their appeals for support in terms of a fight for 'faith and fatherland' shows that they believed that the appeal would resonate powerfully among the leaders of Irish society, and inspire them to risk everything – their lives and revenues, and those of their families and friends – in a rebellion against the English crown. In December 1583, Deputy Grey of Wilton stated that 1,485 of the chief men and gentlemen of Ireland had been killed by the queen's forces in the recent rebellions, not counting men of lesser status, nor yet those executed by martial law and the killing of peasants 'which were innumerable'.[44]

According to the earl of Ormond, Dr Sander, despite being an Englishman, persuaded many in Munster to join in the second Desmond rebellion on religious grounds.[45] After Sander died, another Catholic churchman, Dr Tadhg McDonagho, stirred up much support for the rebellion.[46] Malby, the president

39 SP 63/70/4.   40 LPL, Carew MS 597, fo. 131r; quoted in McCormack, *Earldom of Desmond*, p. 183.   41 LPL, Carew MS 597, fos 243v–246v; quoted in McCormack, *Earldom of Desmond*, p. 180.   42 McCormack, *Earldom of Desmond*, pp 164–7.   43 Ibid., pp 179–80.
44 SP 63/106/62.   45 SP 63/70/8.   46 SP 63/99/48.

of Connacht, was clear that the whole of Ireland was 'terribly infected' with 'papistry', and identified it as the very ground of the rebellion.[47] In September 1580, he re-iterated that 'it is now a quarrel of religion and the expectation of foreign aid does much further it'.[48] Wallop shared the same opinion.[49] St Leger, the president of Munster, complained that all of Munster was 'bent to the Popish religion'.[50] Captain Gilbert Yorke observed that the chief men of all of the Irish cities were committed to 'superstition and idolatry'.[51] Many of the townsmen of Youghal supported the Desmond rebellion, some to the extent of helping the rebels to climb over the walls and capture their town against their loyal fellow citizens.[52] Anthony Power warned the authorities to 'have an eye to the cities that are all Popish'.[53] Barnaby Goche recommended in 1583 that a citadel be built at Galway because the citizens of the city were 'greatly addicted' to the Spanish.[54]

Two Italian envoys arrived at Dingle early in 1580 with further assurances of aid for the rebels.[55] Dr Sander is said to have offered his head if the Spanish did not arrive by 20 April 1580.[56] On 8 April 1580, Desmond and Sander sent letters to McWilliam Burke, to Ulick and John Burke, sons of the earl of Clanrickard, and to others, to draw them into the rebellion.[57] Soon afterwards, a Mass was celebrated for the return of William Burke, another of Clanrickard's sons, who, according to Malby, could not imbrue his hands enough in English heretics' blood.[58] English officials found that they could depend on the loyalty of none in Munster, except for the earl of Ormond.[59] However, support for the rebels ebbed over the summer when the Spaniards failed to arrive.[60]

The arrival of the small papal expeditionary force in September 1580 injected new life into the rebellion.[61] Clanrickard's sons proclaimed themselves to be the pope's men in Connacht and ordered all priests to celebrate Mass in their churches there.[62] The massacre of the foreign force at Smerwick subsequently was a major set-back for the rebels, and was undoubtedly significant in keeping waverers from open action against the crown, but the rebellion continued nonetheless. St Leger, president of Munster, complained in January 1581 that the rebellion in the south was further off from ending than it was at its beginning.[63] Nonetheless, as hopes of Spanish aid were disappointed over the following months of 1581, active support for the rebellion ebbed away again.[64]

Support for the rebellion continued to ebb and flow depending on news of Spanish or papal aid, with a brief period in which Scottish support also seemed possible. The earl of Desmond, despite periods of despair, clung onto hopes of foreign assistance almost to the very end.[65] However, such hope was founded on

47 SP 63/70/3. **48** Brady, *State papers*, no. xxvi. **49** SP 63/103/17. **50** SP 63/70/20. **51** SP 63/70/44. **52** SP 63/71/3i. **53** SP 63/74/63. **54** SP 63/102/18. **55** SP 63/71/45; 63/72/7. **56** SP 63/72/23. **57** SP 63/72/39. **58** SP 63/77/52. **59** SP 63/71/45; 63/73/23, 33. **60** SP 63/75/27, 35. **61** SP 63/77/24. **62** SP 63/77/53, 66; 63/78/41. **63** SP 63/80/29. **64** SP 63/85/15. **65** SP 63/103/7, 14, 22.

faith rather than reason, and the great majority of the surviving rebels submitted even before the earl, injured and unable to walk, was executed on 11 November 1583.[66] As it happened, a ship bringing money and supplies for Desmond arrived in Ireland in January 1584 – but it was too little, too late, as the Desmond rebellion had already ended.[67]

Yet, strikingly, a hard core of rebels did not abandon all hope of succeeding at some future time. Some rebel sympathisers left Ireland to take refuge in the Spanish dominions in the meanwhile. One key clergyman who came to Ireland to rouse support for the second Desmond rebellion, Dr Dermot Creagh, remained in Ireland after its suppression and worked energetically across the south of Ireland to prepare the way for another 'holy war' in the future.[68]

THE BALTINGLASS REBELLION

Ciarán Brady likened the Baltinglass rebellion to, 'another revolt of poets and intellectuals ... [that] was to be far more important in its consequences than in it origins'.[69] He thought it left the vast majority of the Palesmen cold: for them, rebellion 'involved an inconceivable reversal of loyalties'.[70] Deputy Grey was wrong, he argued, in thinking that there was a 'widespread' conspiracy in the Pale, and his reaction to the rebellion was characterised as 'hysterical and ferocious', and involved him in striking out 'wildly at every level of Pale society'.[71] There is evidence, however, that points towards very different conclusions.

Historians have acknowledged that the conspiracies headed by Baltinglass and William Nugent were widely known of in the Pale, and yet kept secret – but they failed to recognise the significance of that general conspiracy of silence in its tumultuous context. The Baltinglass rebellion and the so-called Nugent conspiracy took place during, and were extensions of, the major foreign-backed rebellion that was already taking place across the south of Ireland, with massive military intervention from Spain expected on a daily basis in its support, to free Ireland from the English crown and to restore the Catholic Church in Ireland.

The earl of Kildare was suspected of being the puppet-master of the revolt. Vincent Carey, Kildare's biographer, allows that there was an 'outside chance' that Kildare had Baltinglass set up – as Wallop and Waterhouse suggested in November 1580 – hoping to become the viceroy if the rebels prevailed with Spanish help, or to profit from the confiscation of Baltinglass' estates if the English prevailed.[72] I consider the latter suggestion to be inherently implausible: was Kildare ever likely to be rewarded by the English crown for doing nothing

---

66 McCormack, *Earldom of Desmond*, pp 17, 177–8.   67 SP 63/107/41; 63/111/70i.   68 SP 63/156/12; 63/164/47.   69 Brady, 'Conservative subversives', p. 26.   70 Ibid., p. 21. 71 Ibid., pp 26–7.   72 SP 63/78/6; Vincent Carey, *Surviving the Tudors: the 'wizard' earl of*

to support it in the face of a rebellion supported by Spain and the papacy, or gain materially from a failed rebellion that engulfed his neighbours and affected wide swathes of the country? Carey himself claimed that 'the more likely scenario was that the earl decided to do nothing for or against the rebels, and to let events take their course'.[73] That might seem innocuous but, in fact, it would mean that Kildare was as happy to contemplate a Spanish-backed rebel victory as an English victory. That, in itself, is quite extraordinary.

In fact, Kildare was deeply involved in the Baltinglass rebellion. Carey admitted that 'on the face of it, the evidence against the earl was pretty convincing'.[74] Kildare confessed to prior knowledge of Baltinglass' rebellion, and admitted to maintaining regular contacts with Baltinglass both before and during the rebellion. Christopher Barnewall stated in August 1583 that a letter from Kildare was decisive in persuading the pope to support the Catholic insurrections in 1579/80.[75] The baron of Slane, a Catholic nobleman of the Pale, reported that Dr Dermot Hurley, a papal emissary newly arrived in Ireland from Rome, told him that Kildare and Baron Delvin were the key figures in the recent 'stirs' and 'foreign practices'.[76] Hurley's evidence, given to a friendly source, is particularly persuasive. William fitz James Fitzgarrett, one of Kildare's sevants, and Thomas Meagh, another Palesman, both gave evidence of Kildare's involvement in the conspiracy.[77] The wife of Fiach McHugh O'Byrne, a lord whose military muscle lent real substance to Baltinglass' rebellion, referred to a letter from Kildare to her husband at the time of the planning of the rebellion at the viscount's house at Monkstown, promising that he would join the rebellion at an appropriate time.[78] It was reported in February 1581 that at one point Baltinglass considered submitting to the crown and travelled to within four miles of Dublin to do so, but was dissuaded from doing so by Kildare.[79] The countess of Kildare sheltered Catholic priests who were closely associated with Dr Nicholas Sander, the key clerical advocate of the second Desmond rebellion, and played key roles in rousing support for Baltinglass' rebellion.[80] Rochford, a Jesuit who was the rebel leader's chief adviser, kept his books in Kildare's castle at Rathangan. Another priest, Nicholas Eustace, probably a relation of Baltinglass, resided chiefly at Rathangan and from there visited various gentlemen's houses where, at Mass, he swore them either to join the rebellion or at least not to be against it.[81] The countess' half-brother actually accompanied Sander and Fitzmaurice to Ireland in July 1579.[82] It strikes me as perverse to argue, contrary to so much evidence, that the earl of Kildare and his wife adopted a neutral stance towards the Baltinglass rebellion.

The crown officials who gathered evidence against Kildare identified the

Kildare and English rule, 1537–1586 (Dublin, 2001), p. 210.   **73** Ibid.   **74** Ibid., p. 206.
75 SP 63/104/38, 39.   **76** SP 63/105/29.   **77** SP 63/79/38; 63/81/9, 10.   **78** SP 63/81/10.
79 SP 63/80/52.   **80** Carey, *'Wizard' earl*, p. 207.   **81** SP 63/80/61.   **82** SP 63/76/56.

killing of Captain Garret as yet another strand of evidence of the earl's participation in the rebellion.[83] Garret was one of Kildare's captains but, late in August
1580, he defected to the rebels with fifty musketeers, a significant boost to their
effectiveness.[84] However, on 17 December 1581, Garret was hanged by Fiach
McHugh O'Byrne – at Kildare's instigation.[85] Vincent Carey has shown that
Kildare had resorted previously to killing men who had acted illegally under his
direction when faced with charges of treason in 1575/6.[86]

It may seem that I have laboured the point of Kildare's considerable involvement in the Baltinglass rebellion, but it is critically important for understanding
its nature. My judgment is that the weight of the evidence implicating Kildare
in the Baltinglass rebellion, its varied sources and consistency, is sufficiently
persuasive to warrant the conclusion that the earl and his wife were deeply
involved in the entire affair. The countess was probably motivated chiefly by
religious commitment, for her household was saturated with Catholic influences.[87] His wife's influence may have affected the earl's outlook, though in his
case I suspect that anti-English sentiment, caused by what he considered to be
personal slights, and a sense of wider grievance against the government under
Elizabeth, was more decisive in moving him towards rebellion. I am struck by
Kildare's outburst in the Council of Ireland on the eve of Baltinglass' rebellion
in 1580 – 'all you Englishmen are joined in one and an Irishman can have no
rights or justice at your hands'.[88]

Baron Delvin was identified as Baltinglass' and Kildare's chief co-conspir-
ator. Fiach McHugh himself claimed to have support from Delvin.[89] Fiach's
wife claimed that Delvin was among the chief conspirators who met at
Monkstown to plan the rebellion.[90] Delvin was charged for his part in plotting
the rebellion alongside his brother, William Nugent, and Oliver Eustace.[91] Dr
Hurley confirmed to the baron of Slane that Kildare and Delvin were the
leading conspirators.[92]

Viscount Gormanstown informed Walsingham very early on that the
conspiracy was both greater and wider spread 'than could well be judged of'.[93]
An individual named Eustace, a student of law at the university at Salamanca,
implicated 'many of good living in the Pale'.[94] The scale of the conspiracy
shocked English-born officials.[95] According to one account, most of the families
in the Pale were 'touched with' the conspiracy.[96] Doubtless, much of the support
it enjoyed was tacit rather than active, but even tacit support for a Spanish-
backed rebellion posed a grave threat to the crown's authority. Sir Nicholas
Malby complained on 31 August 1580 that the 'best of the Irish' (presumably the

83 SP 63/93/32. 84 SP 63/75/77. 85 SP 63/86/51, 52. 86 Carey, 'Wizard' earl, pp
173–5. 87 Ibid., pp 190–5. 88 SP 63/72/65; Christopher Maginn, 'The Baltinglass rebellion, 1580: English dissent or a Gaelic uprising?', *HJ*, 47 (2004), pp 210–11. 89 SP 63/75/12
i. 90 SP 63/81/10. 91 SP 63/79/30. 92 SP 63/105/29. 93 SP 63/75/12 i. 94 SP
63/77/31. 95 SP 63/86/78. 96 SP 63/86/55.

lords and gentlemen of the Pale) could not be made to do anything against the 'rebellious Papists'.[97] There were subsequent investigations into the 'slackness' of the Pale's defences.[98] One month earlier, Captain John Zouche had reckoned that the queen had as few good subjects in the Pale as in any place in the world. He suspected that it was only the news of the imminent arrival of Lord Deputy Grey with reinforcements for the English garrison that kept more men from joining the rebellion openly.[99] Pelham reckoned at the time that if foreign aid were to arrive in Ireland, 'few would stick to her majesty'.[1]

When Baltinglass' rebellion began to falter in the summer of 1581, in the absence of the anticipated Spanish military support, the baron of Delvin's brother, William Nugent, who was a key conspirator behind Baltinglass' insurrection,[2] made a determined effort to inject new momentum into it. In October 1581, Wallop informed Walsingham that although Nugent's conspiracy was known to almost one hundred gentlemen over the previous three months, not one of them revealed it to the crown's officials.[3] The fact that so many gentlemen would take the grave risk of participating in such a widespread conspiracy of silence against the English crown during the course of a major on-going rebellion, not to mention the indeterminable number who were willing to commit themselves to support the rebellion actively, gives a good indication of how disaffected so many of the Palesmen were by the early 1580s.

The disaffection exposed in 1580/1 was based on a number of secular grievances, including the demands for cess and the threat that many felt was posed against their constitutional rights and liberties, but it is surely significant that the front-men in the rebellions of 1579–83, and those most willing to risk their lives, were motivated by religious disaffection. Indeed, I would go so far as to suggest that there would have been no rebellion but for the crown's campaign to suppress Catholicism and impose Protestantism. The strength of Catholic commitment in the Pale was clearly very strong *before* the Baltinglass rebellion – hence the wide-scale complicity in the rebellion and in Nugent's conspiracy – and it was not generated by the aftermath of the rebellion as Ciarán Brady proposed. 1580 was no analogue of 1916.

My reading of the evidence leads me to conclude that not only did it enjoy support from some of the most powerful men in the Pale, but it enjoyed (at least tacit) support from large numbers of other élites of the Pale. Also involved in the rebellion were Alderman Walter Sedgrave of Dublin, and William Fitzsimon, a former sheriff of the city, who supplied the rebels with arms and ammunition, as did Walter's father Alderman Christopher Sedgrave.[4] Fr Michael Fitzsimon, a son of Alderman Thomas Fitzsimon and a relation of William Fitzsimon, was also privy to the plotting and travelled to the papal court on the viscount's

97 SP 63/75/82. 98 SP 63/79/3. 99 SP 63/74/66. 1 SP 63/77/75. 2 SP 63/79/30.
3 SP 63/86/20. 4 Lennon, *Lords of Dublin*, pp 152–4.

behalf.[5] Christopher Maginn has highlighted the key role played in the rebellion by the O'Byrnes and O'Tooles.[6] Baltinglass also had alliances with O'Neill of Tyrone, Maguire of Fermanagh and O'Rourke of West Breifne.[7] Had Spanish forces landed in Ireland, as repeatedly promised, it seems clear that they would have been welcomed by many in Ireland, within the Pale and beyond.

According to one report, Viscount Baltinglass had been planning the rebellion since August 1579 – when Sir James Fitzmaurice Fitzgerald arrived back in Ireland.[8] The outbreak of Baltinglass' rebellion took place very shortly before the arrival of a Spanish force off the Dingle Peninsula: it seems at least possible that Baltinglass had some prior knowledge of its arrival. The Munster rebels linked up with Baltinglass and his allies, and fought together for the same cause. The disaffected Palesmen's hesitancy to rebel against their sovereign, or their prudence in waiting for significant foreign support to arrive before they committed themselves openly to rebellion, did at least spare the population of the Pale from the bloodshed and devastation visited on Munster during the second Desmond rebellion.

In trials conducted in November 1580, about twenty men were condemned and subsequently executed. They were mostly sons of leading gentlemen of the Pale.[9] That was no small tally of scalps from the relatively small and endogamous élites in the Pale, and it certainly did not include all of those involved in the rebellion: Baltinglass and William Nugent fled overseas, while Kildare and Delvin escaped the gallows, and literally dozens of gentlemen subsequently received pardons on payment of fines of up to £100.[10] By emphasising the relatively small number of gentlemen who were executed, and their relative youth, and glossing over the dozens of gentlemen who were pardoned, the current historiography has distorted our understanding of the threat posed by the Baltinglass rebellion and the conspiracies surrounding it. The defiantly Catholic commitment shown by a number of those who were executed also needs to be highlighted more, because it shows that the counter-reformation was already well-established among the generation that had grown up since the enactment of the Elizabethan religious settlement in Ireland: while traditional English Catholicism was fading with the passing of the older generations, a revitalised form of Catholicism had captured the enthusiasm of many of the rising generations in Ireland. The disaffection of the Pale community that was revealed by their stance towards the Baltinglass rebellion continued to run deep afterwards. The élites of the Pale conspicuously absented themselves from the official celebrations of thanksgiving for deliverance from the Spanish Armada in 1588.[11] One would have thought that their consciences would have allowed them

5 Ibid., pp 153–5. 6 Maginn, 'Baltinglass rebellion', pp 205–32. 7 SP 63/73/77. 8 SP 63/79/30. 9 Lennon, *Lords of Dublin*, p. 152. 10 Lennon, *Sixteenth-century Ireland* (2005 ed.), p. 206.

a display of loyalty to their monarch in such exceptional circumstances, but apparently it did not.

PERROT'S RELIGIOUS PROGRAMME

Sir John Perrot was appointed as lord deputy on 7 January 1584. His programme for government was overwhelmingly secular, as was that of his predecessor, Deputy Grey de Wilton. Grey complained in April 1581 that

> Rebellion and disobedience to the prince's word are chiefly regarded and reformation sought of, but God's cause is made a second or nothing at all. Be itself the witness. For the many challenges and instructions that I have received for the civil and political government and care taking to the husbandry of worldly treasure, where is there but one article that concerns the looking to God's due service, seeing of his Church fed with true food, and repressing of superstition and idolatry, wherein the groves of Canaan were surely no more filled or infested than this lamentable Ireland is?

Nonetheless, Elizabeth warned Grey against 'being strict in dealing with religion',[12] because she recognised that religious dissent played a major role in the rebellions against her rule in Ireland.

There was nothing novel in the religious terms among Perrot's instructions on taking office,[13] but he demonstrated commitment and tenacity in his endeavours to advancing the Reformation in Ireland. It was Burghley who suggested to him that the ill-fated scheme to transform St Patrick's Cathedral into a university be revived, but Perrot persisted in promoting the scheme after royal support had dissipated. He continued with his immediate predecessors' policies of trying to ensure that parish churches were repaired and maintained, and staffed with resident clergymen, but he was prepared to act unilaterally to that end.

Perrot's resolute approach to advancing the Reformation very quickly ran into problems because he challenged key vested interests in the Elizabethan ecclesiastical establishment in Ireland, and inadvertently galvanised the widespread and profound hostility felt towards the Reformation, while at the same time he was attempting to force through major changes to the system of taxation against well-nigh universal opposition.

Within weeks of Perrot's taking up office in Ireland, W. Johnes, an English official close to the deputy, reported to Burghley on 14 July 1584 on the state of the Elizabethan Church of Ireland.[14] He wrote of the number of churches that

11 SP 63/140/22.   12 Brady, *State papers*, no. xxix.   13 SP 63/108/87.

had fallen down, 'even in that part of the country which should be best reformed [i.e. the Pale]', of the number of benefices held by children on the basis of dispensations that had been granted to them, of the many laymen who held benefices with the cure of souls, and of the many clergymen who held three or more benefices in plurality though they were 'unlearned' and 'not mete men ... to teach and instruct others'. Just over a month later, Deputy Perrot issued a commission to the bishops of 'every diocese' to sequester into their hands all such spiritual livings as were possessed by laymen, or by non-resident clergymen.[15] Perrot personally complained that church buildings were 'generally in pitiful decay, even almost to Dublin gate'.[16] On 4 March 1585, he had letters directed to the officers of every county for enquiries to be made into the extent of decayed churches and chancels, the state of the bridges and the free schools. Evidently, these commissions proved ineffective and Perrot tried to devise new means to reform the Church of Ireland.

A critical problem confronting Perrot was that corruption was rife throughout the Elizabethan Church of Ireland, even at its highest levels. The unqualified boys and men who enjoyed possession of benefices generally did so with dispensations granted (often in return for money) by various bishops, but also by the Ecclesiastical High Commission and by the Court of Faculties, which had been established to *reform* the Church. Wallop complained to Walsingham on 2 January 1585 of Henry Bird, registrar and receiver of the Ecclesiastical Commission, selling advowsons to benefices, and of keeping fines imposed by the Commission.[17] Bird had been Loftus' diocesan registrar until he was deprived for abusing the office by Dr Acworth in 1577.[18] He was suspected of abusing his office in the Commission in 1582, but was exonerated by Loftus and by other commissioners[19] – presumably because they enjoyed a share of the profits of its operations. Bird was subsequently proven to have exercised his offices in the Ecclesiastical Commission 'corruptly'.[20]

Bird's was not a singular case. One of his predecessors as registrar and receiver of the Ecclesiastical High Commission, John Ball, was another disreputable figure. Loftus had appointed him as archdeacon of Glendalough, commissary of Dublin diocese and rector of Newcastle, though Ball was not ordained.[21] As official principal of Dublin, Ball was reported as having granted absolutions for grievous sins ('fornication, adultery or any like offence') in return for money or for sexual favours. Yet Loftus vainly attempted to have Ball restored to the Ecclesiastical Commission in January 1580,[22] before commending Bird instead.

Deputy Sidney had tried to curb the corruption that was endemic in the

---

14 SP 63/111/31. 15 SP 63/125/28. 16 SP 63/139/7. 17 SP 63/114/2. 18 Murray, 'Tudor diocese of Dublin', p. 283. 19 SP 63/94/107. 20 SP 63/155/33. 21 Brady, *State papers*, no. xxiv. 22 SP 63/71/9.

Elizabethan Church of Ireland by establishing the Irish Court of Faculties in 1577. John Garvey, one of its two commissioners, justified its existence on the basis that there was 'no disposition' in the Elizabethan bishops to reform the abuses in the Church.[23] He referred to the widespread practice of bishops appointing 'boys, kerne, laymen and other incapable persons' to benefices in the Church, and cited examples from within the Pale and beyond to illustrate his point. He recounted how Matthew Sheyne, Elizabethan bishop of Cork & Cloyne (1572–82), had admitted to the Court of Faculties in private and then publicly in a sermon delivered in Cork's cathedral, that 'except he sold the livings of his collation [to horsemen and kerne] he were not able to live, his bishopric was so poor'.[24] Loftus retaliated with the information that the Court of Faculties had begun to sell benefices too.[25]

Sidney's hope that the Court of Faculties would help to reform the Church of Ireland was dashed when Archbishop Loftus was appointed as a joint commissioner of the Court along with Garvey in 1579.[26] Anthony Trollope informed Walsingham in September 1581 that

> I was certified and I find it likely to be true that my lord bishop of Dublin is a partner in the profits of the commission of faculties, and anything almost will be suffered [i.e. tolerated] in Ireland for gain and friendship … My lord bishop of Dublin, sure, I think, be a good subject but he has many children and is so desirous to prefer them as he has married [three of his daughters] … and it is said gave £500 a piece in marriage with them, and bought land in Kent, some say as much as is worth £200 a year, and keeps one of his sons at the Temple in London, and has other sons and daughters, all which made him take up money at interest, as he did £400 of Sir William Drury; and to pay this and defray all charges, and get more money for his sons and daughters, many think makes him have a cavalier conscience.[27]

The Court of Faculties continued to withhold its profits from the crown five years later.[28] Sir Henry Wallop, in a letter to Walsingham in April 1585, reported that Loftus, whom he had worked alongside as lord justice, 'chiefly sought his own profit, and the pleasuring of his friends, which are many in respect of the matches made, and to be made, with his children'.[29] Johnes' letter of July 1584 suggests that the problem of simony grew worse following Loftus' appointment in the Court of Faculties.[30] Archbishop Long of Armagh criticised the operation

23 Brady, *State papers*, no. xxi. 24 Ibid., no. xix. 25 Ibid., no. xviii. Garvey acknowledged that the court had dispensed a 10-year-old boy, a son of the impropriator, to hold a benefice for seven years: Brady, *State papers*, no. xix. 26 Murray, *Enforcing the English Reformation in Ireland*, pp 303–4. 27 SP 63/85/39. 28 SP 63/124/82 i. 29 Brady, *State papers*, no. lxvii.

of the Court of Faculties in letters to Walsingham on 20 January 1585 and again on 4 June 1585 – apparently to no avail.[31]

To tackle the corruption, in August 1585 Perrot established a new commission that was empowered to conduct a visitation of the Church 'throughout the land', to correct abuses uncovered, and to imprison and/or deprive delinquents.[32] However, Bishop Jones of Meath, the husband of Loftus' wife's sister, condemned the commission in a letter to Walsingham, claiming that the deputy had established it 'in his fury' (the impression was given that its establishment was a result of personal antagonisms between Perrot and Loftus), and that the commissioners were 'base and infamous persons'.[33] Perrot's commission seems to have been de-commissioned. The deputy was obliged to revert to the type of commission to the bishops that had already proved so ineffective, directing them to sequester into their hands the fruits of such spiritual livings as were possessed by laymen, unqualified individuals, absentees and non-resident clergymen, and to make enquiries as to the state of the churches and chancels, and bridges and free schools, and to discover who was responsible for any defects they uncovered.[34] There is no evidence to suggest that any substantive progress was achieved.

If, as seems to have been the case, Perrot was correct in seeing Loftus as a major obstacle to reforming the Church of Ireland, he failed to devise a convincing case against the archbishop, and he unwittingly allowed the prelate to portray himself as the victim of an unwarranted personal vendetta ('a private mislike').[35] The first really specific damaging allegations made against Loftus came from Robert Legge, deputy remembrancer in the exchequer of Ireland, in a letter to Burghley in February 1590.[36] Legge accused Loftus of keeping 'many churches and [ecclesiastical] livings in his hands to maintain his children, who are unlike to be preachers or ministers, whereby other learned men are kept out'. Legge accused Loftus of having defrauded the crown of the first fruits of four benefices which he had bestowed on his children and kinsmen, and of having rewarded the clerk of first fruits by giving a corrupt verdict in a law suit. He accused him of issuing another corrupt verdict in a case concerning the dean of St Patrick's Cathedral, Dublin. He accused the archbishop of having taken a fine, and concealing it. He observed that it was 'commonly reported' that Loftus had borrowed £120 from certain merchants of Drogheda, but then threatened to sue them for 'Papistry' to avoid having to repay them. He wrote that Loftus acted with impunity because he was 'chief commissioner of the High Commission, and principal for the Faculties and archbishop of Dublin, and lord chancellor, so as he is all in all'.

Loftus was so powerful that no action was taken against him, and his accusers

30 SP 63/111/31.   31 SP 63/114/39; 63/117/7.   32 SP 63/118/66.   33 Ibid.   34 SP 63/125/28.   35 SP 63/127/4.   36 SP 63/150/52.

– Legge and Barnaby Rich 'and others' – were obliged to keep him under surveillance while gathering information against him (as he complained to Burghley), until finally, in September 1592, he had to respond formally to charges of corruption, and even then he resorted to partial answers, some evasions and what seem to have been lies to avoid prosecution.[37] Yet Loftus' answers were not found to be sufficient to exonerate him and, in February 1593, he and Bishop Jones were required to present a 'book' in their defence against the charges made by Legge and Rich to Burghley, Lord Buckhurst and the English privy council.[38] Archbishop Loftus may have held some Calvinist beliefs, but he was certainly not puritanical in matters of money.

Another, perennial problem for the Elizabethan Church of Ireland was the alienation of the Church's assets. Mr Solicitor Roger Wilbraham complained to Burghley on 9 July 1586 that

> Our bishops and clergy make unconsciencably long leases for 200 and 99 years, reserving small rents which may prove greatly to endamage [their] religious successors when God shall call the country to the knowledge of his Word and to the rule of civility and, therefore, where these laws are defective, it were not amiss if by instructions out of England they were upon their installations enjoined not to lease above 21 years; and those already invested to be prohibited.[39]

Sidney's efforts to address the problem in the mid-1560s having failed, the asset-stripping of the Elizabethan Church continued unabated. When John Garvey, bishop of Kilmore, was translated to Armagh in 1589, he found that the archdiocese had been 'ruined' by John Long, his predecessor.[40] A note by Deputy Fitzwilliam in 1589 lamented that 'the late John Long, archbishop of Armagh, loved good cheer but too well'.[41] In February 1592, Garvey complained that the ninety-nine-year leases granted by Long reduced the value of his diocese to £120 a year – a figure which was greatly depreciated by contemporary inflation.[42] Incidentally, Deputy Fitzwilliam also noted that Dr Meredith Hanmer, dean of St Patrick's Cathedral, Dublin, and bishop of Leighlin 'can as well skill to buy and sell matters belonging to the Church as some meaner sort can'.[43] One reflection of the pervasiveness of simoniacal practices in the Church of Ireland in the last quarter of the sixteenth century is afforded by the 'unsufferable wickedness of Walley', warden of the collegiate church at Youghal, who was cited by Deputy Fitzwilliam in 1589 for neglecting his office and selling benefices while allowing his 'honest wife and poor children to wander up and

37 SP 63/165/21, 52, 59.; 63/166/54. 38 SP 63/168/25. 39 Brady, *State papers*, no. lxxxi. 40 SP 63/144/12. 41 SP 63/141/21, vii. 42 SP 63/163/28. 43 SP 63/141/21, vii.

down begging'.[44] Clearly, Perrot's efforts to curb simony had been less than successful.

The scale of the alienation of ecclesiastical benefices and real estate is incalculable, but studies at local level may be able to reveal something of its extent in a number of dioceses. For instance, Niall Byrne, using the records of Christ Church Cathedral, Waterford, showed that during the Elizabethan phase of the episcopate of Patrick Walsh, bishop of Waterford (1547–79), the cathedral chapter engaged in an 'unprecedented liquidation of church property', including an entire row of slated houses in Christ Church Lane and High Street in a single transaction in 1579, which had the effect of making it 'impossible to entice suitably qualified personnel' to the city (by which, I presume, Byrne meant English Protestant ministers).[45] The alienation of ecclesiastical resources was not always motivated simply by greed: Thomas Connors found that Roland Lynch, the Elizabethan bishop of Kilmacduagh (1587–1625) and bishop of Clonfert (1601–25), was persuaded by his Catholic wife and cathedral chapter to alienate his see lands so that no English cleric would accept office there, and Connors observed that John Lynch, Elizabethan bishop of Elphin (1584–1611), 'accomplished much the same there'.[46]

Anthony Trollope, writing to Walsingham on 26 October 1587, informed him that there was

> no divine service in the country, that all the churches in the country[side] are clean down, ruinous and in great decay, and in those in cities and in walled towns is overseldom any service said, and yet that negligently repaired unto. Here are also above thirty bishoprics and not seven bishops able to preach; and yet those which be [capable of preaching], by making of long leases, reserving small rents and sundry sinister devices, so much impair their sees as, if they be suffered, all the bishoprics of Ireland within few years will not yield sufficient maintenance for one man worthy of this calling. ... Here are many most unmeet men bishops, deans, archdeacons and chancellors, treasurers of churches, and such like spiritual officers, as some Papists, yea, some reconciled to the pope.[47]

Beneath the ranks of the beneficed clergy of the Elizabethan Church of Ireland were the 'stipendiary men' who

> will not be accounted ministers but priests. They will have no wives ... but will have harlots which they make believe that it is no sin to live

44 SP 63/141/19, 21.   45 Byrne, 'Reformation in Tudor Waterford', p. 33. Bishop Midleton complained in 1580 that asset-stripping had left the diocese of Waterford & Lismore worth about £30 *per annum*: Brady, *State papers*, no. xxv.   46 Connors, 'Religion and the laity in Galway', p. 133.   47 SP 63/131/64; Brady, *State papers*, no. lxxxvii.

and lie with them and bear them children. But if they marry them they are damned. And with long experience and some extraordinary trial of these fellows I cannot find whether the most of them love lewd women, cards, dice or drink, best. And when they must of necessity go to church they carry with them a book in Latin of the *Common Prayer* set forth and allowed by her majesty, but they read little or nothing of it, or can well read it, but they tell the people a tale of Our Lady or St Patrick or some other saint … and do all they may to dissuade and allure the people from God and their prince, and their due obedience to them both, and persuade them to the Devil the pope. And sure the people so much hear them, believe them and are led by them and have so little instruction to the contrary.

Sir Richard Bingham, president of Connacht, was no less critical of the 'dumb dogs, the idle ministers of Ireland who can neither preach nor teach nor say ordinary service'.[48]

Such criticisms might seem hyperbolic, but they were confirmed by the prebendaries of St Patrick's Cathedral, Dublin, who declared in 1584 that there was 'not one in that land which can or will preach the Gospel, four bishops and the prebendaries of St Patrick's only excepted'.[49] They observed that the number of impropriated churches in Ireland was 'infinite', but there was not a single preacher nor 'scant a minister to be found among them but rather a company of Irish rogues and Romish priests'. The lessees of the impropriated parishes, they stated, sought the cheapest curates, regardless of their qualities, offering stipends of only £2 or £3 *per annum* and obliging the curate to subsist by travelling 'like a lackey to three or four churches in a morning, every church a mile or two asunder, and there once a week reads them only a Gospel in Latin, and so away'. The fact that the prebendaries themselves employed many curates to serve the parishes whose revenues were appropriated to their prebends lends credence to their statements in this regard.

What seems new by the 1580s is a striking level of pluralism, with priests responsible for conducting services in a plurality of churches. Doubtless, the practice had developed over time, partly as a result of inflationary pressures depreciating the value of the paltry stipends typically allowed to the curates of impropriated parishes in Elizabeth's reign, and partly because of increasing difficulty experienced in trying to find sufficient clergymen to conduct services in the Elizabethan Church of Ireland. The commissions established to ensure that clergymen were appointed to parishes, and the complaints of Johnes and the prebendaries of St Patrick's Cathedral, Dublin, indicate that the problem was very considerable in scale by the mid-1580s, and it was not confined to impro-

48 SP 63/148/39.   49 SP 63/113/58; Brady, *State papers*, no. lxv.

priated parishes (which encompassed the great majority of the parishes of the Pale). As far back as September 1581, Trollope wrote to Walsingham that

> A man told me that on the 27th of August, being Sunday, he was at Dundalk, one of the largest country towns in Ireland, and hearing the bell ring went to church, and staring there long could see nobody but the clerk and at length asked him when the people would come to church, and he told him they should have no service there that day for their minister had other benefices, and he used to say service there but seldom.[50]

Dundalk was within the Pale and, as Trollope noted, it was one of the largest towns in Ireland, and its parish church had been impressively augmented on the eve of the Tudor reformations.[51] Yet it had been all but abandoned since the advent of the Elizabethan reformation, and was destined to collapse entirely from neglect.

The reports of Trollope and the prebendaries of St Patrick's Cathedral are very revealing about the degree of conformity offered by Catholic priests working within the parish structures of the Church of Ireland while it was being protestantised in Elizabeth's reign. It seems to have been a great deal more nominal than is often assumed. There was often very little use of the *Book of Common Prayer* in conducting services and, according to the prebendaries, even that use was confined to a reading of the gospels rather than a celebration of the Protestant liturgy. Trollope's more detailed account of the Church services provided by the 'priests' is even more significant because he highlights the earnest efforts made by the priests to persuade their congregations to adhere to Catholicism, and dissuade them from Protestantism. Catholic historians have tended to emphasise the role of the seminary priests in the survival of the Catholic Church in Ireland – and have over-looked the critical role of the far more numerous priests who were educated and trained within Ireland through traditional structures and who ministered to their parishioners within the traditional parish structures despite the insistence on Reformation by the Elizabethan authorities in Church and state. Incidentally, many of the conforming Catholic clergy who operated in the Elizabethan Church of Ireland were not required to subscribe to the royal supremacy, even when being admitted to benefices.[52]

One must always exercise caution when interpreting anecdotal evidence, and recognise that correspondence and tracts designed to bring about 'reform' tend towards pessimism. Yet my own feeling is that there is sufficient evidence, from a range of sources, to demonstrate that the selling of church offices and other

50 Brady, *State papers*, no. xxxv.   51 Jefferies, *Priests and prelates*, pp 24–5.   52 Brady, *State papers*, no. xx.

assets had become general in the Elizabethan Church of Ireland. The Elizabethan Church failed to mount a convincing evangelical challenge for the hearts and souls of the peoples in Ireland, not simply because of economic problems (many of them caused by the dissipation of the financial resources of the Church by the English crown and its appointees to offices in the Church), but chiefly because there were hardly any Protestant preachers available to mount a credible campaign. The absence of Irish Protestant preachers was not simply a reflection of economic problems (there were many more well-endowed benefices in Ireland than there were Protestant preachers), but chiefly because the failure of the Tudor reformations meant that there were remarkably few men in Ireland willing to commit themselves to the Protestant ministry. Finally, it seems clear that those Protestant clergymen in Ireland who were capable of preaching there made little effort to preach: Bishop Jones of Meath diocese was severely berated by Walsingham in 1589 for preaching only once a term, and then in Dublin rather than in his own diocese.[53] He was also condemned for being hypocritical, lewd and corrupt. Perrot's efforts to reform the Church of Ireland made little headway with men like Loftus and Jones directing its affairs.

UNIVERSITY

Perrot had long been a keen advocate for an Irish university.[54] It was Burghley who proposed reviving the old St Patrick's Cathedral project, but Perrot adopted the proposal with enthusiasm.[55] In August 1584, Perrot proposed to Walsingham that the benefices of St Patrick's Cathedral, Dublin, worth about 4,000 marks he reckoned, would suffice to endow two university colleges with £1,000 *per annum* apiece, with the residue transferred to nearby Christ Church Cathedral ('whereby Christ may devour St Patrick and, I hope, a number of his devoted followers too'), while the cathedral building could be converted into law courts and the canons' residences made into an Inn of Court.[56] He wrote 'at large' to both Walsingham and Burghley for their support, arguing in October 1584 that St Patrick's Cathedral was 'superfluous, except it be to maintain a few bad singers'.[57] He made the point to the earl of Leicester in June 1585 that the cathedral served 'little use than for singing men to meet together twice a day to sing badly, rather of custom than devotion'.[58]

However, Archbishop Loftus galvanised the cathedral clergy to petition the lords of the council in England in defence of the cathedral, and he campaigned vigorously in its defence. The prebendaries claimed to be indispensable on the

53 SP 63/149/28.   54 SP 63/107/73; Victor Treadwell, 'Sir John Perrot and the Irish parliament of 1585–6', *PRIA*, 85C (1985), p. 272.   55 Murray, 'Tudor diocese of Dublin', p. 359. 56 SP 63/111/71; Brady, *State papers*, no. lxiii.   57 Brady, *State papers*, no. lxiv.   58 Quoted from Murray, 'Tudor diocese of Dublin', p. 363.

grounds that there were only four Protestant preachers in Ireland apart from themselves.[59] Henry Ussher, archdeacon of Dublin, was despatched to present their case at court.[60] Evidently, the prebendaries' petition bore fruit, because the privy council wrote to Deputy Perrot on 3 January 1585 to express their doubts about the proposal to convert the cathedral, and they directed the deputy to consult with Archbishop Loftus as to how best to proceed, while they suggested that the forthcoming parliament might impose some kind of levy on the leases of impropriated benefices to support the establishment of a university.[61] Loftus consolidated his victory by appealing for Burghley's continued support to preserve the cathedral on 10 January 1585, and again on 18 March 1585.[62] The archbishop reiterated the point that 'in all the whole realm there is not one preacher (three bishops excepted, of whom two were preferred out of this church, but only in St Patrick's'. He observed that Christ Church Cathedral, Dublin, 'neither has nor is able to maintain one preacher'. The deputy's university project would require the removal of those preachers 'in the hope that twenty years hence some divines may spring out of a lecture to be instituted in the intended college. ... I may say schools are provided for in every county here. Oxford and Cambridge are not far off, all under our dominion, but this will not satisfy'. Loftus' defence of St Patrick's was not without substance – but his statement as to the virtual absence of Protestant preachers a quarter of a century after the enactment of the Elizabethan religious settlement is quite remarkable.

Deputy Perrot was not prepared to accept defeat on the university project and tried to brow-beat Loftus into co-operation. Loftus responded by bombarding Walsingham and Burghley with a series of letters against Perrot's complaints,[63] his 'hateful' correspondence,[64] and a 'malicious book' sent to court against him.[65] He also complained of Perrot's threats towards him, and of the deputy's 'heavy displeasure', and of the 'daily indignities and open disgraces' heaped upon him by the deputy.[66] As late as September 1585, Loftus was still writing to Burghley of Perrot's persistent attempts to force through his university project, and he wrote to the queen to pray that his cathedral would not be converted into what he called (tongue-in-cheek) 'Perrot's College'.[67] Finally, the deputy had to accept defeat. James Murray has highlighted Loftus' employment of Richard Bancroft, the absentee prebendary of Mulhuddart and chaplain to Elizabeth's vice-chamberlain, as his emissary at court in the spring of 1585 as being decisive in thwarting Perrot's university project.[68] Certainly by May of 1585, if not already by January of that year, St Patrick's future was assured.[69]

Relations between Perrot and Loftus did not improve after the university project had died. Perrot claimed that his quarrel with the archbishop was not

59 SP 63/113/56; Brady, *State papers*, no. lxv. 60 Brady, *State papers*, no. lxvi. 61 SP 63/114/4. 62 SP 63/114/17, 63/115/32; Brady, *State papers*, no. lxvi. 63 SP 63/115/32, 63/117/42. 64 SP 63/117/43. 65 SP 63/118/45. 66 SP 63/117/11, 63/118/44. 67 SP 63/119/18. 68 Murray, 'Tudor diocese of Dublin', pp 367–9. 69 SP 63/112/68.

caused by their differences about St Patrick's, 'but about his double and under-hand dealings about it'.[70] Perrot had to have Archbishop Long of Armagh and Bishop Jones of Meath deny in writing that they had been abused by him (presumably because of allegations to the contrary by Loftus).[71] Loftus referred to the 'private mislike' between himself and the deputy, while Bishop Jones asked Walsingham to help resolve relations between the two men.[72] In December 1586, Perrot had one of Loftus' daughters and her husband, Thomas Colcought, imprisoned 'for uttering unseemly and contemptuous speeches' against himself.[73] Unfortunately for Perrot, he succeeded in alienating almost all of the English-born councillors in the council of Ireland,[74] which strengthened Loftus' position immeasurably.

Yet Loftus' defence of St Patrick's Cathedral was far from being disinterested. With a second cathedral chapter nearby at Christ Church Cathedral, there is no reason why the dissolution of St Patrick's should have had such irreparably deleterious effects on Dublin's diocesan administration as Loftus alleged.[75] In fact, the archbishop had considerable vested interests in the cathedral, the scale of which were only revealed after Perrot's term of office.[76]

Not only did the archbishop enjoy the revenues of the chancellorship of St Patrick's *in commendam* with his archbishopric, but he bestowed most of the cathedral prebends on members of his extended family, and there were suggestions that one of the prebendaries, a layman, had come to an arrangement whereby he paid some portion of the revenues of his office to the archbishop. In 1592, Loftus' son Edward was the prebendary of Castleknock, 'young Miles' (clearly no clergyman) was the prebendary of Yagoe, a nephew of the archbishop was the archdeacon of Glendalough, while kinsmen of his enjoyed possession of the treasurership and five prebends, and two other prebends were held by brothers-in-law of the archbishop (including Bishop Jones of Meath, who was married to the archbishop's wife's sister), while the prebend of Timothan was held by one William Witherby (described as a 'poor man', and clearly not a clergyman). Henry Ussher, archdeacon of Dublin, was related to Loftus through marriage. Loftus' 'schoolmaster' (presumably the tutor of his children) held the prebend of Maynooth. When charged with nepotism and simony, Archbishop Loftus denied that he leased any of the prebends of St Patrick's Cathedral for profit (though he was not always trustworthy); he pointed out that his school-master was presented to Maynooth by the countess of Kildare (though it is likely to have been as Loftus' request), and that many of the other prebends in question possessed by his family members and kinsmen were held by graduates or by university students, including his son Edward.[77] Interestingly, though, the archbishop identified only two of his extended clan as preachers. It seems that

70 Brady, *State papers*, no. lxxii.   71 SP 63/119/34, 37.   72 SP 63/127/4, 63/128/66.
73 SP 63/127/15.   74 SP 63/127/1.   75 Brady, *State papers*, no. lxvi.   76 SP 63/166/54.
77 SP 63/165/59.

he gave an exaggerated impression of St Patrick's Cathedral as a centre for Protestant preaching during his campaign to preserve it from conversion into a university. A commission was authorised to investigate the charges made against Loftus.[78] However, he remained in office, despite his venality, because of his political utility: Deputy Fitzwilliam stated in 1589 that, 'Ireland has great need of Loftus'.[79]

ENHANCED ENFORCEMENT

Perrot believed that a demonstration of determination would induce conformity, and facilitate conversions by a reformed Church of Ireland.[80] It was a very ill-advised policy, and revealed a fundamental miscalculation of the strength of Catholic commitment in Ireland. Perrot, rather naïvely, hoped to secure parliamentary sanction for his drive to suppress Catholicism. Embedded in his legislative programme, which was chiefly concerned with the form of taxation known as 'cess', was a compendious bill comprised of twenty-seven assorted statutes in force in England and Wales, including the most recent English statutes against Catholic sedition. Victor Treadwell reckoned that 'a more potent instrument for dividing political loyalties and unleashing parliamentary passions would have been difficult to devise'.[81]

In a ham-fisted attempt to cow prospective opposition, Perrot unleashed the Ecclesiastical High Commission without warning in the very week that the Council of Ireland set its seal to his bills.[82] Three 'notorious massing-priests' were apprehended in Dublin and 'a great nest discovered of mass-mongers', including 'diverse gentlemen, whereof some lawyers in places of credit, merchants, ladies and gentlewomen of good sort'.[83] Perrot decided to deal with them 'as shall be meet' at a time of his choosing. His intention was to overawe any Catholic dissidents. Perrot then had the oath of supremacy tendered to Justices of the Peace and other legal officers in the Pale, and he intended to punish defaulters through the Court of Castle Chamber, until he was dissuaded from doing so by wiser councils.[84] Perrot subsequently denied to Burghley that he had tendered the oath 'universally', but only to justices of the peace and other officers 'as the law in that case does necessarily exact'. Yet an entry in the Irish Council Book for December 1584 directing that the 'oath of allegiance' was to be tendered to all men and women over the age of sixteen in County Wexford, suggests that his intention had been to swear-in the entire adult population

---

78 SP 63/171/20.   79 SP 63/144/35.   80 Treadwell, 'Irish parliament of 1585–6', pp 268–71.   81 Ibid., p. 271.   82 Ibid., p. 274.   83 SP 63/112/45.   84 Edwards, *Church and state*, pp 270–1; Treadwell, 'Irish parliament of 1585–6', p. 274.

under English jurisdiction.[85] Such wildly provocative actions formed the backdrop to the parliament convened by Perrot in April 1585.

According to Archbishop Loftus, at the opening of parliament, the deputy was persuaded by Sir Nicholas White, the Irish-born Master of the Rolls, to 'permit this people to have liberty of their consciences and the free use of their religion, assuring Sir John that granting that unto them they would not only condescend to the repeal of Poyning's Act, but to any other reasonable motion which should be propounded in the parliament'.[86] Not only is Loftus' claim inherently implausible given Perrot's determination to suppress Catholicism, and the fact that Perrot did not seek to have Poynings' law suspended at that time, but there is contemporary evidence that suggests that Loftus was guilty of putting his own 'spin' on facts for polemical ends.

Perrot's compendious bill provoked vehement opposition in the Irish House of Commons. A strong commonwealth party emerged which successfully blocked the deputy's legislative programme because they were convinced that if the anti-Catholic legislation were enacted and Poynings' law suspended, 'their freedoms would come in question, to the overthrowing of private men and corporate towns'.[87] Already, the deputy held a Sword of Damocles over the heads of many of the gentlemen of the Pale for refusing to take the oath of supremacy, and he was also investigating town charters and privileges.[88] The commonwealth men could be forgiven for suspecting the worst of Perrot. Their resolute opposition forced him to prorogue the first session of the parliament. Yet, rather than realising the strength of religious feeling, Perrot exacerbated matters greatly by summoning the men who had refused to swear the oath of supremacy to appear before the council of Ireland, and by binding those who refused to submit to appear in the Castle Chamber.[89]

Archbishop Long, who may be counted a reliable observer, wrote a letter to White in July 1586 in which he quoted Bishop Jones' account of what actually happened: Jones complained that White asked Deputy Perrot in a session of the council of Ireland to 'use tolerance in the matter of the oath and religion' so that he might 'draw them in matters of policy to good conformity'.[90] No reference was made to Poynings' law, but reference was made to the 'many gentlemen of the Pale [who] were then called before his lordship [Perrot]'. That suggests that White made his speech for 'tolerance' – and not for 'liberty of their consciences and the free use of their religion' as Loftus misleadingly stated – in June 1585, when Perrot had the justices of the peace and others who had refused to take the

85 *Analecta Hibernica*, 12 (1943), pp 30–1; D.B. Quinn and J.P. Prendergast (eds), 'Calendar of the Irish Council Book, 1 March 1581 to 1 July 1586', *Analecta Hibernica*, 24 (1967), p. 163; Edwards, *Church and state*, pp 270–1.   86 SP 63/94/37; Brady, 'Conservative subversives', p. 11.   87 SP 63/117/62; Treadwell, 'Irish parliament of 1585–6', p. 286.   88 Brady, *State papers*, no. lxix; Treadwell, 'Irish parliament of 1585–6', p. 292.   89 *Cal. Irish Council Book*, pp 166, 178.   90 SP 63/125/12.

oath of supremacy brought before the Council of Ireland to be admonished and then threatened with proceedings in the court of Castle Chamber.[91] Perrot was not, in fact, swayed by White's speech, but was forced to adopt a policy of toleration by the queen herself.

Walsingham, the queen's secretary, wrote to Perrot on 24 July 1585 to express grave concern about the discontentment roused by the deputy's tendering of the oath of supremacy, his enquiries into charters and titles, and his employment of anti-Catholic laws. He informed Perrot that the queen, seeing the 'general mislike' of the proposed religious legislation, wanted it withdrawn. The queen wrote to Perrot personally to make her wishes absolutely clear: she commanded him to follow a moderate line, 'especially in matter of oath and religion, which was charged you not to meddle in'. She went on to declare, 'I marvel, you lack so much discretion in these dangerous days to touch that point of religion, and to leave for this time to scan of patents and privileges'.[92] With Elizabeth on the eve of signing the treaty of Nonsuch, committing herself to supporting the Dutch rebels against Spain, she was desperately anxious to avoid yet another rebellion in Ireland.

Perrot, however, did not capitulate quite yet, and Archbishop Long, for one, shared his conviction that he was running 'the right course towards this reformation'.[93] In September 1585, Perrot justified his firm handling of the religious question, and he tried to secure royal sanction for a 'whittled down' religious bill, but his pleas fell on deaf ears.[94] When Long, possibly at Perrot's behest, wrote to Walsingham, he received a response penned in December 1585 that made it clear that the crown would not condone religious coercion: 'the time is not fit for severity'.[95] The queen's secretary conceded that Perrot's intentions were 'very honourable', but his actions were not appropriate for the time: 'He might have lived in better season in the time of Henry VIII, when princes were resolute to persist in honourable attempts. But our age has been given to other manner of proceedings, whereunto the lord deputy must be content to conform himself as other men do'. Perrot had no choice but to accept the queen's directions.[96] Loftus subsequently complained that when he and Bishop Jones 'and a few others well-affected' on the Ecclesiastical High Commission brought before them the 'principal gentlemen and such as we knew to be ringleaders' of the Catholic cause, they were forbidden by Perrot from taking any action and were informed by him that he had received instructions that the people of Ireland 'should not be dealt with for matters of religion'.[97]

Yet, Perrot did not neglect ecclesiastical affairs altogether. He had the queen's auditor of Ireland investigate the payments due to the crown from the bishops for first fruits and twentieths, from the Ecclesiastical High Commission for fines,

91 *Cal. Irish Council Book*, pp 166, 178.   92 Treadwell, 'Irish parliament of 1585–6', pp 292–3.
93 Brady, *State papers*, no. lxix.   94 Treadwell, 'Irish parliament of 1585–6', pp 293–5.
95 Brady, *State papers*, no. lxxiii.   96 SP 63/131/65.   97 SP 63/154/37.

recognisances and sequestrations, and from the Court of Faculties for its profits, as well as payments due from the crown's secular law officers (including the chancellor, Loftus, and justices of the peace).[98] Suits against churchmen for monies they owed led to protracted and bitter proceedings, and an appeal from the archbishop of Canterbury on behalf of the 'poor clergy of Ireland', but achieved little by way of reforming abuses in the Church.[99]

The efforts made to advance the Reformation in Munster during the course of the plantation there owed nothing to Perrot's initiatives.[1]

Some English officials had hoped that the plantation of Munster would help to advance the Reformation in southern Ireland. Sir William Herbert, a prominent planter with strong connections at Elizabeth's court, offered reasons for optimism in that regard.[2] He gave the impression that he might transform Kerry into a new England. In fact, despite having the *Book of Common Prayer* translated into Irish, and enthusiastically embracing the possibility of creating a native Protestant ministry, his hopes of protestantising even a part of Munster came to nought. Close familiarity with English settlers did not inspire the people of Munster to become Protestants. On the contrary, the English officials and immigrants in the south encountered deep-seated hostility: from the magistrates or ruling classes as much as any others.[3] In the towns too, relations between the English soldiers garrisoned in them and the townsfolk were sometimes very strained.[4] English authority in Munster was strong enough in 1588 to ensure that there were large attendances at the armada thanksgiving ceremonies at Cork (where 2,000 people are reported to have attended), Kinsale and Rosscarbery.[5] However, Protestantism won very few adherents in the province. Archbishop Magrath, whose ecclesiastical province was virtually co-terminus with Munster, lamented in 1593 that 'the general unbridled multitude there [are] notorious Papists and reconciled to the pope and king of Spain'.[6]

Perrot's term as governor ended in June 1588; his programme for government in tatters. Anthony Trollope offered a damning synopsis of the state of the Elizabethan Church of Ireland some months before the deputy's departure: almost all the churches in the countryside decayed or ruinous, no Protestant liturgy in the countryside, while in the cities and walled towns it was rarely celebrated, and then negligently. Preachers were exceptionally few. The average clergyman in the Elizabethan Church considered himself a Catholic priest, and he taught his congregations accordingly. In sum, the Elizabethan Church of Ireland was a chimera.[7] Archbishop Long informed Walsingham in July 1585 that 'It is a hard thing to be thought of that the land is not able to afford, of the birth of the land, forty Christians which have the taste of the true service of

98 SP 63/124/82. 99 SP 63/127/10, 16, 18; 63/128/14; 63/129/70; 63/132/2. 1 SP 63/128/64. 2 SP 63/129/42, 63/135/58. 3 SP 63/126/22; 63/127/2. 4 For example, SP 63/135/42. 5 SP 63/141/19, 21. 6 SP 63/170/4. 7 SP 63/131/64; Brady, *State papers*, no. lxxxvii.

God'.[8] Even if one were to make some allowance for exaggeration, the scale of the failure of the Elizabethan reformation in Ireland, twenty-five years after its enactment by the Irish parliament of 1560, could hardly be more stark.

RECUSANCY

Ciarán Brady sought to define precisely when and why the secular élites in the Pale moved from 'passive church-papistry to active and decisive recusancy'.[9] He cited Nicholas Canny's survey of 'Why the Reformation failed in Ireland' to support his claims that 'for at least a generation, leading Palesmen remained loyal to the [Elizabethan] royal supremacy and to the various doctrines taught under its auspices', and that there existed 'a large body of undecided church-papistry surrounded by small pockets of committed Catholicism and Protestantism ... as ... in ... many parts of contemporary England'.[10] He referred to the Palesmen's 'indifference' to 'a whole range of spiritual and doctrinal matters' and their 'complacency' in religion.[11] According to Brady, 'The cess rather than matters of religion or high policy provided a groundswell of discontent'.[12] That discontent led to the formulation of a constitutional case that had nothing to do with religion until Deputy Grey's 'hysterical and ferocious' reaction to the Baltinglass insurrection of 1580, which Brady likened to the 1916 Rising, decisively changed the Palesmen's outlook in politics and religion.[13] According to Brady, it became clear to the Palesmen during Deputy Perrot's parliament that

> the protection of the old religion ... was not a matter separate from the defence of their ancient constitutional liberties: since both were under siege by an indiscriminately oppressive government, both had to be maintained together. ... recusancy was appropriated as the country cause, not simply as a cover for other underlying discontents, but as an essential element in the Palesmen's new and solidary sense of identity.[14]

This thesis is echoed in most subsequent surveys of the Elizabethan reformation in Ireland.

However, Brady's thesis is flawed by the fact that he mischaracterised the religious disposition of the Palesmen before the Baltinglass rebellion as one of 'complacency' and 'indifference' – contemporary evidence proves it was other-wise. Furthermore, his chief source for the supposedly dramatic transfer of

---

8 Brady, *State papers*, no. lxix.   9 Brady, 'Conservative subversives', p. 13.   10 Ibid., pp 12–13.
11 Ibid.   12 Ibid., pp 16–22.   13 Ibid., pp 25–7.   14 Ibid., p. 29.

Palesmen's religious allegiance, a letter of Archbishop Loftus to Burghley on 22 September 1590, actually offered a very different explanation for the general recusancy that prevailed in the Pale; one that made no reference to the Baltinglass rebellion of a decade earlier.[15]

Archbishop Loftus informed Burghley that

> Albeit there has been in these people a general disposition to Popery, as a thing wherein they were nursled even from the cradle, yet this general recusancy is but of six years continuance at most, and began in the second year of Sir John Perrot's government, in the beginning of the parliament held by him. Before which time, I well remember there were not in the Pale the number of twelve recusants, gentlemen of account.[16]

He went on in his letter to account for the 'general recusancy'. According to Loftus

> In the beginning of the parliament [of 1585–6], Sir Nicholas White, in the name of his countrymen, moved Sir John Perrot before most of this council [of Ireland], to permit this people to have liberty of their consciences and the free use of their religion, assuring Sir John that granting that unto them they would not only condescend to the repeal of Poyning's Act, but to any other reasonable motion which should be propounded in the parliament. His good success with the lord deputy at that time moved another of his country, one Edward Nugent, a lawyer, to come into the lower house with a 'premeditate' speech in defence of the Mass and the Romish religion. By these encouragements and bad example of some persons of credit in this state, this people has ever since grown to wonderful obstinacy and utter detestation of our religion.

Hence, if Loftus may be trusted, the Ecclesiastical High Commission was able to compel people to conform to the Elizabethan Church, 'howsoever they were affected inwardly in their consciences', until Deputy Perrot was persuaded to permit people 'to have liberty of consciences and the free use of their religion'. In other words, Perrot did not inadvertently make the Palesmen more Catholic – he simply allowed them the freedom to demonstrate their pre-existent commitment to Catholicism. Significantly, Loftus made no mention of Baltinglass whatsoever.

---

15 SP 63/94/37; Brady, 'Conservative subversives', p. 13. **16** SP 63/94/37; Brady, 'Conservative subversives', p. 11.

One further observation must be made. Loftus' letter, which Brady used to date the start of the 'general recusancy' in the Pale, is chronologically confusing. The archbishop dated the 'general recusancy' to 'six years' earlier (indicating a date in 1584), but also to the 'beginning' of the parliament convened by Perrot (April 1585), and also to Sir Nicholas White's speech before the council of Ireland appealing for 'tolerance' (probably in June 1585, but not documented until July 1586). Needless to say, these progressively later dates widened the distance in time between the Baltinglass rebellion of 1580 and its supposedly dramatic effects on religious dispositions in the Pale.

Victor Treadwell astutely observed that Archbishop Loftus' letter to Burghley condemning Perrot was a 'travesty', and he noted that this 'polemical attack on Perrot and his Anglo-Irish councillors … has been somewhat uncritically swallowed by students of the period'.[17] It forms a key part of Ciarán Brady's study of the 'Conservative subversives'. The fact is that there was a great deal more recusancy in the Pale before the parliament of 1585–6 than Loftus would have had Burghley believe: the 'nest of massmongers' discovered in October 1584 in Dublin, and the 'great proofs of sundry Masses said in private houses' demonstrate that,[18] and there is a very considerable volume of evidence reflecting general hostility and resistance to Protestantism throughout the Pale from the earliest years of Elizabeth's reign. Archbishop Loftus' reference to the absence of recusants six years earlier, in 1584, is very significant, because he was referring to the time of Perrot's initial 'crackdown' on Catholic Masses and recusancy, when many leading gentlemen and ladies were 'apprehended' and awaited their punishment at what Perrot considered 'an apter time'.[19] In short, Loftus' memory of a time when there were few recusants 'of account', was extremely selective indeed.

What the rebellions of 1579/80 revealed, and what the reactions to Perrot's anti-Catholic measures outside as well as inside the parliament of 1585–6 demonstrated, was the depth of the commitment to Catholicism in the Pale. Deputy Fitzwilliam, Perrot's successor, was obliged to report that not one of the Irish-born judges or learned men communicated at the special thanksgiving service for England's deliverance from the Spanish Armada.[20] According to Archbishop Loftus, the boycott of the thanksgiving service was even more significant and general: Deputy Fitzwilliam and the council of Ireland had directed the sheriffs of every county to warn 'all men' to attend the thanksgiving services organised in the principal church in each county, 'yet', he declared, 'very few or none almost resorted thereunto, but even in Dublin itself the lawyers, in term time, took occasion to leave the town of purpose to absent themselves from that godly exercise'.[21] At least Perrot was spared the ignominy of that debacle.

17 Treadwell, 'Irish parliament of 1585–6', p. 284, fn 139.   18 Quoted in Treadwell, 'Irish parliament of 1585–6', pp 274, 278.   19 Charles McNeill (ed.), 'The Perrot papers', *Analecta Hibernica*, 12 (1943), p. 29.   20 SP 63/140/24.

Yet the story of Perrot's clash with Archbishop Loftus did not end with the viceroy's return to England. Loftus and his clique exacted revenge on both Perrot and Nicholas White by supplying or organising most of the evidence for the spurious charges of treason that resulted in both men dying in the Tower of London.[22]

CONTINUING TENSIONS

The general boycott of the armada thanksgiving services is not, in itself, proof of disloyalty, but it certainly suggests a degree of alienation from the crown.[23] When directed to apprehend any individuals who posed a threat to the state, Deputy Fitzwilliam replied to Walsingham on 14 December 1589 that, 'Considering what fell out in the last rebellion, and the tendency of the wild Irish to rebel, and how far the English race have given themselves to the pope's religion, they are for the most part recusants, it is difficult to set down with certainty the names of those who should be apprehended'.[24] He identified thirteen lords and gentlemen from the heart of the Pale as among the most dangerous men in Ireland.[25] The deputy and others of the council of Ireland wrote in August 1590 of intelligence received regarding the 'disloyal dealings' of the Nugents of Delvin with the Spanish duke of Parma. They wrote that they 'dared not' to investigate the matter because the conspiracy involved some of the 'greatest affinities in the Pale'.[26] In a subsequent letter, they explained that Richard Brady, Catholic bishop of Kilmore, had acted as a medium between Parma and the 'disaffected'.[27] After being directed to enquire into the conspiracy further the deputy, Archbishop Loftus and Bishop Jones wrote that the baron of Delvin and the rest of the Nugents were of 'doubtful' loyalty, that Andrew White, son of the master of the rolls, was 'a most dangerous Papist', and that Sir Lucas Dillon's son-in-law, Rochford (a Jesuit who played a key role in the Baltinglass revolt a decade earlier), was 'an obstinate and dangerous fellow'.[28] In October 1591, Deputy Fitzwilliam identified William Nugent and Andrew White as the 'special ringleaders in all Romish and Spanish actions'.[29] Farannen, Catholic bishop of Kildare, after being found carrying letters addressed to the duke of Parma, admitted to being sheltered by Delvin.[30] However, the administration in Dublin was very reluctant to take action for fear of provoking another rebellion comparable with the Baltinglass revolt a decade earlier.

In March 1591, Archbishop Loftus and Bishop Jones proposed that some of the 'most froward and principal gentlemen of the Pale' be sent to England to be 'severely dealt with' because of the 'general defection of the Irish in causes of

21 SP 63/154/37. 22 Treadwell, 'Irish parliament of 1585–6', pp 304–5. 23 SP 63/137/22; 63/141/19. 24 SP 63/149/33. 25 SP 63/149/32. 26 SP 63/154/8. 27 SP 63/154/12. 28 SP 63/154/35. 29 SP 63/160/50. 30 SP 63/158/7.

religion'.[31] Disaffection ran very deep. There were many treasonous speeches made in the Pale and men were executed as traitors.[32] Roger Wilbraham, the solicitor general, informed Burghley in August 1591 that there were many accusations made against men for using 'traitorous words', some of them for expressing their desire for the advent of the Spaniards.[33] A number of the accusees were executed, with more to follow in the next law term.[34] One of those executed was Patrick Penteney, a lieutenant in the queen's army, for levying cess in Cavan and for declaring that he expected the imminent arrival of Martin Scurlock with a 'great company of Spaniards from the king, and that the bishops placed by the queen should be displaced'. His father, Richard, was subsequently executed for declaring that 'The injury that is done in hanging my son is done by the lord deputy. I pray God I never die until I see him hanged, and her also that made him deputy'.[35] Richard's words may have been voiced in anguish, but sentiments of the father and son were not those of loyal subjects. Sir Robert Dillon was alleged to have had a vested interest in the execution of the Penteneys, which may well be so, given his role in having Sir Nicholas Nugent executed during the Baltinglass rebellion more than a decade earlier,[36] but he himself was accused by one of his bitterest enemies, William Nugent, of failing to take action against another man who spoke treasonous words.[37] Relations among the Pale community were clearly fraught in 1591.

With treasonous speeches and rumours widespread, Deputy Fitzwilliam expressed his wish to Burghley in a letter of 30 December 1591 that twenty gentlemen of the Pale be detained in the Tower of London until Michaelmas of the following year as a precautionary measure.[38] He wrote of a cipher that one William Bathe, a gentleman who lived close to Dublin,[39] left with William Nugent before going to Spain so that they could carry on a clandestine correspondence.[40] Nugent's English brother-in-law, Thomas Wakely, denounced him in a sworn deposition as having boasted of being in receipt of a Spanish pension – a claim that Nugent denied.[41] The evidence, as always, is elusive, though Wakely may be considered a plausible witness, while Nugent had very good reason to be economical with the truth, since his 'neck' was on the line.

It is likely that Baron Delvin and his brother William were among the forty or fifty Palesmen that Deputy Fitzwilliam wanted imprisoned in England in February 1592 (note how the number had swollen since the previous year), 'until this dangerous time is past'.[42] The queen, however, was loathe to take any such provocative action without firm evidence of treason. In September 1592, Delvin

---

31 SP 63/156/35.   32 SP 63/158/51.   33 SP 63/159/50.   34 See, for instance, SP 63/158/52.   35 SP 63/161/25 i.   36 SP 63/160/28.   37 SP 63/159/64.   38 SP 63/161/44.   39 SP 63/161/25. Bathe had been to court and presented 'his late device of the new harp' to Elizabeth herself: SP 63/159/46. His political outlook seems to have changed in the interval.   40 SP 63/161/25.   41 SP 63/161/25 ii.   42 SP 63/163/35.

defended himself against accusations that he had entertained Bishop Dermot Creagh, a papal nuncio, or corresponded with him by word or letter. He also challenged a statement to the effect that all of the noblemen went to Church, apart from him: he replied that the statement was simply untrue, and asked why he should be singled out 'above the rest'.[43] However, the Catholic bishop of Kildare stated that the Nugents were very careful to hide their treasonous activities.[44] Fitzwilliam let matters lie for fear of provoking another rebellion.

CONCLUSIONS

The 1580s marked a watershed for the Reformation in Ireland. From the mid-1560s, it had been possible, through the imposition of fines, the taking of recognances and exemplary imprisonments, to enforce a wide attendance at Elizabethan Church services across some of the Pale, and in the cities across Ireland. From the late 1580s, however, it proved increasingly difficult to force any other than office-holders to attend Elizabethan services, and even office-holders became increasingly reluctant to attend. That was an important development in the course of the Tudor reformations in Ireland, because whatever small prospect there may have been for a Reformation breakthrough while Irish congregations were prepared to attend Protestant services, with no one to preach at, there was no possibility at all of a mass conversion to Protestantism in late Elizabethan Ireland.

A renewed drive by the Elizabethan administration in Dublin and the Ecclesiastical High Commission to enforce conformity from the late 1570s, was soon followed by the second Desmond rebellion and the Baltinglass rebellion. Both were avowedly launched to defend the Catholic religion and, whatever other motives the rebels had, that appeal to religion was central to both of them, and won them widespread sympathy if not active support, even in the Pale itself. The lesson was not lost on Elizabeth, and she obliged her governors in Ireland to desist from forcing men's consciences for fear of the political repercussions of their actions at a time when Anglo-Spanish relations were so fraught.

Deputy Perrot's term of office may well have been a watershed for the Elizabethan reformation, not because of a supposedly dramatic transfer of religious sentiment from 'indifference' to 'determined recusancy', but because the state was forced to acknowledge the strength of Catholic sentiment by relaxing the pressures it had increasingly been bringing to bear to enforce conformity to the Elizabethan Church. Archbishop Loftus was disingenuous in blaming Deputy Perrot for conceding religious toleration *c*.1584–5; it was, in fact, the queen who directed Perrot, forcefully, to terminate his programme for

43 SP 63/166/55.　44 SP 63/158/7.

rigorous enforcement, and to adopt a more *laissez faire* stance in religion. By 1590, recusancy was general, and by that time it was galvanised by 'swarms' of Irish seminary priests, friars and Jesuits. I cannot conceive of the possibility of a Protestant breakthrough from that point in time.

10

Elizabeth's reformation: failure

The defiance of the Pale élites in not attending the special thanksgiving services conducted to celebrate England's deliverance from the Spanish Armada in 1588 demonstrated very publicly their rejection of the Elizabethan religious settlement.[1] In a letter of February 1590, Deputy Fitzwilliam and Archbishop Loftus informed Burghley that in Dublin 'there are now almost none other [than recusants]. The mayor, perhaps for duty, and some few with him for fashion's sake, will come to the ordinary Sunday sermon but none other man or woman'.[2] A state paper of 1600 stated as fact that in Dublin city there were not more than twenty Irish-born house-holders who attended Church of Ireland services, and of them not more than four would receive communion.[3] No statistic could more graphically reflect the scale of the failure of the Elizabethan reformation in Ireland.

A 'SECOND REFORMATION'?

With Perrot gone, Archbishop Loftus launched a vigorous campaign for the re-activation of the Ecclesiastical High Commission. He claimed that when under 'restraint' by the Commission in the past, the Pale élites had shown 'great duty and obedience in resorting to services, sermons and in receiving of the communion' – 'however much they were affected inwardly in their consciences'. Because of the tacit toleration they enjoyed from the mid-1580s, however, they had 'grown to wonderful obstinacy and utter detestation' of the queen's religion. Loftus cited the example of Sir Lucas Dillon, a senior member of the Council of Ireland, who did 'great hurt' by his 'notorious recusancy' since c.1586/7.[4]

Loftus declared in September 1590 that

> The sword without the Word is not sufficient, but unless they be forced they will not once come to hear the Word preached, as we observed at the thanksgiving for the good success against the Spaniards. ... It is a bootless labour for any man to preach in the country out of Dublin for want of hearers.[5]

1 SP 63/140/22. 2 SP 63/150/74. 3 SP 63/207, pt 6/126. 4 SP 63/154/37. 5 SP

Recognizances were exacted to compel a number of men to attend Church of Ireland services, but Barnaby Rich reported in June 1591 that they forfeited their bonds.[6] As noted above, there was tremendous ill-feeling in the Pale, and treasonous speeches and rumours. In July, the queen intervened and declared that she would not have men strained in matters of conscience without some manifest act of disobedience.[7] The problem persisted, however, that the people would not attend services in the Elizabethan Church unless they were compelled to do so, and without their attendance at Protestant services there was no prospect of being able to convert them from Catholicism.

The Ecclesiastical High Commission was re-commissioned anew in 1594,[8] but it hardly had time to function before it was suspended *de facto* in that same year as its activities became politically inconvenient as Hugh O'Neill, earl of Tyrone, moved towards open rebellion.[9] In any case, its value as an instrument of reform may be doubted: the earl of Essex in April 1599 observed tartly that it had been 'a good milch cow' for those in charge of it.[10]

Alan Ford has suggested that in the early 1590s the Court of Faculties was, 'under Loftus' oversight, wielded into an instrument of reform', though I am not entirely convinced that there is hard evidence to sustain that claim.[11] Ford claimed that 'the efforts of the two judges [Ambrose Forth and Justinian Johnson] marked the beginning of the first serious attempt to reform the ministry of the Church of Ireland, and did result in changes being made in the parochial ministry'.[12] However, he noted that there were still examples of clergymen being able to avoid prosecution by the court in the 1590s by paying for its dispensations.

In June 1600, the queen offered the following survey of the state of the Church:[13]

> the most part of churches within the two large dioceses of Dublin and Meath are utterly ruined, insomuch as between Dublin and Athlone, which contains sixty miles, and is the through tract of the English Pale, there are so few churches standing as they will scarcely make a plural number, and so few pastors to teach or preach the Word, as in most of them there is not so much as a reading minister.

> Her majesty has been informed sundry times that many unlettered ministers have been admitted to spiritual livings in her majesty's gift, such as have not the faculty to teach and preach, and many not able to

63/156/37. 6 SP 63/158/51. 7 SP 63/159/22. 8 SP 63/157/35, 63/175/80, CPCR, ii, pp 291–5; Alan Ford, *The Protestant Reformation in Ireland, 1590–1641* (Dublin, 1997 ed.), pp 33–4. 9 Loftus referred to the suspension of the High Commission's activities in 1594: SP 63/207, pt 2/92. 10 SP 63/205/65. 11 Ford, *Protestant reformation*, p. 34. 12 Ibid. 13 SP 63/207, pt 3/139.

read the Word of God distinctly; some also being mere laymen, and all preferred by favour, without examination made of their sufficiency. By which negligence the people remain untaught ...; insomuch as among the Irish themselves this base choice of ministers breeds a contempt of religion and a loathing to come to church, while they see ignorant and profane men set over them, in whom is no ability to instruct either by their learning or their good example of life.

Edmund Spenser, who knew such clergymen from first-hand experience, characterised them thus in his *View of the state of Ireland* (1596):

all Irish priests which now enjoy church livings, they are in a manner mere laymen, saving that they have taken holy orders but otherwise they go and live like laymen, follow all kinds of husbandry and other worldly affairs as other Irish men do. They neither read scriptures, nor preach to the people, nor administer the communion, but baptism they do, for they christen after the Popish fashion, only they take the tithes and offerings.[14]

Such men did nothing to convert their parishioners to the doctrinal tenets of the Elizabethan reformation – probably the opposite.

In the absence of Irish clergymen with Protestant convictions, the Elizabethan Church of Ireland sought to recruit English clergymen but, as Spenser observed, many benefices would not suffice for 'any competent maintenance for any honest minister to live upon, scarcely to buy him a gown'. Irish parishioners were 'intractable' and 'ill-affected' towards English clergymen, as they were 'to all the English', and the clergymen's safety could not be assured over much of Ireland. Also:

the most part of such English as come over thither of themselves are either unlearned, or men of some bad note, for which they have forsaken England. ... [and, in any case] what good should any English minister do among them, by teaching or preaching to them, which either cannot understand him, or will not hear him?[15]

What was needed, Spenser suggested, was that Protestantism

be not sought forcibly to be impressed into them with terror and sharp penalties, as now is the manner, but rather delivered and intimated

---

14 Edmund Spenser, *A view of the state of Ireland* (London, 1809 ed.), p. 142. 15 Ibid., pp 141–2.

with mildness and gentleness so as it may not be hated before it be understood, and their professors despised and rejected. And therefore it is expedient that some discreet ministers of their own countrymen be first sent over amongst them, which by their meek persuasions and instructions, as also by their sober lives and conversations, may draw them first to understand and afterwards to embrace the doctrine of their salvation[16]

The problem was that even by the close of the sixteenth century there were no more than a handful of 'discreet ministers of their own countrymen' available to promote the Reformation in Ireland. The failure of the Tudor reformations was so complete that the fundamental requirement for success, as identified by Spenser, was unrealisable: without a community of Irish-born Protestants it was simply impossible to recruit an Irish-born Protestant ministry. Failure begat failure.

Of course, it has to be noted that the queen's account of the Church was exaggeratedly negative, and Bishop Jones was able to point out that in his diocese of Meath there were no fewer than seventy nine churches in 'good reparation', as well as some impropriated churches whose naves were in good repair but not their chancels, though there were others, including the church at his episcopal residence at Ardbraccan, that were 'in a manner quite pulled down' by the queen's soldiers garrisoned inside them.[17] Nonetheless, the fact remains that the Elizabethan Church of Ireland and its ministry were in a very sorry state, even in the Pale. Archbishop Magrath admitted that 'the churches in the most parts, and within five miles to Dublin itself', were 'like hog-stys, or rather worse', though he pointed out that he was not to blame but rather the rebels, Catholics and particularly the queen's soldiers who, 'although they pull not down the roof and the walls but seldom, yet some of them in former governors' times, have taken the vestments, the doors and the very rotten bones out of [funerary] monuments where they lay more than five hundred years'.[18] Loftus offered no such mitigating excuses, but simply submitted humbly to the queen's criticisms, confessing that she had 'great cause' to be offended 'with us all'.[19]

Loftus' appointment of graduate clergy to the prebends of St Patrick's Cathedral, Dublin, has been cited as proof of his attempt to 'build up a Reformation movement in Dublin'[20] – but this ascription of lofty idealism to Loftus must be qualified by reference to his engaging in nepotism on a grand scale, and the all-too-credible allegations of simony made against him by Legge and Rich. I find it hard to believe that any impulse for reform came from Loftus himself.

16 Ibid., pp 253–4.   17 SP 63/207, pt 5/2.   18 SP 63/208, pt 2/72.   19 SP 63/207, pt 5/17.
20 Ford, *Protestant reformation*, p. 33, quoting Robinson-Hammerstein, 'Erzbischof Adam Loftus', pp 195–7, 255–9.

One very significant measure achieved was the establishment of Trinity College, Dublin – the long-awaited Irish university. Helga Robinson-Hammerstein has recently argued against J.P. Mahaffy's magisterial judgment that 'Loftus, far from being the founder of Trinity College ... was rather the chief obstacle that delayed its foundation till the golden opportunity had been lost'.[21] She conceded that Mahaffy's judgment was based on a close reading of the primary sources, but she offered a very different interpretation. She quoted two contrasting contemporary characterisations of Loftus: one by Barnaby Rich (whom she dismissed as someone who was paid for 'informing' on leading officials in Ireland), claiming that Loftus 'performed his ecclesiastical and secular duties and assignments in Ireland by resorting to trickery, deception and intimidation, untroubled by any scruples of conscience', and another by Meredith Hanmer (whom she represented as 'a cleric and historian, not a government agent') who put Loftus at the top of a list of those he suspected of upholding Puritanism in Ireland.[22] She endorses the latter's characterisation as true, despite the fact that Rich was very far from being alone in criticising Loftus' venality, and despite the fact that Hanmer was a pluralist of 'disreputable reputation'[23] and the term 'Puritan' was a term of abuse at that time. I have yet to see a convincing case presented to the effect that Loftus was a Puritan. Loftus himself, when faced with the accusation of being a Puritan, declared 'I am utterly ignorant of what the term and accusation means'.[24] Certainly, he was influenced by Calvinist doctrines,[25] but I have read nothing to indicate that he held distinctly 'Puritan' beliefs,[26] and consider that the use of the term 'Puritan' to characterise him is unhelpful because of its connotations of dissent from the Established Church, and adherence to a very strict moral code – neither of which was true in Loftus' case.

Robinson-Hammerstein admits to 'assuming', without offering supporting evidence, that Loftus 'never lost sight of the university issue, ... that he was aware that nothing in the matter of the Reformation could ultimately be achieved without a local university'.[27] She asserted that 'he had never advanced any arguments against establishing a university in Ireland' – but, in fact, he did directly argue against the idea of an Irish university in a letter to Burghley on 18

21 Helga Robinson-Hammerstein, 'Archbishop Adam Loftus: the first provost of Trinity College, Dublin' in Helga Robinson-Hammerstein (ed.), *European universities in the age of Reformation and counter-reformation* (Dublin, 1998), pp 34–5, quoting J.P. Mahaffy, *An epoch in Irish history: Trinity College, Dublin, its foundation and early fortunes, 1591–1660* (London, 1903; repr. Port Washington, London, 1970), p. 30. 22 Robinson-Hammerstein, 'Archbishop Adam Loftus', pp 35–6. 23 'Hanmer', A. Ford, *ODNB*. 24 SP 63/214/22. 25 Shirley, *Original letters*, no. lxxvii. 26 There is little hint of a 'Puritan' vision in what Robinson-Hammerstein termed Loftus' 'seemingly bizarre' speech on resigning as provost of Trinity College in 1594 in 'Archbishop Adam Loftus', op. cit., p. 49. 27 Robinson-Hammerstein, 'Archbishop Adam Loftus', pp 44–5.

March 1585.[28] He questioned the 'hope that, twenty years hence, some divines may spring out of a lecture to be instituted in the intended college [proposed by Deputy Perrot]'. He pointed out that 'Oxford and Cambridge are not far off, all under our dominion, but this will not satisfy'. I think his meaning was very clear – he saw no utility in establishing an Irish university.

It is hard to gainsay Mahaffy's judgment that Trinity College, Dublin, owed little to Loftus: '[He] helped by making speeches, and gave the dignity of his name to the college by *posing* as its first provost, but he neither actually governed the society nor contributed more than a decent thank offering (£100) for the profits he had retained from St Patrick's [Cathedral]'.[29] The dowries he lavished on his daughters put his very modest gift to the university into a stark perspective. The strongly Calvinist character of the new university was largely the result of one simple fact above all others: the only Protestant pedagogues who were willing to take up posts in the institution happened to be Presbyterians or Puritans whose prospects of securing posts in Oxford and Cambridge were less than assured. In any event, although the foundation of Trinity College proved to be a major development in the subsequent history of the Church of Ireland, its contribution to the Church in the reign of Elizabeth must be reckoned to have been very small indeed.

An account by an Irish Protestant in July 1600, a man who styled himself 'an Irish native, well-affected in religion', declared that in all of Ireland there were not ten Protestant bishops and twenty-four preachers, by contrast with the 'swarms' of 'Romish bees', Jesuits and others. He stated that eight of the Protestant preachers were Irish-born, and sixteen were English-born (and fourteen of that modest tally of preachers were army chaplains in the queen's employ). Significantly, he stated that there were plenty of 'competent livings' in Ireland, but they were generally held by 'known Massing priests', by laymen and by many English churchmen, 'as well of highest degree in the Church as inferior', who resided in England and offered no service in Ireland. He reckoned that there were hardly 120 Irish-born Protestants in the entire kingdom.[30] However, a more comprehensive application of the 'Word of life' (to be provided by additional English preachers), and the 'sword of death' (he recommended hanging individuals as far more efficacious than the killing of '1,000 with the sword or bullets') would, he argued, lead to a happier result.

There was, nonetheless, a new desire in London to see the Church of Ireland reformed. Bishop Jones was sent a stinging letter by Walsingham in December 1589 that accused him of being hypocritical, lewd, corrupt and negligent.[31] In response, Jones, who only preached once a term, promised that he would preach 'oftener' in future.[32] Loftus was accused of a fairly comprehensive list of corrupt

---

28 Ibid., p. 45. See, however, Brady, *State papers*, no. lxvi.   29 Mahaffy, *An epoch in Irish history*, pp 60–1.   30 SP 63/207, pt 4/3.   31 SP 63/149/128.

practices, and his accusers succeeded in having him called to account for six specific charges in 1592.[33] Loftus' answers were not deemed to be entirely satisfactory, and a commission was authorised to investigate the charges further in 1593.[34] His escape from prosecution may have owed something to his political utility as Tyrone moved towards rebellion. About the same time, Meiler Magrath, the Elizabethan archbishop of Cashel, also came under close scrutiny for a series of allegedly treasonous and corrupt practices.[35] Dr Meredith, the Elizabethan bishop of Leighlin and dean of Christ Church, Dublin, another corrupt prelate, was obliged to pay £3,000 in instalments to the crown in order to keep his diocese.[36] This drive against corruption was overtaken by the outbreak of the Nine Years War, but it seems that the days of official indifference to simony and the wide-scale alienation of the assets of the Church of Ireland were coming to an end.

Towards the final years of Elizabeth's reign, Dublin finally had a sound Protestant ministry. In November 1595, Loftus could declare that if all of Ireland were as well provided for as Dublin was, the Church of Ireland 'might be compared with any Church in Europe for instruction', thanks to his own endeavours, those of his chaplains, the three weekly lectures he paid for from his own purse, and the 'many good and learned preachers' holding benefices there.[37] In early 1603, Loftus could declare that there was 'great plenty of preaching' in the several parishes of Dublin on the Sabbath days, and a public lecture once every week in the city's two cathedrals.[38] Yet, despite the provision of Protestant sermons and lectures in the capital, Loftus conceded that the harvest of souls was poor indeed.

THE CATHOLIC MISSION

The struggle for souls in Ireland entered a new phase from the 1580s – but Archbishop Loftus was clear that the popular attachment to Catholicism that confronted him and his Protestant peers was not new: in 1590 he stated that 'there has been in this people a general disposition to Popery as a thing wherein they were nursled even from the cradle'.[39] Sixteen years earlier, he had asked to be translated to an English diocese where he might be 'more profitable to the Church of God amongst the well-affected people of England' than among the 'stubborn and obstinate' people in Ireland.[40] The stubbornness and obstinacy of the Irish in rejecting Protestantism was a recurring theme in English correspondence from Ireland. Deputy Sidney complained as early as 1566 about 'the

32 SP 63/149/28.   33 SP 63/150/52, 63/168/25, 63/171/20.   34 SP 63/168/25 i. Also 63/65/59.   35 SP 63/140/4, 47; 63/168/78.   36 'Meredith', Helen Coburn Walshe, *ODNB*. 37 SP 63/184/12.   38 *CSPI, 1601–3*, p. 569.   39 SP 63/154/37.   40 SP 63/56/27; 63/55/59.

former errors and superstitions inveterate and leavened in the people's hearts'.[41]

From the start of Elizabeth's reign, there was continued access to Catholic sacraments even in Dublin and the Pale, not only through priests who continued to minister in their benefices, but through networks of Catholic chaplains and tutors operating outside the institutional Church. Catholicism in Ireland did not wither away with the passing of the older generations, as happened to a very great degree in England and Wales, but was inculcated in a more intense form in the young generations of the élites by Catholic teachers and families. Even from the early 1560s, a small but steady and growing stream of students left Ireland for Catholic colleges on mainland Europe. By 1580, the number of Irish students in the continental colleges was considerable, as Archbishop Hurley revealed in the list he compiled in that year.[42] By the 1590s, large numbers of Irish priests were returning from overseas, and there were frequent complaints from Elizabethan officials about the 'swarms' of them in the cities and towns and beyond. In addition, there were mendicant friars, many of them having spent some of their period of formation overseas (though quite a number of them had been educated and trained entirely in Ireland), who operated across the country at large, even in the Pale and in outlying cities where English control was effective.

Colm Lennon emphasised the resilience of popular attachment to Catholic traditions in and around Dublin throughout Elizabeth's reign, despite official disapproval.[43] He showed that Dublin's mercantile community played a key role in supporting the ministry of Catholic priests as pastors and teachers.[44] They sent their sons to Catholic colleges on mainland Europe in increasing numbers, knowing that many of them would return as seminary-trained priests.[45] Lennon asserted that during the Nine Years War, the Jesuits helped to establish a co-ordinated Catholic pastoral network in Dublin parallel to that of the Elizabethan Church.[46]

I doubt that Dublin's Catholic pastoral network was only established at such a late date. Already, a decade earlier, three 'notorious Massing priests' were apprehended in Dublin and 'a great nest discovered of Mass-mongers', including 'diverse gentlemen, whereof some lawyers in places of credit, merchants, ladies and gentlewomen of good sort'.[47] There were 'good proofs of sundry Masses said in private houses' in the capital. Evidently, a Catholic pastoral network was already in place at that time. In May 1590, Archbishop Loftus and Bishop Jones, and Edward Waterhouse informed the privy council that

---

41 Shirley, *Original letters*, no. lxxxii.   42 Ronan, *Reformation in Ireland*, pp 637–43.   43 Lennon, *Lords of Dublin*, pp 130, 145–50.   44 Ibid., pp 142–3, 146, 150.   45 Ibid., pp 158, 159, 160, 212–13.   46 Ibid., pp 164–5, 174, 215.   47 SP 63/112/45.

> Whereof your lordships suppose there be some manifest recusants in points of religion we assure your lordships that there be very few that be otherwise ... And, touching recusants, we conceive that most of the Pale do glory to be so accounted.[48]

Deputy Fitzwilliam and Archbishop Loftus commented in February 1590 that 'Masses are grown more common [in Dublin] than they were wont to be'.[49] There were 'now almost none other' than recusants in the city: 'The mayor, perhaps for duty, and some few with him for fashion's sake, will come to the ordinary Sunday sermon but none other man or woman'. The systematic nature of the boycott of Protestant services indicates that it was organised. It is possible that Bishop Dermot Creagh, who operated across the south of Ireland and in the Pale, was responsible for co-ordinating the boycott.[50]

The Elizabethan bishop, Marmaduke Middleton, had been driven from Waterford in 1582 for trying to make the people Protestant. John Shearman, who was appointed as a schoolmaster in Waterford by Archbishop Long, was also driven from the city for trying to protestantise the children.[51] He informed Long in July 1585 that not one in twenty of the weddings in Waterford were conducted according to the queen's injunctions, but were celebrated at home with a Mass. Christenings were invariably held in the people's homes, either by a priest (and Shearman observed that the wealthiest readily had access to a priest) or by the mothers themselves in the absence of a priest – no one allowed their children to be baptised by a Protestant minister. Funerals too were conducted without resort to a Protestant minister. The 'chief [men] of the city', when obliged to attend Protestant services 'walk round [the church] like mill horses, chopping, changing, making merchandise, so that they in the choir cannot hear a word'. The absolute futility of the conformity demanded by the English crown can hardly have been clearer. Richard Whyte, a Limerick man of Protestant convictions, informed Burghley in May 1590 that Mass was being attended openly in Waterford at that time.[52]

When Whyte visited Cork in 1590, he was accosted for religion (he being a Protestant) by Andrew Skydmore (one of the local mercantile oligarchs) and by Sir Warham St Leger (the English provincial governor), 'with a great train following them, they arrogantly barking condemned the religion established [by law]' and put him 'in great fear' for his life. All of the aldermen of Cork exclaimed against the queen's religion. Meanwhile, a papal legate, presumably Bishop Creagh, had resided at Youghal for a time, and while he was there he granted absolution to the wife of the Elizabethan bishop of Limerick, 'for an angel of gold'. Her husband, Bishop William Casey, had recanted his Protestant

48 SP 63/152/3. 49 SP 63/150/74. 50 The baron of Delvin, one of the leading Catholic peers in the Pale, was accused of harbouring Dr Dermot Creagh: SP 63/166/55. 51 Brady, *State papers*, no. lxx. 52 SP 63/152/15.

beliefs before David Wolfe, SJ, and according to Whyte was actively disrupting the Reformation preaching of Dionise Campbell, a Scottish Protestant who had been appointed as superintendent of Limerick diocese because of its bishop's Catholicism. Turlough O'Brien wrote to Burghley in 1590 to inform him that Galway, 'once the paradise of Ireland in number of professors of the gospel', had 'fallen away so far that where heretofore there was no exception for all sorts and sex to repair to the church, now very few of their men, and not of their chiefest, will be seen to frequent the same'.[53] The collapse of even nominal conformity to the Elizabethan Church was general.

Reports about the open practice of Catholicism in the towns of Ireland prompted the queen and privy council in September 1591 to order that the charters of the Irish cities be perused on the grounds that they were exporting prohibited goods, harbouring priests and Jesuits, and hearing Mass publicly.[54] Threats to their civic liberties obliged the office-holders in the towns to temporise with the crown for a time, but the Nine Years War emboldened them again. John Thornburgh, Elizabethan bishop of Limerick, wrote to the privy council in December 1594 to order the mayor and aldermen of Limerick to bring their wives and children to church to hear his sermons.[55] William Lyon, the Elizabethan bishop of Ross, with Cork & Cloyne *in commendam*, reported in November 1595 that the mayor and sheriffs of Waterford were absenting themselves from Church of Ireland services, while four men had refused the office of mayor in Cork because they would not attend Protestant services as was still required there of office-holders.[56]

The earl of Essex, while Elizabeth's viceroy, observed in April 1599 that during the Nine Years War 'Now they do the more boldly and the more publicly avow [Catholicism] by reason of the necessity they conceive her majesty has to make a party of them to assist her in this war'.[57] At the same time, the English authorities in Dublin received instructions intermittently to curb open displays of Catholic ritual, and to apprehend Jesuits or seminary priests.[58] Boldness could and did lead to priests' arrest and imprisonment.[59] Nonetheless, Essex observed that while

> Some of them have been apprehended and imprisoned, yet quickly enlarged again, but not without some consideration, not only exacted from themselves but their friends have likewise paid dearly to have again their freedom, so that these priests were profitable members to some men's purses and great gain and commodity was raised by them.

53 Canny, 'Why the reformation failed', p. 445.   54 SP 63/160/17.   55 SP 63/177/55.   56 SP 63/184/27.   57 SP 63/205/42.   58 SP 63/168/45.   59 SP 63/202, pt. 1/17, 45, 63/207, pt 2/50. The best example is the arrest of the Jesuit Henry Fitzsimmons, about a year after his return to Ireland and his very public celebrations of elaborate Catholic Masses.

Essex offered the example of Conor O'Devaney, Catholic bishop of Down & Connor, to illustrate his point:

> [O'Devanney] sequestered churches, consecrated priests to say Mass, dispensed with the people for their faith and fidelity to your majesty, absolving them of their sins, confirming them to the pope, and making them upon their book oaths to foreswear all duty and obedience to your highness. The people ran to him on heaps from all parts of the country to receive his blessing. The fame of this bishop was renowned through Ireland, and more renowned coming from Rome than if an angel had come from heaven. ... He was committed to the [Dublin] Castle. There he remained more than a year, christening children after the Popish manner, making holy water which was carried away in bottles, confirming men, women and children (which came flocking unto him) to the pope, making them to foreswear all duty and obedience to your majesty. But in the end ... he was enlarged. ... This holy bishop has since been in Spain upon embassage from the earl of Tyrone.

This is certainly a striking illustration of the appeal of a counter-reformation bishop in Ireland, and it shows *inter alia* that that appeal transcended the traditional divide between the Gaelic Irish and the old colonial community in the Pale.

In Ulster, the counter-reformation was spear-headed by Redmond O'Gallagher, bishop of Derry (1569–1601), a papal legate, *custos* of Armagh.[60] According to Meiler Magrath, writing in 1590, O'Gallagher travelled about Ulster with pomp and company 'as was the custom in Queen Mary's days' and exercised his jurisdiction without any challenge from Elizabeth's viceroys. Magrath remarked that 'The clergy there have even changed the time according to the pope's new invention'.[61] Richard Brady, the Catholic bishop of Kilmore, exercised his jurisdiction unhindered despite English control in County Cavan, and the existence of an Elizabethan bishop of the diocese. Magrath noted too that there were sixteen monasteries in Ulster 'wherein the monks and friars remain, using their habit and service as in Rome itself is used'. The impression I gained from a study of Derry diocese before the Ulster plantation is that the Church was in good order, rooted in an ancient system of erenaghs who not only underpinned episcopal finances and bore responsibility with the beneficed clergy for maintaining the parish churches, but provided a great many of the men who served their local parishes as priests, and oftentimes operated schools

---

60 SP 63/156/12; Ciarán Devlin, 'Some episcopal lives' in H.A. Jefferies and C. Devlin (eds), *History of the diocese of Derry* (Dublin, 2000), pp 120–33.   61 SP 63/156/12.

that educated candidates for the Church and inculcated a sense of commitment to service in the Church.[62] Interestingly, none of Derry's diocesan clergy in 1607 was reported to have been educated or trained in a college on mainland Europe. On the contrary, a couple of priests who were identified as having been educated overseas had studied in Glasgow University.[63] Significantly, George Montgomery, first Protestant bishop of Derry, Raphoe and Clogher (1605–10), himself a Scot, failed to win any of the Scottish-educated priests to Protestantism.[64]

Meanwhile, in the south of Ireland, there was another papal legate, whom Archbishop Magrath characterised as 'one of the most dangerous fellows that ever came' to Ireland.[65] He was Dr Dermot Creagh, Catholic bishop of Cork & Cloyne, and according to Magrath in 1590, he

> came to Ireland in the time of the Desmond rebellion and is still there without pardon or protection; and ... he uses all manner of spiritual jurisdictions in the whole province, being the pope's legate; conse-crating churches, making priests, confirming children, deciding matrimonial cases. And whoever will say that this Creagh is but a poor simple fellow, unable to do harm anyway, he is but a dissembling subject, for it is well known that Creagh is one of the most dangerous fellows that ever came to that land, continued longest there of any of his sort and has done more harm already within these two years than Dr Sander in his time; for Dr Sander could procure the coming of the Spaniards only ... but this Creagh draws the whole country in general to disloyalty and breaking of laws, his credit is so much.

Creagh was from County Tipperary, a scholar of the Irish bardic schools before he joined the Society of Jesus.[66] In his letter of December 1590, Magrath outlined something of the network of counter-reformation priests that Creagh had built up within the archbishop's area of jurisdiction. There was James Kearney, Catholic bishop of Emly, who came from Rome in the previous year accompanied by Dr Thomas Ractor, a native of Fethard, William O'Gorhy, a native of Cashel, and James O'Cleary, a seminary priest like O'Gorhy. Magrath named James Brenagh, another seminary priest who had recently returned from Rome to minister in his native Fethard, and William O'Trehy, yet another seminary priest who had returned from Rome to minister in Cashel, Clonmel and Fethard. Magrath identified Tadhg O'Sullivan as an 'earnest preacher' who

---

62 Jefferies, 'Derry diocese'. See also idem, 'Papal letters and Irish clergy: Clogher before the Reformation' in Jefferies (ed.), *History of the diocese of Clogher* (Dublin, 2005).   63 Jefferies, 'George Montgomery, 1st Protestant bishop of Derry, Raphoe and Clogher (1605–1610)' in Jefferies and Devlin (eds), *History of the diocese of Derry*, p. 163.   64 Ibid.   65 SP 63/156/12.   66 Bolster, *Diocese of Cork*, ii, pp 87–92.

was 'preaching from house-to-house in Waterford, Clonmel and Fethard and in the country about those towns'. In addition, Magrath listed twenty-three others who were either seminary priests, or priests ordained by Bishop Creagh himself or priests who were reconciled to the Catholic Church by Creagh, including Richard Gyauane, who had taken Anglican orders once. These men were based in Cahir, Cashel, Clonmel, Fethard and Kilkenny and in smaller places in the region. Their surnames are representative of the propertied classes of the region, including men with Irish surnames as well as old English. Contrary to a popular misconception, the counter-reformation priesthood was not predominantly drawn from old English communities in Ireland.

It is not possible to draw up a comprehensive outline of Creagh's network because our chief informant, Archbishop Magrath, was, ostensibly at least, an avowed enemy of the Catholic reformers and did not have complete access to the information needed to compile a comprehensive dossier. My impression is that Bishop Creagh's priests probably formed a corps of clerical shock-troops. Given the absence of Protestant progress in the region, the local parish clergy could be depended upon to provide the lay folk with Catholic sacraments and traditional homilies, while the priests named by Magrath provided a leavening, with counter-reformation preaching and exhortations, most particularly in the towns where the English crown's officials were most active in promoting religious change, but not exclusively in the towns by any means.

By 1592, however, Bishop Creagh was more ambitious, demanding that priests and people take oaths disassociating themselves from the Elizabethan religious establishment. Magrath reported that

> This Creagh uses all means to bring all sorts of people to the acknowledging of the pope's authority ... First, he has set down an order that all priests in Ireland, and especially in Munster, shall be denounced as heretics unless they be allowed by himself or such as like authority from the pope amongst them, and to those he allows he has given general instructions to receive none to any part of their seven sacraments but such as will swear, first to keep and obey the pope's laws and authority, and especially to give their help to the pope's army whensoever they shall land, to whom he affirms the whole government, spiritual and temporal, of right to appertain. By this means the most part of the inhabitants of Munster have professed to be subjects to the pope, for as many as communicate, are married, confirmed, absolved or dispensed with are driven to swear to that oath, yea when any infant is baptised the parents are sworn to the pope. Such as shall swear in this sort, their names are written presently in a book which is the register written by the said Dr Creagh's own hand and termed the 'Book of Life', and no Irishman can have life everlasting unless his

name be written in the same book. The said doctor sends a copy to
Rome and Spain once every year with other intelligences of the
incidents and of the states of England and Ireland.[67]

Magrath knew Creagh's *modi operandi* very well. Indeed, at one point Magrath
seriously contemplated having himself absolved by Bishop Creagh: he sent a
messenger to the papal nuncio because he felt that he had led a 'bad course in
matters of religion' for too long and felt that 'it was time for him to amend his
life'.[68] However, Magrath decided to wait a while longer before amending his
life. Instead, he lamented in 1593 that 'the general unbridled multitude there [in
Munster are] notorious Papists and reconciled to the pope and king of Spain'.[69]

   William Lyon, Elizabethan bishop of Ross, with Cork & Cloyne *in
commendam*, found the clergy of his dioceses resigning their benefices *en masse*.
In his visitation of 1592, he found that he had only twenty-five clergymen to
serve the seventy-five parishes in Cork diocese, thirty for the 125 parishes in
Cloyne and thirteen for the twenty-six parishes in Ross.[70] In a letter of
September 1595, Lyon wrote of people being sworn against the Church of
Ireland and of priests forsaking their benefices to become 'Massing priests'.[71] It
was probably part of a general pattern by that time. As Munster was swept by
the Nine Years War, the Church of Ireland was swept away by it.[72] By 1598,
Bishop Lyon had lost all jurisdiction in his dioceses and was obliged to live as an
ordinary man in Cork.[73] Archbishop Magrath too had been displaced from his
diocese by that time.[74]

   Catholic priests in Cork swore the people not to attend Protestant services,
and they also forbade Catholic doctors and surgeons from treating any
clergyman holding a benefice in the Church of Ireland 'in time of sickness'.[75] In
1596, Bishop Lyon depicted the scale of the counter-reformation success in
Cork.[76] Women never attended Protestant services in the city, and only office-
holding men did so. The *Book of Common Prayer* was denigrated as the 'devil's
service' and people crossed themselves in the street 'after the popish manner'
when passing a Protestant minister for fear of diabolical contamination. The
children had abandoned the local grammar school when the teacher was
required to take them to church for Protestant services. The frontispiece and
endleaf of the school's textbooks, where the royal style was reproduced and the
queen prayed for, were systematically ripped out. There were no fewer than ten
'seminary and seducing priests' maintained in Cork. They provided not only
Sunday Masses but a complete round of Catholic devotional liturgies and
practices. The priests perambulated the city streets in the company of the social

67 SP 63/164/47. 68 SP 63/160/49. 69 SP 63/170/4. 70 Ford, *Protestant reformation*, p.
37. 71 SP 63/182/47. 72 SP 63/205/225. 73 SP 63/208, pt 2/154. 74 SP 63/207, pt
4/25. 75 SP 63/183/47; 63/184/27. 76 *CSPI, 1596–7*, pp 13–20; Bradshaw, 'Reformation
in the cities', pp 463–6.

élites and their material needs were met by public subscription. While the Protestant churches were empty, the people thronged to the Catholic services, the young merchants of Cork flaunting swords and pistols as they went to Mass, daring the English authorities to interfere. As Brendan Bradshaw observed, the commitment to the counter-reformation in Cork, and in other Irish cities, 'was to be undeviating'.[77] Nicholas Canny, in a review of the Reformation in Galway concluded that, 'Following the success of the counter-reformation drive, Galway then became to all intents and purposes a Catholic community from the early seventeenth century'.[78] If Turlough O'Brien's report of 1590 may be trusted, the Reformation had already failed in Galway by that date.[79] Turlough lamented that throughout his native Thomond and in Connacht Protestantism had no supporters, other than himself.[80] A discourse of late 1591 stated that the author, whose sister was married to the baron of Inchiquin, had never heard of any Protestant service being used in the earl of Thomond's house, while the baron of Inchiquin had been won back to Rome by the 'superstitious dexterity' of a friar.[81] The same author stated that the Elizabethan bishop of Killaloe, Murtagh O'Brien, was busy confiscating, selling and reselling benefices, and engaging in simony in matrimonial causes before his church court; he was expert in gaming, music and carousing. Any green shoots of Protestantism in the west of Ireland had surely shrivelled.

It is difficult to find evidence of how the Catholic mission actually operated on the ground. One telling observer of the religious scene in Waterford and the towns generally was Sir John Dowdall, the commander of the English garrison in the fort at Duncannon, near Waterford.[82] He informed Burghley that Waterford was the first town in Ireland that refused to attend Church of Ireland services or participate in the rites of the Established Church. The citizens had 'in their town seminaries, Jesuits, Popish priests and friars', and one after another the other towns of Ireland followed their example, and by the time of his writing in 1596, 'all the townsmen of the kingdom are become apostates and do oppose themselves against God and her majesty's laws'. He declared that

> For in the tenth year of her majesty's reign and since, they came very
> orderly to the church, but first their women grew weary of it, and that
> being unpunished their men left it, and they being unpunished the
> mayors, sovereigns and portreeves for the most part have left it: if
> some of them come for a year [their term of office?], the year
> following they refuse it.

---

77 Bradshaw, 'Reformation in the cities', p. 466.   78 Canny, 'Galway: from the Reformation to the penal laws', p. 8.   79 Canny, 'Why the reformation failed', p. 445.   80 Ibid., p. 441.   81 SP 63/161/52.   82 SP 63/187/19.

Every port town and upland town, and also gentlemen's houses for the most part are furnished with superstitious seducing priests. The townsmen and merchants do transport them ... which swarm up and down the whole country, seducing the people and the best sorts, to draw them from God and their allegiance to the prince.

Every town is established with sundry schools where noblemen and gentlemen's sons of the country do repair; these schools have a superstitious or an idolatrous schoolmaster, and each school overseen by a Jesuit, whereby the youth of the whole kingdom are corrupted and poisoned with more gross superstition and disobedience than all the rest of the Popish crew in Europe.

The townsmen do transport into Spain, Italy, Rheims and other places, young men, both of the English and Irish nation, in the company of Jesuits to be brought up in their colleges; and so when they have been thoroughly corrupted they return them again with letters of commendation, with instructions to seduce the people to disobedience and rebellion.

Dowdall's insights on the systematic nature of the education of the young, through Catholic tutors and schools, as well as the continental colleges, are significant, and help to explain why the younger men of the 1580s and 1590s were more rigorous in their attachment to the Catholic Church than their parents were. Significantly, he referred to the role of the traditional priests and friars, as well as the seminary priests and Jesuits, in achieving that result. Back in 1591, Barnaby Rich, a keen observer of events in Ireland, informed Sir Robert Cecil that

Friars, Jesuits, seminaries, Massing priests and such others have free and common recourse throughout the diocese[s] and every city, town and province is so plentifully replenished with them that there is almost neither nobleman nor gentleman but he has some of them in his house and keeps them openly without controlment; and these vowed Catholics, your majesty's vowed enemies, have drawn all obedience from your majesty to the pope.[83]

The earl of Essex in May 1599 complained that 'Jesuits and seminaries have been fostered, bolstered and borne withal, even in Dublin itself', that 'both city, town and country' 'swarmed' with 'Jesuits, seminaries and the rest of that Popish

83 SP 63/206/119.

crew'.[84] Lord Justice Carey used the same metaphor of Catholic priests and Jesuits swarming later in 1599.[85] Meiler Magrath commented that such was the 'swarm' of Catholic priests that there was one for virtually every house (I presume he was referring to the houses of lords and gentlemen).[86]

A Catholic loyalist from the Pale, in an open letter in 1600, took for granted that 'none of us all ... need dissemble that profession [of Catholicism], or go a mile from his house for exercise of our religion'.[87] Piers Hackett, a prisoner in Marshalsea, offered to 'deliver' to Burghley in 1598 the locations of twenty-five Catholic bishops, doctors of divinity and priests who lived in the houses of lawyers, merchants and other great men in one diocese, probably Dublin.[88] A community of Franciscan friars based at Multyfarnham, in the west of the Pale, seems to have operated throughout the Pale with little restraint thanks to the protection afforded by the baron of Delvin. Indeed, the impression given by its critics is that it functioned as a centre of operations for Jesuits and other counter-reformation clergy in the region.[89] The queen herself stated that it was 'the only place of assembly and conventicle of all the traitorous Jesuits of the realm, and where was the first conspiracy and plotting of the great rebellion [i.e. the Nine Years War]'.[90]

Yet the toleration that was conceded was precarious. Henry Fitzsimmons, SJ, was too conspicuously successful to be tolerated. In April 1600, Archbishop Loftus and Bishop Jones informed John Whitgift, archbishop of Canterbury, that ever since his arrival in Dublin a year before

> he has gathered together great multitudes of her majesty's subjects, perverted them in religion and drawn them from the Church. In Dublin, commonly every Sunday, he used to say Mass and to preach. His Mass was sung by note, in prick-song (a number of priests attending upon him with torches, arrayed in the Popish vestments); to which there was an ordinary resort, both of the best sort of citizens and out of the country, of four or five hundred at every assembly. In the week days he used to travel into the country, to houses of gentlemen of the English Pale, where he reconciled many to the Church of Rome, procured them to abjure our service, and by mean of his alliance to many, both in city and country, and of this course of his proceeding in the erection of Popery he was generally received as an angel amongst this ignorant and idolatrous people.

Loftus secured Fitzsimmon's arrest with a bounty of £20.[91] He admitted to Cecil in February 1601 that this success was 'strange', and regarding the other

84 SP 63/205/65. 85 SP 63/206/71. 86 SP 63/207, pt 1/32. 87 Ibid., pt 6/141. 88 SP 63/202, pt 1/70. 89 SP 63/207, pt 2/96. 90 Ibid., pt 3/139. 91 Ibid., pt 2/50.

'Jesuits, friars and seminary priests' who swarmed in the Pale 'we cannot catch one of them'.[92] Patrick Strange of Waterford explained that the crown's officers generally feared excommunication more than any fines or penalties they might incur for not apprehending Catholic clergymen.[93]

The sheer volume of evidence pointing to the general character of Irish people's attachment to the Catholic Church by the end of Elizabeth's reign would make it tedious to attempt to collate each and every one of them. However, even confining oneself to a small number of the best-informed individuals of the time makes the point clearly. Archbishop Loftus was very clear: in 1590, he reported that there was 'almost none other' than recusants in Dublin,[94] and that the people in Dublin did 'glory' in the name of recusant.[95] Trying to preach the Reformation outside of Dublin was, he stated, a 'bootless task'.[96] A report in 1600 stated that only four Irish-born house-holders in Dublin received communion according to the rites of the Church of Ireland.[97] In Cork, Bishop Lyon's Protestant congregation was composed of only five individuals (how many of them were natives of Cork was not stated): 'The Romish priests and seminaries have them in too great awe to obey her majesty's ecclesiastical laws. These men baptise, marry and perform ecclesiastical offices in houses where any may that will be present, and thereof they will vaunt it, saying "This day I have been at Mass: I would you had been there"'.[98] The queen herself admitted in 1600 that 'idolatry is grown to that height as ... Jesuits and other Rome-running priests do so swarm, both in cities and country within the realm, who for want of looking in to in time, have got such an awe over the people that the poor subjects ... dare not but yield to these Romish priests in matters of conscience and faith'.[99]

Meanwhile, it became less acceptable all round for Catholic priests to work within the structures of the Elizabethan Church of Ireland. Congregations in rural districts of the Pale were stated, by Elizabeth herself in 1600, to be meeting together 'on hills, in the open fields and woods, and there spend the time in wicked devices which should be spent in the service and worship of God'.[1] This reference is vague, but she may have been referring to congregations meeting for Mass in the open air. It would take years, of course, to implement the decrees of the Council of Trent comprehensively in Ireland. Nonetheless, the counter-reformation in Ireland had succeeded in thwarting the Tudor reformations, and in winning the allegiance of the vast majority of the indigenous communities in Ireland. The Protestant ministry, by contrast, found that very few, if any, attended their services, particularly outside Dublin, where English immigrants provided some kind of congregations.

92 SP 63/208, pt 1/41.   93 *CSPI, 1601–3*, p. 57.   94 SP 63/150/74.   95 SP 63/152/3.
96 SP 63/207, pt 2/92.   97 Ibid., pt 6/126.   98 SP 63/208, pt 2/154.   99 SP 63/207, pt
3/139.   1 SP 63/207, pt 3/139.

THE NINE YEARS WAR

The Nine Years War (1594–1603) exposed the degree to which the Elizabethan reformation had failed in Ireland by the close of Elizabeth's reign. It is not my intention here to re-write the history of the war, but rather to highlight two neglected features of it: the role of Catholic clergymen in fostering and sustaining the war over a prolonged number of years; and the support it enjoyed (much of it tacit, but significant nonetheless) among a considerable number of lords, gentlemen and urban oligarchs of English descent.

Northern conspiracies

As far back as 1588, Hugh O'Neill, earl of Tyrone, sought to establish secret contact with Philip II.[2] That information was relayed to Deputy Fitzwilliam at the time.[3] A Catholic Palesman identified de Vergas, a commander of one of the Spanish Armada ships wrecked on the Irish coast, as Tyrone's emissary to the Spanish king.[4] The veracity of these intelligences is confirmed by a letter of October 1596 written by Tyrone himself, in which he reminded Philip II that he had been seeking military aid from Spain for the past seven years.[5] Whatever soundings Tyrone had made in 1588/9 were indeterminate in outcome, but following the settlement of Monaghan in 1591 he may have felt a greater impulse to secure support from Spain. Éamon Óg MacDonnell, dean of Armagh and a relation of his, travelled to Spain at the end of 1591, and Hiram Morgan stated that 'the object or at least the result of the dean's mission is obvious – the return of Éamon Magowran, the titular archbishop of Armagh and Catholic primate of [all] Ireland'.[6] Magowran was one of the leading Irish clergymen in Spain campaigning for military support for Ireland. Soon after his return to Ireland late in 1592, the Catholic primate held meetings with six other bishops in the northern province and united the northern nobility by oath in a Catholic Confederacy.[7] In April 1593, he wrote to Philip II's chief counsellor on English and Irish affairs to inform him that the lords of Ireland had promised to support Spanish intervention in Ireland against English tyranny and Protestantism.[8]

The Confederates' emissary to Rome, James O'Hely, Catholic archbishop of Tuam, stated that Tyrone was secretly a member of the Confederacy.[9] Within Ireland itself, there were persistent rumours to the same effect.[10] When he met

---

2 James Perrot, *The Chronicle of Ireland, 1584–1608*, ed. Herbert Wood (Dublin, 1933), p. 65; Hiram Morgan, *Tyrone's rebellion: the outbreak of the Nine Years War in Tudor Ireland* (Woodbridge, 1993), p. 106. 3 SP 63/142/12. 4 SP 63/207, pt 6/141. 5 *CSP Spain*, iv, 642; Morgan, *Tyrone's rebellion*, p. 140. 6 Morgan, *Tyrone's rebellion*, p. 141. See also Micheline Walsh, 'Archbishop Maguaran and his return to Ireland, October 1592', *SAM*, 14 (1990), pp 68–79. 7 SP 63/170/23 i. 8 SP 63/196/30 (3); Walsh, 'Archbishop Magauran', p. 76; Morgan, *Tyrone's rebellion*, p. 141. Sir Richard Bingham, the president of Connacht, held the archbishop chiefly responsible for the rebellion that followed; SP 63/170/19, 23, 26, 66. 9 *CSP Spain*, iv, 611; Morgan, *Tyrone's rebellion*, pp 141–2. 10 SP 63/169/23iii, 23v, 49vii.

with the deputy and council of Ireland at Dundalk in September 1593, Tyrone
was charged with having entertained Magowran and with conspiring to solicit
Spanish military support.[11] Morgan has no doubt that Tyrone was a party to the
'bishops' conspiracy'.[12]

As it happened, Philip II's feeling was that 'What the Irish ask ... is much;
and I think they will require much more still. [He ordered one of his chief
advisers to speak] ... to the archbishop of Tuam and make full enquiry so as to
discover what force they really need. If it be such a small one that we can afford
to give it, it will be a very good thing to help them'.[13] In the event, no force, great
or small, was sent. Yet clerical participation in the Catholic Confederacy did not
cease with the drowning of the archbishop of Tuam, or with the death of
Magowran in June 1593.[14] Redmond O'Gallagher, bishop of Derry and Catholic
vice-primate of all Ireland, continued to play an influential role in the Catholic
Confederacy until his death at the hands of English soldiers in March 1601.[15]

Bishop Dermot Creagh

If the northern bishops' role in promoting war against the English crown is
reasonably well known, that of Catholic clergymen in the southern provinces has
been largely overlooked. The central figure in the south was Dr Dermot Creagh,
Catholic bishop of Cork & Cloyne.[16] Meiler Magrath, Elizabethan archbishop of
Cashel, penned a lengthy report against the Jesuit in 1592.[17] He warned that
Creagh 'ceases not by himself and his ministers to curse her majesty and to
denounce all those who willingly confess themselves to be her subjects and to
keep her laws'. 'This Creagh, with other bishops from the pope, has sworn many
thousands to be in readiness against the coming of the Spaniards'. He compiled
a 'Book of Life' each year in which he inscribed the names of thousands who had
sworn allegiance to the pope in spiritual and temporal matters.[18]

Magrath's account of Creagh's central role in the Nine Years War is
confirmed by the declaration made by Dr James Archer, SJ, in 1598 that Creagh
was 'the greatest in this action of any out of the north of Ireland'.[19] In 1600,
Bishop Lyon of Ross and Cork & Cloyne wrote that 'The whole kingdom is of
a conspiracy by means of the Romish priests which were and are the plotters of
this general rebellion ... the priests rule and direct all things here; and namely
Dermot McCreagh, who has been a practicer of this rebellion this 22 years,
James Archer and Owen Kegan'.[20] During the truce of 1599, Henry Pyne, an
English planter at Mogeely, County Cork, wrote that 'Bishop Creagh, Archer
and other priests of that crew do not cease daily to solicit and persuade those that

---

11 SP 63/171/34. 12 Morgan, *Tyrone's rebellion*, pp 140–1. 13 Quoted in John Silke,
Kinsale: the Spanish intervention in Ireland at the end of the Elizabethan wars (Liverpool, 1970), p.
27. 14 SP 63/170/19, 23, 26, 66. 15 SP 63/183/47; 63/184/31. 16 He was granted
authority to operate in all the dioceses of Munster, save Killaloe: SP 63/150/15. 17 SP
63/164/47. 18 Ibid. 19 SP 63/202, pt 3/161. 20 SP 63/207, pt/ 1/108.

are subjects or neutrals to take part with [the rebels' earl of] Desmond by persuading and assuring them ... of great matters, and aid from the king of Spain and pope'.[21] Creagh's letter to Lord Barry to persuade him to join the Confederate cause or face excommunication survives.[22] Creagh was successful in persuading Lord Mountgarret, and Lord Cahir (Mountgarret's brother-in-law), into open rebellion.[23] Nicholas Walsh, a Waterford loyalist with Catholic sympathies, also commented on Creagh's and Archer's leading roles in the Confederacy in 1599.[24] An anonymous contemporary historian wrote that Creagh had 'confessed among the traitors that he had been in Ireland the space of eighteen years, day and night among them persuading [them] to rebellion, which he termed the Catholic faith. He wrought the combination and effected the whole mischief over Ireland which then took place'.[25] Edward Goeghe's encounter with Bishop Creagh in November 1598 revealed a man who was extremely confident, to the point of arrogance, in his own authority and in the Confederates' prospects for success.[26]

The English captain, John Baynard, had no doubt that the 'devilish Popish priests and seminaries have had, and now have, the means almost without controlment to persuade and draw them to all mischievous and traitorous practices of rebellions both towards God, prince and country'.[27] Sir Thomas Norreys, president of Munster, complained of the Confederacy being 'so strengthened with the ground and pretence of their Popish religion stirred up by the motions of some devilish priests working daily amongst them'.[28] Sir George Carew, Norreys' successor as the president of Munster, concurred, writing that the 'traitorly priests ... are the chiefest firebrands of these unnatural treasons ... (this country people being so much devoted to them as they are)'.[29] Archbishop Loftus,[30] Fenton,[31] and Lord Justice Carey concurred.[32] Archbishop Magrath had no doubt that the number of enemies of the crown increased 'daily' 'by the setting on of seminaries'.[33] He warned Cecil again in October 1600 of their role in procuring Spanish military intervention.[34] A royal proclamation of 1599, when identifying the chief causes of the rebellion, stated *inter alia*, that 'many [were] inveighed with superstitious impressions wrought in them by the cunning of seditious priests and seminaries crept into them from foreign parts'.[35] The queen complained that she was credibly informed

> that James Archer, called the pope's legate, and one McCreagh, usurped bishop of Cork, and sundry other seditious priests, Jesuits, seminaries now resorting to all parts of that our kingdom, especially to that our province of Munster, being (according to the wonted

21 SP 63/202, pt. 3/225. 22 SP 63/207, pt 1/123, ii. 23 SP 63/203/65. 24 SP 63/203/2. 25 SP 63/202, pt 4/57. 26 Ibid., pt 1/161. 27 SP 63/203/116. 28 SP 63/202, pt 4/15, 22. 29 SP 63/207, pt 6/2. 30 SP 63/208, pt 1/41. 31 SP 63/202, pt. 4/40. 32 SP 63/203/71. 33 SP 63/207, pt 5/20. 34 Ibid., pt 5/111. 35 SP 63/203/25.

manner) suborned by the pope and the king of Spain to raise our
subjects to rebellion … have so effectively prevailed in their ungodly
and malicious purposes as, under the pretext and colour of religion,
they have drawn most of those rebels, and some that pretend to be our
subjects in that realm, confidently to believe that we intend not only
to conquer but also utterly to extirp and root out all that nation.

What is significant here is not so much the tactics employed by Creagh and
Archer to rouse support for the Confederacy, meshing political and religious
appeals, but their central role in forging support for the war against England
across the south of Ireland.

'A preparative for Jesuits'

The earl of Essex, while he was lord lieutenant of Ireland, expressed the view
that the disaffection of the people across Ireland 'was a preparative for Jesuits,
seminaries and the rest of that Popish crew to work upon'.[36] Across Connacht,
anti-English sentiment provided a fertile seed-bed for Catholic conspiracies. An
official enquiry identified a catalogue of grievances against Bingham's governance in the western province, including allegations of oppression, gross
corruption and judicial murders.[37] McWilliam Burke of Mayo helped survivors
of the Spanish Armada and, with their encouragement, rebelled in 1589/90.[38]
In a letter of 20 October 1589, Edward White, clerk of the council, wrote that
'They have also established the brehon laws and have Mass and other exercises
of the Popish religion, which they dared not to have hitherto for a long time'.[39]
According to Bingham, the president of Connacht, the rebels declared that every
Englishman was but a devil, and that no Englishman should dwell in
McWilliam's land.[40] Though Bingham succeeded in re-imposing English
authority over Connacht by the end of 1590,[41] McWilliam was not reconciled to
English rule. A conspiracy exposed in 1592, which seems to have involved
McWilliam Burke's son, John, envisaged Galway being given over to Spanish
control by a number of the city's Catholic oligarchs (especially James Blake, a
merchant of Galway dwelling in Spain, to whom the countess of Clanrickard
had sent a priest as a messenger after a secret conference), and then the city being
used as a bridgehead for a massive Spanish force.[42] Bingham condemned
Galway's citizens as being 'in heart wholly Spanish'.[43] That conspiracy was
displaced by the formation of the Catholic Confederacy spear-headed by
Archbishop Magowran in 1592, of which McWilliam was a leading member.[44]
    One English captain complained that 'Albeit the Irish are most commonly

36 SP 63/205/65. 37 SP 63/144/30. 38 SP 63/143/12, iii. It was not until late in 1591 or
early 1592 that the Spaniards were repatriated: SP 63/143/3. 39 SP 63/147/28. 40 SP
63/148/39. 41 SP 63/156/10. 42 SP 63/163/6. 43 SP 63/171/12. 44 Walsh,
'Archbishop Magauran', pp 68–79.

Papists because they know no better Christ; but as for the rebels they take his part for their own profit's sake, otherwise they care neither for God nor man'.[45] Whatever their motives, the people of Connacht were almost unanimous in supporting the Catholic confederates according to President Bingham in September 1595.[46] He warned that Connacht would revolt 'generally' if Spaniards were to land in Ireland.[47] By January 1596, rebellion was general across Connacht, 'to the gates of Athlone', and Bingham felt obliged to send his wife and children from Galway for their safety.[48]

Catholics in Galway were hostile to the English garrison in their city.[49] However, certificates in favour of the garrison were signed by three Protestant clergymen, and by a number of aldermen and other inhabitants of the city.[50] One alderman, Marcus Lynch, was characterised as 'a Protestant and one especially liked of by the state'. Clearly there was still a small community of local Protestants in Galway at the turn of the century who were prepared to nail their colours to the English mast, but they were no less clearly an embattled minority in the city. A hint of why that Protestant community dwindled, apart altogether from the competing efforts of priests and ministers, may be found in the fact that the mayor of Galway in June 1601, 'a Protestant in show', was married to a woman identified as the 'chief' of the recusants in the city. Anthony Trollope noted at the time that even Englishmen who were married to Irish women were not to be trusted – and the suspicions aroused by the conducts of Captain William Warren and Captain John Lee lent some substance to his concerns.[51] As Colm Lennon observed, women played a critical role in maintaining Catholicism in Elizabethan Ireland.

Archbishop Magrath remarked that despite Bishop Creagh's treasonous activities, he was supported by men who maintained an outward appearance of being loyal subjects, though they were really 'dissembling and malicious enemies'. They included 'the strongest, the richest, the wisest and most learned sort; having amongst them divers lords, prelates of the Church, gentlemen, lawyers and merchants, at whose commandments are the cities, corporate towns and havens'. Nor was it only the élites who were bound to the Catholic Church: Magrath informed Sir Robert Cecil in 1593 that the 'general unbridled multitude' in Munster were 'notorious Papists and reconciled to the pope and the king of Spain'.

Magrath's imputation of disloyalty to many of lords, noblemen and citizens of Munster was supported by the testimony of another Irish Protestant, Richard Whyte, a citizen of Limerick.[52] Whyte informed Burghley in a letter of 8 May

---

45 SP 63/146/57. **46** SP 63/183/65. He claimed, though, that some men in Sligo and north Mayo sought his assistance against the rebels. **47** SP 63/183/84. **48** SP 63/186/19. **49** However, it was the mayor of Galway in 1596 who asked for a garrison to be deployed for the defence of the city: SP 63/186/12, iv. **50** SP 63/208, pt 1/68, i, 63/208, pt 3/36. **51** SP 63/131/65, 63/202, pt 1/17, i, 63/202, pt 1/43, 63/203/58, 63/202, pt 1/73. **52** SP

1590 that 'The sting of rebellion, which in times past remained among the Irishry, is transferred and removed into the hearts of civil gentlemen, aldermen and burgesses and rich merchants of Ireland, Papistry being the original cause and ground thereof'. John Thornburgh, Elizabethan bishop of Limerick, warned Robert Cecil in November 1595 that 'divers of great sort, as yet in supposed loyalty' were waiting to hear from Tyrone, and for directions from Rome (of which the 'great number of Popish bishops and seminaries in this land' assured them), before acting: 'They say they labour by Tyrone only for liberty of conscience'.[53]

Anti-English sentiment in Munster, in the wake of the catastrophic English military campaign against the Desmond rebellion and the plantation that followed, was deadly in its intensity. William Saxey, chief justice of Munster, in a letter of 26 October 1598, reported that local rebels had

> effected many execrable murders with cruelties upon the English, as well in the county of Limerick, as in the counties of Cork and Kerry and elsewhere; infants taken from the nurse's breast, and the brains dashed against the walls; the heart plucked out of the body of the husband in the view of the wife, who was forced to yield the use of her apron to wipe off blood from the murderers' fingers; [an] English gentleman at midday in a town cruelly murdered and his head cleft in divers pieces; divers sent into Youghal amongst the English, some with their throats cut but not killed, some with their tongues cut out of their heads, others with their noses cut off; by view whereof the English might the more bitterly lament the misery of their countrymen and fear the like to befall to themselves.[54]

Nonetheless, Saxey informed Cecil that the causes that had 'begotten and bred this common calamity' seemed to be 'first and principally, the seminaries and Jesuits, lurking in every city and walled town of the province, have stolen away the hearts of the Irish from her majesty'.

I am conscious of labouring the point that religion played a significant role in conditioning responses to the Nine Years War in Ireland, yet I do so because it appears that heretofore historians have failed to conceive of the possibility that Catholic convictions could have undermined the loyalties of the communities who would later characterise themselves as the 'Old English' of Ireland. At the same time, I wish to make it very clear that I do not regard the Nine Years War simply as a religious war. Religion was a key component of the war, providing a rationale that appealed to many people across Ireland, and also the means with which to attract Spanish military support against the English crown.

63/152/15.   **53** SP 63/184/41.   **54** SP 63/202, pt 3/127.

Nonetheless, there were other factors involved in the conflict too. Yet, I reckon that if there had been no religious conflict in Ireland in Elizabeth's reign, there would have been no basis on which such a serious challenge to the English crown could have been mounted that was in any way comparable with Tyrone's rebellion.

Support for the Confederates

Sir George Carew observed that prior to his arrival in Munster virtually the entire province was in rebel hands, 'even to the very gates of the cities'.[55] Very few remained loyal to the crown and Sir Thomas Norreys, while president of Munster, referred in December 1598 to the 'specious loyalty' of some gentlemen whose sole concern was for their estates.[56] Lord Barry stood out as an exception to this general pattern.[57] Yet Barry was unable to prevent most of his kinsmen and followers from joining the rebellion.[58] The earl of Thomond, who impressed Carew as a subject as loyal as any from Middlesex, could not prevent his own brother joining in the rebellion.

English Captain Thomas Phillips complained to Cecil in January 1599 that 'such gentlemen as continue subjects can neither command their kinsmen, tenants nor followers in sort as they ought' – a reflection either of popular sentiment against the crown, or of the true disposition of the few remaining gentlemen who pretended loyalty. Essex, Elizabeth's lord lieutenant, observed in April 1599 that

> even of those who serve her majesty, there is scarcely one that does service upon public duty but only as he is led by private quarrels ... he that will bring an hundred horse, or two or three hundred foot, into the field to revenge a private injury, or upon some private quarrel, will protest, yea and proclaim himself utterly unable to bring six men or horse into the field for her majesty's service.[59]

In the same letter, Essex complained that he had not heard of 'any near bordering rebel which has not had a person of quality for his solicitor' nor of any 'such as pretend to be well-affected subjects' who did not have

> a rebel for his client. But the greatest and clearest proof of all others is this, that they do ... suffer their children, kinsfolks and

---

55 SP 63/207, pt. 4/106. 56 SP 63. Edmond Fitzgerald of Cloyne, who pretended loyalty, was accused by William Saxey, chief justice of Munster, an Englishman, of being extremely disloyal. Fitzgerald defended himself from Saxey's charges, and convinced Elizabeth of his fidelity, though Saxey's charges have a ring of verisimilitude: SP 63/ccii, pt 2/43, 60. 57 SP 63/80/65, 74, 82, 63/84/19, 63/91/41, 63/207, pt 1/123, iii, 63/207, pt 2/10, 20, 149. 58 SP 63/207, pt 2/10. 59 SP 63/205/42. For an example, see SP 63/207, pt 3/71.

followers (whom by means they might draw in) to continue in action of rebellion.[60]

Essex's observations on the relations between the queen's pretended subjects and the rebels is salutary; it nicely encapsulates the complexities and ambiguities of relations among Catholics in Ireland who adopted differing stances during the course of the Nine Years War.

Sir George Carew, the president of Munster, warned the privy council on 30 April 1600 that

> the priests have in their devilish doctrine so much prevailed amongst the people in general in this province as, for fear of excommunication, very few dare serve against the rebels or any way aid her majesty. And this infection is so far crept into the hearts of the inhabitants of the cities and corporate towns ... that it is to be feared (if the Spanish do make any invasion, which many of them and the rebels do expect) the cities and towns are in danger to be lost by revolt.[61]

In a letter of 17 June 1600, Carew noted that if a bull of excommunication against Catholics who did not actively join in the rebellion were published in the towns – 'farewell their obedience'.[62] On 2 November, Carew warned that the 'traitorly priests ... are the chiefest firebrands of these unnatural treasons ... (this country people being so much devoted to them as they are)' and, 'if aids out of Spain (daily by them expected) do invade us, I do not believe that either pledges or any other possible assurance that can be devised will hold them subjects; and then likewise of the towns I am as little confident'.[63] He assured Cecil that he would 'handle that matter of religion as nicely as I may, especially in this broken time ... [observing] if it do appear in the least that any part of their punishment proceeds for matter of religion it will kindle a greater fire in this kingdom'. He noted that 'such is the sympathy between them as when the country is strong the towns are proud, and as the forces in the country decay, the towns grow more tractable'.[64]

In a letter of 6 July 1601, Carew was still warning the privy council of his expectation of 'a general revolt throughout the province' if a Spanish military force arrived in Ireland.[65] In his most measured assessment, in a letter of 13 July 1601, he stated:

> What judgment to make of the provincials before they [the Spanish] land, I know not; for until then they will not declare themselves; but

60 Ibid.   61 Ibid., pt 2/149.   62 Ibid., pt 3/114.   63 Ibid., pt 6/2.   64 Ibid., pt 5/113.
65 SP 63/208, pt 3/56.

how well they are affected to them, and how internally they hate our nation, long experience has taught me.[66]

To the testimony of Archbishop Magrath and Richard Whyte, both Irish Protestants, to the effect that the citizens were alienated from the English crown on religious grounds, one may add the testimony of James Goold, justice of Munster, another Irish Protestant, who informed Cecil by letter on 21 June 1601 that 'The seminaries have crept into the hearts of all the people, as well without as within the corporations, and they hold their souls in such bondage as whatsoever they command it is performed', and he highlighted the disloyalty of the corporations.[67]

Carew expressed his greatest doubts about the loyalty of the mayor of Limerick and his brethren – 'the worst people in Ireland'.[68] The earl of Thomond, an Irish-born Protestant whose earldom bordered upon Limerick, presented a damning series of articles against the citizens in March 1600, including allegations that they welcomed rebels into their city and reviled the English garrison among them, that they had issued gunpowder and munitions to rebels, that they boasted that they had cut off the head of the constable of Limerick Castle and 'played football with it', that they boasted that they had killed a lord justice and that they had buried many Englishmen in their cellars, and that the citizens were in constant communication with the earl of Tyrone.[69] Carew condemned the citizens as 'corrupt and traitorous'.[70] Yet they mustered their men 'every day', 'protesting that they purpose and resolve to die before they yield to the Spaniard'.[71] Ambiguity was the order of the day. Nonetheless, the disloyalty of William Stritch, mayor of Limerick, and his father, the 'opprobious speeches' made by one of the aldermen, the virulence of the animosity directed against the English garrison quartered in the city, and the support given to the rebels, certainly demonstrate that the conventional ascriptions of almost universal and unassailable loyalty to the English crown by the urban élites in Ireland stand in need of qualification.

In 1595, Fenton reckoned that Waterford and Cork would probably remain loyal to the English crown, whatever about the other cities and towns.[72] Yet three Irish merchants informed Loftus in January 1590 that 'all Waterford men, as well they which reside in Spain as the rest that do use traffic thither are traitors and do not stick to say when they are in Spain that they ask no other prince but the pope and the king of Spain'. The fact that one of Loftus' informants, James Synnot, a merchant of Wexford, had a brother who was a priest in the court of Philip II at that time, lends some credibility to the claim.[73] Yet, over the years, a

---

66 Ibid., pt 3/66. 67 SP 63/207, pt 3/125. 68 Ibid., pt 3/114. 69 Ibid., pt 2/7. 70 Ibid., pt 3/45. 71 SP 63/208, pt 3/88. 72 SP 63/184/30. 73 SP 63/150/11. Note though that those who were alleged to have been traitors were specifically those who resided in Spain or traded with Spain, not the entire population of Waterford.

number of mayors of Waterford and a number of its merchants provided intelligence to English officials regarding Spanish military preparations for Ireland. Waterford's oligarchs provided labourers to help to build the fortification at Duncannon which was designed to protect the city from a sea-borne assault from Spain.[74] Nonetheless, Sir John Dowdall, the commander of the English garrison at Duncannon, greatly doubted their loyalty.

Dowdall wrote to Burghley in March 1596 that 'the cause and very root' of the rebellion underway in Ireland was the work of Jesuits and 'seducing priests' who 'swarm up and down the whole country, seducing the people and the best sorts, to draw them from God and their allegiance to the prince',[75] even in the towns, even in the 'good town of Waterford', 'which were never but loyal'. Patrick Strange, a Catholic loyalist from Waterford, acknowledged the role of 'our priests' in promoting the Catholic Confederacy and warned that the people were 'hollow hearted' in their attachment to the crown, and that the rumours of foreign aid might affect them, even in the 'settled parts of the country'.[76] However, Carew did 'least mistrust' the citizens of Waterford, because he reckoned that 'although that people be no less superstitious than the rest of the citizens elsewhere, yet I do suppose them to be the best royalists'.[77]

Carew commented in July 1601 that people in Cork were 'no less affectioned to the Spaniard than the rest of the cities in this kingdom'.[78] When the earl of Tyrone led a Confederate army to Kinsale in spring 1600 and passed within a musket shot of Cork, the mayor of the city ordered that no one was to challenge the Confederates, neither to shoot at them nor sally outside the walls. Yet, significantly, there was a 'town Captain' willing to skirmish with the Confederates along with one hundred volunteers from the city.[79] Again, the evidence points to division and ambiguity. John Meade, the city's recorder, and Edmund Tirry, an alderman, were condemned by Bishop Lyon as 'evil-minded men to the state and her majesty's government'.[80]

The Catholic Confederates were confident that the cities would join them once the Spanish arrived. The constable of the English garrison at Boyle Abbey informed President Bingham in a letter of May 1596 that the Spanish were already assured of the support of Waterford, Cork, Kinsale and Limerick.[81] Captain Vaughan reported from Derry in May 1601 that the cities of Waterford, Cork and Limerick had 'bound themselves' to receive any Spanish force that might land in Munster.[82] Because these reports emanated from the north of Ireland, one must have reservations about the quality of their information, but in Munster itself, Dr Archer, the leading clerical Confederate beside Dr Creagh, 'plainly affirmed that all the towns here would revolt at one instant'.[83] The earl

74 SP 63/153/8, iii, 44. 75 SP 63/187/19. 76 *CSPI, 1601–3*, p. 57. 77 SP 63/207, pt 3/45. 78 SP 63/208, pt 3/56. 79 SP 63/207, pt 2/13. 80 Ibid., pt. 1/108. 81 SP 63/190/10, xii. 82 SP 63/208, pt 2/73. 83 SP 63/207, pt 2/7.

of Ormond was told by Dr Archer that Limerick and 'other corporations in those parts' were assured to the Confederate cause.[84]

It is not clear whether Creagh and/or Archer had secured binding commitments from a representative body of the citizens of the towns or, more probably, from smaller coteries of citizens who felt confident that they could 'deliver' their cities or towns to the Confederate cause once the Spaniards arrived. One of Lord Mountgarret's horseboys revealed a conspiracy that involved sixteen or seventeen persons in Kilkenny to allow his master to capture the town.[85] The plot was foiled, but Ormond was very struck at how dangerous it was.[86] A similar conspiracy, involving '30 resolute men set on by 29 priests lying in Dublin', was organised to capture Dublin Castle and the city in October 1598 (which was foiled when it was betrayed by one of the conspirators).[87] All of the conspirators had English surnames. There seem to have been similar conspiracies for the capture of towns in the north of the Pale.[88]

Implicit in these conspiracies is the likelihood that quite small numbers of men were privy to them. However, that does not disprove the judgment of contemporaries that the citizens of several cities and towns would have embraced the Confederate cause openly if a large Spanish force had landed in Ireland. At the same time, one must be cautious about accepting the Confederates' claims at face value: Dr Archer tried exceptionally hard to have Ormond converted to the Catholic cause, and the queen's viceroy proposed that the reason for his endeavour was to win over all of the Pale and the towns.[89] That would suggest that Archer was less confident than he claimed to be of the corporations' support for the war with the English crown.

Deputy Mountjoy claimed that Ormond was offered the crown of Ireland if he would join the Confederacy.[90] While the latter claim cannot be substantiated, and if it were based on fact it may simply have been a negotiating ploy by his captors, it is interesting that another commentator mentioned a proposal whereby Ormond would have been assigned a predominant position south of the River Boyne (where there were communities of old English people), while Tyrone would have been predominant in the north. The same scenario was mentioned again by the former recorder of Cork after the 'flight of the earls'.[91] Such an arrangement would have made sense in the context of divisions between Catholics of Gaelic and old English backgrounds in the late sixteenth century. Justice Nicholas Walsh, a Waterford loyalist of Catholic sympathies, recounted an episode in which a number of Confederates of English descent in the southeast of Ireland were reconciled to the English crown after learning that some Gaelic Confederates had consulted ancient books with a view to recovering lands

84 Ibid., pt 3/111. 85 SP 63/202, pt 4/34, xi. The conspirators seem not to have given up entirely: SP 63/202, pt 4/48, iv. 86 Ibid., pt 4/35. 87 Ibid., pt 3/135. 88 SP 63/207, pt 1/2. 89 Ibid., pt 2/142, 63/207, pt 3/110, 111, 63/207, pt 4/5. 90 SP 63/207, pt 4/5. 91 Kearney Walsh, 'Archbishop Magauran', op. cit.

lost by their ancestors following the English invasion of 1169.[92] In a different letter, dated 2 January 1599, Walsh reported that Creagh and Archer were experiencing difficulties in keeping the Confederates united.[93] Bishop Lyon reported that a rebel who was reconciled to the crown told him that 'the rebels agree not among themselves but by the priests' mighty persuasions'.[94]

Carew's 10,706 pardons in little more than seven months in 1600 is one striking indication of the scale of involvement in the revolt in Munster alone.[95] Yet the involvement of the mercantile oligarchs in the Confederate war effort was even more striking. Not only did they maintain the Catholic clerical 'fire-brands' of the rebellion, they provided the rebels with arms and munitions. Sir John Dowdall wrote in March 1596 that the merchants of Ireland were trading in large quantities of 'muskets, calivers, fowling pieces, swords, murrions, powder and shot'.[96] He warned that Tyrone and the rebels were being furnished with munitions by merchants from 'every town'.[97] He believed that the influence of Jesuits and seminary priests was responsible for such treasonous practices.[98] Lyon, the Elizabethan bishop of Ross with Cork & Cloyne, in a letter of February 1600, was adamant that 'The towns are the nurses of this rebellion, for they furnish the rebels with munition and victual, as wine, salt, *aqua vitae, et cetera.* ... The whole kingdom is of a conspiracy by means of the Romish priests, which were and are the plotters of this general rebellion'. He explained how the trade in war materiel operated from Cork in 1600: 'the merchant of Cork buys his [gun] powder of the Frenchman, sells it to the rebel for a [cow] hide, and that hide he returns back to the Frenchman for a French crown'.[99] Munitions were also imported from England. An Irish-born Protestant from Leinster complained of merchants smuggling gunpowder into Ireland by means of false-bottomed barrels.[1] Again, he ascribed such treasonous trade to the malign influence of Catholic bishops and priests: 'the principal purveyors and procurers of all needful things for the on-setting and upholding of rebellions in Ireland'. An Englishman named Cuff warned Carew in August 1600 that the towns were the 'roots of all these mischiefs', both for sending their sons to Spain to be educated, and for providing gunpowder and other materials to the rebels.[2] In a letter of 16 December 1600, Carew condemned the magistrates and inhabitants of the corporate towns for their 'traitorly' trading with the rebels, by which the 'rebellion has been most nourished'. In his considered opinion, such trade was motivated 'partly out of malice to the state for religion's cause, but especially for their own lucre'.[3] The prevailing assumption that the urban communities of

---

92 SP 63/207, pt 2/10. 93 SP 63/203/2. 94 SP 63/207, pt 1/108. 95 Ibid., pt 6/4. One might quibble about the true meaning of individual pardons, about whether they reflected some innocent individuals' anxiety for some form of 'insurance' against a general land confiscation, yet the fact remains that an enormous number of the men with property in Munster felt obliged to secure pardons for their actions during the war. 96 SP 63/187/19. 97 SP 63/190/10. 98 SP 63/187/19. 99 SP 63/207, pt 1/108. 1 Ibid., pt 4/3. 2 Ibid., pt 4/116. 3 Ibid.,

Ireland were inviolably loyal to the crown of England clearly stands in need of considerable qualification.

In February 1595, Deputy Fitzwilliam wrote of his belief that an English Jesuit named Francis Mountford had been sent to Tyrone by Palesmen, with encouragement to rebel.[4] Mountford gave Tyrone guarantees of a massive Spanish expeditionary force destined for Ireland.[5] Fenton claimed that Mountford, 'more than any other, seduced the earl to fall from his duty'.[6] Bishop Jones of Meath confirmed that 'an English priest' was the 'principal stirrer' in the war in Ulster.[7] Elizabeth herself, at the end of the century, stated that the friary at Multyfarnham was the place where 'all the traitorous Jesuits of the realm' met, and 'where was the first conspiracy and plotting of the great rebellion'.[8] In a summary of the causes of the rebellion among the state papers, penned about the turn of the year 1599, is a statement that, 'divers priests of the English Pale persuaded him [Tyrone] that it were a godly work to restore the Romish religion, which they call the Catholic faith'.[9]

Fenton warned Burghley in September 1595 that if Philip II were to send 4,000 men to Ireland it would create a 'dangerous hazard', as there were 'many parts' that stood 'hovering', waiting to see what transpired, and that included the Pale, where people were weary of their heavy burdens and their minds were 'stirred'.[10] In a subsequent letter, he reiterated that he had no confidence in the loyalty of even the Pale heartlands.[11] Fenton recommended that the earl of Kildare, the most powerful magnate in the Pale, be summoned to England on a seemingly innocuous pretext – a curious move at a time of such crisis, unless he doubted the earl's loyalty.[12] Suspicion is no proof of guilt, but three of the countess of Kildare's 'principal followers' were alleged to have been involved in a conspiracy that embraced key 'furtherers' of the war; the Jesuits Archer, Nangle and Laylor, their fellow Jesuit, Fitzsimmons, some English agents and others.[13] Nonetheless, Kildare and Delvin were still playing the part of loyal subjects in April 1598.[14]

Archbishop Loftus and the council of Ireland reported in October 1598 that Tyrone's rebellion 'is now thoroughly sorted to an Irish war ... to shake off all English government as much as in them lies'.[15] They reported the uncovering of a major Confederate conspiracy to capture Dublin Castle and the city itself, organised by Tyrone with thirty 'resolute men set on by 29 priests lying in Dublin, and should have been assisted with 1,000 of Tyrone's forces, besides the help of 1,000 more from the [Wicklow] mountain rebels, had it not been happily

pt 6/75. **4** SP 63/178/58. **5** SP 63/176/60. Lord Louth's chaplain delivered a letter from Philip II to Tyrone; SP 63/182/71. **6** SP 63/179/85. **7** SP 63/180/32 i. **8** SP 63/207, pt 3/139. **9** SP 63/202, pt 4/61. **10** SP 63/183/9. **11** SP 63/186/25. **12** SP 63/186/90. **13** SP 63/207, pt 2/20, i. **14** SP 63/202, pt 2/11. Baron Delvin informed the deputy of the nature of the Spanish promises to Tyrone and O'Donnell in May 1596: SP 63/189/46 v. **15** SP 63/202, pt 2/135.

discovered by one of the conspirators'. The conspirators whose names were recorded – Friar Nangle, Lapley, Cawell, Shelton, Bethell and Leynan – were all Palesmen. This significant conspiracy was seen at the time as a clear reflection of the Catholic clergy's ability to 'seduce the cities and countries' in Ireland and sway their hearts to their own ends.

Confederates were able to 'burn and spoil near Dublin' (one report stated that they raided within three miles of the capital)[16] at the end of November 1598 without facing any resistance from the local lords and gentlemen.[17] Confederates were also able to raid as far as the south coast of Wexford because the local gentlemen offered no resistance – an occurrence that was virtually unprecedented since the English invasion in 1169.[18] It may not be coincidental that the Jesuit, Archer, had met the seneschal of Wexford several times previously, and had also met with the gentlemen of County Wexford.[19] Wallop summarised the English crown's precarious position in Ireland by November 1598:

> little of Connacht remaining, and that which stands not like long so to continue. We have nothing of substance left, saving a little here about Dublin and part of the country of Wexford, and what assurance we may make of them I rest doubtful by reason first of their affection to the Popish religion and the discontentment they have entered into ... Some gentlemen of good account on the borders are joined to the rebels, and from those which stand in their sons, brethren and servants are fallen, which may give us sufficient cause to doubt the rest.[20]

The chief baron of the exchequer wrote in November 1599 that Tyrone had sent letters into the cities and towns calling for their support against Elizabeth and the English by means of Jesuits and other priests.[21] He observed that the town of Kildare refused to give relief to English soldiers, and Drogheda, Galway, Waterford, Cork, Limerick and others were unco-operative, in part because of genuine grievances but also, he believed, because of Tyrone's 'pestilent libel'. Within the Pale itself, the Berminghams, Husseys, Daltons and some of the Darcys were in open rebellion, and some of Lord Dunsany's company of foot soldiers quit the garrison at Kells to join the Confederates.[22] Soldiers from the garrison at Dundalk also joined the Confederates.[23] William Nugent's son, Richard, along with a number of other young men of the Pale, joined the Confederacy.[24] Lord Justice Carey informed Cecil that Tyrone's 'traitorous and villainous libel' was 'mightily' infecting and seducing 'this bad nation'.[25] Sir Nicholas Walsh, a Waterford loyalist, also warned of 'how much the people were

16 Ibid., pt 4/19.   17 Ibid., pt 3/183.   18 Ibid., pt 4/48.   19 Ibid., pt 1/17, I; 63/207, pt 2/10.   20 Ibid., pt 3/183.   21 SP 63/206/33.   22 Ibid.   23 SP 63/207, pt 1/3.   24 Ibid., pt 2/63, 143.   25 SP 63/206/71.

seduced' by Tyrone's letter to the inhabitants of the Pale.[26] These contemporary observations confound the assumption of historians who assert that Tyrone's calls for support fell on deaf ears.

Viscount Gormanstown informed Lords Justice Carey and Loftus on 20 November 1599 that in response to a general muster of all of the men of the Pale between the ages of sixteen and sixty years, only a few gentlemen and one hundred men made an appearance on the Hill of Tara.[27] Others offered lame excuses. Loftus and Carey were clear in their minds as to how things stood: 'the defection is universal and apparent in the Irish, and no assurance may be reposed in some others that pretend to stand fast who, in the trial, we cannot but think will be ready to run with the rest'.[28] Lord Mountjoy came to the same conclusion: in June 1600, he reckoned that 'the uncertainty of the Spanish hopes has kept the Pale from the boldness to discover themselves' and if Dowcra's expedition to Lough Foyle had 'miscarried', they 'would undoubtedly have presently and almost generally revolted'.[29] A declaration of loyalty by eighteen gentlemen of the Pale was not enough to convince anyone otherwise.[30]

In the summer of 1600, Confederate forces were operating throughout the Pale unchallenged, though they killed 'none'.[31] The council of Ireland was clear in May 1600 that the general 'backwardness' in resisting the Confederates had 'another root, namely that most of them are far gone with a Popish zeal to their Catholic cause (as they term it) wherein the Jesuits and priests have so far poisoned them as they hold it a danger of damnation to do anything to impeach the proceedings of that Catholic cause'.[32] They noted that the people of Dublin were 'far more willing and pliable than the country', and reported that Lord Howth had organised 500 men for the defence of County Dublin and commented that, 'we wish that by their example, the county of Meath and the other shires of the Pale would be drawn to do the like' – but they were not. In Munster, President Carew wrote that the best he could hope for from the queen's subjects in the southern province was for them 'to stand as neutrals'.[33]

A loyalist tract, from December 1600, declared that there were 'great numbers', particularly in the Pale, who were innocent of treason.[34] Actions, however, speak louder than words. Bishop Jones of Meath informed Cecil that while the Confederate army was passing through the Pale on its way to rendezvous with the Spaniards at Kinsale, County Cork, in October 1601, the Pale's élites mustered only sixty horse, forty of them under Lord Dunsany who, from the safety of the walls of Athboy, 'did view and look upon the rebels as they committed those hurts, but they did no service'.[35] The only gentleman in the Pale who took action against the rebels was Sir Garrett Moore, head of a 'new English' family.

---

26 SP 63/207, pt 2/10. 27 SP 63/206/35. 28 SP 63/207, pt 1/86. 29 Ibid., pt 3/93. 30 Ibid., pt 3/109. 31 Ibid., pt 3/70, 71, 73. 32 Ibid., pt 3/63. 33 Ibid., pt 4/106. 34 Ibid., pt 6/123. 35 *CSPI, 1601–3*, p. 135.

Tyrone's forces were greeted in the Pale in a quite extraordinary manner, as Jones testified.[36] Not only did the marcher lords defect to the Confederates, but the Confederates were entertained for four days in East Meath – the very heart of the English Pale. Tyrone sent priests to persuade Lord Dunsany and the other most powerful of the Plunketts to join him in open rebellion. Jones reported that

> What answers they made I cannot directly learn, but their sending unto him of plenty of victuals and of drink, and *aqua vitae*, even out of their castles (where they needed not to fear him or his forces) shows where their sympathies lie in this doubtful time.

Tyrone's priests canvassed for support in Westmeath also, with Delvin entertaining Friar Nangle in his house, and 'the other gentlemen of Westmeath resorted to him as to a market'. Tyrone received better entertainment there than in the Plunkett lordships, with some lords sending him wine. Those were not the actions of loyal English subjects, nor can such actions be explained away as having been prompted by fear of the Confederates – the gentlemen had no reason to fear for their safety inside the tower houses that studded the Pale. Furthermore, when the battered remnants of the Confederate forces returned northwards after the catastrophic defeat at Kinsale, they could have been beaten by 'a troop of women', yet they were able to limp home unimpeded by the Palesmen.[37] As Bishop Jones observed, the Palesmen's gifts of food and drink show where their sympathies lay. Baron Delvin, having previously agreed to send forty-five of his men with the Confederates, now sent one hundred men to fight beside the earl of Tyrone.[38] He provided Tyrone's secretary with a fresh horse, and money.[39] After the defeat at Kinsale, he was imprisoned in Dublin Castle because of his contribution to the Confederate cause.[40]

Loftus and the council of Ireland explained to the English privy council in December 1601 that the 'staggering subjects in Leinster and the English Pale', the 'tottering subjects', were mostly 'so far carried away in heart with their Popish religion and their great expectations that if the Spanish came they shall have freedom of conscience in the kind they desire', and they warned that 'to win the liberty of their religion they will not be curious to put in hazard their temporal estates and freeholds, which at other times they have been as careful to preserve as their lives'. They stated that that was true of 'most of them, though we have no doubt it is not so with all'.[41] They asked the English privy council to 'expostulate' with the gentlemen of the Pale to defend the region in the future.[42] The queen herself was driven to comment that 'those of the Pale who have

36 Ibid., pp 188–9.   37 Ibid., p. 275.   38 Ibid., pp 172, 464–5, 493.   39 Ibid., pp 454, 464.
40 Ibid., pp 405–6.   41 Ibid., pp 218–19.   42 Ibid., p. 156.

hitherto been very loyal in their efforts against the attempts of the unnatural subjects, ... have not been so dutiful in recent times'.[43]

The Confederates' defeat at Kinsale was decisive, though a diminishing number did not accept it as such.[44] Carew remarked of the citizens at Cork that

> While Tyrone with his army lay upon our backs, the townsmen of Cork were proud and would not know those Englishmen with whom they were familiarly acquainted; no sooner was the victory ours but their faces changed, and ever since are tractable. The noblemen and gentlemen of the country came presently unto us, making semblance of joy for our happy success, and some of the relapsed rebels are moving to be received.[45]

In an effort to redeem themselves from their dalliance with a Spanish-backed rebellion, a number of men who had committed themselves to the Catholic cause became 'the most envious and eagerest dogs to serve against the Catholics' in the aftermath of Kinsale.[46] The myth of the inviolable loyalism of the 'old English' was fashioned to obscure an uncomfortable reality about a time when the loyalty of many of them was very anaemic – at best. On 30 March 1603, Tyrone surrendered to Mountjoy. Elizabeth had died only days before.[47] The Nine Years War was over, but the struggle for the souls of Ireland simply entered a new phase.

THE RECUSANCY REVOLT

Following the death of Elizabeth, the citizens and priests of towns across southern Ireland took advantage of the *interregnum* by restoring the public celebration of Catholic liturgies in the parish churches after they had been ritually cleansed from the taint of Protestantism.[48] William Farmer, an English observer, wrote that 'Now came abroad in open show, the Jesuits, seminary priests and friars out of every corner, and walked up and down in every city and corporation. Now they began to alter the churches and religion, bringing forth old rotten stocks and stores of images setting them up in their churches'.[49]

When Mountjoy insisted on their obedience, the sovereign of Wexford wrote

---

43 Ibid., p. 592. 44 Ibid., pp 530–1. 45 Ibid., p. 276. 46 Ibid., pp 398–9. 47 The Catholic Confederates lost the war because England was far stronger demographically, economically and militarily, and the Catholics were still divided by ethnic and cultural allegiances. Without significant Spanish support, success against England was simply impossible, regardless of the disposition of the 'old English' communities: Jefferies, 'Hugh O'Neill, earl of Tyrone, c.1550–1616' in Dillon and Jefferies (eds), *Tyrone: history and society* (2000), pp 221–2. 48 *CSPI, James I*, no. 38. 49 Quoted in Anthony J. Sheehan, 'The recusancy revolt of 1603: a reinterpretation', *Archivium Hibernicum*, 38 (1983), p. 3.

to explain that all of the men of the town, 'few excepted', believed that James VI was a Catholic and he could not restore the churches to the Protestant ministers because of the 'multitudes' who went to Mass daily and 'most incessantly' prayed for the prosperous reign of the king.[50] Faced with the lord deputy and council and 2,000 soldiers, the sovereign and four other leading citizens of Kilkenny swore their allegiance to the king, promised to restore the churches to the Church of Ireland and to perform any other directions that the Council of Ireland might prescribe.[51] They confessed to having been 'seduced' by Dr White, a Jesuit from Waterford, who enjoined them to celebrate the Mass publicly in the parish churches of Kilkenny, after he had first reconsecrated them for Catholic services, and prohibited them from having the Mass celebrated privately in houses as had been their custom. They also blamed a friar named Edmund Barry, allegedly an illegitimate son of Sir James Fitzmaurice Fitzgerald, for their misbehaviour. Robert Walsh, mayor of Waterford, wrote to Deputy Mountjoy in 1603, stating that

> where your lordship is informed of the priests, true it is that some of them, upon the news of our late sovereign's death, entered into the churches here, and the people (being as your lordship do partly know, always given and inclined to the old religion) do flock daily unto them, giving out that they are in good hope the king's majesty will be pleased to let them have the liberty of their conscience.[52]

However, he omitted to mention that the Protestant service books were torn in pieces and/or burned.[53] He made no mention either of the oath levied by the Jesuit, Dr White, 'that they should be true to the pope and maintain the Romish religion with their goods and their lives'. Sir Nicholas Walsh, a Waterford man and member of the Council of Ireland, informed Cecil that he personally heard some people say, 'We will not have a Scot to be our king'.[54]

The citizens of Waterford sent four agents to meet with Deputy Mountjoy early in May 1603 and presented him with a formal request for religious toleration penned by Dr White. Meanwhile, the citizens manned the city's walls against the deputy's forces. Yet, threatened with the fate of traitors, Dr White and the corporation of Waterford capitulated, with Mountjoy offering an assurance that he would seek the king's grace on their behalves.[55]

The citizens of Limerick did not present Mountjoy with any great challenge, 'but in the erecting and frequenting of the Mass, whereunto these people are too much addicted'.[56] Cork, however, was a very different matter. Richard Boyle, the

---

50 *CSPI, James I*, no. 40, iv.   51 Ibid., no. 48.   52 Ibid., no. 40, iii.   53 Ibid., no. 48. In Cashel, a Protestant was tied to a tree and was harangued by a priest, in constant fear of being burned, surrounded as he was by a pile of torn-up Protestant bibles and *Common Prayer* books: Sheehan, 'Recusancy revolt', p. 3.   54 *CSPI, James I*, no. 48.   55 Ibid., nos 48, 49.

secretary of the Munster presidency, declared that the 'recusants' revolt' actually began in Cork and that its citizens had incited the rest of the country about them to stand for liberty of their consciences.[57] According to Boyle, once rumours of the queen's death reached Cork, they manned the city's gates and prevented the entry of any English soldiers, unless they were disarmed. They did not proclaim James Stuart as the new king when directed to do so, but instead sent a messenger (using a false name) to consult with the corporation in Waterford. They imprisoned the royal officers in charge of the English army's ordnance and victuals that were stored in Skiddy's Castle in the city, and they seized the ordnance and the victuals. They sent some men in boats to Hawlbowline to regain possession of the island from the English garrison there. They demolished the fort that President Carew had obliged them to build immediately south of their city walls, to 'bridle' them.[58] The citizens barricaded the two main streets of the city, mounted cannon on the walls and opened fire every day, either on Shandon Castle, the headquarters of Munster's presidency, or on the Protestant bishop's house.[59] When English soldiers approached the city, the citizens trained the cannons on them.[60]

The revolt in Cork was, by any reckoning, an extraordinary affair. The 'greatest and chiefest stirrer up of all these broils' was Cork's Recorder, William Meade, supported by the mayor of Cork and other members of the corporation.[61] He and the mayor, 'with many others', attended a sermon in the city in which a friar 'openly preached that the king's majesty is not a lawful king until the pope has confirmed him'.[62] Meade subsequently became one of Hugh O'Neill's principal agents after the 'flight of the earls'.

Sir Jeffery Fenton stated at the time that the revolt in Cork was really 'a quarrel of state' and that the citizens only proclaimed it as an affair of religion in the hope of winning Spanish support.[63] However, Fenton subsequently changed his mind and complained that Cork's corporation had been poisoned with a blind zeal towards the pope and his 'counterfeit' religion.[64] The citizens of Cork took solemn oaths on sacraments before priests to uphold the Catholic religion with their lives, lands and goods, and even declared they were content to be buried within the city's walls if they were denied it.[65] In the event, the men of Cork found that they were vulnerable to English cannon mounted on the former religious buildings in the suburbs of the city, and once the other cities had capitulated, they decided to submit just before Deputy Mountjoy arrived at the city in person on 10 May.[66]

Anthony J. Sheehan highlighted the economic and constitutional grievances that formed the backdrop to the 'spontaneous popular displays of religious freedom for which the [recusants'] revolt is chiefly remembered'.[67] However, the

---

56 Ibid., no. 48.   **57** Ibid., no. 36.   **58** Ibid., no. 63.   **59** Ibid., nos 55, 59.   **60** Ibid., no. 50.
61 Ibid., no. 66.   **62** Ibid., no. 48.   **63** Ibid., no. 58.   **64** Ibid.   **65** Ibid., nos 55, 59.   **66** Ibid., nos 55, 67.

evidence points very firmly to the centrality of religion in the revolt. 'Liberty of conscience' was the central demand made by the leaders in Cork, and it was the only demand of the other urban communities. The loyal declarations in the letters of the mayors of Waterford and Wexford may give a misleading impression of conditions on the ground, where loyalties to the Scottish king were often more ambiguous than the civic authorities dared to admit to royal officials. Sheehan concluded that 'the townsfolk of Munster acted in a foolish and short-sighted manner'.[68] However, he failed to appreciate how religious passions can colour men's and women's calculations in politics.

Mountjoy did not exact retribution on the participants in the recusancy revolt, apart from an unsuccessful attempt to prosecute the recorder of Cork and a few others.[69] His philosophy was that

> I am persuaded that a violent course therein [the Reformation] will do little good to win men's consciences, but, howsoever, it is too soon to begin it; and it is most sure that it will breed a new war and, as I believe, make all the towns and nobility solicit Spanish aids. ... I am of the opinion that all religions do grow under persecution.

He warned of the danger of a 'new war' unless the matter of religion was handled 'discreetly' in Ireland.[70] However, religious persecution and sectarianism were to form central aspects of life in Ireland in the years that followed.

CONCLUSIONS

Many historians were too sanguine about the prospects of success for the Tudor reformations. They equated some outward conformity to the Church of Ireland with progress for the Reformation. A more meaningful measure of progress, I suggest, would be the degree of actual support for Protestantism. By that criterion, the Tudor reformations showed no true prospect of success. No self-sustaining community of Irish Protestants was formed, even by the end of Elizabeth's reign, after seven decades of state-sponsored religious changes.

To explain why the Reformation failed in Ireland, I think one has to consider two intertwined variables: the strength of the general attachment to Catholicism and the weakness of the state-sponsored Protestant challenge. The variables are reciprocal, in the sense that the English crown did not promote the reformations in Ireland with anything like the rigour or commitment seen in England – partly because royal authority was significantly weaker than it was in England and

67 Sheehan, 'Recusancy revolt', p. 10.   68 Ibid., p. 12.   69 Ibid., p. 3.   70 *CSPI, 1601–3*, pp 556–7.

partly because of the fear that the attachment to Catholicism in Ireland could act as a solvent of royal authority. Successive viceroys, from Grey to Mountjoy, were obliged to exercise discretion in promoting religious change in Ireland. A series of rebellions, and even the small-scale recusants' revolt (1603), all had the defence of Catholicism as their avowed central aim. Modern historians in Ireland have been remarkably loathe to acknowledge the importance of religion in sixteenth-century Ireland, but the policies pursued by successive Tudor monarchs and their viceroys reflected their keen awareness that the imposition of the Reformation in Ireland was unpopular, and threatened to undermine the crown's authority, even among the communities who considered themselves to be English and were traditionally loyal to the English crown.

Historians in today's secular Ireland often fail to appreciate the power of religion in sixteenth-century Europe, despite the fact that religious dissension led to social strife, civil wars and international conflicts across the continent throughout much of the early modern era. Lord Burghley was not alone in thinking that 'there is no enmity so great as that for religion'.[71] The failure to recognise the power of religious dissent as a major cause of political instability in early modern Ireland is compounded by an unspoken assumption that the ethnic identity of many among the people in Ireland with English surnames compelled them towards inviolable loyalty to the reigning English monarch. In fact, the use of English surnames is an extremely poor indicator of ethnic identity in sixteenth-century Ireland (as in today's Ireland). English-speakers in Tudor Ireland were not an integral part of England's political community, which was bound together by mutual experiences and frequent intercourse at the royal court, in parliament and in other institutions of the English state. The relationship of the Anglophone élites in Ireland to the English crown was less direct, less intimate and consequently weaker than that of their fellows across the Irish Sea. Furthermore, even in England, loyalty to the crown as an institution did not guarantee loyalty to any particular monarch – as the 'Wars of the Roses' demonstrated in the fifteenth century, the religion-inspired revolts against Mary and Elizabeth in the sixteenth century and the fates of Charles I and James II testified to in the seventeenth century. Henry VIII and his Protestant daughter did not command the same degree of loyalty from the old English élites in Ireland as they did from the élites in England, and consequently their religious policies did not enjoy the same degree of support.

There was considerable passive resistance offered to the Elizabethan reformation, by non-attendance at Protestant services, by disruptive behaviour by many of those compelled to attend them, and by the withdrawal of financial support from the Church. The records of the Ecclesiastical High Commission show how

71 Quoted in John Coffey, *Persecution and toleration in Protestant England, 1558–1689* (Harlow, 2000), p. 83.

persistent was the problem of Catholic dissent throughout the 1570s and early 1580s, particularly in Dublin, where it seems that about a quarter of the Ecclesiastical Commission's fines were imposed.

Beneath a veneer of enforced conformity in the middle years of Elizabeth's reign, Catholic religious practice and teaching in Dublin, the Pale and beyond was commonly supported by networks of Catholic priests who functioned either inside or outside the institutional Church as chaplains, tutors and dispensers of Catholic sacraments. Fynes Moryson, a keen observer of Irish affairs in the final years of Elizabeth's reign, wrote that the lack of Protestant ministers was such that the queen's bishops in Ireland were 'forced for the most part to tolerate ignorant persons, men of scandalous lives, yea, very Popish readers, rather than parishes should want not only divine service, but the use of baptism, burial, marriage and the Lord's Supper, which the Papists did often cast in our teeth, saying it was better to have the Roman Mass than no service at all, as in many of our churches'.[72] Hence, one must take care not to exaggerate the extent or depth of the conformity achieved or to forget that conformity was imposed through coercion. The veneer of conformity in Ireland was very thin, and there was no credible attempt made by the Elizabethan Church to transform that sullen conformity into anything approaching enthusiasm for Protestantism.

An intensified drive to enforce conformity from the late 1570s was soon followed by rebellions in Munster and the Pale, and whatever other motives the rebels may have had, the appeal to defend the Catholic religion was central to them, and won them widespread sympathy if not active support, even in the Pale itself. The lesson was not lost on Elizabeth, and she directed her officials in Ireland to desist from forcing men's consciences for fear of the political repercussions of their actions at a time when Anglo–Spanish relations were so fraught. However, without employing coercion, it proved to be very difficult to persuade any to attend Elizabethan services, and without congregations in churches to preach at, there was no possibility of mass conversions to Protestantism in late sixteenth-century Ireland.

It is difficult to avoid the conclusion that the Elizabethan Church of Ireland was stymied by poor leadership. None of Elizabeth's appointees to the Irish bench of bishops proved to be inspirational and none devised an effective Reformation strategy for their dioceses, not even Bishop Brady of Meath. Archbishops Curwen and Loftus may have been correct in their scepticism about the utility of an Irish university, while the Irish Church was so poor, but they failed to devise an effective means of educating and training a Protestant ministry for the parishes. There was no training college established for prospective ministers. There were no bursaries established to support young men to study in Cambridge or Oxford universities, though Archbishop Lancaster

72 Moryson, *Itinerary*, pp 93–4.

reckoned that they would cost only £5 *per annum*.[73] There was no in-service training offered to the clergymen who held benefices since Mary's reign to wean them from Catholicism and improve their usefulness as ministers in Elizabeth's Church. No preaching campaigns were organised. No prophesyings or exercises were organised to cultivate Protestant convictions or preaching skills among the Elizabethan clergy in Ireland. Instead, Elizabeth's bishops presided over a situation, even in Dublin diocese and the heart of the Pale generally, wherein many men were employed as parish priests in the Established Church who did not preach, nor even make use of the *Book of Common Prayer*.

Despite the lip-service paid to the need to advance the Reformation through the use of the 'Word' in Ireland, in actual fact, it was the 'Sword', in the form of the coercive measures deployed intermittently by the Ecclesiastical High Commission in the Pale and the pressures exerted on corporations in the outlying boroughs, not to mention the diocesan bishops' traditional means of enforcing ecclesiastical expectations, that was employed as the primary instrument of Reformation in Elizabeth's reign. The use of coercion to force people of Catholic sentiments to attend the services of the Elizabethan Church, without the provision of an effective preaching ministry, was never likely to generate Protestant convictions – but probably proved to be counter-productive in terms of winning hearts and souls. Fynes Moryson reported that Irish people told him that the coercive and corrupt operation of the Ecclesiastical High Commission 'wrought in their hearts a hatred of the government and in time a detestation of our [Protestant] religion'.[74] Such was their strength of feeling that it was 'more easy ... to bring a bear to the stake than any one of them to our churches'.[75] Their passion against Protestantism was such that anyone who became a Protestant was, according to Moryson, 'most hated and molested', and ostracised socially and financially:

> Yea, the Papists generally were so malicious against their countrymen turning Protestants as they not only in life maligned them, but upon their death beds and in the hour of death denied them release or rest, keeping meat and all things they desired from them, and the women and children continually pinching and disquieting them when they would take rest, that they might thereby force them to turn Papists again.

Moryson's colourful tale is not beyond the bounds of credibility, and what his observations serve to indicate (and they are consistent with Bishop Lyon's testimony from Cork) is the strength of the communal pressures exerted on individual converts to conform to the religion of their community. That

73 SP 63/82/58.   74 Moryson, *Itinerary*, p. 92.   75 Ibid.

communal insistence on conformity was so powerful that very few Irish-born individuals lived and died as Protestants in Elizabeth's reign.

It has become customary to emphasise the economic problems of the Irish Church as a critical cause of the failure of the Tudor reformations.[76] However, as I observed earlier, there were more well-endowed benefices in Ireland than there were Protestant preachers available to staff them. Furthermore, the economic weaknesses of the Irish Church were grossly exacerbated by the secularisation and dissipation of the revenues of the Irish Church by the English crown and the clergy it promoted in Ireland. Simony, nepotism and pluralism became endemic in the Elizabethan Church.[77] Absenteeism and pluralism on grand scales were consequences of the Tudor reformations.[78] The so-called 'second reformation' made no discernible impression in Ireland before the reign of James Stuart, by which time a large majority of the parishes and chapelries in the three southern provinces had collapsed.

Nonetheless, the failure of the Tudor reformations was not simply the result of economic weakness or mismanagement. In essence, it was the result of an uneven contest between the commitment of people in Ireland to the Catholic faith, and the vacillating insistence of the Tudor state that they adopt a different version of Christianity without any effective campaign to convince them of the veracity of the new faith. In England, the crown had sufficient allies, in the form of committed Protestants on the ground and a growing cohort of Protestant preachers graduating from Oxford and Cambridge universities, to mount a convincing preaching campaign in the parishes, backed up by a torrent of books and pamphlets. In Ireland, by contrast, there were no communities of local Protestants in Elizabeth's reign, almost no Protestant preachers, apart from a few isolated individuals who failed signally to win communities of adherents, and only one short Protestant book in Irish aimed specifically at Irish audiences. Ireland's was a Reformation with virtually no reformers, and consequently it had no real chance of success.

The advent in Ireland of Irish Catholic priests from colleges on mainland Europe was clearly important in its effects on the course of the Elizabethan reformation. They galvanised the general attachment to Catholicism in Ireland, and strove to make it more intense. Moryson observed that 'howsoever the men grew weary of them, they had the women on their sides'.[79] An important point to bear in mind, though, was that the religious commitment of the continent-trained priests had first been inculcated and nurtured in families, and by teachers and priests at home in Ireland, and reflected their prior commitments to Catholicism. By the 1590s, 'swarms' of Catholic priests who had been trained in

76 Ellis, 'Economic problems', passim; Scott, *Tudor diocese of Meath*, pp 19, 66, 77, 145–6.
77 For example, W.A. Phillips, *History of the Church of Ireland*, iii (Oxford, 1934), p. 550; Robert Wyse Jackson, *Archbishop Magrath: the scoundrel of Cashel* (Cork, 1974), p. 76.   78 Scott, *Tudor diocese of Meath*, p. 83.   79 Moryson, *Itinerary*, p. 94.

mainland colleges returned to Ireland imbued with a zeal for the counter-reformation that impressed even their adversaries, as Spenser exemplifies:

> it is great wonder to see the odds which is between the zeal of Popish priests and the ministers of the Gospel; for they spare not to come out of Spain, from Rome and from Rheims, by long toil and dangerous travelling hither, where they know peril of death awaits them and no reward or riches is to be found, only to draw the people unto the Church of Rome; whereas some of our idle ministers, having a way for credit and estimation thereby opened unto them, and having the livings of the country offered unto them, without pains and without peril, will neither for the same nor any love of God nor zeal of religion, nor for all the good they may do by winning souls to God, be drawn forth from their warm nests to look out into God's harvest, which is even [now] ready for the sickle and all the fields yellow long ago.[80]

Spenser seems not to have realised it at the time, but the failure of the Reformation in Ireland was already irrevocable.[81]

---

80 Spenser, *View of the state of Ireland*, pp 254–5. 81 The suggestion that Moryson's 'very Popish readers' could ever have provided a 'nucleus of local support' for the Church of Ireland in the seventeenth century strikes me as wishful thinking: Moryson, *Itinerary*, pp 93–4.

Bibliography

MANUSCRIPT SOURCES

Bodleian Library, Oxford
Laud Miscellaneous MS 612.

Marsh's Library, Dublin
MS Z 4/2/7 Annals of Dudley Loftus.

Public Records Office, London
State Papers, Ireland Henry VIII–Elizabeth, SP 60–63.

Public Records Office of Northern Ireland, Belfast
MS DIO 4/2/10, Primate Octavian's register of wills.
MS DIO 4/2/11, Primate Cromer's register.
MS DIO 4/2/12, Primate Dowdall's register.

Trinity College, Dublin
MS 567, *Valor in Hibernia.*
MS 808 (5), Statutes of the provincial synod of Cashel, 1453.
MS 10,383, Dioceses of Clogher, Derry and Raphoe.

PUBLISHED SOURCES AND CALENDARS

Public records
Calendar of Carew Manuscripts, i, 1515–1574, ed. J.S. Brewer and W. Bullen (London, 1867).
Calendar of letters and papers, foreign and domestic, Henry VIII, ed. J.S. Brewer et al. (London, 1862–1932).
Calendar of the MSS of the marquis of Salisbury (London, 1893–1973).
Calendar of Patent and Close Rolls, Ireland, Henry VIII–Elizabeth, i, ed. James Morrin (Dublin, 1861).
Calendar of State Papers, Ireland, March–October, 1600, ed. Ernest George Atkinson (London, 1903).

Extents of Irish monastic possessions, 1540–1, ed. N.B. White (Dublin, 1943).

Inquisitionum in officio rotulorum cancellariae Hiberniae asservatarum repertorium, ii ed. James Hardiman (Dublin, 1829).

McNeill, 'Accounts of monastic chattels', *JRSAI*, 52 (1922), pp 11–37.

Statutes at large passed in the parliaments held in Ireland, i (Dublin, 1786).

Statute rolls of the parliament of Ireland: Edward IV, i, ed. H.F. Berry (Dublin, 1914).

The Irish fiants of the Tudor sovereigns, i, 1521–1558, ed. Kenneth Nicholls (Dublin, 1994).

Valor beneficiorum ecclesiasticorum in Hiberniae: or the first fruits of all the ecclesiastical benefices in the kingdom of Ireland, as taxed in the king's book (Dublin, 1741).

Other printed sources

Alexander, A.F. O'D (ed.), 'The O'Kane papers', *An. Hib.*, 12 (1943), pp 67–127.

Annals of Ulster, iii, ed. B. Mac Carthy (Dublin, 1895).

Annals of the kingdom of Ireland by the Four Masters, v, ed. John O'Donovan (Dublin, 1856).

Bale, John, 'The vocacyon of John Bale, bishop of Ossory', *Harleian Miscellany*, 6, ed. T. Park (London, 1813).

Berry, H.F., *Register of wills and inventories of the diocese of Dublin in the time of Archbishops Tregury and Walton, 1457–1483* (Dublin, 1898).

——, 'Documents relating to the wardenship of Galway', *An. Hib.*, 14 (1944), pp 7–18.

Brady, W.M. (ed.), *State papers concerning the Irish Church* (London, 1868).

Calendar of the papal letters relating to Great Britain and Ireland, 14, 1471–84, ed. Victor Tremlow (London, 1960).

Calendar of papal registers relating to Great Britain and Ireland, 15, 1484–92, ed. M.J. Haren (Dublin, 1978).

Calendar of papal registers relating to Great Britain and Ireland, 16, 1492–8, ed. A.P. Fuller (Dublin, 1986).

Calendar of papal registers relating to Great Britain and Ireland, 17, 1503–1513, ed. M.J. Haren (Dublin, 1987).

Collier, J.P. (ed.), *The Egerton papers: a collection of public and private documents* (Camden Society, London, 1840).

Curtis, Edmund (ed.), *Calendar of Ormond deeds*, iii, 1413–1509 (Dublin, 1935).

——, *Calendar of Ormond deeds*, iv, 1509–47 (Dublin, 1537).

Dowling, Thady, '*Annales breves Hiberniae*' in Richard Butler (ed.), *The annals of Ireland* (Irish Archaeological Society, Dublin, 1849).

Empey, Adrian (ed.), *The proctor's accounts of the parish church of St Werburgh, Dublin, 1481–1627* (Dublin, 2009).

Frere, W.H. (ed.), *Visitation articles and injunctions of the period of the reformation*, i (London, New York, Bombay and Calcutta, 1910).

Gwynn, Aubrey, 'Documents relating to the medieval diocese of Armagh', *Arch. Hib.*, 12 (1947), pp 1–26.

Hogan, Edmund (ed.), *Ibernia Ignatia* (Dublin, 1880).

Jefferies, H.A. (ed.), 'Bishop Montgomery's survey of the parishes of Derry diocese: a complete text from *c*.1609', *SAM*, 17 (1996), pp 44–76.

——, 'A catalogue of the bishops of Raphoe to the year 1600', *Donegal Annual*, 49 (1997), pp 106–12.

Kew, Graham, *The Irish sections of Fynes Morysons's unpublished Itinerary* (Dublin, 1998).

Lawlor, H.J. (ed.), 'A calendar of the Liber ruber of the diocese of Ossory', *PRIA*, 27C (1908–9), pp 159–208.

McNeill, Charles (ed.), 'Accounts of sums realised by sales of chattels of some suppressed Irish monasteries', *JRSAI*, 52 (1922), pp 11–37.

——, 'The Perrot papers', *An. Hib.*, 12 (1943), pp 1–65.

——, *Calendar of Archbishop Alen's register, c.1172–1534* (Dublin, 1950).

McNeill, Charles, and A.J. Otway-Ruthven (eds), *Dowdall deeds* (Dublin, 1960).

Moran, P.F. (ed.), *Spicilegium Ossoriense: being a collection of original letters and papers illustrative of the history of the Irish Church from the Reformation to the year 1800*, i (Dublin, 1874).

Moore, Dónal (ed.), 'A relation concerning the estate of the churches within the diocese of Leighlin, 1585–7', *Arch. Hib.*, 41 (1987), pp 3–11.

Nicholls, K.W. (ed.), 'Visitations of the dioceses of Clonfert, Tuam and Kilmacduagh, *c*.1565–67', *An. Hib.*, 26 (1970), pp 144–57.

——, 'The register of Clogher', *CR*, 7 (1971–2), pp 361–431.

Ó Cuív, Brian (ed.), *Aibidil Gaoidheilge & caiticiosma: Seaán Ó Cearnaigh's Irish primer of religion published in 1571* (Dublin, 1994).

O'Sullivan, William, 'Two Clogher constitutions', *CR*, 15:3 (1996), pp 145–55.

Rymer, Thomas (ed.), *Foedera, conventiones, litterae et cujuscunque generis acta publica*, xv (London, 1713).

Scott, Brendan (ed.), 'Administrative documents relating to the pre-Reformation Church in the diocese of Meath, *c*.1518', *Arch. Hib.*, 61 (2008), pp 325–46.

Shirley, E.P. (ed.), *Original letters and papers ... of the Church in Ireland under Edward VI, Mary and Elizabeth* (London, 1851).

Theiner, Augustine, *Vetera monumenta Hibernorum et Scotorum* (Rome, 1864).

White, N.B. (ed.), *Irish monastic and episcopal deeds* (Dublin, 1936).

——, *Extents of Irish monastic possessions, 1540–1* (Dublin, 1943).

——, *Registrum diocesis Dublinensis: a sixteenth-century Dublin precedent book* (Dublin, 1959).

PUBLISHED BOOKS AND ARTICLES

Bagwell, Richard, *Ireland under the Tudors* (London, 1886).

Begley, J., *The diocese of Limerick in the sixteenth and seventeenth centuries* (London, 1927).

Bermingham, Helen, 'Priests' residences in later medieval Ireland' in FitzPatrick and Gillespie (eds), *The parish* (2006), pp 168–85.

Bourke, Cormac, 'Medieval ecclesiastical metalwork from the diocese of Clogher' in H.A. Jefferies (ed.), *History of the diocese of Clogher* (Dublin, 2005), pp 25–40.

Bowker, Margaret, 'The Henrician reformation and the parish clergy' in Haigh (ed.), *English reformation revised* (1987), pp 75–93.

Bradshaw, Brendan, 'The opposition to the ecclesiastical legislation in the Irish Reformation parliament', *IHS*, 16 (1969), pp 285–303.

——, 'George Browne, first Reformation archbishop of Dublin, 1536–1554', *JEH*, 21 (1970), pp 301–26.

——, *The dissolution of the religious orders in Ireland under Henry VIII* (Cambridge, 1974).

——, 'Fr Wolfe's description of Limerick, 1574', *North Munster Antiquarian Journal*, 17 (1975), pp 47–53.

——, 'The Edwardian reformation in Ireland', *Arch. Hib.*, 26 (1976–7), pp 83–99.

——, *The Irish constitutional revolution of the sixteenth century* (Cambridge, 1979).

——, 'The Reformation in the cities: Cork, Limerick and Galway, 1534–1603' in John Bradley (ed.), *Settlement and society in medieval Ireland* (Kilkenny, 1988), pp 445–76.

Brady, Ciarán, 'Conservative subversives: the community of the Pale and the Dublin administration, 1556–1586' in P.J. Corish (ed.), *Radicals, rebels and establishments: Historical Studies*, xv (Belfast, 1985), pp 11–32.

——, *The chief governors: the rise and fall of reform government in Tudor Ireland, 1536–1588* (Cambridge, 1994).

Brady, Ciarán, and James Murray, 'Sir Henry Sidney and the Reformation in Ireland' in Elizabethane Boran and Crawford Gribben (eds), *Enforcing the Reformation in Ireland and Scotland, 1550–1700* (Aldershot, 2006), pp 13–39.

Brady, W.M., *The episcopal succession in England, Scotland and Ireland, 1400–1875*, i (Rome, 1876).

——, *The Irish Reformation* (London, 1867).

Buckley, V.M. and David Sweetman (eds), *Archaeological survey of County Louth* (Dublin, 1991).

Burrows, M.A.J., 'Fifteenth-century Irish provincial legislation and pastoral care' in W.J. Shiels and Diana Wood (eds), *The churches, Ireland and the Irish* (Oxford, 1989), pp 55–67.

Caball, Marc, *Poets and politics: continuity and reaction in Irish poetry, 1558–1625* (Cork, 1998).

——, 'Religion, culture and the bardic élite in early modern Ireland' in Alan Ford and John McCafferty (eds), *The origins of sectarianism in early modern Ireland* (Cambridge, 2005), pp 158–82.

Canny, Nicholas, *The Elizabethan conquest of Ireland: a pattern established, 1565–1576* (Hassocks, Sussex, 1976).

——, 'Why the Reformation failed in Ireland: *une question mal posée*', *JEH*, 30 (1979), pp 423–50.

——, 'Galway: from the Reformation to the penal laws' in Diarmuid Ó Cearbhaill (ed.), *Galway: town and gown, 1484–1984* (Dublin, 1984), pp 10–28.

Carey, Vincent, *Surviving the Tudors: the 'wizard' earl of Kildare and English rule, 1537–1586* (Dublin, 2001).

Clarke, Aidan, 'Varieties of conformity: the first century of the Church of Ireland' in W.J. Shiels and Diana Wood (eds), *The churches, Ireland and the Irish* (Oxford, 1989), pp 105–22.

Cockerham, Paul, and Amy Louise Harris, 'Kilkenny funeral monuments 1500–1600: a statistical and analytical account', *PRIA*, 101C5 (2001), pp 135–88.

Coffey, John, *Persecution and toleration in Protestant England, 1558–1689* (Harlow, 2000).

Connor, Thomas, 'Religion and the laity in early modern Galway' in Moran and Gillespie (eds), *Galway: history and society* (1996), pp 131–48.

Devlin, Ciarán, 'Some episcopal lives' in H.A. Jefferies and C. Devlin (eds), *History of the diocese of Derry* (Dublin, 2000), pp 114–39.

Duffy, Eamon, *The stripping of the altars: traditional religion in England, 1400–1580* (New Haven and London, 1992).

Edwards, David, *The Ormond lordship in County Kilkenny, 1515–1642* (Dublin, 2003).

Edwards, R.D., *Church and state in Tudor Ireland: a history of penal laws against Irish Catholics* (Dublin, 1935).

Ellis, S.G., 'The Kildare rebellion and the early Henrician reformation', *HJ*, 19 (1976), pp 807–30.

——, 'John Bale, bishop of Ossory, 1552–3', *Journal of the Butler Society*, 3:2 (1984), pp 283–93.

——, *Reform and revival: English government in Ireland, 1470–1534* (Woodbridge and New York, 1986).

——, 'Economic problems of the Church: why the Reformation failed in Ireland', *JEH*, 41:2 (1990), pp 257–69.

——, *Ireland in the age of the Tudors, 1447–1603: English expansion and the end of Gaelic rule* (London and New York, 1998).

Elton, G.R., *Policy and police: the enforcement of the reformation in the age of Thomas Cromwell* (Cambridge, 1972).

Empey, Adrian, 'The layperson in the parish: the medieval inheritance, 1169–1534' in Raymond Gillespie and W.G. Neely (eds), *The laity and the Church of Ireland, 1000–2000* (Dublin, 2002), pp 7–48.

Fenlon, Dermot, *Heresy and obedience in Tridentine Italy: Cardinal Pole and the counter-reformation* (Cambridge, 1972).

FitzPatrick, Elizabeth, and Caimin O'Brien, *The medieval churches of County Offaly* (Dublin, 1998).

Fitzpatrick, Elizabeth, and Raymond Gillespie (eds), *The parish in medieval and early modern Ireland: community, territory and building* (Dublin, 2006).

Fitzsimons, Fiona, 'Wolsey, the native affinities and the failure of reform in Henrician Ireland' in David Edwards (ed.), *Regions and rulers in Ireland, 1100–1650* (Dublin, 2004), pp 78–121.

Flynn, T.S., *The Dominicans in Ireland, 1534–1641* (Dublin, 1993).

Ford, Alan, *The Protestant Reformation in Ireland, 1590–1641* (Dublin, 1997 ed.).

Gillespie, Raymond, 'The shaping of reform, 1558–1625' in Kenneth Milne (ed.), *Christ Church Cathedral, Dublin: a history* (Dublin, 2000), pp 174–94.

Gwynn, Aubrey, *The medieval province of Armagh* (Dundalk, 1946).

Haigh, Christopher, *Reformation and resistance in Tudor Lancashire* (Cambridge, 1975).

——, *English reformations: religion, politics and society under the Tudors* (Oxford, 1993).

—— (ed.), *The English reformation revised* (Cambridge, 1987).

Hall, Dianne, *Women and the Church in medieval Ireland, c.1140–1540* (Dublin, 2002).

Hardiman, James, *The history of the town and county of Galway: from the earliest period to the present time* (Dublin, 1820).

Haren, M.J., 'A description of Clogher cathedral in the early sixteenth century', *CR*, 12 (1985), pp 48–54.

——, 'Social structures of the Irish Church: a new source in papal penitentiary dispensations for illegitimacy' in Herausgegeben von Ludwig Schmugge (ed.), *Illegitimitat im spatmittelalter: schriften des historischen kollegs kolloquien*, 29 (Oldenbourg, 1994), pp 207–26.

Harris, Walter (ed.), *The whole works of Sir James Ware concerning Ireland*, i (Dublin, 1764).

Haugaard, William, *Elizabeth and the English Reformation* (Cambridge, 1970).

Heal, Felicity, *Reformation in Britain and Ireland* (Oxford, 2005).

Heath, Peter, *The English parish clergy on the eve of the Reformation* (London, 1969).

Houlbrooke, Ralph, *Church courts and the people during the English Reformation, 1520–1570* (Oxford, 1979).

Hutton, Ronald, 'The local impact of the Tudor reformations' in Haigh (ed.), *English reformation revised* (1987), pp 114–38.

Jackson, R.W., *Archbishop Magrath: the scoundrel of Cashel* (Cork, 1974).

Jefferies, H.A., 'The Irish parliament of 1560: the Anglican reforms authorised', *IHS*, 26 (1988), pp 128–41.

——, 'The Church courts of Armagh on the eve of the Reformation', *SAM*, 15 (1993), pp 1–38.

——, 'Diocesan synods and convocations in Armagh on the eve of the Tudor reformations', *SAM*, 16 (1995), pp 120–32.

——, *Priests and prelates of Armagh in the age of reformations* (Dublin, 1997).

——, 'The diocese of Dromore on the eve of the Tudor reformation' in Lindsay Proudfoot (ed.), *Down: history and society* (Dublin, 1997), pp 123–40.

——, 'Derry diocese on the eve of the plantation' in Gerard O'Brien (eds), *Derry and Londonderry: history and society* (Dublin, 1997), pp 175–204.

——, 'The laity in the parishes of Armagh *inter Anglicos* on the eve of the Tudor reformations', *Arch. Hib.*, 52 (1998), pp 73–84.

——, 'The visitation of the parishes of Armagh *inter Hibernicos* in 1546' in Charles Dillon and H.A. Jefferies (eds), *Tyrone: history and society* (Dublin, 2000), pp 163–80.

——, 'The early Tudor reformations in the Irish Pale', *JEH*, 52 (2001), pp 34–67.

——, *Cork: historical perspectives* (Dublin, 2004).

——, 'The Kildare revolt: accident or design?', *JCKAHS*, 19 (2004–5), pp 447–59.

——, 'Papal letters and Irish clergy: Clogher before the Reformation' in Jefferies (ed.), *History of the diocese of Clogher* (Dublin, 2005), pp 81–107.

——, Review of Murray, *Enforcing the English Reformation, History Ireland*, 17:3 (May/June 2009), p. 61.

Kearney Walsh, Micheline, *Destruction by peace: Hugh O'Neill after Kinsale* (Armagh, 1986).

——, 'Archbishop Maguaran and his return to Ireland, October 1592', *SAM*, 14 (1990), pp 68–79.

Lander, Stephen, 'Church courts and the Reformation in the diocese of Chichester, 1500–1558' in Haigh (ed.), *English Reformation revised* (1987), pp 34–55.

Leask, H.G., *Irish churches and monastic buildings*, iii (Dundalk, 1960).

Lehmberg, S.E., *The Reformation of the cathedrals* (Princeton, NJ, 1988).

Lennon, Colm, *The lords of Dublin in the age of reformation* (Dublin, 1989).

——, 'The chantries in the Irish Reformation: the case of St Anne's guild, Dublin, 1550–1630' in R.V. Comerford, M. Cullen, J.R. Hill and Colm Lennon (eds), *Religion, conflict and coexistence in Ireland: essays in honour of Monsignor Patrick J. Corish* (Dublin, 1989), pp 6–25.

——, *Sixteenth-century Ireland: the incomplete conquest* (Dublin, 1994).

——, 'The urban patriciates of early modern Ireland: a case-study of Limerick', *The 26th O'Donnell Lecture* (Dublin, 1999).

——, *An Irish prisoner of conscience of the Tudor era: Archbishop Richard Creagh, 1523–86* (Dublin, 2000).

——, 'Mass in the manor house: the counter-reformation in Dublin, 1560–1630' in James Kelly and Daire Keogh (eds), *History of the diocese of Dublin* (Dublin, 2000), pp 112–26.

——, 'The confraternities and cultural duality in Ireland, 1450–1550' in Christopher Black and Pamela Gravestock (eds), *Early modern confraternities in Europe and the Americas* (Aldershot, 2006), pp 35–52.

——, 'Pedagogy and reform: the influence of Peter White on Irish scholarship in the Renaissance' in Thomas Herron and Michael Potterton (eds), *Ireland in the Renaissance, c.1540–1660* (Dublin, 2007), pp 43–51.

Loades, David, *The reign of Mary Tudor: politics, government and religion in England, 1553–1558* (London, 1979).

Lynch, Anthony, 'The archdeacons of Armagh, 1417–71', *CLAHJ*, 19 (1979), pp 218–26.

——, 'Religion in late medieval Ireland', *Arch. Hib.*, 36 (1981), pp 3–15.

——, 'The administration of John Bole, archbishop of Armagh, 1457–1471', *SAM*, 13 (1991), pp 39–108.

Lyons, Mary Ann, *Church and society in County Kildare* (Dublin, 2000).

MacCuarta, Brian, *Catholic revival in the north of Ireland, 1603–41* (Dublin, 2007).

MacCulloch, Diarmaid, *The later Reformation in England, 1547–1603* (Basingstoke, 2001).

——, *Reformation: Europe's houses divided, 1490–1700* (London, 2004).

McCabe, Brian, 'An Elizabethan prelate: John Garvey (1527–1596)', *Breifne*, 26 (1988), pp 594–604.

McCafferty, John, 'Defamation and the church courts in early sixteenth-century Armagh', *Arch. Hib.*, 48 (1994), pp 88–99.

McCormack, A.M., *The earldom of Desmond, 1463–1583: the decline and crisis of a feudal lordship* (Dublin, 2005).

McCorristine, Laurence, *The revolt of Silken Thomas: a challenge to Henry VIII* (Dublin, 1987).

McMahon, Mary, *Medieval church sites of north Dublin* (Dublin, 1991).

McMahon, Mary, *St Audoen's Church, Cornmarket, Dublin: archaeology and architecture* (Dublin, 2006).

Maginn, Christopher, 'The Baltinglass rebellion, 1580: English dissent or a Gaelic uprising?', *HJ*, 47 (2004), pp 205–32.

——, *'Civilising' Gaelic Leinster: the extension of Tudor rule in the O'Byrne and O'Toole lordships* (Dublin, 2005).

Mahaffy, J.P., *An epoch in Irish history: Trinity College, Dublin, its foundation and early fortunes, 1591–1660* (London, 1903; repr. Port Washington, London, 1970).

Marshall, Peter, *The Catholic priesthood and the English Reformation* (Oxford, 1994).

——, *Reformation England, 1480–1642* (London, 2003).

Martin, F.X., 'The Augustinian reform movement in the fifteenth century' in John Watt, J.B. Morall and F.X. Martin (eds), *Medieval studies presented to Aubrey Gwynn SJ* (Dublin, 1961), pp 230–64.

——, 'Confusion abounding: Bernard O'Higgins, OSA, bishop of Elphin' in Art Cosgrove and D. McCartney (eds), *Studies in Irish history presented to R. Dudley Edwards* (Dublin, 1979), pp 38–84.

Mason, W.M., *The history and antiquities of the collegiate and cathedral church of St Patrick's, near Dublin, 1190–1819* (Dublin, 1820).

Mayer, T.F., *Reginald Pole: prince and prophet* (Cambridge, 2000).

——, (ed.), *The correspondence of Reginald Pole, 1500–1558* (Aldershot, 2002, *et seq.*).

Meigs, S.A., *The reformations in Ireland: tradition and confessionalism, 1400–1690* (London and New York, 1997).

Mooney, Canice, *The Church in Gaelic Ireland: thirteenth to fifteenth centuries* (Dublin, 1969).

Moran, Gerard, and Raymond Gillespie (eds), *Galway: history and society* (Dublin, 1996).

Moran, P.F., *History of the Catholic archbishops of Dublin since the Reformation*, i (Dublin, 1864).

Morgan, Hiram, *Tyrone's rebellion: the outbreak of the Nine Years War in Tudor Ireland* (Woodbridge, 1993).

Moss, Rachel, Colmán Ó Clabaigh and Salvador Ryan (eds), *Art and devotion in late medieval Ireland* (Dublin, 2006).

Murphy, Margaret, 'The high cost of dying: an analysis of *pro anima* bequests in medieval Dublin' in W.J. Shiels and Diana Wood (eds), *The Church and wealth: studies in Church history*, 24 (Oxford, 1987), pp 111–22.

Murray, James, 'Archbishop Alen, Tudor reform and the Kildare rebellion', *PRIA*, 89C (1989), pp 1–16.

——, 'The sources of clerical incomes in the Tudor diocese of Dublin, *c.*1530–1600', *Arch. Hib.*, 45 (1990), pp 139–60.

——, 'Ecclesiastical justice and the enforcement of the Reformation: the case of Archbishop Browne and the clergy of Dublin' in A. Ford, F. Mc Guire and K. Milne (eds), *As by law established: the Church of Ireland since the Reformation* (Dublin, 1995), pp 33–51.

—— *Enforcing the English reformation in Ireland: clerical resistance and political conflict in the diocese of Dublin, 1534–1590* (Cambridge, 2009).

Murray, Laurence, 'The ancient chantries of County Louth', *CLAHJ*, 9 (1939), pp 181–208.

Neely, William G., *Kilkenny: an urban history, 1391–1843* (Belfast, 1989).

Nicholls, K.W., 'Rectory, vicarage and parish in the western Irish dioceses', *JRSAI*, 101 (1971), pp 53–84.

——, 'Medieval Irish cathedral chapters', *Arch. Hib.*, 31 (1973), pp 102–11.

Ní Ghabhláin, Sinéad, 'Late twelfth-century church construction: evidence of parish formation?' in FitzPatrick and Gillespie (eds), *The parish* (2006), pp 147–67.

Ní Mharcaigh, Máirín, 'The medieval parish churches of south-west County Dublin', *PRIA*, 97C (1997), pp 245–96.

Nugent, Patrick, 'The dynamics of parish formation in high medieval and late medieval Clare' in FitzPatrick and Gillespie (eds), *The parish* (2006), pp 186–210.

O'Brien, W.P., 'Two sixteenth-century Munster primates: Donnchadh Ó Taidhg (1560–62) and Richard Creagh (1564–85)', *SAM*, 14:1 (1990), pp 35–57.

Ó Clabaigh, Colmán, *The Franciscans in Ireland, 1400–1534: from reform to reformation* (Dublin, 2002).

Ó Cuív, Brian, 'The Irish language in the early modern period' in T.W. Moody, F.X. Martin and F.J. Byrne (eds), *A new history of Ireland* (Oxford, 1976), pp 509–45.

O'Dwyer, P., *The Irish Carmelites* (Dublin, 1988).

O'Keeffe, Tadhg, 'The built environment of local community worship between the late eleventh and early thirteenth centuries' in FitzPatrick and Gillespie (eds), *The parish* (2006), pp 124–46.

O'Neill, Michael, 'The medieval parish churches of County Meath', *JRSAI*, 132 (2002), pp 1–57.

——, 'St Patrick's Cathedral, Dublin, and its prebendal churches: gothic architectural relationships' in Seán Duffy (ed), *Medieval Dublin V* (Dublin, 2004), pp 243–76.

——, 'The medieval parish churches of Kildare', *JCKAHS*, 19 (2004–5), pp 406–46.

Ó Siochrú, Micheál, 'Foreign involvement in the revolt of Silken Thomas', *PRIA*, 96C2 (1996), pp 49–66.

Palliser, D.M., 'Popular reactions to the reformation during the years of uncertainty, 1530–70' in Haigh (ed.), *English reformation revised* (1987), pp 94–113.

Perrot, James, The *Chronicle of Ireland, 1584–1608*, ed. Herbert Wood (Dublin, 1933).

Phillips, W.A., *History of the Church of Ireland*, iii (Oxford, 1934).

Pogson, R.H., 'Reginald Pole and the priorities of government in Mary Tudor's church', *HJ*, 18:1 (1975), pp 3–20.

——, 'Revival and reform in Mary Tudor's Church: a question of money' in Haigh (ed.), *English reformation revised* (1987), pp 139–56.

Quinn, D.B., and J.P. Prendergast (eds), 'Calendar of the Irish Council Book, 1 March 1581 to 1 July 1586', *An. Hib.*, 24 (1967), pp 91–180.

Rex, Richard, *Henry VIII and the English Reformation* (Basingstoke, Hampshire and London, 1993).

Robinson, J.L., 'Churchwardens' accounts, 1484–1600, St Werburgh's Church, Dublin', *JRSAI*, 44 (1914), pp 132–42.

Robinson-Hammerstein, Helga, 'Archbishop Adam Loftus: the first provost of Trinity College, Dublin' in Helga Robinson-Hammerstein (ed.), *European universities in the age of Reformation and counter-reformation* (Dublin, 1998), pp 34–52.

Ronan, M.V., *The Reformation in Dublin, 1536–1558* (Dublin, 1926).

——, *The Reformation in Ireland under Elizabeth* (London, 1930).

Rothe, David, *Analecta et de processu martyriali*, ed. P.F. Moran (London, 1884).

Scarisbrick, J.J., *The Reformation and the English people* (Oxford, 1984).

Scott, Brendan, *Religion and Reformation in the Tudor diocese of Meath* (Dublin, 2006).

Sheehan, A.J., 'The recusancy revolt of 1603: a re-interpretation', *Arch. Hib.*, 38 (1983), pp 3–13.

Simms, Katharine, 'The brehons of later medieval Ireland' in D. Hogan and W.N. Osborough (eds), *Brehons, serjeants and attorneys: studies in the history of the Irish legal profession* (Blackrock, Co. Dublin, 1990), pp 51–76.

——, 'Frontiers in the Irish Church: regional and cultural' in T.B. Barry, Robin Frame and Katharine Simms (eds), *Colony and frontier in medieval Ireland: essays presented to J.F. Lydon* (London, 1995), pp 177–200.

Stalley, Roger, *The Cistercian monasteries of Ireland: an account of the history, art and architecture of the White Monks in Ireland from 1142 to 1540* (London and New Haven, 1987).

——, 'The architecture of the cathedral and priory buildings, 1250–1530' in Kenneth Milne (ed.), *Christ Church Cathedral, Dublin: a history* (2000), pp 95–128.

Swanson, R.N., *Church and society in late medieval England* (Oxford, 1989).

Tait, Clodagh, *Death, burial and commemoration in Ireland, 1550–1650* (Basingstoke, Hampshire and New York, 2002).

——, '"As legacie upon my soul": the wills of the Irish Catholic community, *c.*1550–*c.*1660' in Robert Armstrong and Tadhg Ó hAnnrachain (eds), *Community in early modern Ireland* (Dublin, 2006), pp 179–98.

Treadwell, Victor, 'The Irish parliament of 1569–71', *PRIA*, 65C (1966), pp 55–89.

——, 'Sir John Perrot and the Irish parliament of 1585–6', *PRIA*, 85C (1985), pp 259–308.

Walshe, Helen Coburn, 'The response to the Protestant Reformation in sixteenth-century Meath', *Ríocht na Midhe*, 7 (1987), pp 97–109.

——, 'Enforcing the Elizabethan settlement: the vicissitudes of Hugh Brady, bishop of Meath, 1563–84', *IHS*, 26 (1989), pp 352–76.

Walsh, Katherine, 'The beginnings of a national protectorate: curial cardinals and the Irish Church in the fifteenth century', *Arch. Hib.*, 32 (1974), pp 72–80.

——, 'Deliberate provocation or reforming zeal? John Bale as first Church of Ireland bishop of Ossory (1552/3–1563)' in Ciarán Brady (ed.), *Worsted in the game: losers in Irish history* (Mullingar, 1989), pp 42–60.

Walsh, Paul, 'An account of the town of Galway', *Journal of the Galway Archaeological and Historical Society*, 44 (1992), pp 47–118.

——, 'The topography of the town of Galway in the medieval and early modern periods' in Moran and Gillespie (eds), *Galway: history and society* (1996), pp 27–96.

Watt, John, *The Church in late medieval Ireland* (Dublin, 1972).

Westropp, J.T., 'The churches of County Clare, and the origins of the ecclesiastical divisions in that county', *PRIA*, 3 (1900–2), pp 100–80.

Whiting, Robert, *The blind devotion of the people: popular religion and the English Reformation* (Cambridge, 1989).

Wilkie, William E., *The cardinal protectors of England: Rome and the Tudors before the Reformation* (Cambridge, 1974).

UNPUBLISHED THESES

Byrne, Niall, 'Reformation in Tudor Waterford, 1547–1603' (MA, UCC, 1998).

Lyons, Mary Ann, 'Church and society in early sixteenth-century Kildare, 1500–1540' (MA, NUI Maynooth, 1991).

Murray, James, 'The Tudor diocese of Dublin: episcopal government, ecclesiastical politics and the enforcement of the Reformation, c.1534–1590' (PhD, TCD, 1997).

Preston, S.M., 'The canons regular of St Augustine in medieval Ireland: an overview' (PhD, TCD, 1996).

Scully, Siobhán, 'Medieval parish churches and parochial organisation in Muintir Eolais' (MA, UCG, 1999).

Index